MEDIEVAL DUBLIN VIII

Dedicated to the memory of
Anne Walsh (†2008)
BA (Mod.), MA (NUI), DLIS (NUI), ALAI,
History Subject Librarian, Library of Trinity College, Dublin,
a true friend to a whole generation
of Friends of Medieval Dublin

Medieval Dublin VIII

Proceedings of the Friends of Medieval Dublin Symposium 2006

Seán Duffy

EDITOR

FOUR COURTS PRESS

Typeset in 10.5 pt on 12.5 pt Ehrhardt by
Carrigboy Typesetting Services for
FOUR COURTS PRESS LTD
7 Malpas Street, Dublin 8, Ireland
e-mail: info@fourcourtspress.ie
and in North America for
FOUR COURTS PRESS
c/o ISBS, 920 NE 58th Avenue, Suite 300, Portland, OR 97213.

A catalogue record for this title is available
from the British Library.

ISBN 978–1–84682–042–7 hbk
ISBN 978–1–84682–043–4 pbk

This book is published with the active support of
Dublin City Council/Comhairle Chathair Átha Cliath.

Dublin City
Baile Átha Cliath

Printed in England
by MPG Books, Bodmin, Cornwall.

Contents

Contributors

CHRISTINE BAKER is field monument advisor with Fingal County Council.

TERESA BOLGER is a senior archaeologist with Margaret Gowen & Co. Ltd.

HOWARD B. CLARKE is associate professor emeritus of medieval history at University College Dublin and secretary of the Royal Irish Academy.

BERNADETTE CUNNINGHAM is deputy librarian of the Royal Irish Academy.

SEÁN DUFFY is a Fellow of Trinity College, Dublin and chairman of the Friends of Medieval Dublin.

ALAN J. FLETCHER is associate professor in the school of English and drama at University College, Dublin.

MICHAEL GIBBONS is an archaeologist based in Clifden, County Galway.

MYLES GIBBONS is a graduate in history from NUI Galway.

RAYMOND GILLESPIE is associate professor of history at NUI Maynooth.

R. ANDREW McDONALD is Director of the Centre for Medieval and Renaissance Studies at Brock University, Canada.

EDMOND O'DONOVAN is a senior archaeologist with Margaret Gowen & Co. Ltd.

LINZI SIMPSON is senior project manager with Margaret Gowen & Co. Ltd.

NESSA WALSH is operations manager with Margaret Gowen & Co. Ltd.

Editor's preface

This volume contains the proceedings of the eighth annual Friends of Medieval Dublin Symposium, held in Trinity College Dublin on Saturday, 13 May 2006. We are very grateful to the speakers for presenting their work to a packed house on the day and for allowing us to publish it in this volume. We are similarly grateful to those scholars who were not on the programme but subsequently submitted contributions for publication here, which have added significantly to the merits of the volume, and we take this opportunity to encourage others to follow suit for future volumes.

2006 was an important year for our group. Thirty years earlier, on 8 April 1976, a number of people in Dublin – representing archaeology, medieval history, historical geography, architecture, town planning, as well as aldermen of the city – met and formed the association that became known as the Friends of Medieval Dublin. The Friends is essentially a study group that exists for the purpose of increasing knowledge about medieval Dublin, and promoting public interest in it. But the decision of the then Corporation of Dublin to proceed when it did and where it did with the construction of the Civic Offices complex, and the opposition of the Friends to it, has meant that this study group has been synonymous ever since with the 'Save Wood Quay' campaign, which pitted it in opposition to the Corporation.

Just how different the ethos of Dublin City Council is from that of the Corporation in 1976 was demonstrated when, on 10 April 2006, in the same Civic Offices which had been the *casus belli* thirty years earlier, the City Manager, Mr John Fitzgerald, hosted a reception to mark the anniversary of the Friends' founding. On the same occasion, the launch took place of the beautifully illustrated book *Viking Age Dublin*, written by Dr Ruth Johnson, the Dublin City Archaeologist and a longstanding member of the Friends. And on 1 September of that same year, in the impressive surroundings of Dublin Castle, a major conference was held on the subject of the city walls, organized by the City Heritage Officer, Donncha Ó Dúlaing. Truly, much had changed in the intervening years.

It is a pleasure, therefore, to acknowledge here the support given to the cost of publishing the *Medieval Dublin* series by the city Manager, John Fitzgerald, and since his retirement by his successor, Mr John Tierney, whom we wish well in this challenging role, and with whom we look forward to many years of fruitful collaboration. We would like also to thank the Department of History, School of Histories and Humanities, Trinity College Dublin, who covered the costs of the Symposium, and our gratitude remains undiminished to Michael Adams, Martin Fanning, and the rest of the team at Four Courts Press.

Seán Duffy
Chairman
Friends of Medieval Dublin

The search for the ninth-century *longphort*: early Viking-Age Norse fortifications and the origins of urbanization in Ireland*

MYLES GIBBONS AND MICHAEL GIBBONS

> In Ireland the Scandinavians encountered economic and political conditions that differed in several respects from those pertaining elsewhere. The foundation of *longphuirt* and towns – unknown, for instance, in Norse Scotland – formed one such unique response to Irish conditions (Sheehan 2004, 178).

> '*Longphort oile ag Duibhlinn*' (Another fortress [was erected by them] at Duibhlinn) (O'Donovan 1856, 461).

In the mid-ninth century Viking fleets are described in the Irish annals as establishing *longphuirt* (sing. *longphort*) at a series of coastal locations in Ireland. Scholars render *longphort* into English in a variety of different ways. Wallace observes that 'Ó Corráin talks of a "defended ship enclosure", Clarke of "an *emporium* or trading station" and de Paor of "a shore fortress". The *R.I.A. Dictionary* defines "longphort" as "a camp, encampment, temporary stronghold (or a) mansion, princely dwelling, stronghold, fortress"' (Wallace 1982, 138).

A small number of the early *longphuirt* locations later came to play host to walled coastal cities. Twelfth-century Dublin was referred to as a *civitas* or city (Clarke 1998, 331). But, while archaeological investigations in Dublin, Cork and Waterford have helped to clarify our understanding of the tenth- and eleventh-century settlement, the mid-ninth century *longphort* phase remains unclear (Clarke 1998; Hurley 1986; Hurley 2003). The nature of the original *longphort* and hence of the origins of urbanization in Ireland remain the subject of intense debate. Over the past decade many scholars have drawn on one possible meaning of the term – that of fortress – and have tried to locate Scandinavian fortresses in the field.

* The authors would like to acknowledge the assistance of the staff of the Library of the Royal Irish Academy.

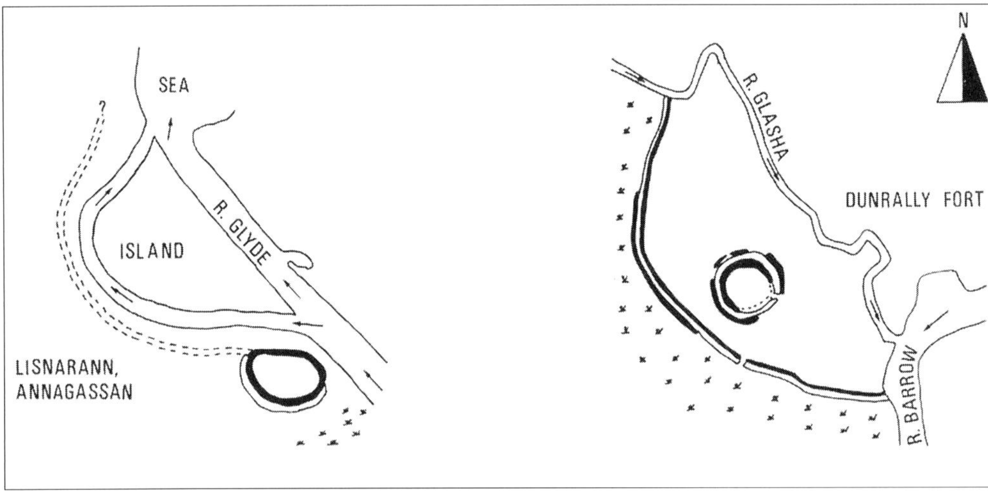

1 Annagassan and Dunrally (not to scale) after Kelly, E.P. (1995), 'Vikings on the Barrow', in *Archaeology Ireland*, 33 (Autumn 1995)

PROPOSED 'LONGPHUIRT' IN IRELAND

In Ireland, Lisnaran fort near Annagassan in Co. Louth has long been identified as the *longphort* of Linn Duachaill (see fig. 1). There does not, however, seem to be any archaeological evidence for this belief. The only finds evidence from the site is a fourteenth-century coin hoard from the bottom of the related cliff and the surviving buildings inside the walls are undated (Buckley and Sweetman 1991, 97–8). Ballykieran Little in Co. Westmeath on Lough Ree was partially excavated in the belief that it might be a *longphort* or *dún* connected with the campaign of AD 845. The site was surrounded by a substantial earthen bank on the landward side and contained a number of hollows on the shore adjacent to the mouth of the Breensford River. The site produced iron slag and fired clay but no conclusive evidence of a Scandinavian presence (O'Sullivan 1998, 150).

Charles Dyer's 'Earthworks of the Danelaw frontier' proposed that a series of earthworks in England between Wessex and the old Danelaw might be of Danish origin. He identified three types of Danish earthwork: roughly D-shaped or semi-rectangular enclosures on the edge of navigable rivers or else roughly circular fortifications on high sloping ground and heavily fortified artificial harbours. Dyer drew on political probability, historical and saga material as well as perceived resemblances to the Trelleborg-type circular fortresses in Denmark to make his identifications. Although none of these have, as yet, produced Viking material, Dyer's proposed Danish forts at Church

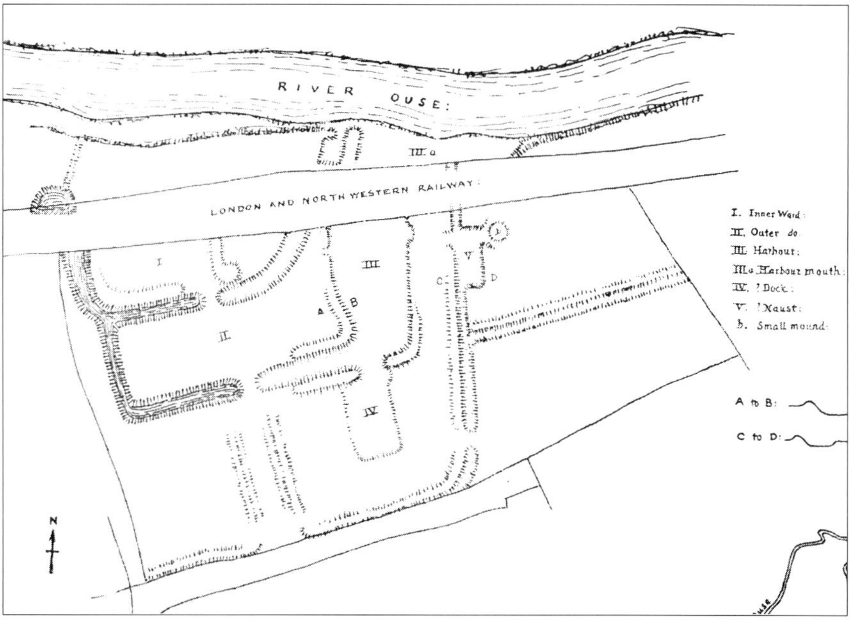

2 Possible Danish Earthwork on the Ouse near Tempsford after Dyer, James (1972), 'Earthworks of the Danelaw Frontier' in Fowler (ed.), *Archaeology and the landscape: essays for L.V. Grinsell* (London), 222–36

Spanel and Beeston-Berrys (Dyer 1972, 206) are often cited as possible parallels for the Irish *longphort* (see fig. 2).

One of Dyer's proposed models for Danish earthworks – a D-shaped enclosure on the edge of a navigable river – has been extremely influential in Ireland. Similar Irish sites, including Rathturtle in Co. Wicklow (Etchingham 1994), Dunrally in Co. Laois (Kelly and Maas 1999), and Athlunkard in Co. Clare (Kelly and O'Donovan 1998), have been proposed as Scandinavian fortifications. The identification of all of these earthworks as *longphuirt* has been based on political probability, place-names, and a perceived resemblance to the Dyer model. None have produced Scandinavian material and none can be considered to be unquestionably Scandinavian in origin (Gibbons 2004).

THE TERM 'LONGPHORT'

A series of other earthworks and surviving remains – notably Ballylongford (Co. Kerry), Lonart (Co. Kerry) (Connolly et al. 2005, 158–9), Lonehort (Co. Cork) (Sheehan et al. 2001, 114), and Kilongford (Co. Waterford) (O'Brien and Russell 2005, 123) – have been proposed as Viking in origin. This method is based almost entirely on the inclusion of the element *longphort* in their names, a method of doubtful utility. The origins of the term *longphort* are unclear although it is found as a place-name throughout the Gaelic-speaking world, in both Ireland and Scotland, a fact that has not received sufficient emphasis in the Irish debate.

It is initially used in the annals to describe the camps/landing-places associated with the activities of ninth-century Viking fleets (Kelly and Maas 1999). The elements which make up the term, however, *long* (ship) and *port* (landing-place) were in use in close proximity substantially earlier in the phrase *gab port a long* ('to take a landing-place for a ship', meaning to find a place to come ashore), and it is not certain that the term *longphort* itself was not already in use without any ethnic connotations prior to its appearance in the annals. By the eleventh century, the term had come to mean 'field encampment', initially without any necessary connection with the sea or any suggestion of even semi-permanence (Bhreathnach 1998).

By the mid-twelfth century the *mórlongphort* or 'great-camp' played an important role in Irish warfare. It was often occupied for several months at a time, constructed outside an army's home kingdom, and seems to have acted as a semi-fortified base (less well-defended than a *dún* or fortress but distinguished from an unfortified collection of huts), from which armies could conduct extensive raiding campaigns (Flanagan 1997, 60). In the thirteenth and fourteenth centuries, the term came to refer to 'strongholds' (later simply high-status dwellings), often permanently inhabited, in the hands of Gaelic lords (O'Connor 1998, 84–5). It seems likely that it was this meaning that later scholars drew upon when translating *longphort* as fortress. In Scotland the term seems to refer primarily to encampments and by the seventeenth century to simple hunting-booths (Watson 2004, 493–5). Interestingly, there does not seem to have been any effort in Scotland to correlate the use in place-names of the term *longphort* with Viking settlement. The popular use of *longphort* has become so strong that it has even been mistaken for an actual Nordic name (O'Brien and Russell 2005), although this was discontinued in a later article (O'Brien, Quinney and Russell 2006).

This wide range in possible meanings makes it impossible to use the term as an indicator of ethnic origin unless there are already strong reasons to believe that the name dates back to the ninth century.

SCANDINAVIAN FORTIFICATIONS OUTSIDE IRELAND: PARALLELS FOR THE 'LONGPHORT'?

Given the difficulty in identifying the Scandinavian-built *longphort* in Ireland, it is tempting to look elsewhere for examples of Viking fortifications. The walled Scandinavian trading towns at Birka and Hedeby and the geometrical forts at Trelleborg and Fyrkat are often quoted in the Irish *longphort* debate but both came into being under different circumstances to the *longphuirt* and fulfilled different roles. The walled settlements seem to have been established as planned, fortified trading-centres under royal authority (Holmquist Olausson 2002, 159–67). The *longphort* by contrast were, at least initially, established in contested and hostile terrain. Their transition to planned towns seems to have followed 'the return' from York in 917 and to draw on the experience of Anglo-Scandinavian and Anglo-Saxon town building (Clarke 1998). Similarly, the geometrical forts date to the mid- to late tenth century. They seem to have been built under royal authority, although they remained in service for a very short period of time and their design may be based on Carolingian prototypes such as that at Oost Souburg (Trimpe Burger 1975).

WINTER CAMPS AND FORTIFICATION IN BRITAIN

Ninth-century Viking fortifications or camps are similarly difficult to locate in both Scotland and Wales. Eric Talbot has proposed a series of sites but, like Dyer's examples from England, these have not yet produced Scandinavian material and the available historical sources are late (Talbot 1974). In Wales a low-lying enclosed farming settlement, *c.*80m in diameter and dating to *c.*600, has been rediscovered at Llanbedrgoch. The site was later (AD540–770) expanded to incorporate an area of *c.*1ha and shows evidence of seventh-century trade. It appears to have been refortified in the ninth century, whether as a response to attack or due to occupation by Vikings remains unclear, as does the original ethnicity of the builders, which is undiscussed but could be either native Welsh or evidence of pre-Viking Irish settlement. Scandinavian and Hiberno-Scandinavian remains including hack silver, merchants' weights, ringed-pins and buckles have been discovered on site as have five burials oriented north-south and buried without ceremony, possibly the victims of violence. The site was abandoned by the late tenth/early eleventh century (Redknap 2004, 139–75).

Few of the winter-camps of the Great Army in England in the late 860s and 870s have been discovered or excavated but their locations may provide a clue as to the nature of the early *longphuirt*. The camps at York (Roman city with Anglo-Saxon settlement of Eoforwic, and monastery), Nottingham (Middle Saxon enclosure), Thetford (royal/ecclesiastical centre), Reading (royal estate), London (established settlement and wic), Torksey (evidence of eighth-century trade), and Repton (Mercian royal minster) were all established at or near established administrative or population centres (Richards 2004). The Great Army's winter-camp at Repton has been excavated. The Mercian minster had been incorporated into the ramparts as a gatehouse for a

D-shaped earthen enclosure on the edge of a bluff, above the old route of the river Trent. Little Scandinavian material was discovered inside the ramparts and the fortified area seems too small to accommodate large numbers of troops or to protect their accompanying shipping. This suggests that the majority of the army did not remain in the camp and the accompanying fleet may not have been based in the immediate area either. The illustrations that accompany discussions of Repton almost invariably show at least one longship but this may be misleading.

This interpretation of Viking use of camps is supported by Asser's description of the creation of one such camp at Reading:

> In the year of the Lord's Incarnation 871, the Viking army of hateful memory left East Anglia, went to the kingdom of the West Saxons, and came to the royal estate called Reading (situated on the southern bank of the River Thames, in the district called Berkshire). On the third day after their arrival there, two of their earls, with a great part of the force, rode out for plunder, while the others constructed a rampart between the two rivers Thames and Kennet, on the right hand [southern] side of the same royal estate. (Keynes and Lapidge 2004)

The Reading camp remains undiscovered but, as described by Asser, it acted more like a fortified centre-piece, around which the raiding army could manoeuvre and to which it could retreat at need, than a single inhabited area. The early *longphuirt* are likely to have been built and operated on similar lines. If the *longphuirt* were similar to the winter-camps described in England, then it is likely that they were established at or near existing centres with good communications links and plentiful stocks of food.

It has been objected that, unlike the winter-camps described in England and Frankia, the *longphuirt* were not abandoned after a single season's use but operated as permanent settlements. This was the ultimate result of the mid-ninth-century Viking campaigns. It may not, however, have been the original intention. The Vikings did try to move inland immediately after the establishment of the first *longphuirt* but these campaigns were unsuccessful. After the establishment of *longphuirt* at Dubh Linn and Linn Duachaill in 841, fleets established themselves at Linn Rois on the Boyne and at Cáel Uisce (Narrow Water, Co. Down). An additional fleet led by Turgéis attacked along the Shannon system until he was defeated and drowned by Máel Seachnaill in 845 (Kelly and Maas 1999). It seems likely that the campaigns of the early 840s represented a large-scale effort at conquest rather than a simple extension of the intermittent raids of earlier years. Defeat at the hands of the Irish and the arrival or a second wave of hostile Scandinavians in 849, who attacked both Dubh Linn and Linn Duachaill in 851, weakened the armies established around the original *longphuirt*.

Later ninth-century efforts to extend their control also ended in failure. A Viking fleet under Rothlaiobh or Rodulf campaigned in the Waterford harbour area in the 850s and early 860s but were defeated in 867 (Kelly and Mass 1999). Similarly, the Dublin Vikings attempted to extend their area of control inland through the creation of a *dún* near the monastery at Clondalkin but this was also destroyed in 867 (Clarke 1998). For the remainder of the ninth century the Viking armies in Ireland acted as mercenaries for various Irish kingdoms and power groupings opposed to the ruling Uí Néill rather than as an independent threat. The *longphort* at Dubh Linn/Áth Cliath became a permanent settlement due to failure and defeat rather than as a matter of policy.

IRISH PARALLELS FOR THE WINTER-CAMPS

The obvious Irish equivalents to Carolingian towns or Roman fortifications are the large monastic settlements of which there are many. Both Linn Duachaill and Dubh Linn (*longphuirt* established in the early 840s) share their names with monastic settlements whose abbots are recorded in the annals (at Linn Duachaill the abbot is recorded as being burned by 'foreigners and Irish' the year after the establishment of the *longphort*). It seems likely that the original *longphort* was within the monastic enclosure and incorporated elements of the Christian architecture into the defences (Gibbons 2004).

The recently discovered site at Woodstown appears to represent an Irish riverside settlement, with enclosed and unenclosed elements, on the river Suir. One of the two larger enclosures (C-shaped, *c*.200m in length) has had its outer ditch dated to the fifth century AD. A second adjacent enclosure (*c*.260m in length and 100–60m in width) remains undated. The site appears to have played host to limited industrial activities and may have been associated with the ecclesiastical centre in the neighbouring townland of Killoteran. The site may have been occupied by Vikings at some point between the ninth and eleventh centuries and have played host to ship-building/repair activities and to at least one pagan burial, possibly several. The broad range of artefacts are relatively common on Irish crannóg (lake-dwelling) sites of a similar date which leaves the question open as to what degree the site is a Viking one at all (O'Sullivan 1998, 139). Quantities of hack silver demonstrate an accumulation of wealth on the site although whether this was acquired by the Vikings, or the local Irish, as a result of trade or raiding activity is unclear. Woodstown did not develop into a town and, like many indigenous early settlements, had been abandoned by the late eleventh century (O'Brien et al. 2006, 13–17). The site appears to represent more evidence of temporary Viking occupation of native sites. The development of towns seems to have followed a slightly different pattern.

DUBLIN AND THE DEVELOPMENT OF THE HIBERNO-SCANDINAVIAN TOWNS

At Dublin the original *longphort* seems to have been established near the 'Black Pool' – probably at the monastery of Dubh Linn – and then to have relocated to Áth Cliath in about 843. Settlement was probably not concentrated in a single location but was dispersed in a similar fashion to that in Scandinavia and Viking Scotland. Unlike the Northern Isles of Scotland, however, Ireland did not prove to be a permissive environment for large-scale rural settlement. Recent attempts to suggest the existence of a series of Hiberno-Scandinavian way-stations with a hybrid archaeology and building style along the south and west coasts are unconvincing (Sheehan et al. 2001; Kelly-Gibbons and Kelly 2003; for counterarguments see Gibbons, Gibbons and Higgins 2005).

Ninth-century material and structures are now beginning to come to light near Dublin's 'black pool' and efforts are being made to estimate the location of the original *longphort* (Simpson 2005). No defensive structures or earthworks dating to the ninth century have been located, however, and the proposed *longphort* locations (illustrated in Simpson 2005, 55) seem to be based on the idea of a single defended area or enclosure. Since the ninth century remains seem to reflect a semi-rural spread of settlement this is unlikely to yield positive results.

Excavations have revealed that Dublin was not completely abandoned after its destruction in 902 but have also revealed extensive changes following the 'return' of the Viking leadership from England in 917 (Simpson 2005, 30). A planned Hiberno-Norse town seems to have developed in the mid-tenth century. This is first referred to as a *dún* in 944 and the earliest defensive enclosure so far identified dates to *c.*950. It seems that while the locations of the Hiberno-Norse towns were based on the presence of the earlier *longphuirt* their later development as urban centres took place in parallel with that of the Anglo-Scandinavian towns.

Rather than being planned and specially fortified towns established as an act of Danish policy, the Five Boroughs (Derby, Leicester, Lincoln, Nottingham and Stamford) may have been established as strongholds and urban centres in the early tenth century (910–20) and have been modelled on the Wessex burhs (Richards 2004, 101). Similarly, York appears to show a shift in population in the mid-ninth century but seems to have begun to acquire urban characteristics in the early tenth century when long narrow property plots were established along the southeast side of Coppergate. In the mid- to late tenth century both the usable space within buildings and the density of buildings per plot increased. Overall the pattern is one of developing urbanization in the tenth century rather than immediate urbanization following Scandinavian conquest in the ninth (Hall 2004, 289–90).

DIAGNOSTIC FEATURES FOR SCANDINAVIAN FORTIFICATION?

Despite decades of intensive work no diagnostically identifiable early Viking fortified camps have come to light. If the early *longphuirt* actually consisted of defensive adaptations of an existing Irish site and surrounded by a wider area of unenclosed and unplanned settlement, then they may prove extremely difficult to identify in the field, especially given the sheer volume and variety of earthwork sites in the Irish countryside (running into tens of thousands) and the absence of an agreed diagnostic type of early Viking fortification. Recent work in Norway and Denmark may help to clarify at least some of their likely features, however.

Firstly, it seems likely that the walled or enclosed area of these camps did not contain the bulk of the armies involved or of their accompanying fleets. Anne Norgard Jorgensen has commented on the area of waterfront needed to prepare a Scandinavian fleet to go to sea:

> With a working area of some 2m on each side of the ship, the 100 ships would require a flat coastal stretch around 600m long. Even the amount of sail material for 100 ships of 50m (squared) amounts to half a hectare or 5,000m (squared) of sail of linen or wool – but this is just mentioned to give an impression of the size and resource consumption (Norgard Jorgensen 2002).

Based on Norgard Jorgensen's work, defending the fleets of *c.*60 ships each on the Liffey and the Boyne in 836 would have required a defended space over 300m long. The fortified enclosures that have been excavated, such as the one at Repton, seem too small to have defended such large numbers of ships and it seems unlikely that the fleets operating in Ireland were defended by earthworks on this scale either. It seems more likely that they may have been dispersed outside the fortifications.

Secondly, given the predilection of Scandinavian armies for occupying established towns, estates and ecclesiastical centres, the surviving remains of a Viking camp may not be diagnostically identifiable on the ground. Their seaward defences may be, however. A system of sea-control structures connected with 'naval bases' dating to the late Iron Age, Viking Age and medieval periods have been identified Denmark. These consist of long barrages of wooden stakes used to seal entrances to anchorages and landing areas. Early versions of the technique were in use between the first and fifth centuries and a series of fleet levy areas and anchorages were defended by sea-control barrages throughout the Viking Age, from at least AD 700 until the twelfth century (Norgard Jorgensen 2002).

Since a system of sea defences played a central role in Scandinavian naval warfare it seems possible that they also played a role in the defence of coastal and riverine camps in Ireland. This is particularly likely at Linn Duachaill and Dubh Linn where the original set of invaders faced other Scandinavians in the early 850s. In Scandinavia the sea-control system was extended and repaired into the twelfth century and this may have also been the case in Ireland. Naval warfare, between different Irish groups, rival Hiberno-Scandinavian towns, and by Hiberno-Scandinavian fleets in the service of Irish kings, was a feature of Irish warfare in the pre-Norman period and wooden or stone barrages may have played a role in the defence of important maritime centres, where topography permitted. Wexford, Waterford, Cork and Limerick harbours are the most likely locations for the discoveries of such barrages if they did in fact exist. These might, however, be misidentified as fish-traps or causeways, especially due to the increasing number of these being located by intertidal surveys and the general lack of awareness that coastal defence features might be encountered.

Efforts to locate early *longphuirt* in the field through the use of place-names and field surveys have failed to produce any incontestably Viking evidence. The Woodstown discoveries may ultimately shed some light on the problem but the extent and duration of Viking activities there have not yet been fully elucidated. In view of this, rather than continuing to look for earthworks on river bends that fit a preconceived model of a Viking *longphort* it might be wise for scholars and researchers to shift their attentions to the intertidal zone and to areas commanding the entrances to landing places. Wooden barrages of ninth-century date are likely to prove the most reliable evidence that an area was used as a Scandinavian *longphort*.

CONCLUSION

The supposedly unique nature of Scandinavian settlement in Ireland has been shown to be illusory. While at present we have no evidence for early Viking-Age Norse fortifications in Ireland, the available evidence suggests that the ninth-century *longphuirt* may have had no identifiable form as permanent settlements. In spite of the importance of some of the *longphort* locations as the setting for later urbanization in Ireland, they seem rather to have retained their original roles as military strong-points surrounded by a semi-rural hinterland. Successful Irish resistance prevented the establishment of a rural Scandinavian-style society across any large region of Ireland, leaving the ninth-century invaders tied to their original temporary raiding bases. Rather than developing out of the ninth-century *longphuirt*, the tenth-century towns appear to have developed in parallel with both the Anglo-Scandinavian and Anglo-Saxon centres with which they shared the Irish Sea province.

BIBLIOGRAPHY

Biddle, M. and Kjolbye-Biddle, B. 2001 Repton and the 'great heathen army', 873–4. In J. Graham-Campbell, R. Hall, J. Jesch and D.N. Parsons (eds) *Vikings and the Danelaw: select papers from the proceedings of the thirteenth Viking Congress*, 45–96. Exeter.

Bhreathnach, E. 1998 Saint Patrick, Vikings and Inber Dée–longphort in the early Irish literary tradition. *Wicklow Archaeology and History* 1, 36–9.

Buckley, V. and Sweetman, D. (eds) 1991 *Archaeological survey of County Louth*. Dublin.

Clarke, H.B. 1998 Proto-towns and towns in Ireland and Britain in the ninth and tenth centuries. In H.B. Clarke, M. Ní Mhaonaigh and R. Ó Floinn (eds) *Ireland and Scandinavia in the early Viking Age*, 331–80. Dublin.

Connolly, M., Coyne, F. and Lynch, L. 2005 *Underworld: death and burial in Cloghermore Cave, Co. Kerry*, Bray.

Duffy, S. (ed.) 2004 *Medieval Dublin VI: proceedings of the Friends of Medieval Dublin symposium 2003*. Dublin.

Dyer, J. 1972 Earthworks of the Danelaw frontier. In Fowler (ed.) *Archaeology and the landscape: essays for L.V. Grinsell*, 222–36. London.

Etchingham, C. 1994 Evidence of Scandinavian settlement in Wicklow. In K. Hannigan and W. Nolan (eds) *Wicklow history and society: interdisciplinary essays on the history of an Irish county*, 13–138. Dublin.

Flanagan, M.T. 1997 Irish and Anglo-Norman warfare in twelfth-century Ireland. In T. Bartlett and K. Jeffrey (eds) *A military history of Ireland*, 52–75. Cambridge.

Gibbons, M. 2004 The longphort phenomenon in Early Christian and Viking Ireland. *History Ireland*, 12, no 3.

Gibbons, M. 2005 Athlunkard (Ath-an-longphort): a reassessment of the proposed Viking fortress in Fairyhill Td County Clare. *The Other Clare* 29, 22–5.

Gibbons, M. & M. and Higgins, J. 2005 Hiberno-Norse ringed pin from Omey Feichín, Connemara–its historical and cultural setting. *Journal of the Galway Archaeological and Historical Society*, 57, 150–65.

Hall, R. 2004 Jórvík: a Viking-Age city. In Hines et al. (eds) 2004, 284–95.

Hines, J. Lane, A. and Redknap, M. (eds) 2004 *Land, sea and home*. Society for Medieval Archaeology Monograph 20. Leeds.

Holmquist Olausson, L. 2002 The fortification of Birka–interaction between land and sea. In Norgard Jorgensen et al. (eds) 2002, 159–67.

Hurley, M. 1986 Late Viking Age settlement in Waterford city. In W. Nolan and T.P. Power (eds) *Waterford history and society: interdisciplinary essays on the history of an Irish county*, 49–72. Dublin.

Hurley, M. 2003 The defences. In R.M. Cleary and M.F. Hurley (eds) *Excavations in Cork city 1984–2000*, 171–181. Cork.

Kelly, E.P. 1995 Vikings on the Barrow. *Archaeology Ireland*, 9, no. 3.

Kelly, E.P. and Maas, J. 1999 The Vikings and the kingdom of Laois. In P.G. Lane and W. Nolan (eds) *Laois history and society: interdisciplinary essays on the history of an Irish county*, 123–59. Dublin.

Kelly, E.P. and O'Donovan, E. 1998 A Viking *longphort* near Athlunkard, Co. Clare. *Archaeology Ireland*. 12, no. 4, 13–16.

Keynes, S. and Lapidge, M. (eds) 2004 *Alfred the Great: Asser's Life of King Alfred and other contemporary sources*. London.

Norgaard Jorgensen, A., Pind, J., Jorgnesen, L. and Clausen, B. (eds) 2002 *Maritime warfare in northern Europe: technology, organisation, logistics and administration 500BC–1500AD*. Copenhagen.

Norgard Jorgensen, A. 2002 Naval bases in southern Scandinavia from the seventh to the twelfth century. In Norgard Jorgensen et al. (eds) 2002, 125–52.

O'Brien, R. and Russell I. 2005 The Hiberno-Scandinavian site of Woodstown 6, County Waterford. In J. O'Sullivan and M. Stanley (eds) *Recent archaeological discoveries on national road schemes 2004*. Archaeology and the National Roads Authority, Monograph Series no. 2, 111–124, Bray.

O'Brien, R., Quinney, P. and Russell I. 2006 Preliminary report on the archaeological excavations and finds retrieval strategy of the Hiberno-Scandinavian site of Woodstown 6, County Waterford. *Decies* 61, 13–95

O'Conor, K.D. 1998 *The archaeology of medieval rural settlement in Ireland*. Discovery Programme Monograph no. 3, Dublin.

O'Donovan, J. (ed.) 1856 *The annals of the kingdom of Ireland by the Four Masters*, 7 vols, Dublin.

O'Sullivan, A. 1998 *The archaeology of lake settlement in Ireland*. Discovery Programme Monograph no. 4, Dublin.

Richards, J.D. 2004 *Viking Age England*, Stroud.

Redknap, M. 2004 Viking-Age settlement in Wales and the evidence from Llanbedrgoch. In Hines et al. (eds) 2004, 139–76.

Simpson, L. 2005 Viking warrior burials in Dublin: is this the longphort? In S. Duffy (ed.) *Medieval Dublin VI. Proceedings of the Friends of Medieval Dublin symposium 2004*, 11–62. Dublin.

Sheehan, J., Stummann Hansen, S., Ó Corráin, D. 2001 A Viking Age maritime haven: a reassessment of the island settlement at Beginish, County Kerry. *Journal of Irish Archaeology* 10, 93–119.

Sheehan, J. 2004 Social and economic integration in Viking-Age Ireland: the evidence of the hoards. In Hines et al. (eds) 2004, 177–206.

Talbot, E. 1974 Scandinavian fortification in the British Isles. *Scottish Archaeological Forum* 6, 37–45

Trimpe Burger, J.A. 1975 The geometrical fortress of Oost Souburg (Zeeland). *Chateau Gaillard*, 7, 215–19.

Wallace, P.F. 1982 The origins of Dublin. In B.G. Scott (ed.) *Studies on early Ireland: essays in honour of M.V. Duignan*, 129–42. Belfast.

Watson, W. 2004 *The Celtic place-names of Scotland*. Edinburgh.

Pre-Romanesque churches in County Dublin and its hinterland: the Golden Ratio

NESSA WALSH

This paper is based on a thesis presented in partial fulfilment of a MA degree completed by the author in 1993 at UCD. The original thesis documented and catalogued a total of eighteen pre-Romanesque churches in the modern province of Leinster. This type of church had been referred to by Leask in the first volume of his landmark publication *Irish churches and monastic buildings* (1955). In his chronology these churches were placed after the early dry stone ecclesiastical buildings predominant along the west coast of Ireland, which Leask suggests date to the seventh century and earlier and before the churches of the Romanesque period dating from the twelfth century, hallmarked by carved and sculptural decoration.

In the last decade, publications on churches of this type have discussed regional variations with a particular focus on masonry and construction (Ó Carragáin 2005). Manning has provided studies of individual buildings, such as those of the cathedrals at Glendalough, Co. Wicklow (2002) and Clonmacnoise, Co. Offaly (1998) and has also documented references to early timber and stone churches in the annals (2000).

Five of the eighteen churches documented in the writer's thesis are located in County Dublin: Dalkey Island, Kill o' the Grange, Killiney, Kiltiernan and Palmerstown. These are the subject of this paper, which also includes references to the other thirteen churches in Leinster: Agha and Kiloughternane, Co. Carlow; Kilree and Clonamery, Co. Kilkenny; Ardagh, Co. Longford; Dulane, Co. Meath; Temple Doolin, Clonmacnoise, Co. Offaly; Fore, Co. Westmeath and the cathedral, Reefert, St Kevin's, St Mary's and Trinity all at Glendalough, Co. Wicklow.

For the five County Dublin churches, I present below a discussion of the current presentation and dimensions of their primary pre-Romanesque surviving remains, while the dating, relative chronology and nave length/breadth ratios of all eighteen churches will also be considered.

INTRODUCTION

The defining characteristics of these churches are as follows: they are of mortared stone construction; the majority were originally constructed as

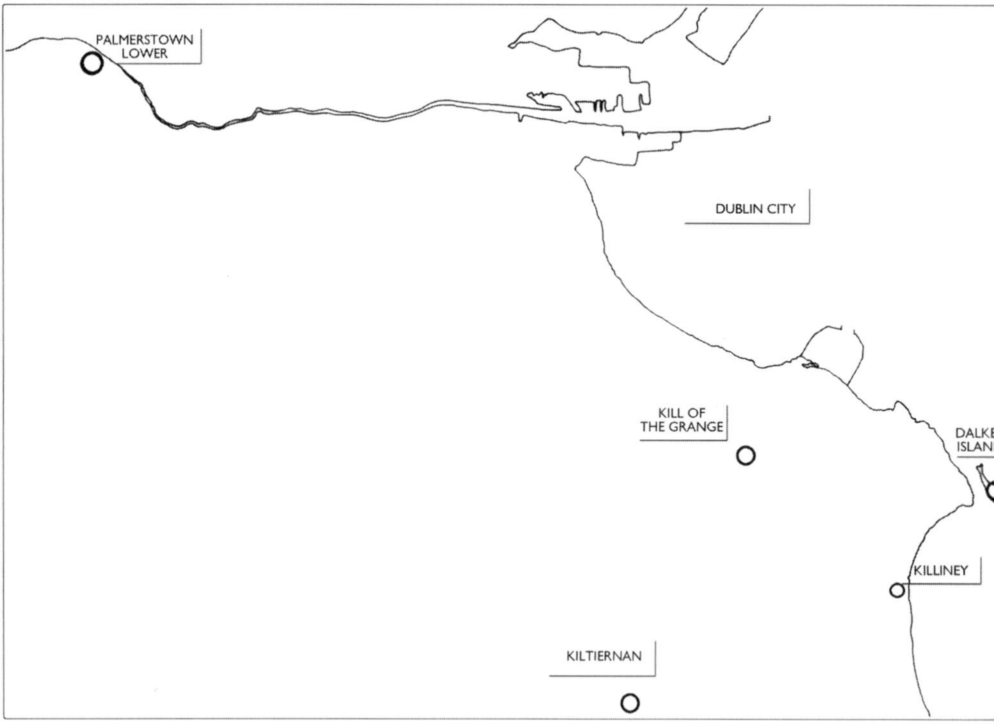

1 Distribution map of County Dublin churches

single-cell buildings with an original square-headed doorway, located in the centre of the west gable; all are orientated east-west; their interiors were lit by a small number of simple round- or square-headed windows which splayed inwards; any decorative sculpture that survives in the original church fabric is confined to the west doorway. The pre-Romanesque churches can be divided further into two groups by the presence or absence of antae (projections of the nave side walls past the west and east walls) that most authors agree are a skeuomorph from earlier timber constructed churches.

The following is a catalogue of the five pre-Romanesque County Dublin churches; interestingly all these churches are located to the south of the River Liffey and all except that at Palmerstown are located within six miles of each other (fig. 1), a fact which would be interesting to explore in further research.

2 Dalkey Island, view from SE

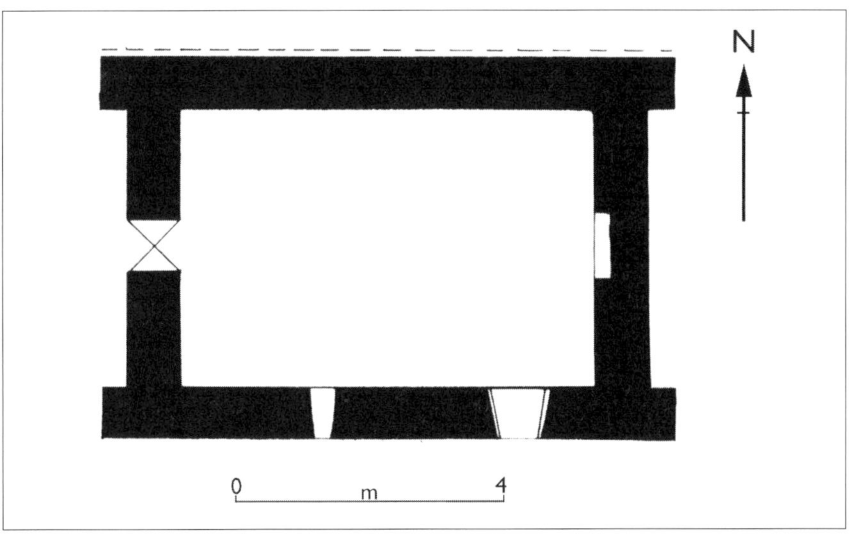

3 Plan of Dalkey Island

THE PRE-ROMANESQUE COUNTY DUBLIN CHURCHES

Dalkey Island, Dalkey, County Dublin

This church, dedicated to St Beccnat, is situated on Dalkey Island, opposite Coliemore Harbour.

This is a single-cell church, with a square-headed doorway at the centre of the west wall. The doorway lintel comprises a single stone, dressed on its external face. The door jambs incline and have been created by simply squaring off the wall masonry. Three square-headed windows survive in the south wall and antae are present at both the east and west gables. The bell cote on the west gable is a later addition.

The antae project by an average of .37m. The nave measures 6.25m x 4.14m with a length/breadth ratio of 1.504:1 (figs 2 and 3).

Killiney, County Dublin

This church is located in a graveyard on Marino Road off Killiney Hill Road. It is dedicated to the six daughters of Léinín *c.*sixth century.

It is a three-cell church comprising contemporary nave and chancel and a third, later cell added to the north wall of the nave and chancel. The nave has a square-headed doorway in the west wall. No original nave windows survive. The soffit of the west doorway lintel-stone displays a Latin cross carved in relief. The nave is connected to the chancel by an arch, the piers of which were constructed by squaring off the chancel walls. The chancel has a window in its south, east, and west walls; the east window is square-headed and the lintels of the north and south windows are missing. The east and west gables of the nave are intact, as is the east gable of the chancel cell. The third, later cell is located at the north of the nave and chancel and is accessed internally by a later doorway in the north wall of the nave.

The nave measures 6.15m x 3.90m; the chancel 3.52m x 2.70m. The length/breadth ratio of the nave is 1.57:1 (figs 4 and 5).

Kill o' the Grange, Clonkeen, County Dublin

The church at Kill o' the Grange is located within a walled graveyard at the edge of a housing estate off the Abbey Road. It is associated with St Fintan.

The church currently stands as two interconnecting cells, an original nave and a later eastern chancel. The nave's west gable survives to its full height, including a later belfry, while its east gable also appears to be relatively intact. In the nave a square-headed doorway is located at the centre of the west gable. The lintel of this doorway is composed of two individual stones lying parallel to each other, dressed on their exposed faces. The jambs, which incline, were constructed by squaring off the wall masonry. North and south wall windows each have external round heads carved from single stones, while the interior

4 Killiney, view from SW

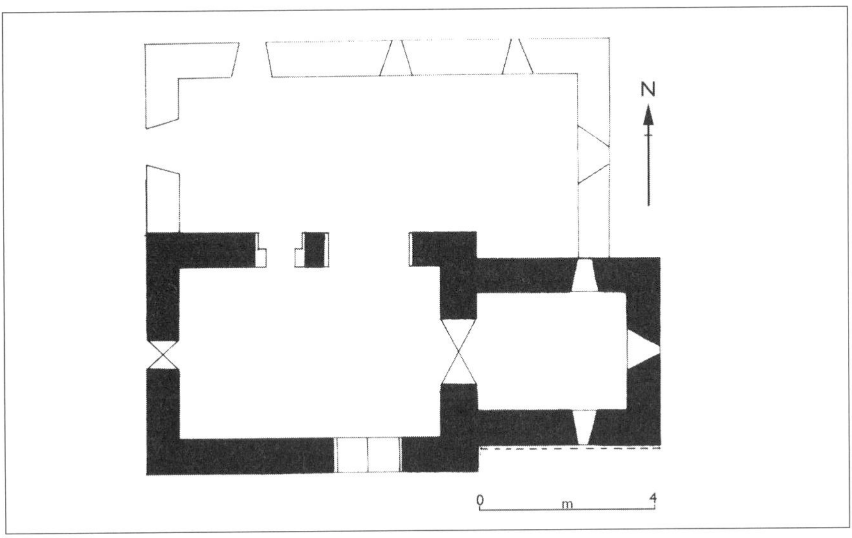

5 Plan of Killiney

window heads are composed of a number of individual thin stones. Two further square-headed windows and a later pointed-headed doorway are present in the south nave wall. Antae are present at each corner of the nave projecting forward by an average of .27m.

6 Kill o' the Grange, view of west gable

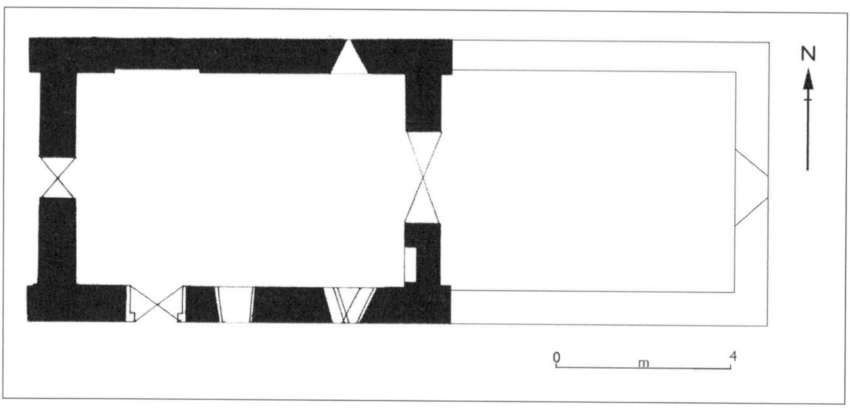

7 Plan of Kill o' the Grange

Only the east wall of the chancel survives to any height and a window is present at the centre of this wall. The north and south walls of the chancel were bonded directly onto the east antae of the nave. A round-headed arch in the nave's east wall connects the nave to the later chancel cell.

The nave measures 7.67m x 5.03m with a length/breadth ratio of 1.55:1 (figs 6 and 7).

8 Kiltiernan, view from NW

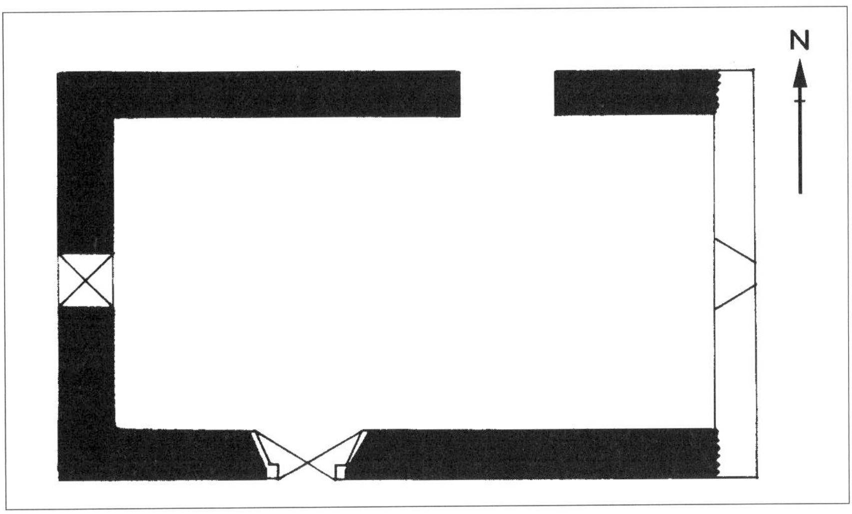

9 Plan of Kiltiernan

Kiltiernan, County Dublin
Located on Bishop's Lane off Ballybetagh Road, standing in a graveyard on ground that falls away steeply at the south of the graveyard to a river. This church is associated with St Tigernán.

This is a single-cell church with a square-headed doorway (now blocked) located at the centre of the west wall. A later pointed-headed doorway has been inserted in the south wall and a round-headed window is present in the

10 Palmerstown, view from SW

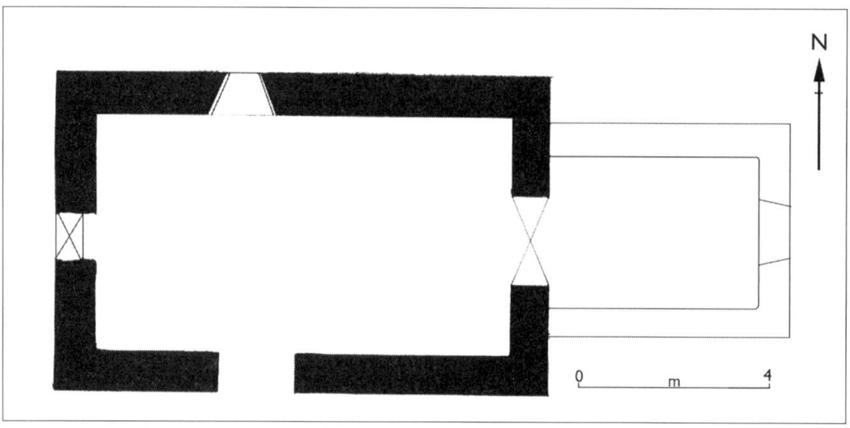

11 Plan of Palmerstown

east gable. Two phases of building can be recognised from a change in masonry type in the south wall and the different type of masonry in the surviving east wall (smaller, rounder stones). The remains of a wall extend south from the exterior of the south wall. Although there is no standing chancel cell, records from the Regal Visitation of 1615 and 1630 note 'a church and chancel' at Kiltiernan.

As the eastern end of the church is certainly a later extension, the length of the original nave is not known. The width of the nave is 5.40m (figs 8 and 9).

Palmerstown, Palmerstown Lower, County Dublin

This church stands in a walled graveyard .25 miles northwest of St Steward's Hospital on the southern slopes of the Liffey Valley and is notably eleven miles from the nearest of the other four churches.

Presently it stands as a two-cell church consisting of a nave and narrower eastern chancel. The original nave had a square-headed west doorway (now blocked) and a large window has been inserted above this doorway. The nave's east gable survives to what appears to be its original height. The second cell, an eastern chancel, is a later addition; it is narrower than the nave and its walls are not integrated with those of the nave. The two cells are connected by an archway in the nave's east wall.

It is likely that a doorway was inserted in the nave's southern wall where there is currently a gap in the wall. A belfry was added to the nave's west gable. The north nave window was subsequently reduced in size, as was the east window of the chancel cell.

The nave measures 8.80m x 5.02m with a nave length/breadth ratio of 1.75:1 (figs 10 and 11).

THE OTHER THIRTEEN CHURCHES

The location and length (**L**)/breadth (**B**) ratios of the other thirteen pre-Romanesque churches included in the original study group are:

Church	L x B	L/B Ratio
Agha, Co. Carlow	? x 4.60m	n/a
Kiloughternane, Co. Carlow	5.71m x 3.65m	1.568:1
Kilree, Co. Kilkenny	8.57m x 5.67m	1.511:1
Clonamery, Co. Kilkenny	? x 5.70m	n/a
Ardagh, Co. Longford	8.55m x 5.88m	1.454:1
Dulane, Co. Meath	10.49m x 6.30m	1.665:1
Temple Doolin, Clonmacnoise, Co. Offaly	8.05m x 3.50m	2.3:1
Fore, Co. Westmeath	11.41m x 7.20m	1.584:1
Glendalough, Co. Wicklow:		
The cathedral	14.76m x 9.01m	1.638:1
Reefert	8.80m x 5.24m	1.679:1
St Kevin's	6.95m x 4.45m	1.56:1
St Mary's	9.78m x 6.10m	1.603:1
Trinity	8.96m x 5.30m	1.69:1

ANALYSIS

Of the total of eighteen pre-Romanesque churches studied, fifteen were originally constructed as single-cell churches while three, those at Killiney, County Dublin and Reefert and Trinity at Glendalough were built as two-cell churches. Only four (those at Kiloughternane, Dalkey Island, Ardagh, and Dulane) stand today as single-cell churches whose plans have not been added to or altered. The other eleven churches survive as two- or three-cell churches; the second and/or third cell being a later addition.

Antae

Antae – the projections of the nave side walls past the west and east walls – are present at two of the five churches in County Dublin – Dalkey and Kill o' the Grange. Of the other thirteen Leinster churches, nine have antae projecting from both the nave's east and west gable; at two churches, Agha, Co. Carlow and Clonamery, Co. Kilkenny, the nave's east wall was demolished when the later chancel cell was added. Antae are not found at any of the later chancels. The depth of the antae projection ranges from .20m at Temple Doolin in Clonmacnoise to .70m at Dulane, Co. Meath.

In a comparison of nave areas and lengths and antae projection it is found that the three churches with the greatest antae projection (the cathedral at Glendalough, Fore, Co. Westmeath and Dulane, Co. Meath) also have the largest nave area and longest nave lengths. However, the remaining churches represent a mixture of nave areas and their nave lengths appear to be unrelated to the projection of their antae.

Antae are also present at Irish churches with Romanesque doorways and windows but their presence is likely to indicate the insertion of Romanesque features into an earlier church. For example, the cathedral in Clonmacoise has antae but a Romanesque doorway, and, as Manning (2000) documents, it is mentioned in the annals as having been constructed in 909AD.

Antae are not a feature of any standing British churches but have been found during excavations, notably at sites with an Irish connection: St Columba's Shrine on Iona had antae extending from each of its four corners; St Dunstan's church of St John the Baptist at Glastonbury, uncovered during excavation, had antae and a break in the centre of its west wall and finally, on St Patrick's Isle at Peel, Isle of Man, remains of what appear to be antae were found during the excavation of St Patrick's church.

Decoration

Of the larger group of eighteen Leinster churches studied, original decorative sculpture is present only at their western doorways, and of the five County Dublin churches, decoration is only found at Killiney (although the possibility

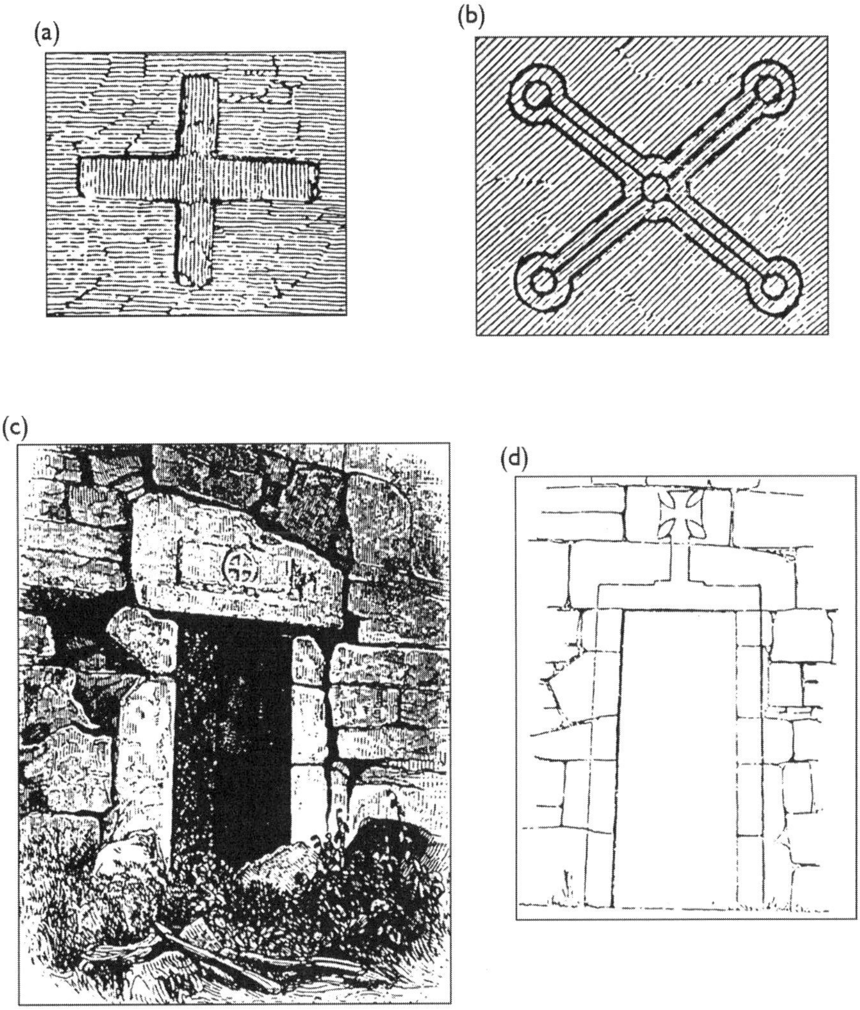

12 Decorated doorways: a) Killiney, lintel soffit (after Petrie); b) St Mary's, lintel soffit (after Petrie); c) Fore, exterior west doorway (after Petrie); d) Clonamery, exterior west doorway (after Leask)

of decoration being present at Kiltiernan and Palmerstown cannot be ruled out as their doors are blocked and the soffits of the lintel are not visible). Crosses are carved in the external lintels of the west doorways at Fore, Clonamery and, as in Killiney, on the soffit at St Mary's in Glendalough (fig. 12).

Dating

Dating of these pre-Romanesque churches is considered by an analysis of their architectural features, annalistic references, and scientific evidence.

Manning (1998) in his study of the churches at Clonmacnoise suggests that shallower antae may indicate a later date and Ó Carragáin generally supports this view (2005), suggesting that shallower antae are more likely to be found in churches that have other architectural features supporting a later date, i.e., round-headed doorways and windows, minor sculptural embellishments, and raises the possibility that in general churches without antae are of a later date. Accepting this view, the church at Killiney, which has no antae, a plain round-headed chancel arch and a carved cross on the lintel of the west doorway would be the latest church in this group. However when the main group of pre-Romanesque churches is considered in light of Ó Carragáin's suggestion, two of the three churches where sculptural decoration is found have antae – Fore (with an average antae depth of .55m) and Clonamery (with an average antae depth of .31m).

Manning (2000) has documented references in the annals to early churches; one of the eighteen Leinster pre-Romanesque churches is mentioned when it is recorded that a *damliac* (stone church) at Dulane, Co. Meath was burnt in 920AD. The antae at the church at Dulane with a depth of .70m are the deepest antae of the eleven churches catalogued in Leinster with antae and the relatively early reference in the annals to a stone church at Dulane supports Manning's suggestion that shallower antae may indicate a later date.

In 1995 Berger published results from his radiocarbon analysis of mortar samples taken from a selection of early stone ecclesiastical buildings around Ireland. While none was taken from a pre-Romanesque church included in this study, a sample was taken from Temple Ciarán at Clonmacnoise. This single-cell building was included in an appendix to the writer's thesis rather than in the main catalogue because, despite the presence of antae, the west doorway had been altered and it is not clear if it was originally square-headed. The date Berger obtained for Temple Ciarán was 660–980 AD which would confirm that this building is pre-Romanesque and does in fact belong to this study group.

Ratio of nave length to nave breadth

Leask first raises the topic and significance of the length/breadth ratio of early stone churches. He refers to a Brehon law tract dealing with the payment of the builders of stone churches with specific dimensions of 15 feet x 10 feet. Leask claims this 1.5:1 length/breadth ratio is seen at many early stone churches. Ó Carragáin (2005) believes that the proportions of the pre-Romanesque churches relate primarily to the size of the church and that larger churches generally had longer proportions. However in this study

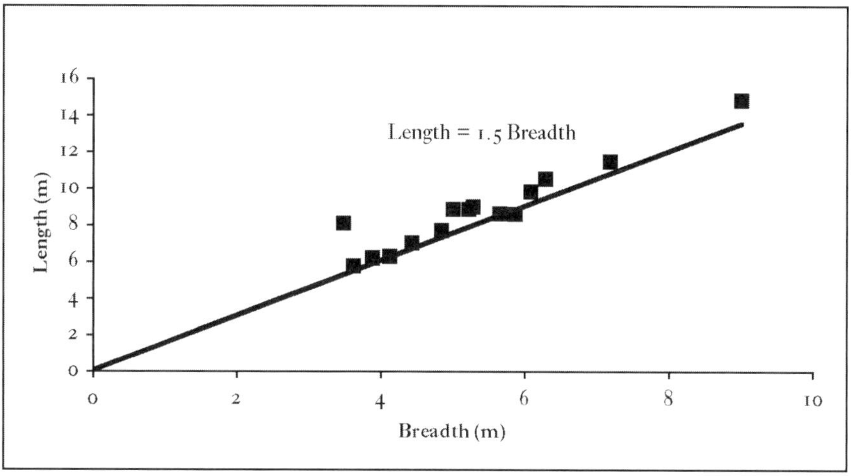

13 Graph 1: Leask's hypothesis rejected

group of pre-Romanesque churches those with the three longest naves and largest nave areas (the cathedral at Glendalough, Fore, Co. Westmeath and Dulane, Co. Meath), with nave length/breadth ratios of 1.638:1, 1.584:1 and 1.665:1 respectively, cannot be said to have significantly longer proportions than the rest of the study group.

Leask's hypothesis may be tested statistically using fifteen of the eighteen pre-Romanesque churches originally studied for which the original length/

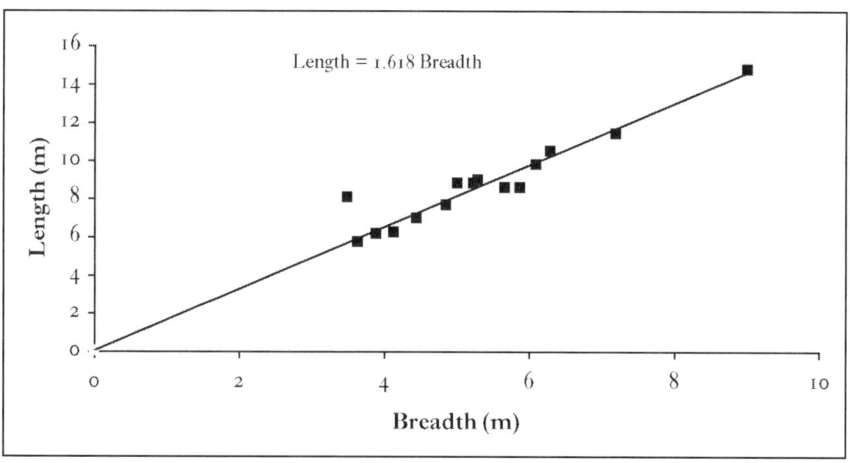

14 Graph 2: The Golden Ratio

breadth can be determined with certainty. In Figure 13 a line representing a length/breadth ratio of 1.5:1 has been drawn against a scatterplot of the lengths and breadths of the naves of the fifteen churches. It may be seen that most of the points do not lie on this line and in fact a formal statistical test rejects this line as the 'best fit' to the data (fig. 13).

It is proposed that the guideline length/breadth ratio for these churches was that of the Golden Ratio, namely, 1.618:1 which will be explained below. As a test of this hypothesis, Figure 14 shows a scatterplot of the lengths and breadths of the naves of fifteen pre-Romanesque churches in Leinster, along with a line with a slope of 1.618. It may be seen that six of the churches fall on this line.

What is the significance of the Golden Ratio?
When a line is divided into two parts so that the ratio of the whole line to the longer part is equal to the ratio of the longer part to the shorter part, we obtain the Golden Ratio. The formula, defined by the third century BC Greek mathematician Euclid, is (fig. 15):

$$(ac + cb)/ac = ac/cb$$

15 Euclid's formula

where *ac* is the longer segment and *cb* the shorter one. When a line is divided in this way, the *a*/*b* ratio is 1.618:1. A rectangle whose length to breadth ratio is 1.618:1 is said to be a Golden Rectangle.

It has been claimed that the Golden Rectangle is the most aesthetically pleasing shape for a rectangle. It was used in the composition of the Great Pyramid at Giza, the Parthenon in Athens, in medieval cathedrals such as Chartres in France and in the layout and arrangement of paintings by Renaissance artists such as Leonardo da Vinci, Michaelangelo and Raphael and later by nineteenth- and twentieth-century artists such as Seurat and Dali.

SUMMARY

In summary, there is a recognizable group of pre-Romanesque churches in Leinster with distinguishable architectural features which can be dated to the tenth century by radio-carbon evidence and annalistic references, and the evidence from this group of churches supports the writer's suggestion that the builders of these churches had a knowledge of the Golden Rectangle, a sophisticated and aesthetically pleasing ideal that has been in use in architecture in Mediterranean Europe since 3,000 BC.

ACKNOWLEDGMENTS

I would like to thank Linzi Simpson for encouraging me to publish and for assisting with the editing; Brendan Walsh for his help with the statistical analysis, his enthusiasm and support; and the graphics department of Margaret Gowen & Co. Ltd.

BIBLIOGRAPHY

Berger, R. 1995 Radiocarbon dating of early medieval Irish monuments. *R.I.A. Proc.* 95C, 159–74.

Ní Ghabhláin, S. 1995 Church and community in medieval Ireland: the diocese of Kilfenora. *R.S.A.I. Jn.* 125, 61–84.

Leask, H.G. 1995 *Irish churches and monastic buildings Vol. I. The first phases and the Romanesque*. Dundalk.

Manning, C. 1998 Clonmacnoise cathedral. In H. King (ed.) *Clonmacnoise Studies 1. Seminar papers 1994*, 56–86. Dublin.

Manning, C. 2000 References to church buildings in the annals. In A.P. Smyth (ed.) *Seanchas. Studies in early and medieval Irish archaeology, history and literature in honour of F.J. Byrne*, 37–52. Dublin.

Manning, C. 2002 A puzzle in stone: the cathedral at Glendalough. *Archaeology Ireland* 60, 18–21.

Ó Carragáin, T. 2005 Regional variation in Irish pre-Romanesque architecture. *Antiquaries Journal* 86, 23–56.

O'Keeffe, T. 2000 Romanesque as metaphor: architecture and reform in early twelfth-century Ireland. In A.P. Smyth (ed.) *Seanchas. Studies in early and medieval Irish archaeology, history and literature in honour of F.J. Byrne*, 313–22. Dublin.

Paulos, J.A. 1991 *Beyond numeracy, an uncommon dictionary of mathematics*. London.

Walsh, N. 1993 The pre-Romanesque mortared stone churches of Leinster. MA, University College Dublin (unpublished).

The Irish, the Vikings and the English: new archaeological evidence from excavations at Golden Lane, Dublin

EDMOND O'DONOVAN

with contributions from Niamh Doyle and Siobhán Scully

This paper describes the results of an archaeological excavation on Golden Lane in 2005 adjacent to the site of the church of St Michael le Pole in Dublin. The text describes the medieval archaeological deposits uncovered at the site and is followed by an account of the principal medieval artefacts discovered during the excavation. The prehistoric and post-medieval discoveries on site are not described in any detail.

HISTORICAL AND ARCHAEOLOGICAL BACKGROUND

The topography of the site

The site was situated on the southern fringe of the church site on a low-lying ridge separated from the medieval town by the River Poddle and the *Dubhlinn* located half way between St Patrick's cathedral and Dublin Castle. The Poddle flows down Patrick Street and turns east along the base of the city wall on the western and southern edge of the site; it has been culverted and is now underground. The great 'pool' of Dublin from which the place-name *Dubhlinn* ('Black Pool') is derived, lies to the northeast. The old riverbed of the Poddle meandered across the valley in the Ship Street/Bride Street area and it was diverted into the city fosse in the late 1170s (Simpson 1997, 17). The ridge on which the excavation was conducted forms a parallel parcel of land to the ridge of Dublin on which the Viking and later medieval walled town developed. The southern suburban hinterland of the medieval walled town of Dublin developed as a result of the inertia created by St Patrick's cathedral and the ancient route way, the *Slighe Chualann*, to the south.

The church of St Michael le Pole

The historical sources indicate that the church of St Michael le Pole was in existence before the arrival of the Anglo-Normans at Dublin in 1170. It formed part of a series of early churches with native dedications in the area, such as St Kevin's, St Brigit's and St Patrick's (Clarke 1977, 39). It has been suggested that

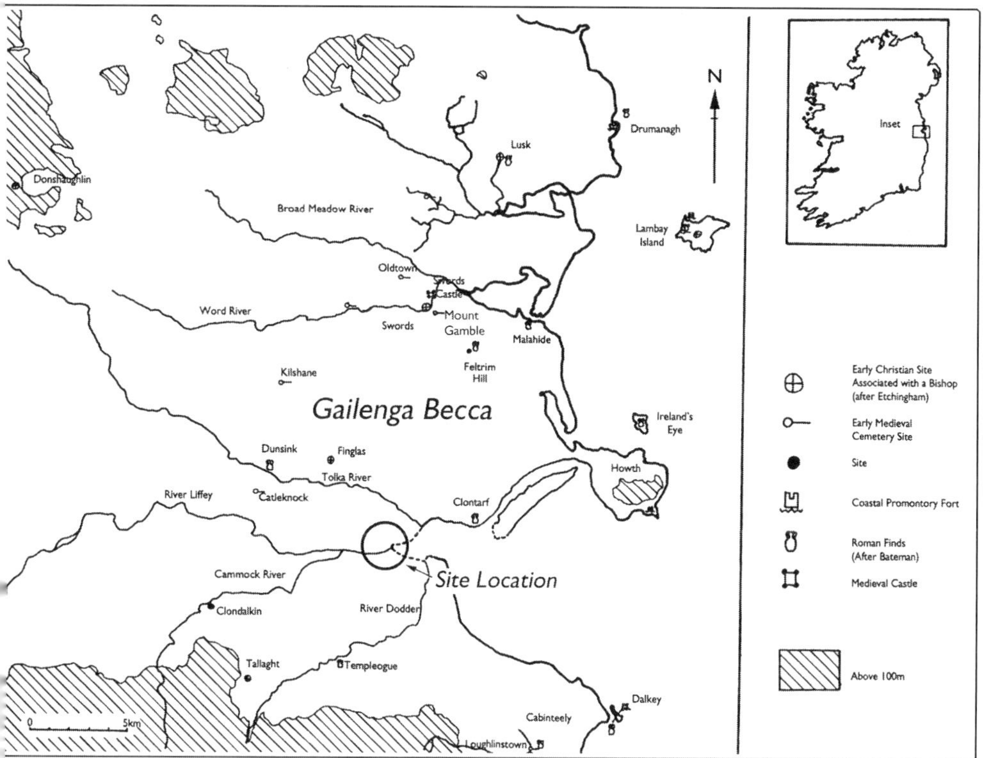

1 Early medieval Dublin

St Michael's is possibly a corruption of St Mac Táil, a seventh-century saint associated with County Kildare. A stone church and round tower were located at the site, another indication of its pre-Norman date (Gowen 2001, 31). However, it does not appear to have been an important church in the medieval period as demonstrated by the fact that in the late thirteenth century it is described as 'not worth the service of a chaplain' and was evidently not functioning as a parish church (McEnery and Refaussé 2001, no. 150, 61). The southern precinct and cemetery associated with the church of St Michael le Pole was uncovered as part of the 2005 excavations. An earlier campaign of archaeological excavations was

2 Church of St Michael le Pole *c.*1751

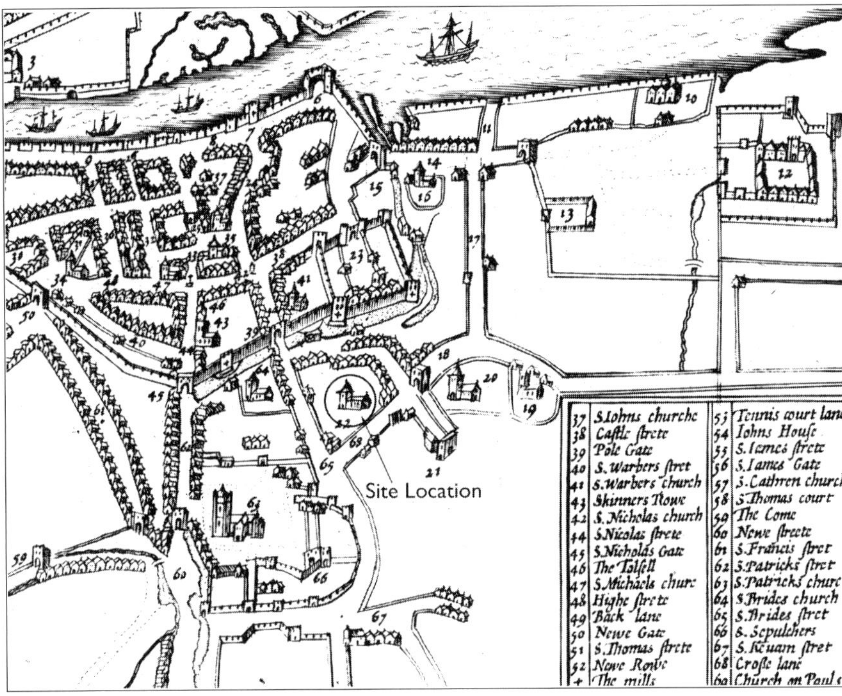

3 John Speed's map of Dublin, 1610

carried out in 1981 on the site by the Dublin Archaeological Research Team or DART (Gowen 2001). These investigations were located on the church site itself and exposed the west wall of the medieval church and the foundations of what was thought to represent an 'engaged' round tower (i.e., one forming part of the church structure). The latter was interpreted as the location of the round tower illustrated in the eighteenth century. A significant unexpected discovery was the identification of archaeological deposits dating from the pre-Viking era.

The earliest deposits (AD 675–900) uncovered by DART consisted of habitation layers. These layers consisted of hearths and substantial post-holes and a series of early ditches cut into the boulder clay. The Phase I evidence was derived from settlement-related occupation at the site, but these deposits were not fully investigated and more extensive excavation at the church site may provide definition on house plans or a pre-masonry timber church. The second phase of evidence at the site consisted of early-medieval burials that pre-dated the foundation of the church and the 'engaged' round tower *c.*AD 1100. Some of these early burials were interred in the Irish Insular tradition and this suggests that an Irish population was buried at the site either before or after the establishment of Dublin as a Viking town. The medieval stone church has been dated to *c.*AD 1100 and continued in use throughout the medieval period, with burials interred within the rectangular walled graveyard

Plate 1 The Viking burial LXXXV under excavation (Photo by Kevin Weldon)

up to 1830. The church of St Michael le Pole was granted to the priory of the Holy Trinity before 1170 and appears to have functioned as a parish church throughout the medieval period.

The growth of Dublin and demise of St Michael le Pole's

The city of Dublin grew in parallel with the church site and Chancery Lane is recorded as a street in the medieval period dating from *c.*AD 1230 and Golden Lane is first referenced in AD 1382 (Clarke 2002, 13). The church is recorded as impoverished and depopulated in the mid-sixteenth century when it was annexed to St Werburgh's church (ibid., 17). It was then deconsecrated and from 1690 the church building was used as a school into the eighteenth century. The building is illustrated as an Alms House on the Ordnance Survey map of 1864. The foundations of the post-medieval buildings were discovered above and abutting the medieval church walls (Gowen 2001). These post-medieval buildings had triangular fireplaces suggestive of 'Dutch Billy' houses built at the site after 1690. An illustration of the church taken from a sketch by J. Grogan in 1751 depicts the building that was finally demolished in the early twentieth century; the site of the church and graveyard is marked on the Ordnance Survey map of 1837. The site of St Michael le Pole's was completely surrounded by houses and other buildings in the city by the eighteenth century and no trace of the monument survives above ground-level today.

Plate 2 Dublin Archaeological Research Team (DART) excavation at the Church of St Michael le Pole, stone-lined grave dating to AD 895–1269 pre-dating the church wall, post-dating boulder clay, hearth on the boulder clay dated to AD 663–872 (after Gowen 2001)

The possible monastic Enclosure aligned on St Stephen's Street

Annalistic references to abbots of Dublin in the seventh and eighteenth century (Clarke 1977, 40) bear witness to the presence of a significant early ecclesiastical site or sites in Dublin prior to the establishment of Viking settlement in the ninth century. These references in conjunction with cartographic evidence led Fr Myles V. Ronan to comment (Ronan 1940, 482) on the peculiar 'rath-like' morphology of St Stephen's Street Upper and Lower, which Howard Clarke (1978 and 2002) has speculated may reflect the location of an early-Christian enclosure and possibly ancient Dublin's episcopal centre. Many archaeological excavations have been conducted within the Stephen's Street enclosure area, however, and no definitive early-Christian ecclesiastical remains have been uncovered to date.

Archaeological excavations at Bride Street and Chancery Lane

Mary McMahon directed archaeological excavations at Bride Street in 1993 (McMahon 2002). The discovery of a small number of early-medieval burials on the site led the director to suggest that the Bride Street site was originally enclosed within a boundary associated with the church of St Michael le Pole some 100m to the east. The burials dated from between AD 726 and 979 (ibid., 81). The discovery of burials, medieval 'garden soil' and post-medieval deposits at the Bride Street site are entirely consistent with Claire Walsh's recent findings

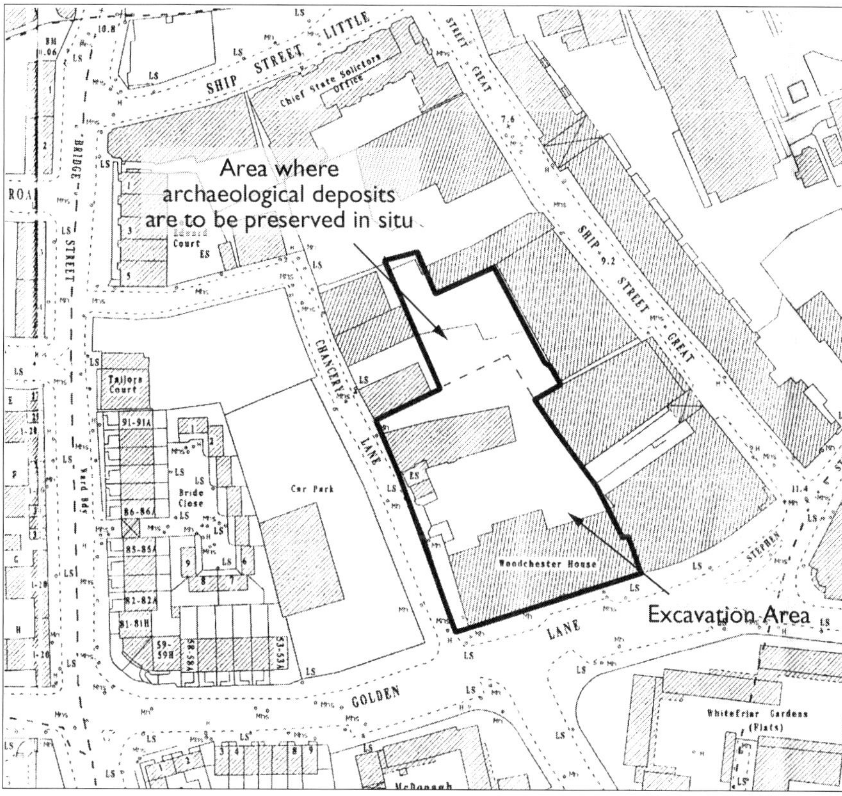

4 Site location

on a neighbouring site on Chancery Lane in 2004 (Walsh, pers. comm.). The Bride Street and Chancery Lane sites back onto one another.

Archaeological excavations at George's Street and Ship Street Great

Two archaeological excavations directed by Linzi Simpson were carried out to the east of the church site of St Michael le Pole. Viking burials were discovered on both sites. An early Viking burial was discovered immediately adjacent to the eastern boundary of the Golden Lane excavations on Ship Street Great (Simpson 2005, 11). The archaeological deposits were almost completely removed from the site by basements; however, a Viking burial was uncovered accompanied by fragments of a sword and a ring. A second archaeological excavation located on the corner of South Great George's Street and Stephen Street Upper revealed four early Viking-Age burials dating from the ninth century. These burials were located on the old south-eastern shore of the Black Pool or *Dubhlinn* and were associated with areas of burning, and possible contemporary habitation deposits. The deposits lay beneath medieval soils and the remains of early post-medieval buildings (ibid., 11).

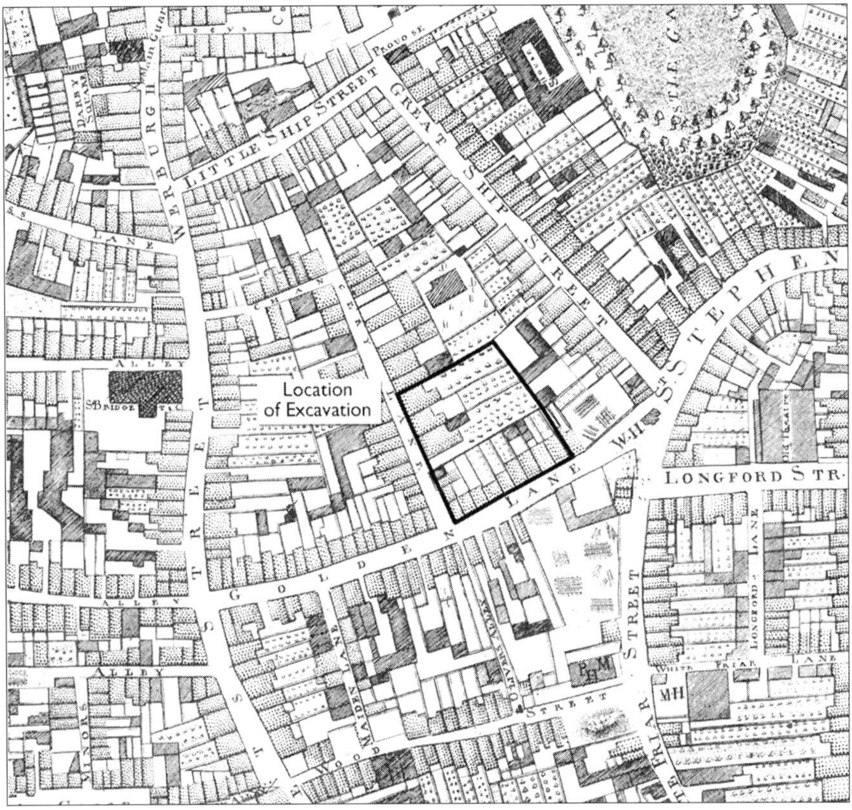

5 Site location (John Rocque, 1756)

ARCHAEOLOGICAL EXCAVATIONS AT GOLDEN LANE

The excavations at Golden Lane in 2005 uncovered early-medieval and Viking-Age settlement activity, a cemetery, four outlying burials (including two Viking burials) and Anglo-Norman settlement activity. The following is a summary description of some of the principal deposits uncovered at the site from the period *c.*AD 600–1500 on the corner of Golden Lane and Chancery Lane. Considerable quantities of post-medieval archaeological deposits were also recorded during the excavation and are not discussed or described here. The text is presented in chronological order and attributed a cultural background where possible.

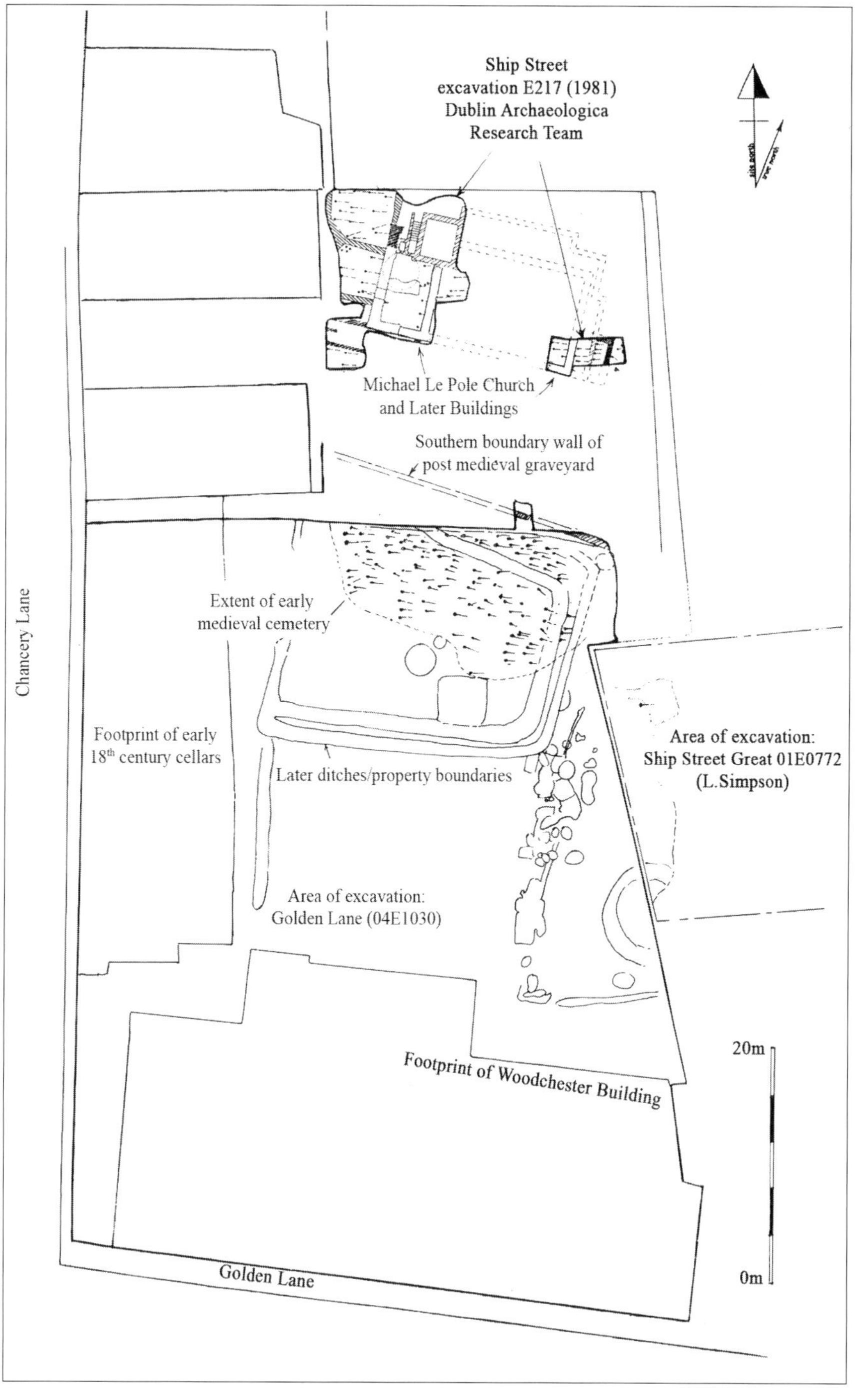

6 Layout of excavations at Golden Lane

Plate 3 Site location superimposed on Dublin's streetscape looking east

Pre-cemetery early-medieval occupation activity

A series of shallow pits (F753, F1830 and F1828) were recorded in the northeast corner of the site. These pits predated the use of the area as an early-medieval cemetery. No direct stratigraphic relationship between these pits and the actual church structure was determined as the church site is located beyond the northern limit of the 2005 season of excavations. However the 1981 campaign of excavation by the Dublin Archaeological Research Team located pits and post-holes predating the masonry structure of the church. The features recorded in the northeast corner of the site may be related in function to the 'pre-church' deposits identified in 1981 (Gowen 2001). The origin of the pits could be associated with activity prior to the establishment of the ecclesiastical site (pre-AD 600–700). Conversely, these pits may be contemporary with the earliest phase of graves predating the masonry church structure and may represent activity on the boundary of the site prior to its use as a cemetery at a later stage. The pending study of the charcoal and macro-fossil analysis from these pits may shed further light on their cultural background.

The pit (F753) was sub-circular in plan (measuring 1.74m long, 1.68m in width and 0.50m maximum depth) with concave sides and a concave, slightly flattened base. The uppermost fills of this feature were truncated by two later burials (Burial nos CVII and CI). The base of the pit was filled with a rich organic clay silt fill (F1130) lying on the base of the pit, with occasional small rounded gravel inclusions and charcoal flecking, as well as animal bone, and was sealed by a layer of yellow brown sandy silt material (F1129). A secondary deposit of organic-rich clay silt (F1128) was similar to primary fill (F1130), containing small sub-rounded gravel inclusions, charcoal flecking, land-snail shell inclusions and disarticulated animal bone. The final layer (F754) sealed the secondary deposit and consisted of grey brown silty clay. It is likely that the lower fill (F1130) and secondary fill (F1128) represent dumps of organic waste or possibly cess and were subsequently deliberately sealed by re-deposited natural subsoil (F1129 and F754).

The pit (F1830) was sub-circular in plan with gradual breaks of slope, sloping *c.*35° concave sides and a flattened concave base. This pit (measuring 1.04m in length, 1m wide and 0.25m in depth) was filled with a homogenous dark greenish grey clay silt deposit (F1831), containing frequent sub-angular limestone pebbles, lenses of charcoal flecking and dark orange mottling throughout the soil matrix. The fill of the pit was truncated by a later burial (Burial no. CCLXXVII).

Due east of pit F1830 was a similar pit, F1828. The full extent of this pit was not located as it was truncated by a medieval ditch and post-medieval drain. The pit (F1828), measuring at least 1.85m in length, 1.54m wide and 0.22m deep, showed evidence of primary silting as a thin layer of dark orange/brown silty clay with frequent charcoal inclusions (0.17m in depth), followed by a secondary deposit of light greyish brown silty clay (F1836). This feature was truncated by a series of burials (Burial nos CCLXXV and CCLXXIII).

Early-medieval cemetery and Viking-Age burials at St Michael le Pole's

A total of 272 burials were excavated on the Golden Lane site. Two hundred and sixty eight of these burials were located in a dense cemetery one on top of the next in a halo, defining the extent of the early church site of St Michael le Pole. The excavated portion of the cemetery measured 22m x 10m and formed the southern and south-western perimeter of the church site. The church itself lies 15m to the north of the 2005 campaign and was partially uncovered by the DART excavation in 1981. The burials have provisionally been dated to the early-medieval period and the Viking Age (*c.*AD 700–1200) prior to the capture and establishment of Dublin by the Anglo-Normans; no medieval pottery was found associated with the grave fills. The cemetery was clearly an element of the early church site at St Michael le Pole. The potential cultural associations of this pre-Norman church site are particularly intriguing as the site appears to span both the early medieval and the Viking Age, culturally and chronologically. No ditch or enclosing feature was

Plate 4 Burials CXVII, CXIV & CIX looking west

identified cut into the boulder clay defining the extent of the cemetery; however the burials clearly demark a boundary between church activity and activity relating to 'secular' settlement beyond it. The radiocarbon dating program for burials within the cemetery is not complete and thus far the burials within the main cemetery have only been dated by comparison of grave morphology with comparable sites and artefactual association.

The burial rite at Golden Lane The burials at the Golden Lane site were interred in the supine position as extended inhumations orientated with the head to the west. However, in common with other cemeteries there was some variation within this rite. Burial CIV is a good example of a typical burial from the site (note that the lower legs of Burial CIV below the knee have been removed in the medieval period by the digging of a later ditch). The burials were largely contained within a tight elliptical grave-cut and were uncovered with their arms either tightly by the side or loosely crossed above the pelvis. This occurred in common with the placing of the legs together and the upright placing of the head, occasionally augmented by stones on either side of the head (ear-muff stones). This burial position is consistent with the early-Christian burial rite where a body is placed in a grave wrapped in a shroud. The process of wrapping the body in a shroud is illustrated on the Cross of the Scriptures at Clonmacnoise (O'Brien 2003). The tight clustering

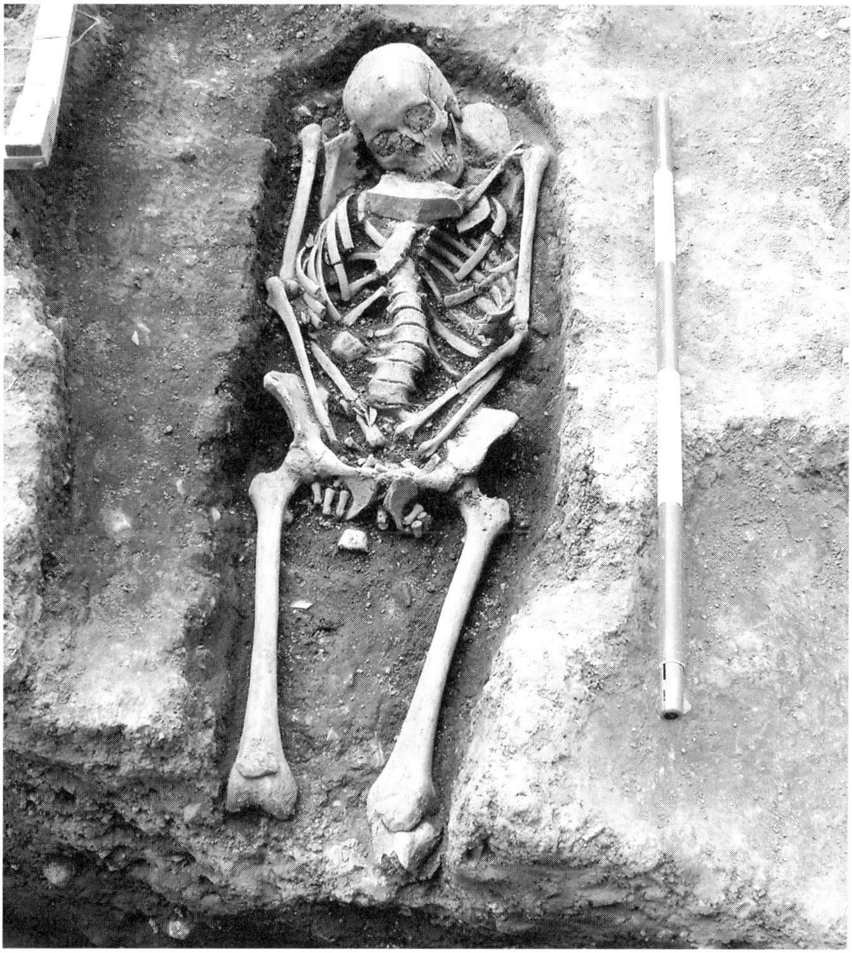

Plate 5 Burial CIV

of the burials (in a cemetery) is consistent with 'early-Christian' burial practices at church sites in Ireland.

A number of examples of graves containing ear-muff stones were recorded during the excavation along with a variety of hand positions in common with other 'early-Christian' cemeteries in Ireland. Burials II and CCXXXIV are clear examples of this rite where stones are used to support the head within the grave. This suggests that the arrangement of the head and chin on the upper torso looking east over the body is deliberate. The reuse of disturbed skulls as ear-muffs was a feature of the cemetery. Burial CXXV is a striking example of the skull/ear-muff variant and it compares with similar examples from early-Christian cemeteries in Dublin, such as Cabinteely (Conway 1999).

Plate 6 Burial CXXV and CXXVII

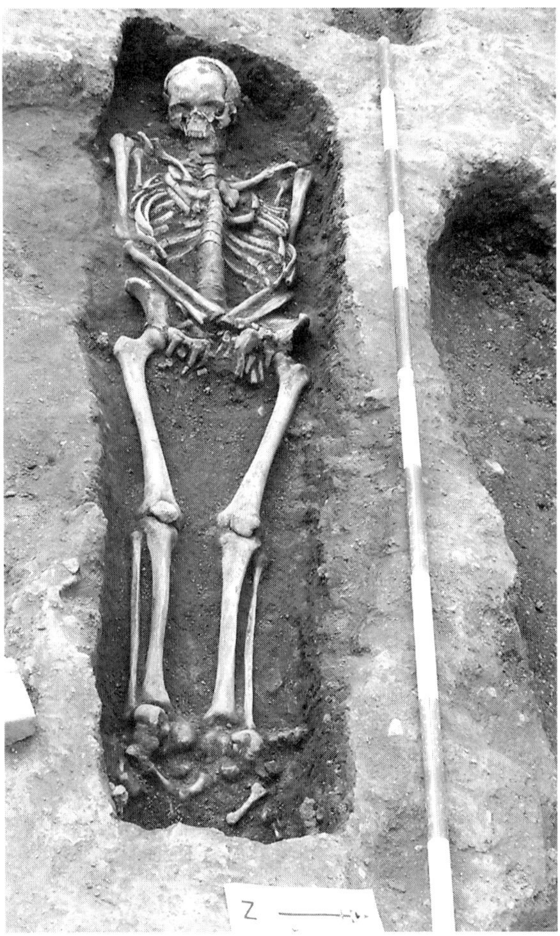

Plate 7 Burial CCXXVII

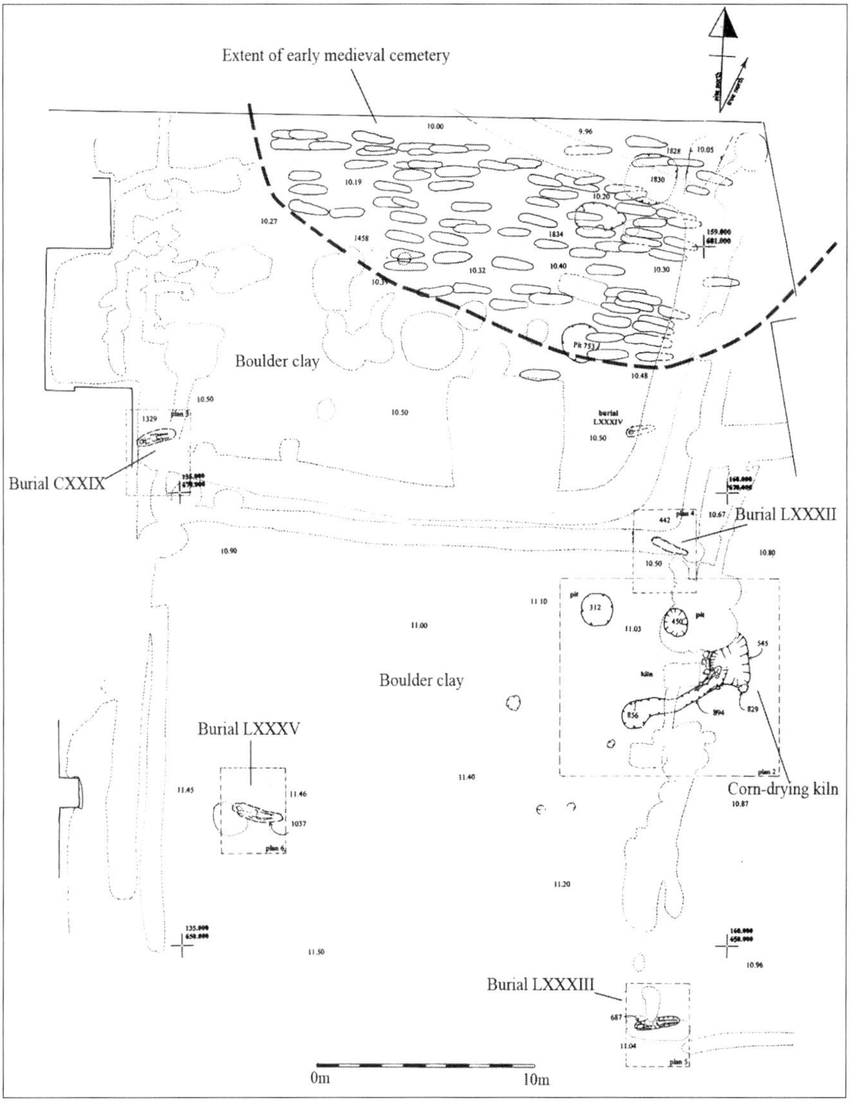

7 Location of the early habitation deposits, cemetery and the outlying burial

No stone-lined or lintel graves were uncovered at the Golden Lane site in contrast to other early-medieval cemeteries, such as at Mount Gamble in Swords, Co. Dublin (O'Donovan 2006, 182). However, the presence of burials that were plank-lined demonstrates that a wooden equivalent of lintel graves existed at the Golden Lane site. A number of rectangular grave-cuts were identified during the excavation, such as Burial CCXXVII, this burial contained large metal nails at cardinal points within the grave-cut. These nails presumably held the timber planks in position prior to the placing of the

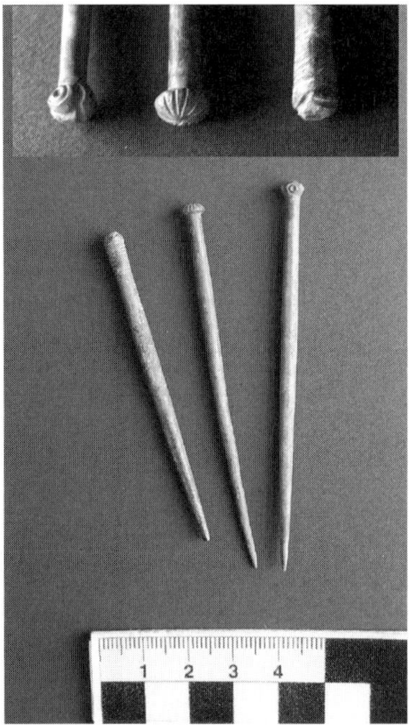

Plate 8 Stick Pins (left to right lower photo; 1160:1, 12:7, and 17:1)

shrouded body in the grave. Very faint traces of linear organic planking were recorded at the site.

The ninth century AD is currently the earliest date for a burial at the St Michael le Pole cemetery. This is based upon a C14 date of an 'Irish-type' lintel grave that was uncovered under the stone church during the 1981 DART campaign (895–1269 AD, Gowen 2001). It is highly likely that earlier phases of Irish burials exist at the site. This dated burial along with the other examples of culturally Irish burial- and grave-morphologies indicates that the church of St Michael le Pole is derived from an Irish population or a population significantly absorbed into the Irish Christian tradition. Six stick-pins were found at the site; two of these artefacts (Find nos 12:7 and 17:1) were recovered from archaeological deposits between and above burials and indicate that burial continued in the eleventh and twelfth centuries after the Norse town of Dublin was founded. These are significant findings both in terms of the debate on the site of the monastery of *Dubhlinn* and in respect to the cultural background of the individuals interred in the cemetery in the Hiberno-Norse period.

Satellite burials on the periphery of the cemetery Four burials (nos LXXXV, LXXXIII, LXXII and CXXIX) were recorded between 10–30m beyond the edge of the cemetery. The southernmost grave (LXXXIII) was largely intact. Only the lower torso and legs of a male burial, a 'Viking' (LXXXV) accompanied with grave goods, survived. A partially complete female grave (CXXIX) was recorded at the western side of the site associated with a decorated bone Viking buckle, and a very disturbed burial (LXXXII) was revealed under a later medieval property-boundary ditch. Significantly, two of the satellite burials (LXXXV and CXXIX) were found in association with Viking artefacts or grave goods. The association and find circumstances of burial LXXXV were the best preserved on site and are discussed in detail below.

The Viking burial (LXXXV) contained the remains of a young adult male (*c*.20–30 years, Laureen Buckley, pers. comm.). The strong stature of the young Viking man was also noted by the site osteologist. He was buried on the

Plate 9 Burial CXXIX

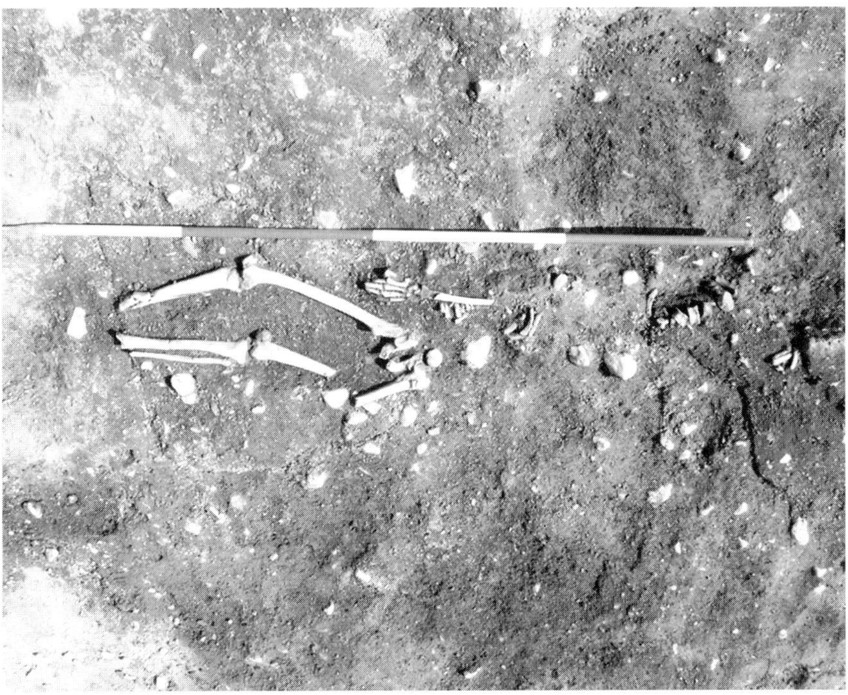

Plate 10 Burial LXXXV

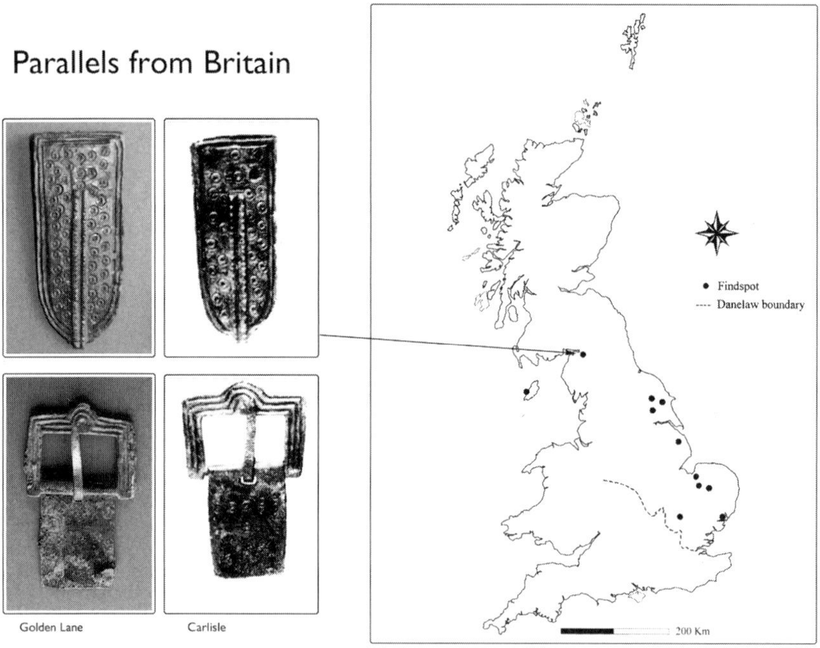

8 Golden Lane strap-end and belt-buckle (1038:1–2) and
a parallel from Carlisle (after Thomas 2000)

boulder clay in a shallow grave in a curious 'fire-reddened clay', 20m to the south of the cemetery. A thin deposit of 'garden soil' lay above the burial from which an iron spearhead (Find no. 1032:1) was recovered. The burial was not shrouded and the presence of artefacts and the loose body-position within the grave demonstrated that the young man was buried in his clothing. The fact that the Viking burial survived to the extent that it did was very fortunate. The upper torso was truncated by a later medieval pit. It is tempting to suggest that the location of these graves was known to the Anglo-Norman inhabitants of the city and that they were plundered.

It was as the skeleton was being lifted that a belt buckle (Find no. 1038:1), a strap-end (Find no. 1038:2), an iron knife (Find No: 1038:4) and lead weights (Find no. 1038:3) were discovered under the left femur of the burial. The position of the grave goods demonstrated that a belt hung around the Viking's waist. A leather scabbard containing the iron knife must have been attached to the belt and slipped under the left leg at burial. It is likely that the lead weights were also suspended in a leather pouch on the belt as they were discovered adjacent to the knife. A faint organic stained soil was traced where the belt and scabbard were present. Only the lower limbs of the burial survive.

The C14 date obtained from the Viking burial (LXXXV) at Golden Lane suggests that the individual was buried in Dublin prior to AD 832. This conclusion is based upon the two sigma (95.4% certainty) radiocarbon date (See Appendix below). The grave goods accompanying the burial have been dated stylistically to the early tenth century in Britain (James Graham-Campbell, pers. comm.). The most notable parallels are from the Isle of Man and Carlisle (Thomas 2000, 249), in the Irish Sea Area around Dublin, Anglesey, Cumbria, and Galloway (Graham-Campbell 1998). The implications of the finding at Golden Lane are significant because it suggests that the strap-end and buckle date from the early ninth century (as opposed to the early tenth century) on the basis of the C14 date and, hence, that Vikings were being buried in Dublin before AD 832.

The Golden Lane satellite burials form part of a series of early Viking graves stretching from Bride Street across to Golden Lane, Ship Street Great to George's Street (where Linzi Simpson has recently excavated five ninth-century Viking burials). The newly discovered burials provide a context for the mid-nineteenth century discovery of a Viking buried with a sword, spear and shield on Bride Street (Ó Floinn 1998, 132, 139). These discoveries represent a heretofore unknown early Viking cemetery in Dublin where individual graves were interred over a wide area skirting the perimeter of St Patrick's church (the later cathedral) and the church site of St Michael le Pole, on an axis parallel to and south of the ridge of Dublin outside the later walled town.

Viking Age/early-medieval occupation activity

A variety of non-burial pits and other archaeological features were located during the excavation. These were interpreted as evidence for secular occupation of the site. The pits (F753, F1020, F1828 and F1830) pre-dated the early-Christian cemetery (described above). Other pits (F312 and F450) were contemporary with the use-period of the cemetery and were found to contain datable Viking-Age finds; the function of these pits remains uncertain. The discovery of a corn-drying kiln with a 'fire box' (F545), flue (F594), and drying chamber (F856) containing oats, is significant because it demonstrates the secular nature of the occupation of the site in the tenth century. The cultural background or ethnicity (Irish/Viking) of the population involved in cereal production at the kiln site is not certain. It is not clear whether such clear distinctions within the local population, as presented in material culture, relate to ethnicity. However, the kiln type as categorized by Monk and Kelleher (2006) conforms to their L- or comma-shaped type found on rural 'Irish' settlement sites such as at Brooklodge in Co. Cork, and other sites in Cos Kildare, Meath and Westmeath.

The corn-drying kiln A corn-drying kiln was excavated and recorded 15m due south of the edge of the cemetery. The kiln dated from the tenth century and was clearly pre-Norman in date (see Appendix). It was located stratigraphically under a series of medieval pits and later property boundaries

Plate 11 Corn-drying kiln flue looking west-southwest

Plate 12 Corn-drying kiln drying chamber looking east

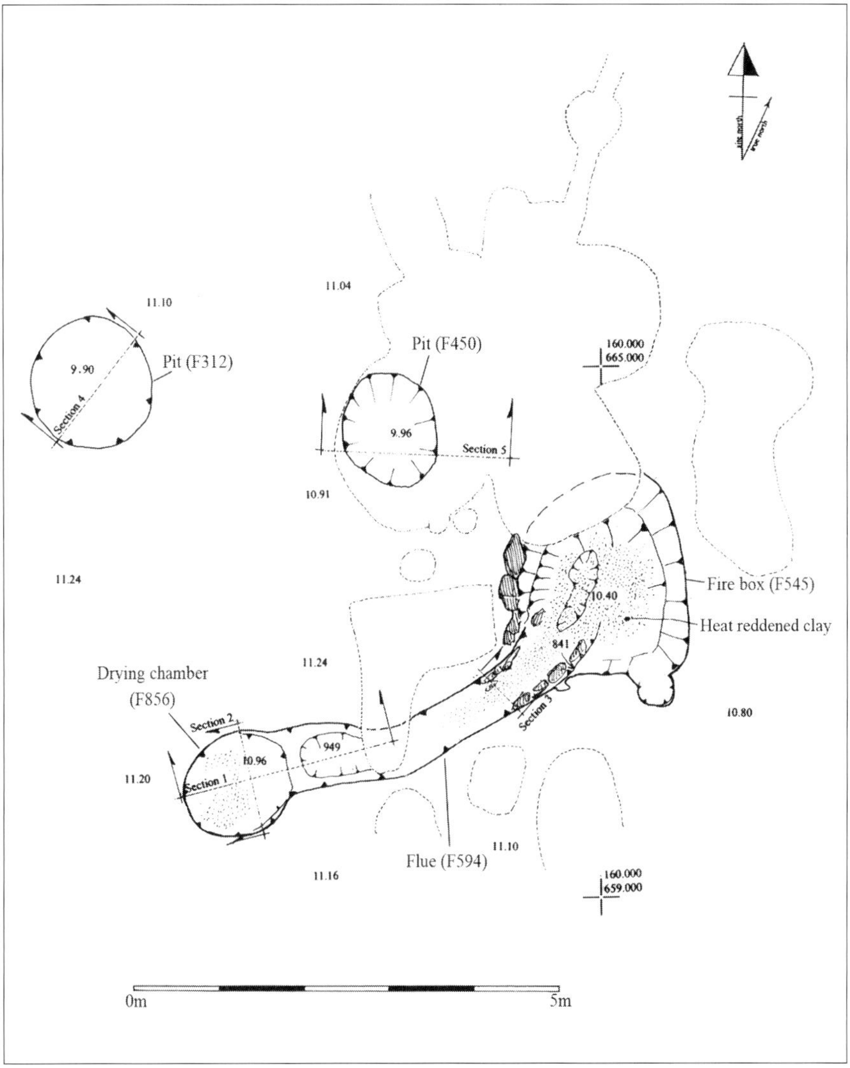

9 Corn-drying kiln and pits (F312 and F450)

dating from AD 1200–1500. The kiln consisted of a 'fire box' (F545), flue (F841) and drying chamber (F856). The corn-drying kiln functioned by creating heat in a fire in the 'fire box' and creating a draught of hot air transferred via the flue from the 'fire box' into a drying chamber where the dry air lowered the moisture content of the grain in the kiln, thus ensuring that the grain could be stored and lessening the likelihood of it becoming moldy whilst in storage. The preliminary analysis of the grain retrieved from the kiln indicates that it was predominantly used for the drying of oats; small amounts of barley were also noted in the fills within the kiln (Sara Halwas, pers. comm.). Porridge, oatcakes or oatmeal-based stews are all possible foods derived from oats; barley can be used in the production of beer or malt cakes, or used in soups and stews.

The drying chamber of the kiln (F856) was oval in plan measuring 2.20m in length, 1.20m wide and was cut into the natural boulder clay to a depth of 0.40m. A curving flue extended from the eastern side of the kiln from east to west (measuring 3.5m in length, 0.90m wide and 0.60m at its deepest point). The flue was lined on both sides by large and medium-sized angular and sub-angular limestone blocks (F843) ranging in size from 0.25m x 0.20m x 0.20m, to 0.15m x 0.20m x 0.07m, and 0.16m x 0.14m x 0.09m. These were aligned along the edge of the flue with no evident bonding and showed evidence of being heat-cracked. The 'fire box' (F841) was located at the north-eastern extent of the flue, orientated north-south and was oval in plan (measuring 1.12m in length, 0.98m wide), with a drop in level from the flue of 0.29m. The base of the 'fire box' contained a number of large limestone blocks (F943) also performing a lining function. Those not found *in situ* may represent the collapse of a roof superstructure.

A series of fills and deposits were recorded within the 'fire box', flue and drying chamber, representing phases of use and abandonment. The 'fire box' contained a series of charcoal-rich fills. A layer of grey clay silt (F914) with frequent charcoal and pebble inclusions lay along the base and continued along the length of the flue towards the drying chamber. This layer is contemporary with the primary deposit (F944) within the drying chamber.

A reddish black silty clay deposit (F948) sealed the primary deposit (F944) in the drying chamber and continued into the flue of the kiln. A later black silty clay (F894) sealed these earlier deposits. This layer (measuring 5.70m in length and 0.08m in depth) contained a high density of charcoal lumps and flecks, as well as an abundance of charred cereal grains, and continued into the flue of the kiln. The drying chamber was sealed by a succession of flat, irregular, angular limestone slabs (F950/F857) (measuring from 0.28m x 0.25m x 0.05m, to 0.40m x 0.25m x 0.05m, to 0.16m x 0.15m x 0.07m) within a matrix of mid-orange/brown sandy clay (F858/F895), containing frequent gravel inclusions and charcoal flecking. The uppermost layer within the drying chamber (F895) is contemporary with the tertiary fill of the flue (F842) and represents the final phase of activity within the kiln when the top of the drying chamber collapsed.

Several episodes of cereal-/grain-drying were evident in the kiln. Oats dominated the assemblage of cereals present in the kiln with a small amount of barley also being noted (Sara Halwas, pers. comm.). The high density of charred grain excavated from the drying chamber suggests that the kiln collapsed before the grain could be recovered, possibly as a result of the grain in the drying chamber catching fire. The backfill material from the flue, with a

Plate 13 Viking-age pit (F312)

high content of charcoal and scorched earth or fire-reddened clay, is suggestive of the collapse of a superstructure of wattle and daub. Likewise the backfill material of the drying chamber, containing overlapping, flattened limestone slabs and high charcoal content, suggests that a superstructure or roofing of wattle and stone construction may have collapsed into the drying chamber during an overly zealous drying process. The morphology of the corn-drying kiln compares closely to a site in Brooklodge, Co. Cork cited by Monk and Kelleher (2006, 81) in their article on corn-drying kilns. The Golden Lane kiln parallels closely with their L- or comma-shaped type. The date of the Golden Lane kiln clearly overlaps with the establishment of Dublin as a Viking-Age town and it is highly likely that the oats produced at the kiln were for consumption within Dublin.

Viking-Age pits Two pits (F312 and F450) were excavated adjacent to the corn-drying kiln; these appeared to be rubbish pits. The pits have been dated to the Viking Age on the basis of the recovery of bone (in fact, pig fibulae) pins from one and a fragment of a belt buckle from another. The pits were stratigraphically pre-Norman in date.

The pit (F312) was located 4m north of the corn-drying kiln. This pit (measuring 1.59m in length, 1.35m wide and 0.98m in depth) contained nine

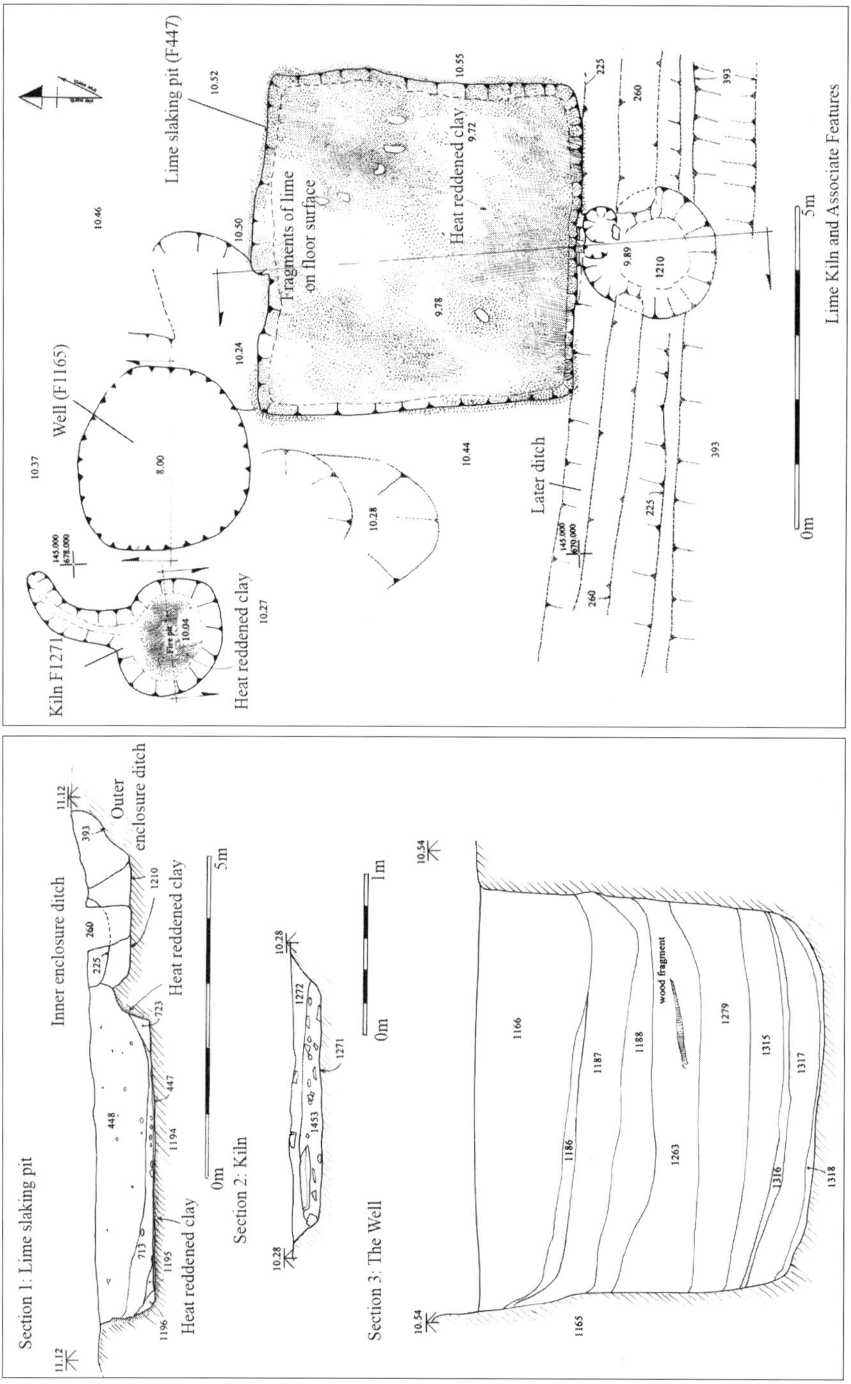

10 Plan and section of the lime-production area

fills. The primary fill (F348) lay along the base of the pit and consisted of very dark grey, humic silt with high organic content. A radiocarbon date (AD 830–1018, 94.5% certainty) was obtained from charcoal from the primary fill of the feature. The basal fill was sealed by a secondary thick layer of yellowish brown silty clay (F337). Later deposits lay along the sides of the pit possibly representing individual dumps of material. Along the northern edge a dark yellow brown clay silt (F339) contained a high density of charcoal as well as burnt bone and scorched clay, similarly along the southern edge a layer of dark brown charcoal-rich silt (F347) contained scorched earth, sealed by a layer of light yellowish brown clay silt (F338). A further discrete deposit of dark brown silty clay (F349) lay above these layers and contained frequent inclusions of scorched orange clay and flecks of charcoal. This was partially sealed by a deposit of greyish brown clay silt (F336).

The pit appears to have been deliberately backfilled and sealed by a succession of similar well-sorted fills. These mid-orange/brown sandy clays (F313/F350) contained occasional animal bone and charcoal inclusions. These layers represent the final backfill of the pit.

Large quantities of animal bone were recovered from lower fills as well as charcoal and burnt bone, while five perforated bone pins (Find nos 348:1–5) were recovered from the primary fill (F348), suggesting an early-medieval to Viking date for the pit. The function of the pit is unclear; it was originally excavated to below the water table and may have been a water source or a pit for cold storage. The sides of this pit were slightly convex in profile suggesting that the lower sides may have been eroded by water action during the use of the feature. A high density of charcoal and scorched earth in the secondary deposits suggests that the pit was utilized as a refuse pit for dumping of waste, possibly associated with activity from domestic hearths or from the corn-drying kiln to the southeast.

A smaller pit (F450), measuring 0.98m in diameter and 0.52m in depth, was located 2m to the north of the corn-drying kiln. It was filled with a primary layer of mid-brown sandy clay (F451) and was sealed by a layer of dark brown sandy clay (F456). These two fills were sealed by a layer of fine sandy clay (F457) and the upper half of the pit was cut by a later medieval pit (F317).

Lime production and construction of the church?

A complex of features associated with lime production was excavated on the southern margin of the cemetery. The features were located immediately outside the burial ground and appeared to have been sited to deliberately avoid cutting through graves. The structures were all cut into the boulder clay and included a large slaking-out or mortar pit (F447), a deep and wide well (F1165) and a pit/kiln with evidence for burning of stone (F1271). A radiocarbon date was established from a fragment of wood found in a fill from the well (F1318). The 2-sigma date from the wood dates the lime production site

(95.4% certainty) to between AD 1022 and 1164. A substantial stone church and round tower dating from AD 1000–1100 were identified in the Dublin Archaeological Research Team's excavations in 1981 on the St Michael le Pole site (Gowen 2001). It is highly likely that the lime-production complex found in the Golden Lane excavation was used to build the stone church at the site in the eleventh century.

Lime mortar is used as the basic bonding unit in the construction of masonry structures from the medieval period. The complex of features described below managed the process of converting limestone through the firing of the stone in a kiln into powdered calcium carbonate. The dry lime was then mixed with water and aggregate to make lime mortar. Lime mixed with mortar on its own can also be used to make whitewash. The identification of a kiln, well and slaking-out pit records the presence of the different structural elements in the lime mortar/wash manufacturing process.

Hearth/lime kiln A shallow key-hole kiln (F1271) was located on the southern edge of the cemetery. The kiln (F1271) was circular in plan (diameter *c*.1.90m) with a curving linear flue extending from the northeast side of the bowl of the feature. This feature contained a primary dark grey/black charcoal-rich sandy silt (F1453) and frequent medium-sized angular lime and sandstone fragments. These deposits were similar to the stone layers (such as F1175) in the base of the slaking-out pit (F447). The kiln was sealed by a layer of reddish brown sandy clay (F1272), containing animal bone, frequent charcoal and evidence of scorched clay along the edge of the cut. The presence of limestone within the feature (F1453), coupled with the large amount of charcoal, may suggest that this feature was used to extract lime from the stone as powder or dry calcium carbonate prior to mixing with water and gravel for the production of mortar. The inclusions of scorched earth within the upper fill (F1272) may be suggestive of a collapsed roof structure.

Slaking-out/mortar pit A large rectangular pit (F447) measuring 5.17m north/south, 4.91m east/west and 0.94m deep was recorded at the edge of the cemetery. The pit had almost vertical sides and a flat base. An irregular sub-circular-shaped hollow (F1210/F1212) was present in the southern side of the feature. The uppermost fills were truncated by a later medieval enclosure-ditch (F225).

The base of the pit (F447) was irregularly covered with an uneven, greyish white lime mortar deposit (F1207), 0.02m deep. The base and edges of the pit were scorched red by the heat given off when powdered lime was mixed with water. A loose deposit of heat-shattered, medium-sized angular limestone and sandstone (F1175) was recorded towards the northeast and southwest corners of the pit. The deposit (F1175) contained a high percentage of charcoal, ash and lime inclusions. This was sealed by a thin layer (approximately 0.04m

Plate 14 Rectangular slaking out pit (F447) and other features under excavation

deep) of dark grey clay silt (F1194). A layer of orange/brown clay silt (F1196) lay along the base of the northern edge of this pit, which was partially sealed by an organic deposit of dark grey clay silt (F1195), containing charcoal and shells. Along the southern internal edge a layer of blackish red charcoal, ash, cinders and burnt clay (F723) sealed a deposit of light brown gravely, silty clay (F724) and was contemporary with F1195 and F1196, all being sealed by a later deposit of yellowish brown silt (F713). This material appeared to have been deposited from a northerly direction as it lay deepest along the northern edge of the pit and contained pockets of yellow clay with tip lines falling to the south. The final backfill of this feature was represented by a thick deposit of mid-brown silty clay (F448), containing burnt clay, charcoal, animal bone and lime flecking.

A distinct hollow pit (F1210/F1212) was present on the southern edge of the pit (F447). It contained a layer of charcoal-rich clay (F1270) lining the base of the cut and was sealed by a deposit of compact mortar (F1213) at its junction with the pit (F447). These layers were sealed by a primary layer of greyish brown silty clay (F712/F716) lying along the base of the flattened cut and was sealed by a layer of orange grey clay silt (F715/F718). This material was very similar to a greyish brown silty clay layer (F713), forming the upper backfill of the slaking-out/mortar pit (F447) and suggests that both features silted up and were backfilled over the same period of time after the lime production ceased at the site.

Plate 15 The well (F1165)

The well A deep well measuring 2.70m wide and 2.48m deep was located adjacent to the kiln and slaking-out pit. It was sub-circular in plan with a level base and contained a series of organic-rich, waterlogged deposits. The primary layer consisted of very dark brown silty clay (F1318) sealed by a layer of greyish black silty clay (1317). These contexts also contained a number of wooden artefacts. These include a semi-circular plank/bucket-base, a twisted withy and several bucket staves. These primary deposits were sealed by a series of organic-rich deposits of greyish brown silty clays (F1316, F1315, F1279, and F1263), with increased silt content, becoming more humic, and darker in colour with depth. These secondary layers contained well-preserved wood chippings, fragments of withy, leather fragments and a semi-circular wooden barrel-base. The lower fills of the well are consistent with its use as a source of water on site, and the organic preservation and discovery of bucket fragments supports this interpretation.

A stony deposit of reddish brown silty clay (F1188) sealed the earlier organic layers (F1316, F1315, F1279, and F1263). This (F1188) was sealed by a layer of very dark grey clay silt (F1187), with a lens of orange/brown sandy clay (F1186). A greyish brown silty clay layer (F1166) sealed these less organic deposits and represented the final backfill of the pit (F1165). These contexts had a lower organic content but contained frequent crushed sea shells (oyster, cockle and mussel), animal bone and charcoal flecking. These later deposits in

Plate 16 Edward IV farthing (226:6)

the well suggest that this pit was subsequently abandoned as a water source, and functioned as a refuse pit.

Medieval settlement and the establishment of property plots

A large double-ditched medieval sub-rectangular enclosure (*c.*AD 1200–1500) was uncovered during the excavation. The external dimensions of the enclosure measured 25m east-west and *c.*22m north-south, with an entrance or gate-house structure located on its western side fronting towards present-day Chancery Lane. The ditches enclosed an area measuring 20m east-west and 15m north-south. The enclosure was cut through and was later than the cemetery. The cemetery continued in use to the north of the enclosure and was identified during the excavations by the Dublin Archaeological Research Team in 1981, where medieval (AD 1200–1540) and post-medieval (AD 1540–1800) burials were uncovered. The northern enclosing element of the enclosure evolved into the southern boundary of the medieval and post-medieval cemetery. This is illustrated on the historic maps of the site, such as John Rocque's map of 1756 and the first edition of the Ordnance Survey in 1837.

The fill of the ditches contained many sherds of medieval pottery and the final tertiary fill of the ditches contained an Edward IV farthing dating from 1460–61 (Find no. 226:6). The preliminary interpretation based upon the finds suggests that the earth-cut enclosure was constructed in the thirteenth century and continued in use up to the end of the fifteenth century. It is tempting to classify the medieval enclosure as a moated site constructed

Plate 17 Inner U-shaped enclosure ditch (F225)

immediately outside the walls of the city, especially as the southern and eastern boundary were water-filled; however, the depth and width of the ditches falls short of a typical moated site and hence the Golden Lane example is peculiar. A pit located within the enclosure was the find spot for an extremely well-preserved bronze medieval hand-bell (Find no. 1334:1). The bell may have had an ecclesiastical function and this, coupled with its discovery adjacent to the church of St Michael le Pole, suggests that the enclosure functioned as the site of the priest's house in the Anglo-Norman period.

A series of medieval field boundaries and refuse pits were identified throughout the site; these features are indicative of land enclosure and domestic settlement that occurred outside the town walls. This more dispersed occupation was linked by field systems. The field systems were dated by medieval pottery retrieved during the excavation.

The medieval sub-rectangular enclosure The enclosure was surrounded by two rectilinear ditches (F393 and F225) that were largely not inter-cutting. The ditches drained the natural water that soaked out from the higher northern ground to the southeast towards the *Dubhlinn*. The ground at the church site is low-lying and the water table would have been (and remains) high, arising from the proximity of the Poddle and the *Dubhlinn*. The ditches did not appear to have a significant defensive function.

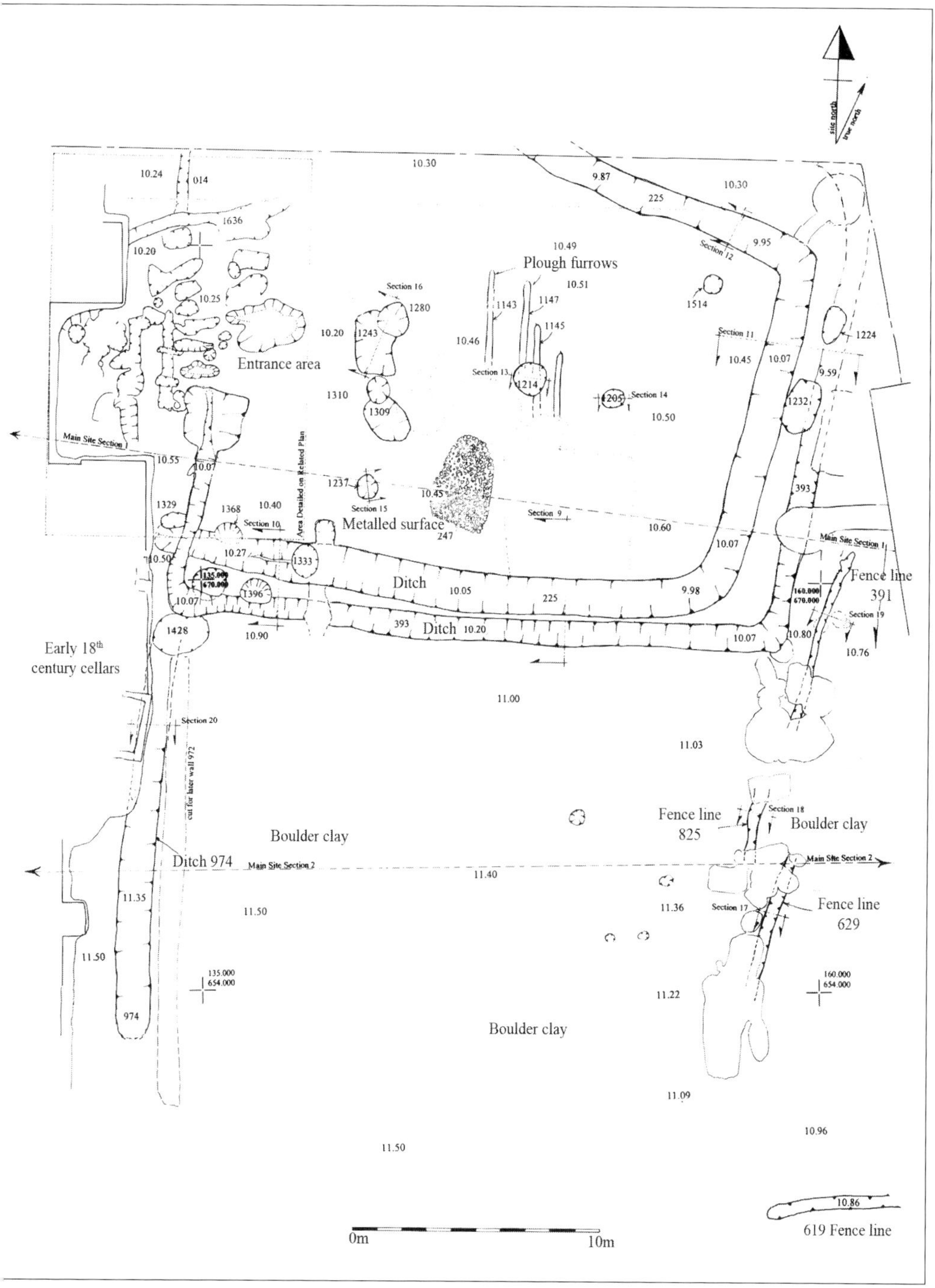

11 Medieval rectangular enclosure

Plate 18 Outer V-shaped enclosure ditch (F393)

The inner enclosure (F225) was U-shaped with concave sides and base. The fill of the ditch consisted of a primary greyish brown clay silt material (F429/F496/F1336) with gravel inclusions and charcoal flecking, sealed by a secondary deposit of mid-brownish grey clay silt (F493/F497/F1337) containing inclusions of shell, animal bone and charcoal flecking. The uppermost backfill of this ditch consisted of mid-brown clay silt (F226/F1338), containing occasional sub-rounded gravel inclusions, animal bone and isolated charcoal smears and flecking throughout, sealing the lower deposits.

This ditch was cut 1m into the boulder clay at its deepest in the northeast corner of the site, where it truncated a series of earlier burial deposits. The full extent of the northern side of the enclosure-ditch (F225) is unknown as it continued into an unexcavated area. The southern boundary of the enclosure was much shallower where it continued parallel to the outer enclosure-ditch (F393). The southern boundary ditch was only 0.10m deep in this location and continues west where it is truncated by later post-medieval structural features. The relatively shallow nature of the ditch may be explained by local truncation on the southern side of the enclosure.

The southern and eastern side of the outer enclosure-ditch (F393) was revealed during the excavation. The ditch (F393) varied in width and depth along its length (measuring from 0.90m to 1.20m wide and 0.65m to 1m in depth). It had a pronounced V-shaped profile, straight sides and a concave base. Several phases of use were evident, from initial primary silting, secondary deposits, and eventual tertiary backfills indicating the abandonment of the enclosure area.

A phase of primary silting of material (F510, F511, F369, F489, F1132 and F1394) was identified along the length of the ditch, indicating a gradual accumulation of material during the initial use after the ditch was excavated. This was represented by layers of well-sorted, greyish clay silt with occasional inclusions of the shells of land-snails, and orange mottling. The deposits were remarkably consistent throughout the length of the ditch, indicating semi-waterlogged conditions with a low constant flow of water along the ditch base. The silt accumulated to its greatest depth in the north-eastern end of the feature.

The silts were sealed by a series of secondary deposits (F394, F435, F512, F513, F564, F565 and F566), which varied along the length of the ditch, and may indicate the nature of the activity that occurred within the enclosed area. The analysis of the macro-fossil plant remains and charcoal from these features is pending and it is hoped these results may lead to a greater understanding of function within the enclosure. A final phase of backfilling followed the secondary deposits in the form of a series of mid-brownish grey silty clays (F397, F398 and F434).

Although the enclosure-ditches (F225 and F393) appear to respect each other along most of their length, the upper fills of the inner enclosure-ditch (F225) were truncated by the outer enclosure-ditch (F393) in the southwest, where it turned north forming the western boundary of the enclosure. Whilst both enclosure-ditches were possibly contemporary and functioned adjacent to each other, the outer enclosure-ditch was clearly constructed after the inner ditch. The sequential nature of the ditches is supported by the differing profiles (U-shaped and V-shaped).

Post-medieval settlement

A small number of significant high-status early post-medieval artefacts were discovered on the site. These include Schnellen drinking tankards from Siegburg in Germany dating to the 1570s, an inverted baluster-stem drinking glass dating to *c.*1620 and a shaft and globe wine bottle, dating to *c.*1650, with a seal marked with the letter 'B'. The relatively complete state in which some of the artefacts were recovered suggests that they were discarded close to the place where they were used, in the immediate vicinity of Golden Lane.

The cellars (basements) of four 'Dutch Billies' were excavated along Chancery Lane. The buildings are likely to have been built after 1690 and involved a significant rebuilding effort and alteration to the streetscape along that portion of the lane. Each cellar measured 12m east/west and was between 9m and 13m wide. The four properties can best be summarized as two pairs of

Plate 19 'Dutch Billy' house foundations on Chancery Lane

Plate 20 Montelupo olive jar (902:1) in the floor within the 'Dutch Billy' house

buildings, each one subdivided in two. The buildings were constructed around a shared central triangular chimney-stack between each pair of houses, with rooms to the front and rear with a corner fireplace in each. The individual properties varied in plan and the building sequence recorded in the excavation suggests that nos 19 and 20 were built before nos 17 and 18.

The cellars at nos 17–20 were cut deep into the boulder clay and little evidence of the pre-existing sixteenth-century buildings survived on site. Reused early post-medieval house timbers were discovered and the party cellar wall of nos 19/18 was built over a well. The presence of the well built under the wall is evidence for an earlier phase of building. This, in combination with the variation in plan of the basements, is highly suggestive of earlier buildings influencing the layout of the post-restoration Dutch Billy buildings on Chancery Lane.

The continuity of property plots from the Viking Age down to the present day is a feature that was first identified in excavations in medieval Dublin (Wallace 1994) and subsequently in Waterford (Hurley et al. 1997, 149) and Cork (Hurley 1997, 4), where post-medieval and medieval property plots were superimposed on the earlier Viking and medieval property divisions. This feature is again uncovered at the Golden Lane site where the medieval rectangular enclosure and other field boundaries are fossilized in the property plot walls laid out at the site in the seventeenth and eighteenth centuries. This evidence is indicative of continuity in property ownership and inhabitation of the site from at least AD 1200 to the present day.

DISCUSSION

The interpretation of the archaeological findings of the Golden Lane excavations is still at an early stage and any conclusion here should be considered as preliminary. The chronology of the deposits on site is unlikely to alter substantially; however further radiocarbon dating of the early-medieval burials may extend the date range of the cemetery. The analysis of the human bone is currently in progress by Laureen Buckley, osteo-archaeologist. The results arising from her study should provide the first scientific assessment of the health status and population demographics for the early-medieval and Viking population of Dublin.

An analysis by Lorna O'Donnell and Sara Halwas of the environmental remains on deposits from the site will hopefully allow for the function of the pits and other features to be determined. It is likely that these features were for storage, refuse, etc., or simply for the extraction of gravel and clay. Evidence for the local diet will result from an analysis of the animal bone and macro-fossil plant remains (cereal grains, etc.) that survive as carbonized deposits in the soil from the site.

The earliest burial horizon around the church cut into the boulder clay forms a very regular series of graves. Few instances of intercutting burials were recorded from the early levels. The osteological analysis of these burials is intriguing as it is possible that these represent a clerical or non-secular graveyard. This interpretation is pending the results of the analysis of the human bone. The later cemetery uncovered many intercutting burials containing adults and children and was more likely to be derived from the local secular population.

The Viking burial (LXXXV) fits into an emerging pattern of widely dispersed Viking graves discovered in an area from Bride Street to South Great George's Street, where eight ninth-century Viking burials have been recorded (Simpson 2005, 11). Raghnall Ó Floinn describes the Viking cemetery at Kilmainham and Islandbridge as 'grave-fields' (1998, 132) where burials were interred over a widespread yet definable area. This definition of a Viking cemetery distinguishes it from the dense early-Christian cemetery tradition where hundreds of burials can be located in an area measuring 10m x10m as opposed to a 'grave-field' where burials may be 10–20m apart. Thus the 'grave-fields' site is an element of the landscape rather than the early-Christian cemetery that appears as an element within it.

The Viking burials (LXXXV and CXXXIX) date, at the very latest, to the mid-/late ninth century, however statistically the burial LXXXV is 90% more likely to have been interred before AD 832. The dates from the George's Street site also appear to be potentially this early (Simpson 2005) and therefore the evidence from Golden Lane supports the view that a Viking 'grave-field' existed between present-day Bride Street and George's Street with pagan Viking burials dating from the first quarter of the ninth century.

Clearly burial also continued in the cemetery of St Michael le Pole in the Viking Age, suggesting that an element of the Viking population became Christian or a local native Irish population survived the proximal establishment of Dublin as a Viking town. In fact a combination of both explanations is likely and the later phases of the cemetery can be characterized as 'Hiberno Scandinavian'. The corn-drying kiln is further evidence for native technologies and types being uncovered immediately adjacent to the Viking town. This coupled with the construction of the masonry element of the church of St Michael le Pole between AD 1000–1100 in the 'Irish' tradition with a round tower further emphasizes the diverse cultural elements evident on the site.

The sense of continuity between the Irish and the Viking deposits at the site contrasts with the Anglo-Norman deposits that postdate them. The rectangular enclosure cut through the earlier cemetery and a new rectilinear settlement pattern with field systems is imposed upon the earlier land structure. The Anglo-Norman land-parcelling units are maintained and further subdivided in the post-medieval property plots that are present on the historic maps. This suggests that land enclosure and occupation continued in an unbroken sequence from AD 1200 to the present day.

THE MEDIEVAL SMALL FINDS FROM GOLDEN LANE

Siobhán Scully

INTRODUCTION

The archaeological excavations at Golden Lane (04E1030) produced a variety of medieval artefacts. There were non-pottery ceramic finds, ferrous and non-ferrous metal finds and artefacts worked from stone and skeletal material of medieval date. A large quantity of post-medieval artefacts was also recovered such as glass and metalwork. The majority of the glass finds were wine bottles but spirits, beer and mineral bottles were also represented as well as a well-preserved early seventeenth-century wine glass. The post-medieval metalwork was dominated by a large amount of structural iron. The post-medieval finds are not described here. The medieval pottery and timber artefacts from the site are not presented in this report either.

Included in the medieval ceramic building material are decorated and undecorated floor-tiles and roof tiles consisting of ridge-tile and plain roof tile fragments. The ferrous and non-ferrous metal finds include artefacts of personal dress, household objects, personal possessions and some structural and decorative items. Of special note are the finds associated with the Viking Burial LXXXV. The metalwork also incorporates the structural iron recovered from the graves excavated at Golden Lane. There are a small number of artefacts of stone, all of which were functional items, and a slightly larger number of artefacts of skeletal material which included personal possessions, items of dress and possibly some functional items in the case of the bone pins.

The author wishes to thank Noël Siver for her identification of the Edward IV coin (226:6). The excavation at Golden Lane had the licence number 04E1030. This number has been removed from before the finds numbers in the text below for the sake of brevity. The following abbreviations for measurements have also been used: Length (L), Width (W), Thickness (T), Height (H), Diameter (Diam.).

CERAMIC BUILDING MATERIAL

Floor-tiles

Introduction Thirty-nine medieval floor-tile fragments were recovered from the excavations at Golden Lane. Twenty-six are decorated with line-impressed designs and the remaining tile-fragments were dated by their fabric-type. All the medieval tiles have a red earthenware fabric sometimes with a grey reduced core. They have a coarse fabric which is less homogenous than the body fabric of post-medieval tiles (Eames and Fanning 1988, 6, 13). There are no complete tiles in the assemblage but the tile-fragments have a combined weight of 2.176kg.

Line-impressed tiles Eames and Fanning (1988) developed a catalogue and index of medieval tile designs then known from Ireland and recording where they were found. Sixteen of the line-impressed tiles from Golden Lane correspond to the motifs they recorded. The remainder are small fragments of which too little remains for the design to be identified or which have design elements that were common to a large

12 Medieval line-impressed floor tiles: L4 Lion rampant sinister (195:148); L8 Double-headed eagle (1152:82); L12 Vine scroll border (195:149 and 1338:2)

range of tiles. The identifiable designs are described below and are organized according to the design numbers allocated by Eames and Fanning.

L4 (Lion rampant sinister) There are two tile-fragments with this design (195:148, 226:112). It consists of a lion rampant sinister within a pointed quatrefoil frame and is one of the most popular designs in Ireland (Eames and Fanning 1988, 41). It has been found on a large number of ecclesiastical and some secular sites in Dublin, Kildare, Kilkenny, Louth, Waterford and Wexford (ibid., 86). In Dublin city it has been found

13 Medieval line-impressed floor tiles: L20 4-tile cusped circular band enclosing foliage (63:218); L60 Rosette within intersecting vesicas with trefoils (553:181); L86 Unidentified fragment (13:108, 217:150 and 676:56); L90 4-tile circular band with 4-foils enclosing foliate spray (676:55); Fragments which may be from a number of designs or unidentified (261:95 and 745:50)

in Dublin Castle, Kilmainham, St Audoen's church, St Kevin's church, St Nicholas's church, St Patrick's cathedral and Ship Street (ibid.).

L8 (Double-headed eagle) One fragment of tile (1152:82) with this design was found at Golden Lane. The design has a double-headed eagle within a cusped frame and is known from sites in Dublin, Kildare, Louth and Wexford including Dublin Castle, St

Kevin's church, St Mary's abbey and St Patrick's cathedral in Dublin city (Eames and Fanning 1988, 42, 87).

L12 (Vine scroll border) Two tile-fragments (195:149, 1338:2) have this design. It is also known from Christ Church cathedral, Dublin and St Mary's church in Drogheda (Eames and Fanning 1988, 87).

L19/20 (4-tile cusped circular band enclosing foliage) One tile (63:218) has similar decoration to this. Unfortunately only the part which has the cusped circular band remains. This design is known from a large number of sites in Dublin, Kildare, Kilkenny and Meath including Dublin Castle, Kilmainham, St Audoen's church, St Mary's abbey, St Patrick's cathedral and St Saviour's church within Dublin city (Eames and Fanning 1988, 87–8).

L60 (Rosette within intersecting vesicas with trefoils) The tile-fragment (553:181) with this design only has the trefoil in the corner of the tile remaining. This design, a variant of the more widespread L59, is found at Dublin Castle and Christ Church cathedral (Eames and Fanning 1988, 90).

L63 (Rosette within intersecting vesicas with trefoils) One tile (195:147) has a corner fragment of this design. It is also a variant of L60 and has been found at St Mary's abbey, Dublin (Eames and Fanning 1988, 90).

L69 (4-foil within 4 quarter-circles enclosing vine leaves) A small tile-fragment (428:10) has a similar design to L69 but unfortunately the design is quite worn. It is known from St Saviour's friary and Timolin church in Dublin (Eames and Fanning 1988, 90).

L86 (Unidentified fragment) Only part of this design is known from James Street and St Mary's church in Drogheda (Eames and Fanning 1988, 92). It consists of a trefoil in the corner of the tile. Three fragments (13:108, 217:150, 676:56) from Golden Lane have the same trefoil design but more of the design survives on the Golden Lane fragments, which consists of a roundel with cusps and possibly with a floral design in the centre.

L90 (4-tile circular band with 4-foils enclosing foliate spray) Four tile-fragments (226:111, 614:8, 676:54, 676:55) have this design. It is also found at St Patrick's cathedral, Dublin (Eames and Fanning 1988, 92).

Two other line-impressed tiles from Golden Lane have partial designs which could come from a number of known tile motifs. One tile-fragment has a leaf or fleur-de-lis in the corner (261:95) and another has a floral loop (1152:82) at the edge of the tile. A third fragment (745:50) has an unidentified design. The seven remaining fragments with line-impressed decoration are too small for them to be attributed to any particular design.

Many of the line-impressed designs found on the tiles from Golden Lane can be found on tiles from Christ Church cathedral, St Patrick's cathedral and the excavations at Dublin Castle as well as numerous other church sites in Dublin (Eames and Fanning 1988). It is possible that the Golden Lane tiles were produced by the same tile-manufactory from which the other tiles came and were used in the church of St Michael le Pole. Wasters have been recovered from excavations at Wood Quay and Kilmainham, attesting to the manufacture of tiles in the city (ibid., 12). Only three small fragments of line-impressed tile were recovered from the excavations of the church site of St Michael le Pole (Gowen 2001, 46).

The Golden Lane line-impressed tiles are all made from a red earthenware fabric and many have a grey core. Below is a table showing the colours of the glazes used on the line-impressed tiles from Golden Lane:

Glazes on line-impressed tiles

Colour	*No. of tiles*	*% of line-impressed tiles*
Olive green	11	42%
Dark green	4	15%
Yellow/Brown	4	15%
Yellow	2	8%
Brown/Green	1	4%
Brown	1	4%
Black	1	4%
No glaze remaining	2	8%

Only one tile, which had a yellow/brown glaze, was seen to have a white slip underneath the glaze (63:218) but a slip was probably also used for the two tiles with yellow glazes (428:10, 676:57) and possibly some of the tiles with a yellow/brown glaze too. The most commonly occurring colours were variations of green, followed by the yellow-brown groups of colours.

Undecorated medieval tiles Thirteen medieval tile-fragments were undecorated but many of these only survived as small fragments so they may once have belonged to decorated tiles. They are suggested to be medieval in date due to their body fabric, which is the same as the medieval line-impressed tiles. Eight of these fragments have the remains of a glaze. Below is a table showing the colours of the glazes found on the undecorated medieval tiles:

Glazes on medieval floor-tiles

Colour	*No. of tiles*	*% of medieval tiles*
Yellow/Brown	3	23%
Brown/Green	1	8%
Green/Yellow/Brown	1	8%
Brown	1	8%
Yellow/Green	1	8%
Olive green	1	8%
Unglazed	5	37%

Roof Tiles

Medieval ridge-tile fragments Five fragments of medieval ridge-tile were recovered from Golden Lane. These include a V-shaped ridge-tile fragment (261:92) decorated with thumb impressions along the apex of the ridge and has patches of olive green glaze remaining, a U-shaped ridge-tile fragment (745:49) with some yellow/brown glaze remaining and three fragments of decorative cresting. The decorative crests survive only as fragments and it is difficult to tell if they were integral to the tile or applied, although one (554:61) definitely seems to have been applied. Although

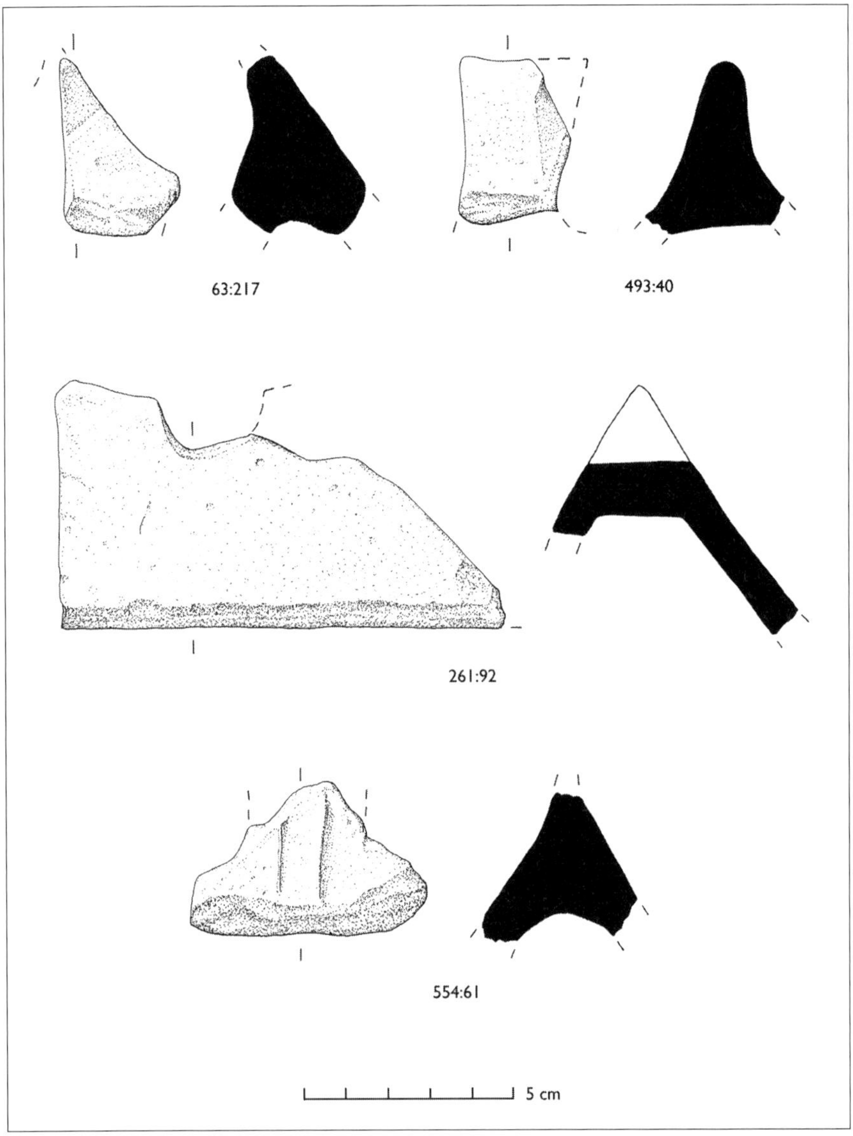

14 Roof Tiles: Medieval ridge-tile fragments (63:217, 493:40, 261:92 and 554:61)

damaged, it was probably a flat-topped crest. It has thumb and stab marks. The two other crest fragments are hook crested, one of which is glazed and has stab marks (43:40) and the other has some patches of glaze (62:217).

Medieval tile-fragments There are six tile-fragments which are probably medieval in date but they only survive as very small portions of tile. They have red earthenware fabrics, some with a grey core and some with micaceous inclusions. Two have a yellow/green glaze, one has a light green glaze, and the remainder are unglazed.

NON-FERROUS METAL ARTEFACTS

Possible shroud pin Only one of the thirty-six household pins from the Golden Lane excavations came from a grave fill (1576:2). It has a short, circular shank and globular head and is much different in appearance than the other pins from the site and may have been used as a shroud pin for Burial CLXXXIX.
1576:2 L 9mm Diam. of head 3mm Diam. of shank 2.2mm.

Stick-pins There are six stick-pins from Golden Lane, although one (1142:2) only survives as a fragment of shank. O'Rahilly (1998) developed a typology for stick-pins from the Dublin excavations 1962–1972, based on the form of the head and this typology is used to categorize the stick-pins from Golden Lane.

There are two stud-headed stick-pins (12:7, 1308:1). O'Rahilly describes this group of pins as having a hemispherical or stud-like head, the underside being flat and convex, usually without a collar (O'Rahilly 1998, 28). This type of stick-pin did not lie flush against the cloth, indicating a change in fashion and they date from the end of the eleventh century to the mid-thirteenth century (ibid.). One of the stud-headed pins from Golden Lane (12:7) has radiating grooves on the head of the pin and the other (1308:1) has a ring-and-dot motif in the centre of the head surrounded by radiating lines.

There is one club-headed stick-pin (17:1). These have a knop-shaped head and are usually decorated with one out of five different designs (O'Rahilly 1998, 28). O'Rahilly (ibid.) suggests that they are a typological development of the stud-headed pins and notes that they were the most numerous type of stick-pin in her assemblage. They were also the most numerous type of stick-pin from the Waterford excavations (Scully 1997, 438). The club-headed pin from Golden Lane has O'Rahilly's Type 3 decoration, which consists of three dot-in-circle decorations around the head. O'Rahilly (1998, 28) dates these pins from the last quarter of the eleventh to the end of the thirteenth century. Those from Waterford dated mostly from the early twelfth to the early thirteenth century (Scully 1997, 439), while those in Cork dated from the early to late thirteenth century.

Two stick-pins with undifferentiated heads (226:8, 1160:1) were found at Golden Lane. The heads of these pins are only slightly wider than the shanks and they are usually, but not always, decorated either on the head or on the shank or both (O'Rahilly 1998, 27). One of the undifferentiated pins from Golden Lane (226:8) has O'Rahilly's Type A decoration. The upper portion of the shank is decorated with three ring-and-dot motifs with a series of short horizontal stabs below each ring-and-dot. The other undifferentiated pin (1160:1) has three series of short horizontal stabs on the upper portion of the shank. It has no ring-and-dot motifs but the top of the head has Type 2 decoration (ibid., 25), consisting of three incised lines which join at the edge of the head to form a triangle. O'Rahilly dates these pins from the early twelfth century to the first quarter of the thirteenth century.
12:7 Stud-headed pin (O'Rahilly Class 8). Hemispherical head with radiating grooves on the top, flat on underside. Circular shank tapering to point. Slight kink in shank,

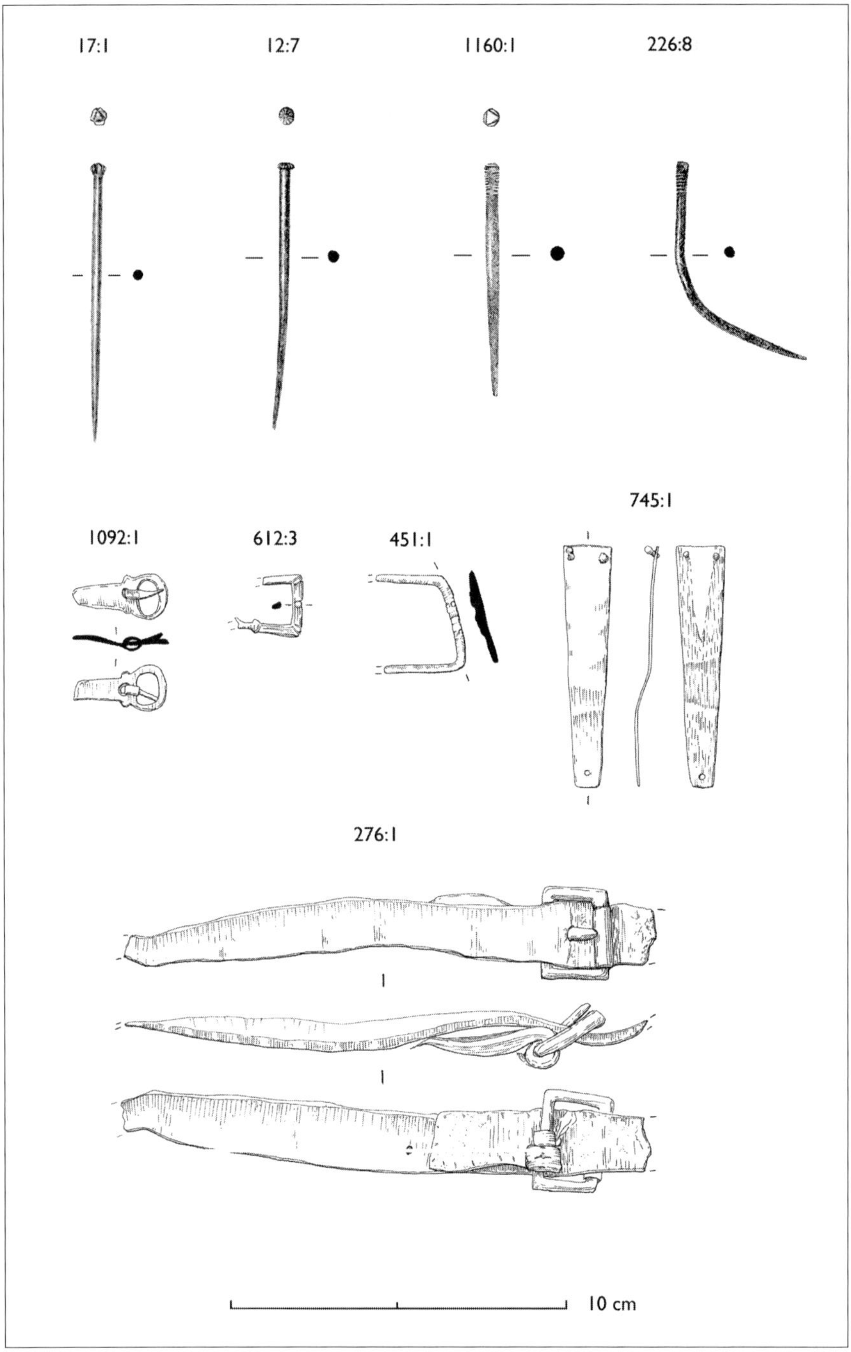

15 Non-ferrous metal artefacts: Stick Pins (17:1, 12:7, 1160:1 and 1308:1); Buckles (1092:1, 612:3 [1], 451:1 and 276:1); Strap-End (745:1)

three-quarters of the way down. Late eleventh to mid-thirteenth century. L 77.9mm Diam. of head 5.1mm Diam. of shank 3.2mm.
17:1 Club-headed pin (O'Rahilly Class 9, Type 3). Knop-shaped head with three dot-in-circle decorations around the head. Circular tapering shank. Mid-eleventh to late thirteenth century. L 81.5mm Diam. of head 4.7mm Diam. of shank 3.2mm. Associated with Burial II.
226:8 Undifferentiated headed pin (O'Rahilly Class 7, Type A). Head only slightly wider than shank, decorated with three dot-and-circles with a series of short horizontal stabs below them (roughly six to seven). Circular tapering shank, bent at middle. Early twelfth to early thirteenth century. L 81mm Diam. of head 3.mm Diam. of shank 3mm.
1142:2 Possible stick-pin fragment, point only. Oval in section. Remaining L 11.5mm Wth of shank 2.2mm T of shank 1.9mm. Associated with Burial CIII.
1160:1 Undifferentiated headed pin (O'Rahilly Class 7). Head only slightly wider than the shank. Shank decorated with three series of short horizontal stabs (about seven in each series). The head is decorated with three grooved lines which meet at the edge to form a triangle (O'Rahilly Type 2 decoration). Circular tapering shank with slight swelling one-third of the way down the shank. Early twelfth to early thirteenth century. L 67.8mm Diam. of head 4mm Diam. of shank 3.9mm. Associated with Burial CVII.
1308:1 Stud-headed (O'Rahilly Class 8). Hemispherical head decorated with a dot-and-ring in the centre surrounded by radiating grooves. Flat on underside of the head. Circular tapering shank, which becomes square in section towards the point. Late eleventh to mid-thirteenth century. L 78.6mm Diam. of head 5mm Diam. of shank 3.8mm.

Buckles Five buckles were found at Golden Lane. There are two single-loop rectangular buckles. This type of buckle was popular during the fifteenth and sixteenth centuries (Whitehead 2003, 16). One is broken (451:1). It has a small rivet on one side of the frame, so it is possible that there may have been a spindle attached. The pin would have rested between two animal heads facing each other and the remainder of the frame is decorated with small incised lines. The other has a looped pin and an attached sheet-metal roller (276:1). Rollers were added to make fastening easier and tighter (Egan 1991a, 54). There are also two leather straps still attached to the buckle. The fragmentary sub-rectangular buckle (1463:1) also has the remains of a sheet-metal roller.

The double-loop trapezoidal buckle (612:3 [1]) has incised lines as decoration on the frames. Double-loop trapezoidal buckles date mainly to the seventeenth century but are also known from the fifteenth and sixteenth centuries (Whitehead 2003, 81). It is possibly a spur buckle.

There is a small oval buckle with an integral strap (1092:1). It has a looped pin. It was also possibly a spur buckle.

Two possible buckle pins (689:128, 1527) were also recovered. The former, which tapers to one end, has two small rivets at the wider end and the latter, which is also tapered, has the remains of gilding and is associated with Burial CLXII.
276:1 Single loop rectangular buckle, rounded at edges. Sheet-metal roller attached to one side. Looped pin attached, sub-rectangular in section. Two fragments of leather strap still attached. Shorter strap decorated with oblique slits on either edge. Buckle: L 27mm Wth 22mm T 4mm. Strap 1: L 133mm Wth 18mm T 4mm. Strap 2: L 40.5mm Wth 17.5mm T 2.5mm.

451:1 Rectangular buckle fragment broken at one end. D-shaped in section. Pin would have rested between what appear to be two small animal heads. Small incised lines along the remainder of the external surface. L 29mm min. Wth 25mm T 2–3.2mm.
612:3 (1) Small trapezoidal buckle, part of the frame is broken. Has incised lines as decoration at the corners and in the centre of the short side. L 18mm min. Wth 19mm T 2mm.
689:128 Possible buckle pin. Tapers at one end. Other end possibly has the remains of two small rivets. L 13.6mm Wth 1.8–3mm T 0.9mm.
1092:1 Small oval buckle with integral strap. Looped pin attached, rectangular in section. L of buckle and strap 28.5mm Buckle: Wth 13.8mm T 1.2mm Strap: Wth 6.5mm T 1.5mm.
1463:1 Possible fragment of sub-rectangular buckle frame with some of the sheet-metal roller still attached. L 26.2mm Wth 6.8mm T 5mm.
1527:1 Possible buckle pin. Rectangular in section, tapered and bent towards one end. Remains of gilding on front near wider end. L 23.3mm Wth 2.4–2.9mm T 1.2mm. Associated with burial CLXII.

Strap-end Strap-ends were attached to straps, belts and girdles and were commonly made of metal alloy (Pritchard 1991a, 126). They prevented the ends of the strap from fraying (Hinton 1990, 505). There is one strap-end, apart from the Viking strap-end (1038:2), from Golden Lane. The sub-rectangular tapering strap-end (745:1) is a two-piece strap-end of which only one plate survives. The two circular perforations at the wide end still have the rivets *in situ* and there is a single perforation at the narrower end which would have held another rivet. The strap would have been held between this plate and another metal plate with the rivets holding them in place. It has the remains of silvering on the front.
745:1 Sub-rectangular strap-end, narrow at one end. This end has one small circular perforation and the wider end has two. These two have rivets still *in situ*. Silver coating on one side of strap-end. L 70mm Wth 8.9–14.5mm T 0.9mm.

Lace chapes Lace chapes or aiglets are folded sheets of metal alloy that were used to prevent the ends of laces fraying. The tighter-fitting fashions of the fourteenth century and later meant a greater demand for laces (Egan 1991c, 284). Lace chapes were recovered from fourteenth- to sixteenth-century contexts at Winchester; although an earlier type is known from twelfth- to fourteenth-century contexts (Biddle and Hinton 1990, 583). A number of lace chapes from the excavations at Patrick Street, Dublin were from sixteenth- and seventeenth-century contexts (Hayden and Walsh 1997, 137) and ten lace chapes were recovered from the Waterford excavations in contexts which dated between the thirteenth and the seventeenth centuries (Scully 1997, 484–5).

The nine lace chapes from Golden Lane fall into two types; rolled tubes with edge-to-edge seams or rolled tubes with overlapped seams. There are five of the former and four of the latter, although one of the lace chapes with an overlapped seam (217:2) has a slightly flattened tube. Six of the lace chapes have an untrimmed overlap at the end, while two (734:1, 842:1) appear to have been trimmed. One of the lace chapes (217:3) is broken at each end. They range in length between 17.5mm and 52mm, though the longest one (1152:4) is much larger than any of the rest of the lace chapes and is more crudely made. One of the lace chapes (598:2) has two small perforations near the

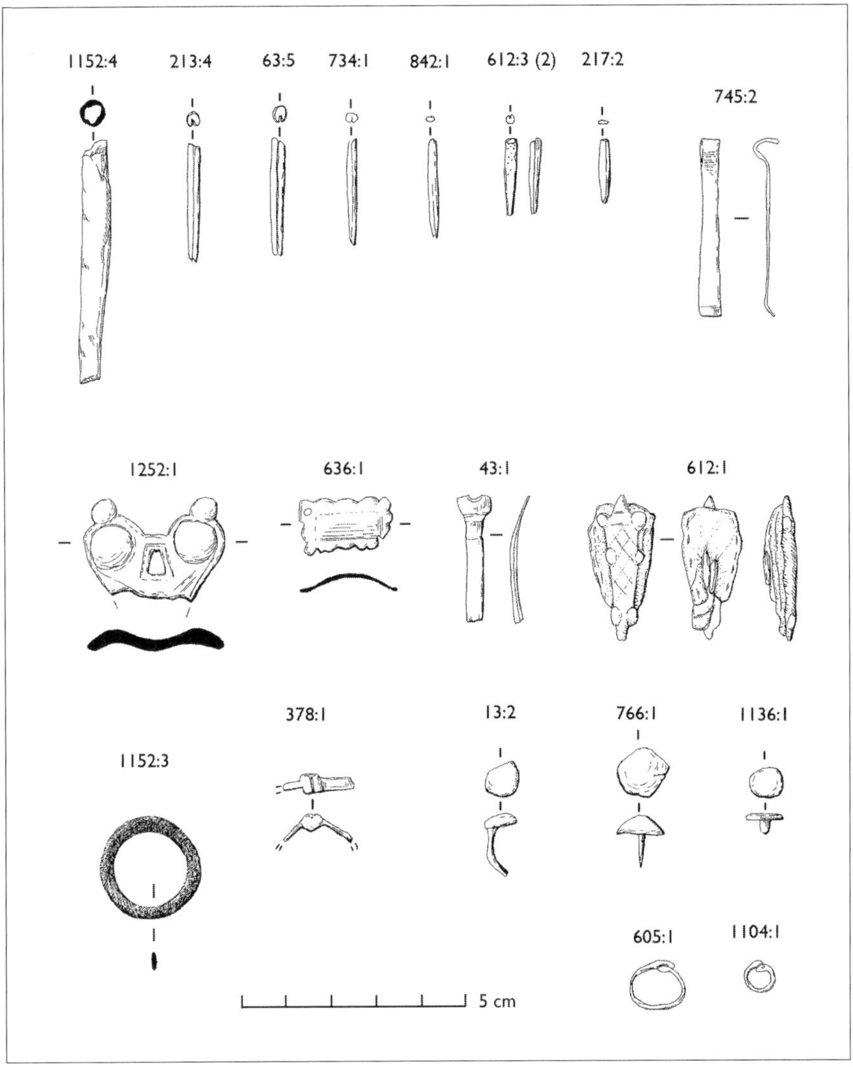

16 Non-ferrous metal artefacts: Lace chapes (1152:4, 213:4, 63:5, 734:1, 842:1, 612:3 (2) and 217:2); Tweezers (745:2); Mounts (1252:1, 636:1, 43:1 and 612:1); Finger Rings (1152:3 and 378:1); Copper Alloy Tacks (13:2, 766:1 and 1136:1); Chain Mail (605:1 and 1104:1)

seam. These holes were where the chape was riveted to the lace (Biddle and Hinton 1990, 581). The surface of one of the chapes (612:3 [2]) is decorated with small punch marks and another (842:1) possibly has the remains of gilding. Five of the lace chapes retain material within the tube (63:5, 217:2). Leather and textiles, including silk, have been found in lace chapes from London (Egan 1991c, 281, 285). A number of lace chapes from Winchester contained leather (Biddle and Hinton 1990, 581). None of the lace chapes from Golden Lane were associated with burials.

63:5 Rolled tube, edge-to-edge seam. Untrimmed overlap at end. Material in the middle of the lace chape. L 25.8mm Diam. 2.2–3.2mm.
213:4 Rolled tube, edge-to-edge seam. Untrimmed overlap at end. L 26mm Diam. 2.1–2.9mm.
217:2 Made from one folded sheet of copper-alloy. Tube slightly flattened, overlapped seam. Untrimmed overlap at end. Material in the middle of the lace chape. L 13.6mm Wth 2.2mm T 1.4mm.
217:3 Folded copper-alloy sheet, broken at each end. Rolled tube, edge-to-edge seam. L 9mm Diam. 3mm.
598:2 Rolled tube, edge-to-edge seam. Untrimmed overlap at end. End appears to be also slightly damaged. May have two small circular perforations. Material in middle of chape. L 26mm Diam. 2.5–3mm.
612:3 (2) Rolled tube, edge-to-edge seam. Untrimmed overlap at end. Decorated all over with small punch marks. Material in middle of chape. L 17.5mm Diam. 1.8–2.5mm.
734:1 Rolled tube, overlapped seam. End looks trimmed. Material in middle of chape. L 23mm Diam. 2–3mm.
842:1 Rolled tube, overlapped seam. End looks trimmed. Possible remains of gilding. L 22mm Diam. 2.5mm.
1152:4 Rolled tube, overlapped seam. Crude in shape. Untrimmed overlap at end. L 52mm Diam. 5–6.5mm.

Finger Rings Two finger rings were recovered from the excavations at Golden Lane. One of the rings (378:1) has a heart-shaped bezel but its hoop is broken. Rings with bezels began to be used during the thirteenth century but most of those found from the London excavations date to the late fourteenth and early fifteenth centuries (Pritchard 1991b, 334). Rings with bezels would have been cast in a three-piece mould (ibid.). The other ring (1152:3) is a simple copper-alloy hoop which was cast in one piece. The hoop also has a slight flange around the outside. Cast rings with plain, and occasionally decorated, hoops were found in London and it was suggested that some of these may be guard rings used to protect stone-set rings (ibid., 325, 332). They all dated to the first half of the fifteenth century (ibid., 332).
378:1 Ring fragment with heart-shaped bezel. Ring is broken and rectangular in section. The heart-shape is in the thickness of the ring and does not face outwards. L 14.8mm Wth 2.8–4mm T 1.3–3.8mm.
1152:3 Finger ring. Plain and crudely made. Elliptical in section. Widens at one point in the circumference. Diam. 22mm Wth 4mm T 2mm.

Tweezers One half of a pair of tweezers (745:2) was found at Golden Lane. They are made from one flat strip of metal which was folded, although one side is now missing. There is a rounded loop at the top and the remaining terminal is flat. The surface of the metal has been scratched away where the slide would have been. Slides on tweezers appear to be a medieval type (Biddle 1990b, 690).
745:2 Possible tweezers fragment, rectangular in section, curved at one end. One arm broken off, remaining tip inturned. L 38.8mm Wth 5mm T 1mm.

Chain Mail Two chain mail links were found at Golden Lane. Both rings have expansions where each end of the hoop was riveted together. Earlier chain mail could be made of alternating rows of riveted and solid rings but by the late fourteenth century, chain mail consisted of mostly riveted links, except in cases where an area needed to be stiffer such as a collar, where the riveted and solid rings could be alternated in rows (wallacecollection.org).

605:1 Oval ring, oval in section. Expanded at the join where the two ends were riveted together, now separated. L 11.3mm Wth 10mm T 0.8mm.

1104:1 Ring expanded where the two ends meet and are riveted together. Small circular rivet hole on one of the expanded ends. Ring circular in section. Diam. 6mm T 0.9mm.

Mounts Metal alloy mounts were decorative objects attached to textile and leather articles of personal dress such as belts, straps and girdles, or on the leather straps of horse harness, though they could also have been fixed to caskets, book covers or pieces of furniture (Ottaway and Rogers 2002, 12; Egan 1991b, 162). Mounts were usually attached by means of rivets but occasionally another means of attachment was used (Egan 1991b, 162). Ten mounts were recovered from Golden Lane and all were attached by means of rivets, except for one (1252:1), which was too fragmentary to tell how it was attached, and another (43:1) which has no visible means of attachment. Only two of the mounts (61:2, 612:1), however, still have their rivets *in situ*. One of the mounts (612:1), which is in the shape of an animal with herringbone decoration on its back, is still attached to leather. The leather is folded over in a roughly triangular shape with the edges stitched together and the mount is attached by means of two copper-alloy projections which pierce the leather and are folded over. The mounts can be divided into a number of different categories; circular, square/rectangular, figurative, non-figurative, bar mounts and those which just survive as fragments and their original shape is unknown. There is one circular mount (31:2). It had two raised rings and a central perforation but it is now much broken. There is one small, plain, square mount (376:3) and a rectangular mount (636:1) which has a scalloped edge and is raised in the middle. There are two figurative mounts; one in the shape of an animal described above (612:1) and another (1166:1) which is possibly flower-shaped, has a central perforation and has a small projecting bar. The non-figurative mounts are a small square mount with a central perforation and a projecting arm and a fragment which has raised decoration (1252:1). There is one possible bar mount (43:1), although there is no apparent means of attachment. It is a narrow strap which expands and flattens at one end. Bar mounts were attached to belts or straps in rows (Egan 1991b, 209). There are two more possible mounts (61:2, 83:1) which survive just as fragments and their original form is unknown.

31:2 Possible mount. Broken, probably circular with central perforation. Two raised rings. L 16mm Wth 11mm T 2.5mm.

43:1 Possible bar mount. Linear strap, semi-circular in section. Expands and flattens at the head. Two decorative grooves before head. Head rounded and has semi-circular indentation at top. L 27.5mm Wth 4.3–7.6mm T 0.9–2mm. Associated with Burial XII

61:2 Two fragments, possibly mounts. Irregular in shape, both have split rivets. 1. L 23mm Wth 15mm T 1.8mm 2. L 16.8mm Wth 12.5mm T 2.2mm.

83:1 Possible fragment of mount. Small, flat fragment, irregular in shape, with one small circular rivet. L 13mm Wth 6–9mm T 0.7mm. Associated with Burial XXVIII.

376:3 Possible mount. Small square fragment. One small punch mark which looks under x-ray to be a perforation. L 10.2mm Wth 9mm T 1mm.

612:1 Mount in the shape of an animal with herringbone incised decoration on its back. Still attached to a fragment of folded leather. L 30.5mm Wth 6.5–13.5mm T 7mm.
636:1 Small, rectangular mount with scalloped edges. Raised and hollow in the middle. One small circular perforation in one corner. L 19.7mm Wth 11mm T 3mm.
1152:1 Possible mount. Small, square with small circular perforation and small strap, semi-circular in section. L 16.5mm Wth 3–7mm T 2mm.
1166:1 Possible mount. Small, possibly flower-shaped (?) head with small circular perforation. Small arm extended from base of object. L 9mm Wth 2.2–7.5mm T 1.2mm.
1252:1 Mount. Broken. Two roughly teardrop-shaped discs, joined at the top and in the middle with two raised circles at the widest part, which are hollow at the back. There is one semi-circular knop at the end of each teardrop. L 31.5mm Wth 22.5mm T 4mm.

Copper-alloy tacks Copper-alloy tacks, while being functional structural objects, could also be decorative in nature (Groves 1990, 1102). They were used in fabric, leather and wood (ibid.). Groves (1990) classified the copper-alloy tacks from excavations in Winchester according to their morphology. Those from Golden Lane are of types that would have been used to decorate leather or furnishings (ibid., 1106). There is one Groves Type 12 copper-alloy tack (1136:1) from Golden Lane. It has a flat, circular head and a short circular shank. The head and shank are unitary and it has the remains of gilding. There are two Groves Type 13 copper-alloy tacks (766:1, 840:13). They have hemispherical, hollow-domed heads and square, tapering shanks. The head and shanks were made separately. The remaining copper-alloy tack (13:2) from Golden Lane cannot be classified according to Groves's typology. It has a sub-rectangular head, slightly raised in the middle. The shank is off-centre to the head and the head and shank were made separately.
13:2 Head broken along two sides, may have been sub-rectangular, slightly raised in the middle. Short rectangular shank, bent at tip. Shank off-centre to head. Head and shank made separately. Unclassified. Head: L 7.9mm Wth 7.8mm T 2mm Shank: 10.5mm Wth 3mm T 2mm.
766:1 Hemispherical, hollow-domed head. Square, tapering shank. Head and shank made separately. Groves Type 13. L 13mm Diam. of head 10mm H of head 3.5mm Shank: 0.9mm x 0.9mm.
840:13 Hemispherical, hollow-domed head. Square, tapering shank. Head and shank made separately. Groves Type 13. L 14mm Diam. of head 11.2mm H of head 5mm Shank: 1mm x 1mm.
1136:1 Flat, circular head, short circular shank. Head and shank unitary. Remains of gilding on head. Groves Type 12. L 3.8mm Wth 7.2mm Diam. 1.8mm.

Coin Only one medieval coin was recovered from the excavations at Golden Lane. It is a copper half farthing or 'Patrick' (226:6) of Edward IV. It is an issue of 1461 and is of the rare variety with 'P' in two angles of the cross on the reverse of the coin. Before Edward IV had ascended the crown, his father Richard, duke of York, had promised the Anglo-Irish parliament that he would issue a separate Irish coinage in return for their support against his Lancastrian opponents. Shortly after Edward gained the throne the Anglo-Irish parliament appointed Thomas Brady as master of the mint and some months later Edward appointed his own choice for the position, Germyn Lynch.

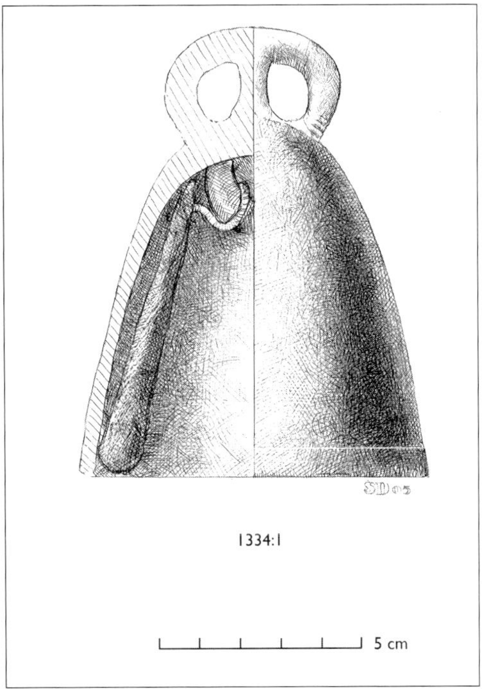

17 Non-ferrous metals: Hand-bell (1334:1)

Brady's were the first to be struck in 1461 and these are known as the 'anonymous issue' as they have no reference to Edward IV. Lynch did not begin to strike coins until 1463, while Brady was responsible for the farthings and the copper half farthings, although not many of the copper coins seem to have been struck. The copper half farthing has a small crown in a beaded circle with the legend 'PATRIK' on the obverse and an equal armed cross on the reverse. A very rare variety has the letter 'P' in the angle of the cross on the reverse. The copper half farthings are thought to have been struck in Dublin (Colgan 2003, 39–41).
226:6 1460–61 Edward IV copper half farthing. Obv: in the central field there is a crown ringed by a beaded circle. The legend, divided by a branch, reads: PA TRIK. Because the obverse design was struck off-centre, only a portion of the outer beaded circle appears on the surface. Rev: a cross with arms of equal length, framed by four sets of arches. Between the arms of the cross, in two positions 180 degrees apart, are the letters P, P. Diam. 14.5mm T 1.1mm.

Hand-bell A conical, 'beehive' hand-bell was recovered from the pit F1333. This pit contained pottery dating from the twelfth to the fourteenth centuries. The bell may have belonged to the church of St Michael le Pole. It could have served a variety of functions. A round tower or *cloicthech* ('bell-house') is shown on the site of the church of St Michael le Pole in de Gomme's map of 1673 and in drawings by J. Grogan in 1751 and Beranger in 1766 (Gowen 2001, 20, 22–3). Hand-bells were rung from the top windows of round towers (Edwards 1990, 128). This could have been to call people for services or to warn of danger such as fire or attack. Hand-bells were also rung during the liturgy of the Mass.

1334:1 Copper-alloy conical, or 'beehive', bell. Two oval suspension loops at apex of bell. Shallow incised line on exterior near rim. Clapper *in situ*, now stuck to internal wall, hung from an S-shaped hoop which was in turn attached to a suspension loop. Conservator noted remains of a rope around the top and sides of the bells and the interior had been packed with straw or wood. H 106.2mm Diam. 88.2mm T 2.6mm.

FERROUS METAL ARTEFACTS

Iron buckle There is one small, double-loop, iron buckle (63:8) from Golden Lane. It is corroded but was probably trapezoidal in shape and had a knop at the pointed end. It has a detached pin which is flat and rounded at one end and tapers to a point at the other.
63:8 L 32mm Wth 13.5–21.5mm T 2.5–5.5mm.

Mounts There are five possible iron mounts or straps from Golden Lane. One is flower-shaped with a circular perforation and a rectangular strap (65:1). It was associated with Burial XX so may have been binding from a coffin or attached to a wooden object placed in the grave. A short length of iron tubing (612:11) has the remains of copper-alloy on the exterior and may have been used as a binding. From the same context there is a flat iron strap (612:15) which tapers at one end and has a rectangular notch at the other end. There is one possible mount from a casket or chest (1152:5). Forty-eight iron mounts for chests or caskets were recovered from excavations in London and they mostly dated from the late thirteenth to the mid-fifteenth century (Brenan 1998, 65). One other object from Golden Lane may be a fragment of a mount or decorative piece of ironwork (612:19) but the full form of the object is unknown.
65:1 Possible iron decorative strap or mount or binding. Rectangular strap and flower-shaped head with circular perforation. L 50mm Wth 15.7–33.8mm T 3mm. Associated with Burial XX.
612:9 Possible mount or decorative piece of ironwork. Shank rectangular in section. One rectangular branch in the middle and is Y-shaped towards one end, possibly where it branches in two. L 80mm Wth 11.5mm T 12.5mm.
612:11 Short length of iron tubing. Remains of copper-alloy on the exterior. Possibly used as binding on a wooden object. L 29.6mm Diam. 15.5mm T 1.4mm.
612:15 Iron strap, flat and rectangular in section. Tapered towards one end and has rectangular notch in the other end. L 78.3mm Wth 19–27.5mm T 4mm.
1152:5 Iron mount for chest or casket. Rectangular terminal with tapering strap. Possible central perforation in the rectangular terminal. L 45mm Wth 5–28mm T 6mm.

Keys Six iron keys were found during the excavations at Golden Lane. One key is possibly a Goodall Type 6 key (Goodall 1990a, 1007). It has a kidney-shaped bow, a solid, circular stem and a bit which is in line with the end of the stem. Kidney-shaped bows date to the late fourteenth or early fifteenth centuries but can sometimes be found in later contexts (ibid., 1008). Another key with a kidney-shaped bow is probably a Goodall Type 8 key (Goodall 1990a, 1007). This type of key has a stem which extends beyond the bit but also narrows halfway over the bit. Type 8 keys could

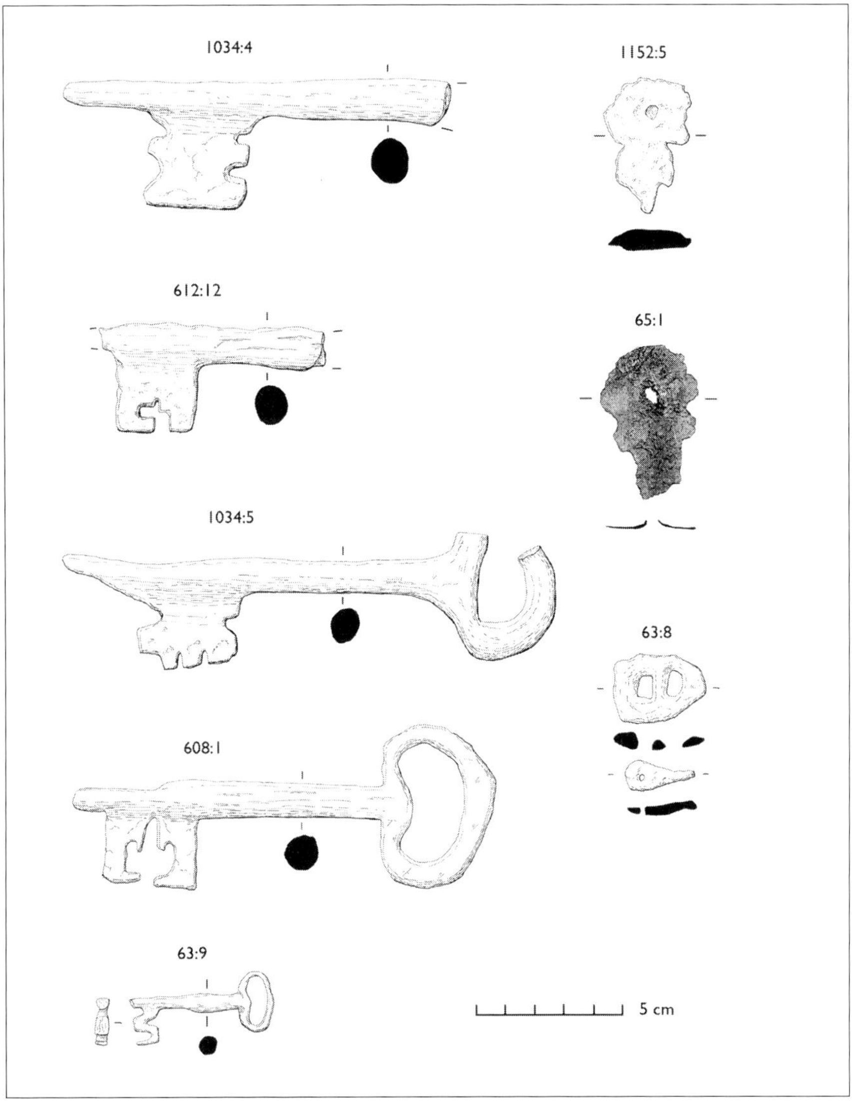

18 Ferrous metal artifacts: Keys (1034:4, 612:12, 1034:5, 608:1 and 63:9); Mounts (1152:5 and 65:1); Iron Buckle (63:8)

be used on both sides of the lock and also continued in use into the post-medieval period (ibid.). Another key (612:12) has a stem which projects beyond the bit but it is missing its bow. Similar keys have been found in London and have been dated to the fourteenth century (Egan 1998, 115, 117).

Two of the keys (1034:4–5) are from a pit (F1033) which cut the Viking Burial LXXXV and is thought to be medieval in date. Unfortunately one of the keys is missing its bow and the other has a partial oval bow, which was a common bow form used throughout the medieval period and later (Goodall 1990a, 1008) and so the keys cannot be closely dated. Their stems and bits are similar to Goodall Type 7 keys (ibid., 1007) which are medieval in date. There is also one partial stem (840:38) which could not be classified.

63:9 Key for mounted lock. Kidney-shaped bow. Solid stem, circular in section, with swelling in middle of stem. Bit perpendicular to the stem and in line with end of stem. Wards cut parallel to stem. L of Key: 48.8mm Remaining H of Bow: 21.5mm Wth of Bow: 12mm Wth of Stem: 36.8mm Wth of Bit: 8.2mm T of Bow: 4.8mm T of Stem: 3.8mm T of Bit: 4.5mm. Goodall Type 6. Medieval.

608:1 Key for mounted lock. Kidney-shaped bow. Solid stem circular in section, extends beyond the bit. Stem narrows halfway over the bit. Bit has wards cut through a central opening. L of key: 143mm H of Bow: 54mm Wth of Bow: 38mm Diam. of Stem: 13mm Wth of Bit: 32mm. T of Stem: 8mm T of Bit: 5mm. Goodall Type 8. Late fifteenth/early sixteenth century.

612:12 Key for mounted lock. Bow missing. Solid stem circular in section, extends beyond the bit. Wards of bit cut through a central opening. L 74.5mm Diam. of Stem: 14.5mm Wth of Bit: 28mm T of Bit: 7mm.

840:38 Key for mounted lock. Partial stem, circular in section. Bow broken off. Only very small fragment of bit remains. L 76mm Diam. of Stem: 4mm.

1034:4 Key for mounted lock. Stem circular in section, extends beyond the bit. Bow missing. Bit is solid with wards cut parallel to the stem on the outside edges of the bit. L 129mm Diam. of Stem: 15mm Wth of Bit: 35mm T of Bit: 5mm.

1034:5 Key for mounted lock. Oval bow, broken. Stem sub-rectangular in section, extends beyond bit. Bit is solid with wards cut into the sides and base. L of Key: 166mm Remaining H of Bow: 43.5mm Wth of Bow: 37.5mm Wth of Stem: 13.5mm Wth of Bit: 33mm T of Bow: 10mm T of Stem: 10.5mm T of Bit: 4.5mm.

Blades and Knives There are eight knife blades and a possible pivoting knife or pocket-knife (247:3) which is in fragments. All the blades are typically triangular in section, except for one (226:11) which is so encrusted with adhering corrosion products that the shape of its section is unknown. One of the blades is possibly a whittle-tang (1038:4), used throughout the medieval and later periods (Goodall 1990b, 835). One corroded and encrusted blade may be a razor (13:3). It has a narrow tang at one end which has a small, circular rivet hole. The possible pivoting or pocket-knife (247:3) is fragmented and corroded but has a small double-ended, copper-alloy rivet intact and another fragment of a copper-alloy rivet.

12:6 Iron blade, triangular in section. Broken at one end, possibly rounded at the other. L 58.8mm Wth 18mm T 3.2–4.8mm.

13:3 Iron blade. Triangular in section. Heavily encrusted with adhering corrosion products. A rivet hole visible in x-ray. L 86mm Wth 10–17mm T 5.5mm.

25:5 Blade fragment, triangular in section. L 80.6mm Wth 16mm T 2.5–3.5mm.

217:6 Blade fragment. Tip of blade broken off. Triangular in section. L 39mm Wth 13.5–17.5mm T 3–5.5mm.

217:8 Blade fragment. Triangular in section. Encrusted with adhering corrosion products. L 27mm Wth 14mm T 4.5mm.

226:11 Blade fragment. Heavily encrusted with adhering corrosion products, section of blade unclear. L 38mm Wth 26mm T 3.8mm.

247:3 Iron blade from a pivoting or pocket knife in four fragments. Blade fragments triangular in section. One fragment has two copper-alloy rivets, one with a circular head intact. 1. L 62.8mm Wth 11–14mm T 3.2mm 2. L 52.7mm Wth 13mm T 3mm 3. L 46.5mm Wth 13mm T 3.2mm 4. L 23mm Wth 14mm T 9.2mm.
689:16 Small blade fragment, triangular in section. Heavily encrusted with adhering corrosion products. L 28mm Wth 15mm T 1.5–3mm.
1038:4 Blade, triangular in section with straight back and curved blade. Possibly whittle tang. Rectangular tang tapers to a point. L 210mm Wth 5–16mm T 3–6.5mm.

Structural iron from graves Fifty of the burials excavated at Golden Lane had structural iron in their grave fills. The location of where in the grave fills the structural iron came from is recorded for thirty of the burials. The other twenty burials have no find location for the nails as they may have come from the grave fill before the burial was fully excavated and it was not recognized what they were and some were retrieved only during the cleaning of the skeleton in post-excavation work. Most had only a single nail, though a few had between two and five nails, so in some cases they may be just intrusive finds and not directly related to the burial. Two of the burials (CI, CVII), however, had a large number of nails from their grave fills, twelve and fifteen respectively, and these probably represent some kind of structural element used within the grave. The nails for which find locations are known can be divided into three groups; nails which possibly form a coffin or plank lining, nails found to the sides of the burials which may represent the remains of coffins or plank lining and nails found over the upper torso.

The nails from ten burials appear to form a coffin shape or represent plank lining placed in the grave. The positions of these nails form a sub-rectangular shape which narrows towards the feet and many of these burials have a large number of nails, for example, Burials CCLIX and CCXXVII. The nails are found at the sides of the burials, to the west of the head and to the east of the feet. Those at the sides are most commonly found at the hips, the shoulders, the knees, the ankles and occasionally the elbows. Interesting, one of these burials, Burial CLXXIV, has ear-muff stones either side of the head and the nails are found outside of the stones, suggesting that a form of plank lining may have been used, as it is unlikely that ear-muff stones would be placed in a coffin. Unfortunately only four nails were found with this burial and a pit (F1490) had been cut to the south of the lower legs, so it is difficult to say whether there was a structure, if any, surrounding the entire burial. Evidence for wood lining has been found at a number of sites in Ireland. Two of the burials from Phase I at Cabinteely had graves lined with elm (Conway 1999, 21). Most of the Period I burials from St Peter's, Waterford had timber-lined graves (Hurley and McCutcheon 1997, 193). Only seven graves had preserved timbers but in many other cases timber lining was suggested by square-cut graves where the cut is larger than the burial and to a lesser extent wood staining or slots. Occasionally nails were found, but not more than one or two. These burials dated to the eleventh and twelfth centuries and predated the stone-lined graves at St Peter's (ibid.).

Fourteen other burials had low numbers of nails located somewhere to the side of the body and in some cases the burial has been severely truncated, for example, Burials CCXXXIII and CCXXXV. The nails from this group of burials were found at various areas around the body: at the right side of the upper body (Burial CCXXXV), to the left and right of the lower body (Burial CXXIII, Burial CCXVII, Burial CCXXVI,

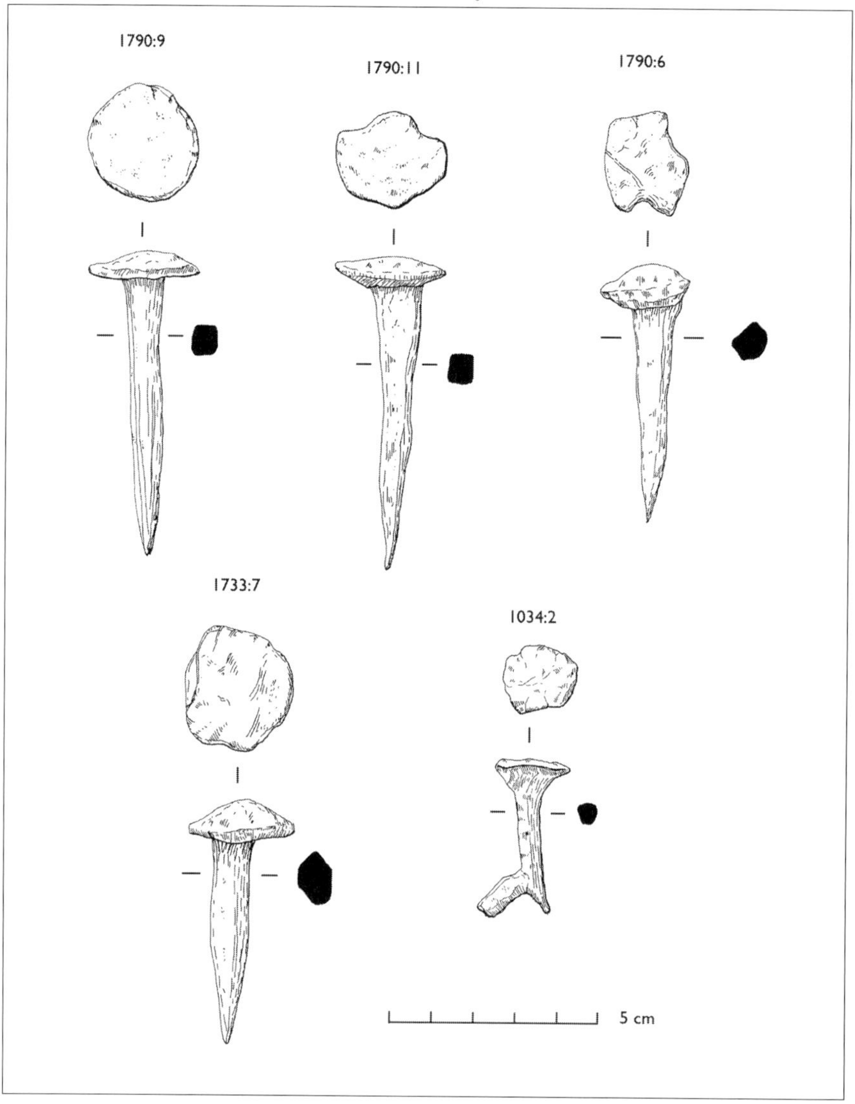

19 Ferrous metal: Structural Iron from Graves (1790:9, 1790:11 and 1790:6 from Burial CCLIX, 1733:7 from Burial CCXXXI and 1034:2 from Burial LXXXV)

Burial CCXXXIII), at the left and right elbows (Burial LXXXVI, Burial CXVII), at the right shoulder (Burial CCLVI), at the left elbow and right hand (Burial CCXV), at the pelvis (Burial XII, Burial CLIX, Burial CCXXIV), above the skull (Burial CXLVII) and to the left of the skull (Burial CLXXII).

The third group of burials are those where nails were found over the upper torso. There are four burials with single nails found over, or (in the case of Burial CXVIII which had been truncated) just below the torso. During the excavations at Winchester large numbers of copper-alloy tacks were found in the area of the cathedral, with nearly half of them having been found in the graveyard (Groves 1990, 1104). While it was suggested that tacks in the cemetery may have represented small reliquaries buried with the dead, only single tacks were found in the graves and it was suggested that these could represent the attachment of a wooden tablet or a parchment to the lid of the coffin which bore the name of the dead person and a prayer for their soul (ibid., 1104–5). While the Golden Lane nails are made from iron and not copper-alloy and it is speculative at best to suggest that single nails found above the torsos of burials at Golden Lane performed the same function, it is at least a possibility. One of the burials included with the coffin or plank-lined burials, Burial CCXXVII, also had a nail on the upper torso which may help to support this interpretation.

THE VIKING FINDS

Six metal artefacts accompanied Burial LXXXV; a copper-alloy buckle and strap-end, an iron spearhead and an iron knife and two lead weights. The spearhead was found in a layer of soil that sealed the pit F1034 which cut the burial to the west. This pit is thought to have been a robbing pit, dug in order to extract grave goods from the burial. The remainder of the finds were found close together beneath, and to the right of, the right femur of the burial.

The tongue-shaped strap-end (1038:2) with the central rib and ring-and-dot ornament is of a type that has been previously found in Viking graves at Peel Castle, Isle of Man and Cathedral Green, Carlisle and as stray finds in eastern England (Thomas 2000, 249). Thomas notes that those found in eastern England are of a lesser quality and are probably copies. Examples are also known from Domburg, Holland and from Scandinavia. Those found from graves in the Irish Sea region were accompanied by matching buckles (ibid.). The strap-end and buckle from Carlisle cathedral are almost identical to the strap-end (1038:2) and buckle (1038:1) from the Viking grave at Golden Lane, the only differences being the arrangement of the ring-and-dot ornament. Sets of matching strap-ends and buckles were common throughout Scandinavia during the ninth and tenth centuries (ibid.). The buckle (1038:2) from Golden Lane is a square, single-loop buckle with a folded sheet copper-alloy buckle plate. The edge of the buckle is decorated with a raised rib between two grooves, similar to the decoration on the edge of the strap-end. It also has ring-and-dot ornament on the front of the buckle plate. The strap-end was found under the right femur of the burial and the buckle was found just above and a little to the right of this.

Two lead weights (1038:3) were found below the left hip of Burial LXXXV. They were found together and traces of organic material around them were noted during excavation so they may have been placed in a pouch which hung from the person's belt. One is in the shape of a truncated cone and has a central perforation in which a blob of lead had been placed and the other is cylindrical in shape. The lead alloy weights from Anglo-Scandinavian contexts in York were cylindrical, truncated conical, inverted truncated conical and spherical in shape (Mainman and Rogers 2000, 2561). Plain lead weights were the most common from York but occasionally they had incised marks or perforations (ibid.). Over two hundred and fifty lead weights were recovered from the excavations at Wood Quay. They all appeared to be based around a basic unit of 26.6g (Wallace 1984, 125–6). The lead weights from Golden Lane are as follows:

Weight before conservation	**Grams**	**Grains**	**Oz Troy**	**Oz Avoirdupois**
Truncated conical	13.98	215.7	0.4495	0.4931
Cylindrical	17.27	266.5	0.5552	0.6092
Weight after conservation	**Grams**	**Grains**	**Oz Troy**	**Oz Avoirdupois**
Truncated conical	12.49	192.8	0.4016	0.4406
Cylindrical	16.38	252.8	0.5266	0.5778

It can sometimes be difficult to determine the intended value of a weight found during an archaeological excavation as it may have received damage or it may not be known what system of weights was used (Biddle 1990c, 910). The truncated conical weight is just less than half of the basic 26.6g of the Viking weights from Wood Quay and the conical weight is roughly three-fifths of 26.6g. They may originally have been intended as divisions of 26.6g but as a result of their deposition and subsequent retrieval and conservation their weights may have altered.

The iron knife (1038:4) is a whittle-tang knife. It has a straight back and a blade which curves slightly upwards towards the tip. The blade is triangular in section. Knives were common possessions which would have been carried by most people and used for a variety of purposes (de Neergaard 1987, 51). Its handle could have been made of wood or bone. Considering that the knife was found by the side of the right femur with the blade pointing downwards, it is possible that it had been held in a scabbard which was suspended from a belt. An organic-stained soil was detected around the knife and this may have been trace-remains of the scabbard (O'Donovan 2005, 17). This organic staining was also thought to be present where the belt that held the strap-end and where the buckle would have been (ibid.).

The iron spearhead (1032:1) has a circular socket. The socket has a series of bulbous mouldings which are each decorated with a series of incised lines. The blade is lozenge-shaped in section and is broken near the top.

1032:1 Spearhead. Iron. Circular socket, tapering towards where the socket meets the blade. Socket was broken near the end but has been repaired during conservation. Socket has bulbous mouldings, each with a set of four incised lines. There are five mouldings above where the socket was broken. Slight collar between the socket and blade. Small circular rivet head *in situ* near the base of the socket. Blade widens just above the socket and then tapers again. Tip of blade is broken. The blade is diamond-shaped in section, being thinner at the edges. L 194mm L of socket 111mm Diam. of socket 13.2–20.2mm Wth of blade 28–36mm T of blade 2–8mm.

1038:1 Copper-alloy buckle. Square, single-loop buckle with folded sheet copper-alloy buckle plate. Rectangular buckle has a lip and the outer surface of the frame and lip are decorated with a raised rib between two deeply incised lines. Buckle plate folded with a notch in the fold to accommodate the buckle pin. Plate is decorated on the outer surface with three rows of ring-and-dot decoration, one on each side and one down the middle. It is riveted together by two copper-alloy rivets near the edge of the

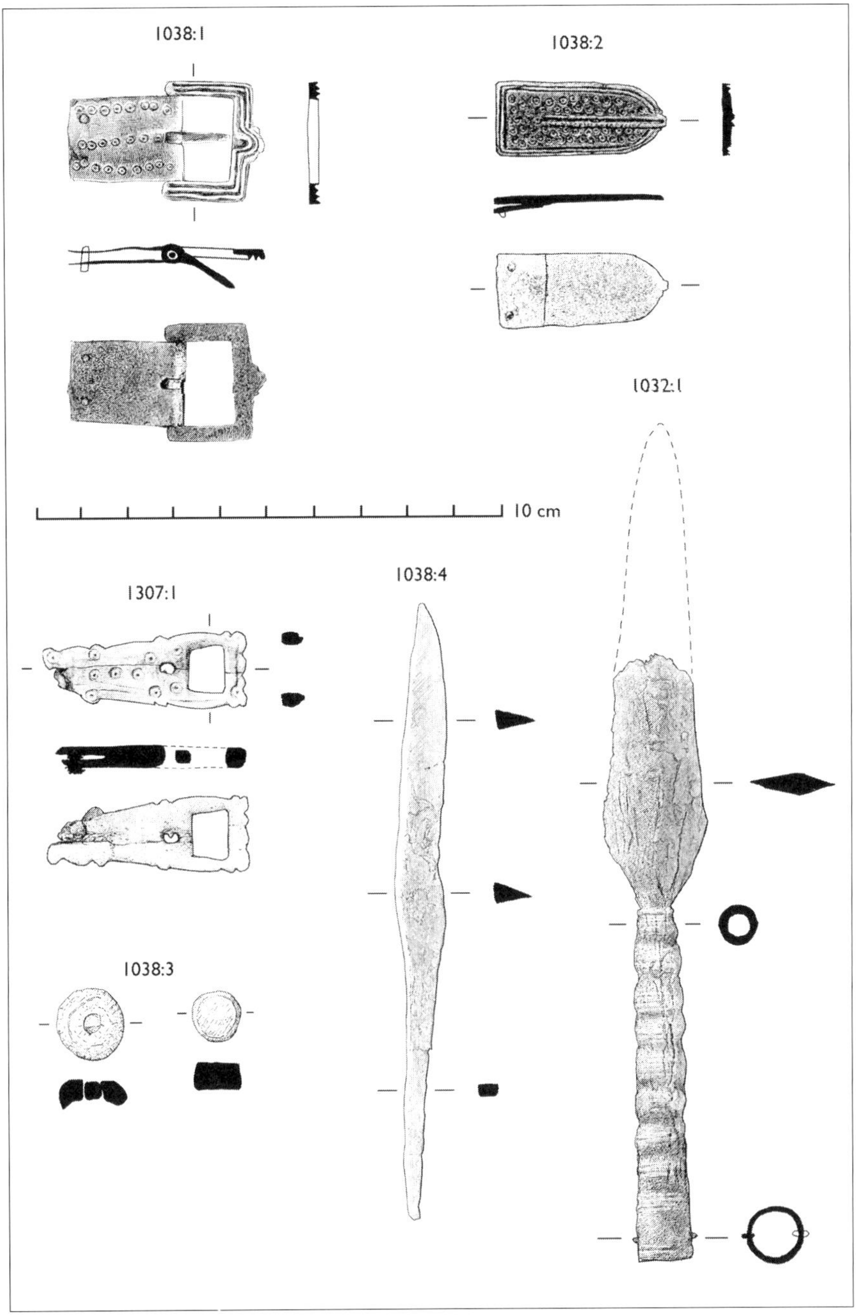

20 Finds associated with Burial LXXXV and CXXIX: Copper alloy buckle (1038:1), Copper alloy strap-end (1038:2), Bone buckle (1307:1), Lead weights (1038:3), Iron knife (1038:4); Iron spearhead (1032:1)

plate. Looped buckle pin *in situ*. It appears to have the remains of gilding on the buckle pin. L 60mm Loop: Wth 35.2mm T 2.2mm Plate: Wth 25mm T 4mm.
1038:2 Copper-alloy Viking-Age strap-end. The tongue-shaped strap-end has a median rib with a groove in the middle of the rib and small horizontal nicks across the rib. The surface surrounding the rib has punched ring-and-dot ornament. The border of the strap-end is formed by a low, narrow rib between two grooves. The strap-end's split-end terminal was secured by two small copper-alloy rivets. L 51mm Wth 18–22.2mm T 1.2–5mm.
1038:3 Two lead weights. 1. Truncated conical. Circular, flat on top and base, widens towards base. Central perforation which widens towards the base and is filled with a blob of lead. Surface is cracked. Diam. 21.8mm T 8mm. 2. Cylindrical. Circular, flat on top and base, only slightly wider at base. White patches of lead corrosion on the base and side. Diam. 12.8mm–15.2mm T 8.6mm.
1038:4 Iron knife. Whittle-tang. Blade back rises after the tang and then is straight to the tip. Tang curves up towards the cutting edge, which curves slightly upwards to meet the blade back. Blade triangular in section. Tang is also triangular in section, though not as pronounced as the blade. The tip of the tang is curved. Tang was repaired during conservation. L 210mm Blade: Wth 4–13.5mm T 7.3mm Tang: Wth 4.2–15mm T 3.8–6.3mm.

STONE ARTEFACTS

Hone The hone/whetstone found at Golden Lane (226:9) was designed to be held in the hand and has a sharpening groove on one side at the widest end. Smaller, fine-grained hones were used for sharpening small blades and craftsmen's tools (Ellis and Moore 1990, 869).
226:9 Hone/Whetstone. Sub-rectangular in shape, tapered at one end. The two ends are rough but all the sides are smooth and one has a groove near the wider end. Fine-grained.

Loom weight One stone loom weight (1152:2) was recovered from Golden Lane. It is bun-shaped with a straight perforation.
1152:2 Loom weight. Sandstone. Circular with central cylindrical perforation. Small hole near the edge on one side. Indentation running around the circumference of the weight. Surface is rough. Diam. 46mm T 22.5mm diam. of perforation 4.8mm.

Rotary quern stone There is one incomplete rotary quern (1697:1) from Golden Lane. It is broken but was circular in shape and probably had a cylindrical central perforation. Rotary querns could have been used for grinding flour for bread but Biddle and Smith (1990, 882) suggest that they may also have been used for grinding other foodstuffs such as malt or mustard. The fragment of rotary quern from Golden Lane was found in the grave fill of Burial CCXIV.
1697:1 Incomplete rotary quernstone. Red sandstone. Circular. Broken in half. Probably had a cylindrical central perforation. Associated with Burial CCXIV.

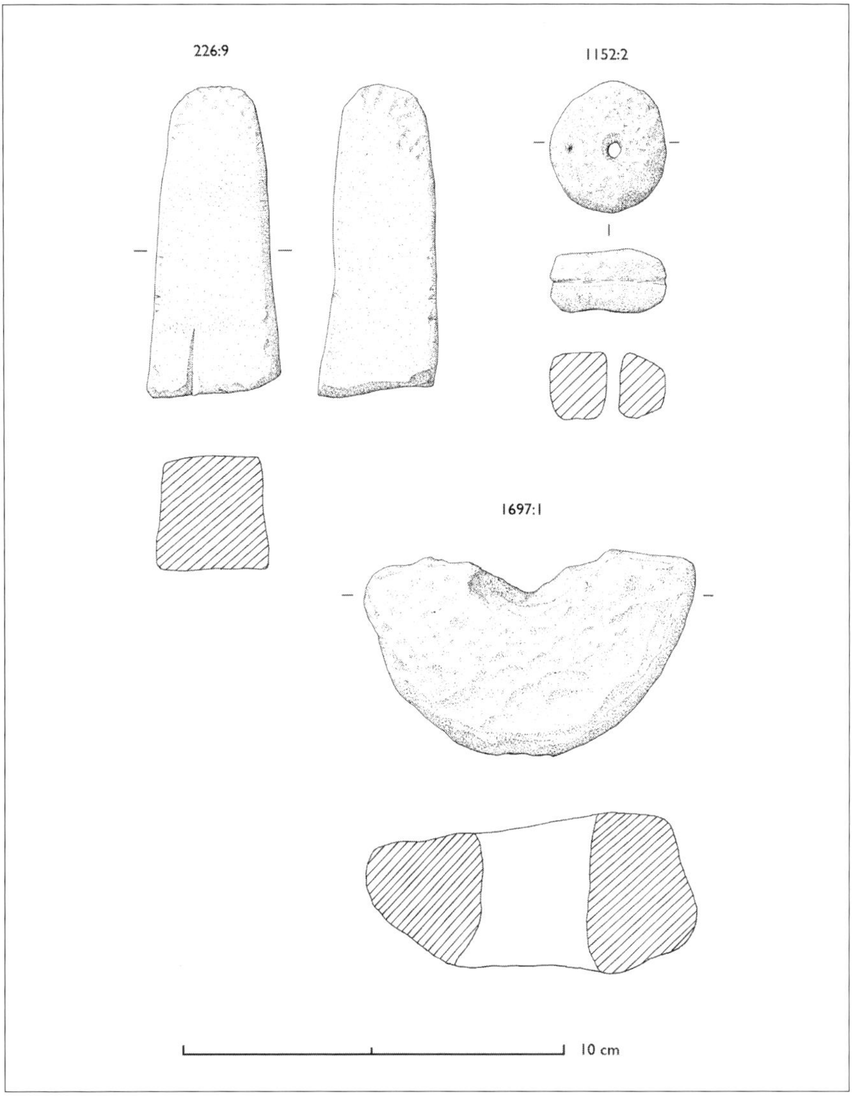

21 Stone artefacts: Hone (226:9); Loom Weight (1152:2); Rotary Quernstone (1697:1)

ARTEFACTS OF SKELETAL MATERIAL

Tuning peg One bone tuning peg (63:2) for a stringed instrument was recovered from Golden Lane. It has a sub-rectangular head, a circular shaft and a notch at the end of the shank. Many tuning pegs have been found from medieval and post-medieval sites in Ireland and Britain and their variations in size would suggest that they were used for a number of different instruments (Lawson 1990, 711; Hurley

1997, 665). The longer pegs are probably harp pegs while the shorter ones are possibly for smaller psaltery-type instruments (Hurley 1997, 665). The tuning peg from Golden Lane is only 59.5mm in length, which would suggest it falls into the latter category. The string was usually attached to the peg through a small circular perforation at the bottom of the shaft but the Golden Lane peg has a small notch instead. The notch appears to be original and not a perforation that was broken, as the end of the shaft is smooth but also may have been reused.
63:2 Bone tuning peg. Shaft circular in section, head is expanded and sub-rectangular in section. Notch in end of shaft. L 59.5mm Wth 5–7.5mm T 4.2–5mm.

Combs One possible complete bone-comb and four bone-comb fragments were found on Golden Lane. They are simple single-sided or double-sided combs. There are no composite combs. Three of these were double-sided combs (151:2, 840:7, 945:1) and two are single-sided combs (415:1, 1703:1). Double combs usually have teeth of different sizes on either side as each side would have had a different function (Galloway 1990, 665). Two of the double-sided combs from Golden Lane (151:2, 945:1) have differently-sized teeth but one (840:7) appears to have same-sized teeth on each side of the comb. One of the single-sided combs (415:1) appears to be complete apart from two broken teeth. It was probably used as a hair decoration. The other single-sided comb was associated with Burial CCXVII.
151:2 Bone-comb fragment. Double comb, teeth finer on one side. Most of the teeth are broken off. Broken at each end. L 43mm Wth 13.5–21.5mm T 3mm.
415:1 Small bone-comb. Single-sided. Originally had eight long teeth, two of which are missing and one is broken. Small semi-circular indentation on one side of comb. L 29mm Wth 14mm T 2.8mm.
840:7 Bone-comb fragment. Double comb, teeth appear to be the same size on each side. One end still intact. Teeth mostly missing on one side. L 42mm Wth 20mm T 1.2mm.
945:1 Bone-comb fragment. Double tomb, teeth finer on one side and thicker and much more widely spaced on the other. One end intact. L 58.8mm Wth 51.9mm T 2.8mm.
1703:1 Bone-comb fragment. Single-sided comb. One side intact. The broken edge possibly has the remains of a rivet hole and some staining from an iron rivet. L 23.8mm Wth 14.8mm T 2.5mm. Associated with Burial CCXVII.

Buckle The bone buckle from Golden Lane (1307:1) is a single-loop buckle with strap made from one piece of bone. The edges are carved as if the buckle had been made from metal and the front of the buckle is ornamented with ring-and-dot decoration. The end of the strap was deliberately split and there are the remains of an iron rivet here. However, between the iron rivet and the oval perforation near the loop the bone has cracked. The buckle probably dates to the late ninth or tenth century.
1307:1 Bone buckle. L 62mm Wth 15–20mm T 6.5mm.

Bone pins There are two types of bone pins from Golden Lane. One is similar to dress or stick-pins that are made of copper-alloy and the remainder are pins which are made from pig fibulae. The pin (715:1), which is like a copper-alloy stick-pin but is of bone, has an undifferentiated head. The heads of these pins are only slightly wider than the shanks and they are usually, but not always, decorated either on the head or

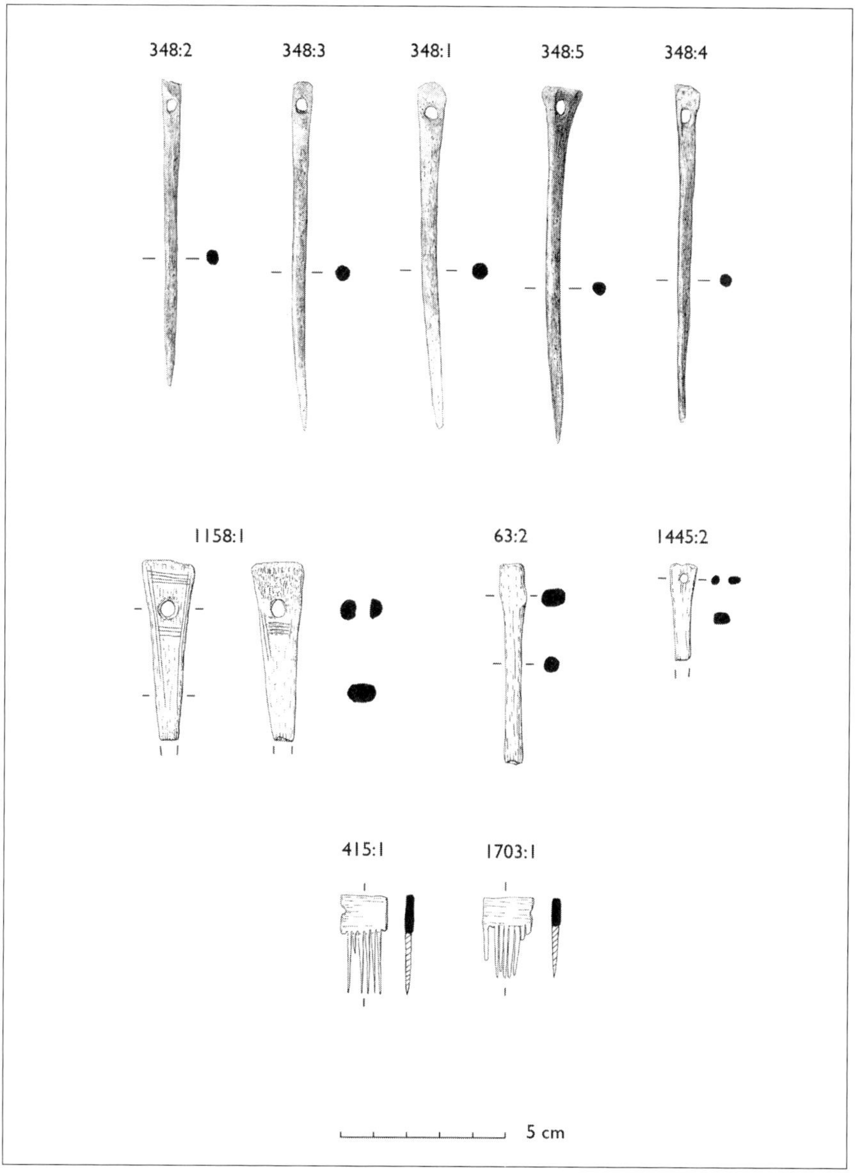

22 Artefacts of skeletal material: Bone Pins (348:2, 348:3, 348:1, 348:5, 348:4, 1158:1 and 1445:2); Tuning Peg (63:2); Combs (415:1 and 1703:1)

on the shank or both (O'Rahilly 1998, 27). The bone pin has two incised lines near the top of the shank and narrows just below these. The other seven pins are modified pig fibulae. The distal end of the bone has been shaped to form the head and the shaft has been cut and then formed into a pointed shank. The heads all have circular or oval holes. Five of these pins were recovered from the pit F312, one (1158:1) is associated with Burial CVI and one (1445:2) is associated with Burial CXXXIII. These pins could have had a number of different functions. They could have been used as dress pins, needles or weaving tools.

The modified pig fibulae from York were separated into groups according to how they had been worked and the variety of different shapes present suggested that the pins could have been used for a number of different functions (MacGregor, Mainman and Rogers 1999, 1950). Some may have been used as needles. These are more likely to be those which have been trimmed at the perforated end rather than those that are splayed (ibid. 1951) and the tops of the heads are usually cut straight across (Keene 1990, 232). As they are quite large needles they would only have been used for sewing coarse materials (ibid.). Only two (348:2, 348:3) of the bone pins from Golden Lane could possibly have been needles. They have much narrower heads than the others but the heads are still quite wide and they could only have been used for very coarse sewing.

It is also possible that the bone pins could have been used as dress pins. Many of the bone pins found in York were thought to have been dress pins and it was suggested that the pins that were perforated would have been held in place by a cord strung through the perforation (MacGregor, Mainman and Rogers 1999, 1950). Five pins made from modified pig fibulae were found during excavations in Waterford and it was suggested that they may have been used as dress pins (Hurley 1997, 671). Large numbers have been found on early-Christian sites in Ireland such as Lagore crannog, Ballinderry crannog no. 2, and Cahercommaun (ibid.). Two of the modified pig fibulae from Golden Lane (1158:1, 1445:2) were associated with burials and it is possible that these were dress pins, especially the pin associated with Burial CVI (1158:1) as this pin, unlike the other modified pig fibulae, is decorated with incised lines. Such incised lines, as well as being decorative, also helped to grip the material so that the pin would not slip out of place (MacGregor 1985, 116).

The other possibility is that modified pig fibulae were used as weaving implements. Those found in Winchester were thought to have been used in weaving due to the fabrication marks and their highly polished surface (Keene 1990, 232). They were probably used to lift groups of threads while weaving and the perforations may have been used to attach the pins to the weaver so they would not get lost (ibid.). The pins with perforations from Golden Lane may have been used for this purpose. They all have highly polished surfaces. The five pins from the pit F312 all have perforations of similar size and it was possible that they have been threaded together through the perforations, possibly as part of a weaver's toolkit. Groups of pins have been found in other places such as the three modified pig fibulae with perforated heads which were found together in the corner of a tenement building dating to the late tenth century at 16–22 Coppergate, York (MacGregor, Mainman and Rogers 1999, 1880).

348:1 Bone pin. Made from pig fibula. Shank oval, head is flattened and splayed and rounded at the top. Head has circular perforation. Tip has a blunt point. Polished surface. L 102mm Wth 5–9mm T 3.2–4.2mm.

348:2 Bone pin. Made from pig fibula. Roughly worked with large circular perforation near head. Tip is pointed. Polished surface. Shank circular in section, while head is flat and rectangular in section. L 90.7mm Wth 4.6–6.8mm T 2.5–4.6mm.

348:3 Bone pin. Made from pig fibula. Circular shank and flattened head with circular perforation. Tip is pointed. Polished surface. L 103mm Wth 4–6.2mm T 3.2–4.2mm.

348:4 Bone pin. Made from pig fibula. Circular shank and flattened head with circular perforation. Tip is pointed. Polished surface. L 100mm Wth 4–7.7mm T 3.1–4mm.

348:5 Bone pin. Made from pig fibula. Circular shank with flattened and expanded head with circular perforation. Tip is pointed. Polished surface. L 105mm Wth 4.5–12mm T 3.8–4.7mm.
715:1 Bone pin. Circular shank which is wider towards the head. Top of head flat. Shank narrows below head and there are two raised rims forming the head. The shank tapers to a point. L 67mm Diam. 2.2–5.9mm.
1158:1 Bone pin. Made from pig fibula. Oval shank with expanded head. Circular perforation near the head. Decorated with incised lines. On one side there are four horizontal incised lines above the perforation and three below. A single vertical incised line near each edge forms a border. On the other side there are four horizontal incised lines below the perforation and two vertical incised lines to one side of the perforation. End of the pin broken. L 53mm Wth 7–16.3mm T 5.8mm–6.2mm. Associated with Burial CVI.
1445:2 Fragment of bone pin. Made from pig fibula. Expanded head with circular perforation. Sub-rectangular shank, broken. Polished surface. L 28.9mm Wth 5.8–9.3mm T 4mm. Associated with Burial CXXXIII.

MEDIEVAL AND POST-MEDIEVAL POTTERY FROM GOLDEN LANE

Niamh Doyle

INTRODUCTION

The pottery assemblage from Golden Lane contained a total of 4,304 sherds of medieval and post-medieval pottery from stratified contexts. The pottery from the main assemblage is discussed in the archaeological report in one group, which is separated chronologically into medieval and post-medieval pottery. This paper will focus on a description and discussion of the medieval and late medieval assemblages with a short summary of the post-medieval assemblage.

A further 1,410 sherds of post-medieval pottery were retrieved from the backfilled cellars of buildings fronting onto Chancery Lane. The pottery from these unstratified layers was retrieved, identified and recorded separately from the main assemblage and is discussed separately in the main archaeological report.[1]

METHODOLOGY

These fragments were identified visually in accordance with existing typologies. A brief description of fabric and decoration is given. The different types of pottery are presented in tabular form and discussed further in detail. Medieval vessel types and

1 The pottery from the unstratified basement layers of Golden Lane was identified with Clare McCutcheon, whom I would like to thank for her help and time.

styles of manufacture were identified in accordance with the Medieval Pottery Research Group's classification of ceramic forms (MPRG 1998). Both medieval and post-medieval types were identified based on information from published excavations in Ireland and existing typologies. Reference is made to specific fragments of pottery in the text by find number as per National Museum of Ireland guidelines; however, the licence number has been omitted in the text, the reference being given in the format of feature number: find number.

DATING

Date ranges for the pottery types are based on published dates for the production and distribution of pottery excavated from archaeological sites in Ireland, England and the United States of America. The medieval pottery dates refer more particularly to the occurrence of Dublin-type, French, and English wares on published excavations in Ireland.

QUANTIFICATION

The tables in figures illustrate the number of sherds found within each type and their percentage within the whole assemblage. The Minimum Number of Vessels (MNV) is a vessel count based on a frequently occurring diagnostic feature of the vessels represented in the assemblage. The high instance of jugs within the medieval assemblage means that basing the MNV on the occurrence of rim-handle fragments, as representative of handled jars, is suitable. The tables shown in figures illustrate the MNV for each medieval and post-medieval pottery type. A count of the Minimum Number Represented (MNR) of each vessel type is included for the post-medieval wares. Date ranges and the origins of types are shown on the tables for both the medieval and post-medieval pottery assemblages.

TWELFTH- TO FOURTEENTH-CENTURY POTTERY

The medieval pottery from Golden Lane consists of 1,922 fragments of Irish medieval pottery and 347 fragments of imported pottery, ranging in date from the twelfth to the late fourteenth century. The pottery is discussed here in groups based on place of origin and date of use in Ireland.

Table 1. Irish and imported medieval pottery based on sherd count

Irish 84.45%	French 8.04%	Flemish 0.48%	English 7.03%

The imported medieval wares include English imports from Bristol, Wiltshire and Chester, French imports from southwest and central France, as well as Flemish imports. The imported wares represent 15.55% of the medieval pottery, and range in date from the second half of the twelfth century to the late fourteenth century.

The Irish medieval pottery represents 84.45% of the medieval assemblage; with 'Leinster cooking ware' comprising 23% of the Irish medieval assemblage and the remainder represented by Dublin wares. Dublin-type ware was the most prolific, representing 29% of the Irish wares; it was produced from the late twelfth to the early fourteenth century.

Table 2. Irish and imported medieval pottery from Golden Lane

Type	Number of sherds	MNV	MVR	Form	Date range	Origin
ENGLAND						
Minety-type	4		3	jug	M 12th-E 13th C	English
Ham Green A	5		3	jug	E 12th-L 12th C	English
Ham Green B	70		4	jug	M 12th-13th C	English
Ham Green cooking ware	9		2	jugs, cooking pot	12th-M 13th C	English
Bristol Redcliffe	5		2	jug	M 13th-14th C	English
Chester-type	23	1	3	jug	13th-14th C	English
Southeast Wiltshire-type	16		4	jug	L 11th-L 12th C	English
Miscellaneous English	28	0	5	jug	12th-14th C	English
FRANCE						
Saintonge mottled green glazed	136	1	11	jug	13th-14th C	French
Saintonge green painted	10		2	jug	L 13th-E 14th C	French
Saintonge polychrome	4		2	jug	L 13th-E 14th C	French
Saintonge sgraffito	1		1		L 13th-E 14th C	French

→

Type	Number of sherds	MNV	MVR	Form	Date range	Origin
Unglazed Saintonge	12		2	jug	L 13th-E 14th C	French
BPT 192	6		1	jug	L 12th-E 13th C	French
Paris-type	2		1	jug	L 12th-13th C	French
Céramique Onctueuse	1		1	jug	13th C	French
Normandy gritty ware	2		2	jugs, cooking pot	11th-13th C	French
Rouen-type	4		2	jug	12th-13thC	French
Miscellaneous French ware	2		2	jug	L 12th-E 13th C	French
FLANDERS Flemish highly decorated ware	11	1	4	jug	13th-14thC	Flemish
IRELAND Dublin-type coarseware	281	4	15	jugs, cooking pots, pipkin	L 12th-M 13th C	Local
Dublin-type ware	666	5	26	jugs, storage and cooking pots, pipkin	E 13th-14th C	Local
Dublin-type fineware	371	6	22	jugs, storage pots	L 13th-14th C	Local
Dublin-type cooking ware	77		23	cooking pots	L 12th-13th C	Local
Leinster cooking ware	527	5	15	handled jugs, storage jars, cooking pots, 2 heavy platters	12th-14th C	Local
Overall Total	**2273**	**22**	**158**		**12th-14th C**	

IMPORTED MEDIEVAL POTTERY

The assemblage contains 326 fragments of imported medieval pottery from England, France and Flanders ranging in date from the twelfth to the fourteenth centuries and constituting 15.55% of the medieval pottery assemblage.

English medieval wares

The English medieval pottery within the assemblage counts for 7.03% of the medieval assemblage. The English pottery comes from both north and southeast Wiltshire and also from the port towns of Bristol and Chester, both of which had strong economic and cultural links with medieval Dublin.

Minety-type Minety-type pottery was produced in the North Wiltshire region of England from the twelfth to the fifteenth centuries and was imported into Ireland from the mid-twelfth to the early thirteenth centuries (Vince 1988, 262). This type appears as a coarse grey fabric with quartz inclusions and a characteristic pitted interior surface where the limestone inclusions have burnt away during firing. All four fragments of this type within the assemblage are jug fragments. The assemblage contains three body-fragments with the characteristic pitting, one glazed on both sides from the shoulder of a jug, and one collared rim-fragment.

Southeast Wiltshire Type Southeast Wiltshire Type is a hand-built glazed English ware manufactured in southeast Wiltshire and imported into Ireland from the late eleventh to the late twelfth centuries (Vince 1988, 264). The fabric is a light to mid-grey colour with red surfaces, some quartz and occasional red-brown inclusions. The assemblage contains sixteen jug fragments of this type, all with a patchy light to mid-brown/green glaze with occasional combing (195:42) and applied decoration on the body of jugs. Rim types represented are everted, and squared with thumbing along the lip of the rim and an applied strip running parallel below the rim (1100: 1). The medieval pottery assemblage from Wood Quay (McCutcheon 2006, 39) also contained a small number of pitchers and crucibles of this type, while excavations in Waterford city (Gahan and McCutcheon 1997, 293) and Hanover Street, Cork (McCutcheon 2003, fig. 4.1.1:1–2) yielded pitchers, storage vessels and crucibles.

Ham Green wares The products of the Ham Green potteries in Bristol, England were widely imported into Ireland in the twelfth and into the thirteenth century (Gahan and McCutcheon 1997, 293–4). The occurrence of Ham Green wares within medieval assemblages from Dublin was first studied by Barton (1988) with accompanying thin-section analysis carried out by Vince (1988). These hand-built glazed and cooking wares are found on rural and urban sites throughout Ireland and their stylistic influence can be seen on much locally-produced pottery from Ireland from the twelfth and thirteenth centuries. The glazed wares have been divided into Ham Green A and Ham Green B types based primarily on form and decoration and also on fabric (Barton 1963). The fabric of 42 sherds of pottery have been identified as Ham Green, but lack any diagnostic or decorative elements that would identify them as either Ham Green A or B. Due to the difficulty in visually separating fragments of Ham Green A from Ham Green B ware based on fabric alone, it is the practice to differentiate between the two based on the presence of diagnostic elements of decoration and form when referring to pottery assemblages from excavations in Ireland (McCutcheon 2003, 203). Body-fragments without the characteristic applied decoration of Ham Green A body-sherds have been included in the sherd count with

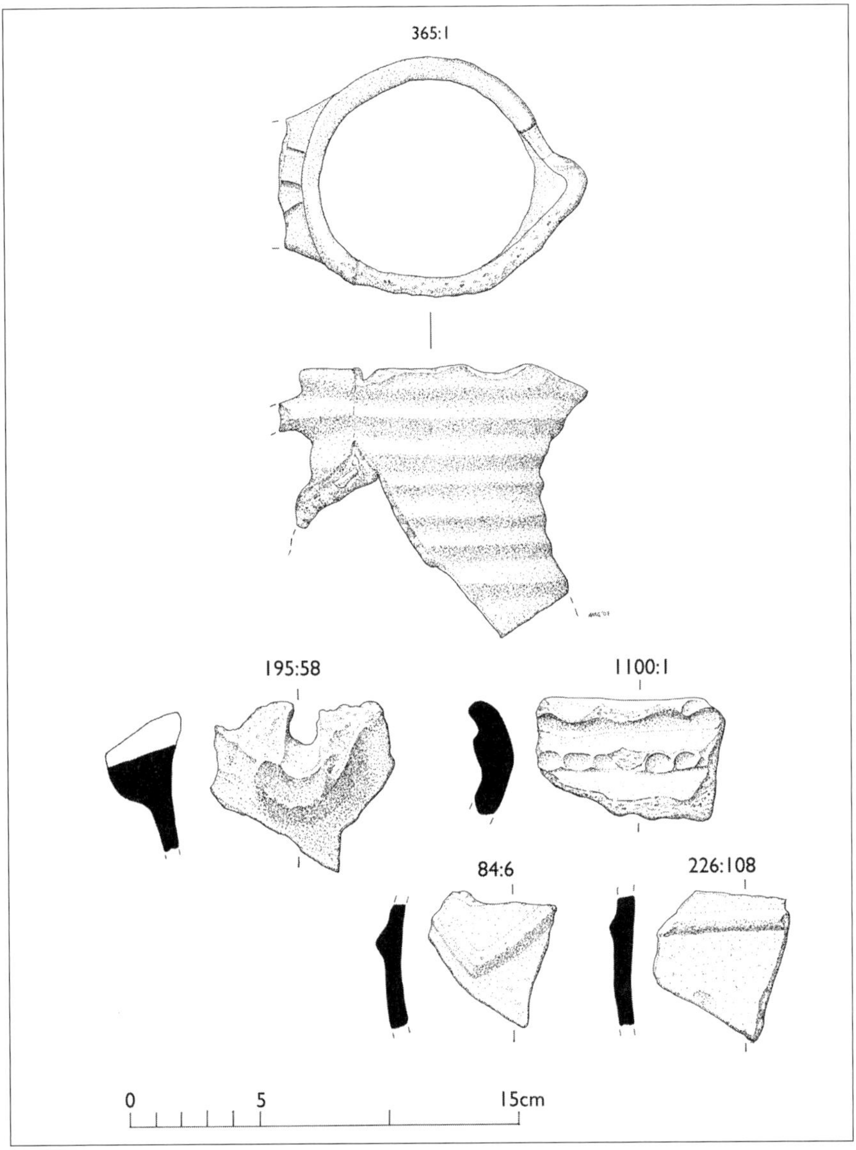

23 Medieval pottery imported from England: Chester ware, rim and pulled handle spout of jug (365:1), tubular spout/fume (195:58); South East Wiltshire type, jug rim fragment with applied strip (1100:1), body fragments with decoration (84:6, 226:108)

Ham Green B wares. Although this method alters the sherd count in favour of Ham Green ware, the MNV for both is based on diagnostic rim-handle elements, providing an accurate representation of vessel numbers for each.

Ham Green A This pottery was produced in Bristol, England and imported into Ireland *circa* 1120–1175 (Gahan and McCutcheon 1997, 293–4). It consists of a fine grey fabric with a brown-green lead glaze. It is characterized by a roller stamp/

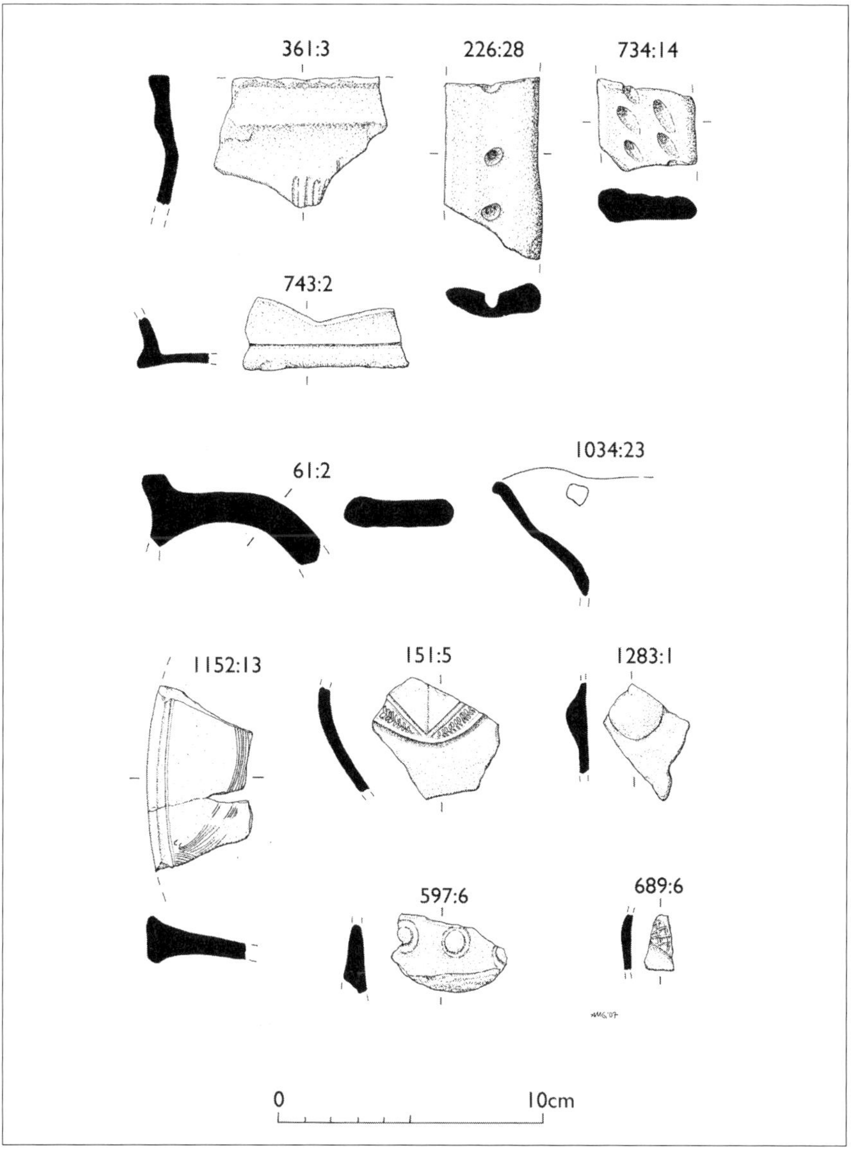

24 Medieval pottery imported from England and France: Ham Green B, rim fragment (361:3), handle fragments (226:28, 734:14); Redcliffe base fragment (743:2); Saintonge Mottled Green Glazed handle fragment (61:2), rim/spout fragment (1034:23), rim of large platter/serving dish (1152:13), body fragments with a shield (151:5), with applied pellet (1283:1), with impressed horseshoe shapes (597:6) and with rouletted applied strip (689:6)

roulette decoration on the rim and base ridges of the vessel body and an applied thumbed/frilled strip along the rim edges. Ham Green A jugs are comprised of everted rims, bridge spouts, strap-handles decorated as above and flat/sagging bases (Barton 1963). All diagnostic parts within this assemblage represent jugs which appear in Ireland from 1120–1175. This assemblage contains two body-fragments with diagnostic rouletted design, one plain strap-handle fragment and two everted squared rim-fragments with rouletted design along the edge.

Ham Green B Ham Green B pottery was produced in Bristol and imported into Ireland between 1170 and 1250 (Gahan and McCutcheon 1997, 294). The fabric of Ham Green B is typically a dark grey colour, containing inclusions of quartz and calcite and glazed a mid-dark green. Decoration is typically in the form of horizontal and/or wavy combing with anthropomorphic or zoomorphic incised and applied designs (Barton 1963). Diagnostic fragments within this assemblage represent jugs or pitchers. Although the MNV based on rim-handle count is zero for this type, it can be said that there are more Ham Green B vessels represented than Ham Green A. Body-fragments exhibiting diagnostic Ham Green B decorations, including bands of horizontal (195:63) and wavy combing (689: 4) and grooves, occasionally with perpendicular slashing (361: 2) and applied strips (1136: 53) or applied strips in a contrasting colour (745: 44). The assemblage contains three collared rims, one with possible faint stabbing along the top and a fragmented bridge spout. There are two decorated strap-handles; one with two vertical lines of stabbing along the centre and one with a central line of punched holes and two sagging bases with applied frills within the assemblage.

Ham Green cooking ware Ham Green cooking ware appears as a fabric rich in calcite and black particles with a red-brown surface and grey-black core (Barton 1963). The assemblage contained nine unglazed body-fragments of this type, some with external sooting from their use as cooking pots. Small quantities of this type of cooking ware within the assemblage are indicative of the prevalence of locally-produced cooking wares in the area, as was the case at Wood Quay (McCutcheon 2006, 48).

Bristol Redcliffe ware Redcliffe pottery was produced by the Ham Green kilns in Bristol and imported into Ireland from the late thirteenth century. The fabric is a characteristic sandwich of grey core between buff to salmon coloured surfaces, with a yellow-green lead glaze. The assemblage contains five fragments representing at least one jug if not two. It is suggested that the small quantity of Redcliffe pottery from medieval pottery assemblages from Dublin is due to the prevalence of locally-produced pottery at this time (McCutcheon 2006, 50).

Chester-type Chester type is a wheel-thrown ware produced in Chester, England and exported to Ireland in the thirteenth and fourteenth centuries particularly to major Anglo-Norman towns along the east coast. Dublin and Drogheda both appear to have traded extensively with Chester, resulting in the importation and imitation of Chester-type vessel forms and decoration in Drogheda wares in particular (Sweetman 1984, 183; Doyle 2004). The similarity between Chester-type and Dublin-type wares could mean that Chester-type pottery has been underrepresented in medieval pottery reports from Dublin. Chester-type pottery has a hard-fired sandy fabric, decorated with a thick lead glaze that has a white speckled, gooseflesh surface. The fragments of this type within the assemblage represent jugs, with a MNV of one based on the presence of a rim-handle fragment with a simple rim, a pulled spout and strap-handle with slash marks at the join and an internal rim-diameter of 75mm across. Some body-fragments are decorated with horizontal combing and applied strips. The assemblage contains two strap-handle fragments with slash and stabbed decoration, one possible tubular spout characteristic of Chester wares and one base-fragment with thumbing, created by pressing the thumb into the base. Small quantities of Chester-type pottery were found in Dublin at Essex Street West and at Wood Quay (McCutcheon 1995, 43; 2006, 54).

English miscellaneous Two groups of unidentified pottery from this assemblage have been grouped together based on appearance. The first has a very hard-fired sandy fabric with a dark grey-black core and orange-red exterior. Forms include a pulled spout, everted and simple rims and rilling around the shoulder of a vessel. The second group of unidentified wares is made from an extremely open tempered gravelly fabric fired to a white-grey colour with frequent grey, brown and red inclusions. This second fabric is possibly Dyfed gravel-tempered ware which originates in the western region of Wales (Papazian and Campbell 1992, 56–8).Vince confirmed the presence of this type within the Waterford assemblage by petrological analysis (Vince 1997, 337–8).

Continental medieval pottery

The medieval pottery assemblage from Golden Lane contains examples of pottery imported from various regions in France as well as Flemish pottery, accounting for 8.52% of the medieval assemblage.

Saintonge mottled green glazed Saintonge mottled green glazed was produced in south-west France and imported into Ireland in the thirteenth and fourteenth centuries as part of the trade in wine from the Bordeaux region of France to Ireland and England (Clarke 1983; Deroeux and Dufournier 1991). Of a total of 136 fragments of this type the assemblage contained 102 body-fragments all with characteristic copper mottled lead glaze, several of which are decorated with applied thumbed strips or horizontal and wavy combing. One example is decorated with a rouletted applied strip (689: 6), one with an applied pellet (1283: 1), another with a shield, a heraldic motif of Saintonge wares (151: 5) and another with impressed horseshoe shapes (597: 6). The rim-handle of a jug with a simple rim and strap-handle represented a single vessel. At least seven jugs/pitchers were represented by seven spout fragments from jugs with simple rims and bridge spouts; there are also five strap-handle fragments with the characteristic Saintonge folded-under strap design. The assemblage contained four flat-based, obtuse-angled jugs although none with makers'/owners' marks as described from Wood Quay (McCutcheon 2006, 114–115) and Waterford (Gahan and McCutcheon 1997, 308–317). Eleven jugs are represented with squared, everted rims and collared rims. A single thick squared rim possibly represents a large platter/serving dish, glazed internally with a combed semicircular design (1152: 13). Some fragments of unglazed and partially glazed jugs were present, some of which have heavily sooted exteriors, indicating they were used to heat their contents. The fabric is white to grey in colour with occasional quartz and red inclusions, probably haematite.

Saintonge polychrome and sgraffito This pottery was imported to Ireland in the late thirteenth and early fourteenth centuries, and it appears as a fine wheel-thrown fabric decorated with bird and shield motifs (Dunning 1968). The assemblage contained six fragments of this type including body sherds and part of a bridge spout from jugs. Body-fragments were decorated with white slip and green and brown paint, others with an orange-red slip on the exterior and green, yellow and brown paint, with horizontal combing also possibly representing Saintonge sgraffito ware.

Saintonge green painted Saintonge green painted jugs have an even, consistent glaze achieved by painting a copper-rich solution beneath a layer of clear lead glaze

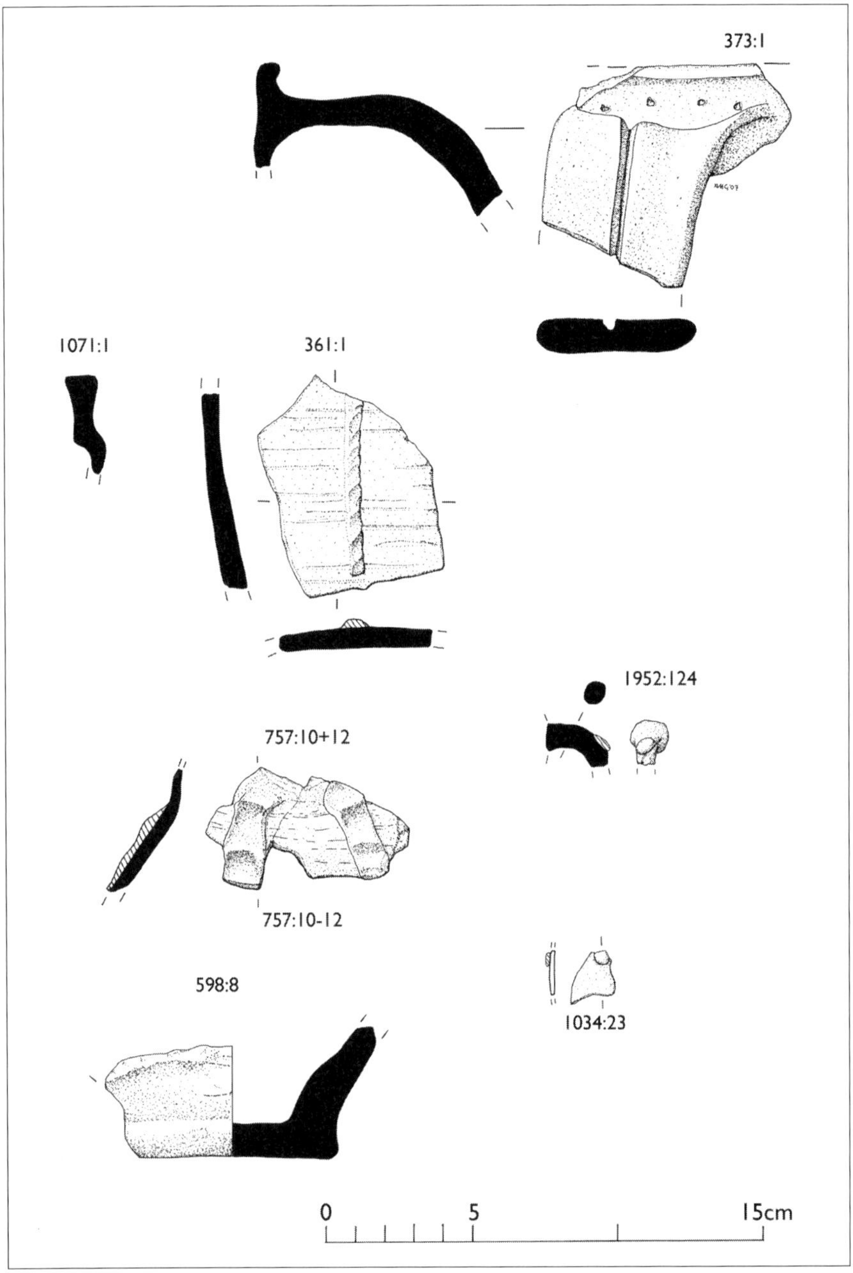

25 Medieval pottery imported from France and Spain: Normandy Stoneware, rim-handle fragment (373:1); Normandy Gritty Ware, rim sherd (1071:1); Céramique Onctueuse, body sherd with applied rouletted strip (361:1); Rouen-type, decorated body fragments (757:10 + 12); Paris-type, decorated body fragment (1952:124); Seville Coarse Ware, base of olive jar (598:8).

(Dunning 1968). The assemblage contains ten fragments of this type, all from fine jugs, including two simple rim-fragments, two fine thin strap-handle fragments and a fragment of a bridge spout.

Bristol pottery type 192 (BPT 192) The assemblage from Golden Lane contains six fragments of BPT 192, consisting of a fine buff fabric, with thick consistent glaze and including one simple rim-fragment, presumably a jug. This pottery type has been found to represent 80% of miscellaneous French ware from Irish excavations, particularly in port towns (McCutcheon 2006, 96).

Céramique Onctueuse The assemblage contains one fragment of possible Céramique Onctueuse; this type was found in a thirteenth century pit in Waterford (Gahan and McCutcheon 1997, 306). It is thought to originate in the Morbihan district of Brittany, constituting 96% of pottery excavated there (ibid, 306). The body sherd present is identified on the basis of a mid-brown fabric which has an oily/soapy texture, characteristic of the type due to the presence of talc in the clay (Hodges 1978). The sherd is decorated with an applied rouletted strip.

Normandy gritty ware Normandy gritty ware consists of an unglazed gritty fabric with frequent quartz inclusions; the gritty wares occurred as two groups in the Waterford excavations report (Gahan and McCutcheon 1997, 304), both of which are represented in this assemblage. A single rim sherd (1071: 1) which is white in colour with occasional mica and quartz inclusions can be identified as belonging to the first group. The rim-fragment found is unglazed and collared as with vessels of the first type of Normandy gritty ware described from Waterford where it was dated eleventh to thirteenth century (ibid). There are two examples of the second type, which is a grey micaceous fabric with a dark-grey/brown core. Both fragments have a sooty exterior from exposure to fire. The assemblage also contains a single flat obtuse-angled base from a jar.

Rouen-type Rouen-type originates from the northwest of France (Barton 1965, 74–5) and was imported to Dublin in the twelfth and thirteenth centuries (Gahan and Walsh 1997, 112). The assemblage contains decorated body-fragments from a Rouen-type jug. The fabric is an orange-red colour with a characteristic red slip and is decorated with applied strips in white clay that appear yellow under a clear lead glaze that indicates this jug belongs to Barton's di-chrome grouping (Barton 1965, 74). The assemblage contains fine grey wheel-thrown pottery, which is highly decorated and has been grouped with Rouen-type here but is possibly Paris-type pottery. There are two body-fragments in this assemblage with reddish-brown glaze and green painted decoration and fine, thin rod-handle fragments possibly from a cup or small jug, both decorated with an applied pellet painted green.

Miscellaneous French ware The assemblage contains two fragments of pottery from a jug that has been identified as French medieval ware based on fabric and glaze but cannot be attributed to a particular source. Instead, they have been included here as Miscellaneous French wares, as discussed by McCutcheon (2006, 86–8), which are thought to have originated in the mid-west region of France in the late twelfth to early thirteenth century.

Flemish highly-decorated ware Flemish highly-decorated ware has a red fabric covered in a thick white slip, with a lead glaze that appears green applied over the slip (Janssen 1983). This ware was imported into Ireland in the thirteenth and fourteenth centuries (Gahan and McCutcheon 1997, 321). The assemblage contains eleven fragments of this type, including four body sherds, one with applied strip decoration, and four collared rim-fragments one with strap-handle fragment attached giving a MNV of one. A single near-complete vessel of this type was retrieved from excavations at Wood Quay, Dublin (McCutcheon 2006, 131); it has been found in Cork (Gahan et al. 1997, 121) while the largest known assemblage of Flemish Redware outside its country of origin was found in Waterford (Gahan and McCutcheon 1997, 321–2).

Local medieval pottery

The assemblage contains a total of 1,922 sherds of medieval Irish pottery, constituting 83.4% of the medieval pottery assemblage. Dublin-type wares comprise the largest group within the overall assemblage at 29% and form 35% of the Irish wares, with Leinster cooking ware forming 27.4% of the Irish wares. Details of form and decoration noted within the imported medieval assemblage are discussed within the text, while the large number of medieval Irish types recommended their discussion in tabular form.

Table 3. Form and decoration in Irish medieval wares

Type	MNV	MVR	Vessel part	No.	Description of forms present
Dublin-type coarseware	4	15	rim	10	2 with applied frill, 3 everted bevelled, 5 straight/simple
			body	229	Lead glaze, 6 decorated
			base	32	14 sagging, 8 thumbed and frilled, 1 splayed
			handle	15	13 strap-handles: 13 slashed, 1 undecorated, 1 hooked rod-handle.
			spout	0	
Dublin-type ware	5	26	rim	37	4 everted, 6 squared with frills, 3 collared, 8 squared
			body	523	Lead glaze, 28 internal slip, 28 with horizontal combing, applied rosettes and strips
			base	59	4 splayed, 4 straight-sided flat bases, 23 sagging, 7 decorated with thumbing, 7 decorated with frilling

→

Type	MNV	MVR	Vessel part	No.	Description of forms present
			handle	26	25 strap-handles: 3 plain, 6 single central incised line, 16 slashed and 1straight rod-handle
			spout	1	1 possible bridge spout fragment
Dublin-type fineware	6	22	rim	18	7 simple, 1 frilled, 3 with applied frills
			body	310	Lead glaze, 1 internal slip, horizontal combing, applied strips and pellets
			base	27	3 sagging, 15 thumbed
			handle	15	15 strap-handles: 14 plain, 1 with central incised line
			spout	6	3 bridge spouts, 1 pulled, 2 fragmented
Dublin-type cooking ware	0	23	rim	25	5 everted internally-bevelled, 3 everted with grooved rims, 15 everted squared
			body	46	4 glazed, most with sooty exteriors, 1 slip coated
			base	12	Sagging
			handle	0	
			spout	0	
Leinster cooking ware	5	15	rim	65	32 everted, 1 everted decorated, 8 everted flat-topped, 3 frilled, 2 simple
			body	396	Undecorated
			base	47	Pitted base, 6 straight-sided, 23 sagging, 16 undiagnostic
			handle	15	7 strap-handles: 5 plain, 1 stabbed, 1 central incised line and 1 tubular handle
			spout	0	

Leinster cooking ware The assemblage contains 527 fragments of Leinster cooking ware, representing a variety of handled jugs, storage jars, cooking pots and at least two heavy platters. Leinster cooking ware is a hand-built ware found on most sites in south-eastern Ireland from the twelfth to the fourteenth centuries. The fabric is coarse and contains large plates of quartz, mica and occasionally decomposed feldspar (Ó Floinn 1988).

There are five rim handle fragments indicating a MNV of five vessels within the assemblage, all of which appear to be jugs with simple rims and strap-handles, two of which are decorated at the rim-handle join. The assemblage contains a further two strap-handle fragments. One example is quite wide with a curved cross-section and bands of vertical stabbing. The other is broken but was decorated with a central incised line. There is a single example of a hollow handle possibly designed for use with a stick or rod that could be placed into the socket to safely remove a vessel from heat. This fragment (161: 56) measures 24mm diameter with an opening of 11mm diameter. The assemblage contains 65 rim-fragments, the majority of which (33) are tall, everted rims with one or more internal channels, typical of the type found predominantly in north Leinster (Ó Floinn 1988, 328). One such is decorated with vertical slash marks radiating out from the centre (63:20).There are eight examples of everted, flat-topped, thickened rims, described by Ó Floinn (ibid.) as typical of assemblages from Dublin (168:8). There are three decorated rims with frilled/crimpled borders, created by pinching the edge of the rim, found mostly in the southern portion of Leinster (Ó Floinn 1988, 329). There are two examples of heavy thick rims pinched into corners or rough lug handles. These probably represent two large, heavy sub-square platters (61:8 and 61:9). There are 47 base-fragments, all exhibiting the diagnostic and characteristic basal pitting of Leinster cooking ware from drying on a bed of sand (ibid). Ó Floinn describes a technique of slab building used for manufacturing Leinster cooking ware (1988, 327), and evidence of this technique is clearly visible on a single base-fragment with some internal glaze that possibly indicates it was fired alongside glazed vessels (520:3).

Dublin-type wares

It is a convention in medieval pottery analysis to name pottery after its production site. In the absence of a definite production site the pottery is named after the area in which it has been found to be most prolific (Blake and Davey 1983, 39–40). While archaeological evidence has been found for tile production in Dublin at Cornmarket (Wren 2006, 181), there is still no known pottery production site in Dublin. Documentary research has highlighted twelfth- and thirteenth century-references to a street of potters in the Register of the hospital of St John the Baptist without the New Gate (Brooks 1936), located west of Cook Street along the line of the modern Oliver Bond Street (McCutcheon 2000, 118). Research on the medieval pottery produced and consumed locally has provided a classification of Dublin-type pottery by fabric, form and date as carried out by Barton (1965), Papazian (1989) and re-designated by McCutcheon (2000 2006).

Dublin-type coarseware Dublin-type coarseware is a hand-built glazed ware that dates from the middle of the twelfth to the middle of the thirteenth century. The fabric is micaceous with occasional quartz inclusions and varies from an orange-red exterior and grey to black core. There were 281 sherds of Dublin-type coarseware fragments in the assemblage, with a MNV of four jugs represented. Although there are no spout-fragments remaining for this type, the majority of vessels represented appear to be jugs or jars. The body of the vessels was decorated with an uneven brown to green lead glaze including some sherds decorated with horizontal combing or incised zigzag patterns, some with applied strips, with either rouletting or slip-painted decoration or a combination of both. The majority of the rim-fragments in the assemblage are from vessels with straight, simple or thickened rims, with further examples of an applied frill decoration below the rim and everted externally-bevelled rims. Most of the strap-handles are decorated with slashed patterns, which McCutcheon's study of handle types from the medieval assemblage at Wood Quay has shown to be the most prolific for this type (McCutcheon 2006, 49). A jug with a plain strap-handle is represented as well as one with a hooked rod-handle (520:5).The majority of the base-fragments are from vessels with sagging bases, several with thumbed decoration, reminiscent of Ham Green B jugs.

Dublin-type ware Dublin-type ware is a wheel-thrown, glazed pottery produced locally that dates from the late thirteenth to the fourteenth centuries. This type superseded Dublin-type coarseware; it is less coarse and is heavily influenced by Bristol Redcliffe pottery of the same date (McCutcheon 2000, 122). The assemblage contains 666 fragments altogether, and there are a MNV of five represented in the assemblage, all of which represent jugs or pitchers. This type represents the largest group of Irish medieval pottery within the assemblage, as was also the case with other Dublin assemblages at Isolde's Tower, Essex Street West and Wood Quay (McCutcheon 1994, 53; 1995, 52; 2006, 59).

Small to average-sized jugs are represented by various types of rim-fragments (table fig b) and a possible bridge spout fragment of this type. Small storage jars are also represented within the assemblage some with a groove possibly for a lid and a large dish/platter is represented by a deep everted rim-fragment. There are 25 examples of strap-handles within the assemblage, five of which are rim handle fragments, representing a minimum of five vessels. Of all these, three are plain, six are decorated only with a central incised line and the remaining are decorated with slashes and stabbing along the handle. The handles of Dublin-type ware vessels from Wood Quay showed a trend towards plain handles and those decorated with a band of diagonal slash marks between two vertical incised lines (McCutcheon 2006, 73). There is a single straight handle from a pipkin; the handle features a central line more as a result of its manufacture than as a decoration; it is glazed on the upper portion only (217: 48). Base-fragments include those from four vessels with splayed bases, four with straight-sided flat bases, possibly dishes or platters, and twenty-three with everted sagging bases decorated by pressing the thumb into the base or decorated with pinched or applied frills at the base. The base-fragments represent jugs, all of which exhibit external lead glaze and some of which are glazed on the base, indicating that the jugs were stacked for firing, allowing glaze to run down the jugs and pool at the base.

Dublin-type fineware Dublin-type fineware is a fine, wheel-thrown type dated to the late thirteenth-fourteenth century. This type possibly overlaps with the later period of Dublin-type ware but contains many fewer inclusions and follows on from Dublin-type ware stylistically (McCutcheon 2000, 122). The assemblage contains six rim-handle fragments from jugs/pitchers giving an MNV of six for this type. There are 371 fragments of this fine ware, including 310 body-fragments with green/brown lead glaze, some of which were decorated with bands of horizontal combing and one with an internal coating of slip. Applied decoration on the body of the jugs occurs in the form of rosettes and strips, some with rouletting or painted in a contrasting colour to the body of the pot; this form of decoration was probably influenced by contemporary English Redcliffe pottery. Rims within the assemblage represent jugs or pitchers, the majority of which are simple rounded rims with examples of frilled rims and rims with applied frilled strips also represented. Of the six spouts represented, three are bridge spouts on simple and collared rims, one is a small pulled spout and two are too fragmented to classify. All jugs of this type within the assemblage have got strap-handles, the majority of which are plain while some exhibit slashing where the handle meets the rim and one example is decorated with a single central incised line. Plain handles and those decorated with single central lines are typical of this type, as represented within the Wood Quay assemblage also (McCutcheon 2006, 80). While straight-sided, everted sagging-based jugs/jars are represented; the majority of Dublin-type fineware vessels here have sagging, thumbed bases, eleven of which were decorated by pressing the thumb into the base. The remaining five were decorated by pinching the pot base and wall together, including one vessel that retains a crease mark between the wall and base, indicating that the technique was developed as much to join wall to base as to steady and decorate the vessel.

Dublin-type cooking ware Dublin-type cooking ware is an unglazed, micaceous type used to manufacture cooking and storage vessels in Dublin from the twelfth to the thirteenth centuries. It occurs in both hand-built and wheel-thrown forms and was used alongside all Dublin-type wares (McCutcheon 2000, 122). The Minimum Number of Vessels (MNV) is a vessel count based on a frequently occurring diagnostic feature of the vessels represented in the assemblage. The high instance of jugs within the medieval assemblage means that basing the MNV on the occurrence of rim-handle fragments, as representative of handled jars, is suitable for most pottery types. Cooking vessels are less likely to have handles than glazed jugs or jars, with the result that this method of counting the MNV is less applicable to cooking vessels.

All diagnostic pieces represent small to medium jars used for cooking and/or heating food over a fire. There are 46 body-fragments, four with glaze, and several with sooty exteriors from use. One example has a slip-coated exterior, a feature noted in Leinster cooking wares, possibly representing an attempt to imitate the light coloured surfaces of imported French cooking wares (Ó Floinn 1988, 329). Most of the vessels represented have everted, squared rims and obtuse-angled sagging bases. This vessel type was the most common Dublin cooking ware vessel type from Wood Quay also, McCutcheon noting that this vessel type was characteristic of the twelfth and thirteenth centuries and was used alongside metal cooking vessels of the same form (McCutcheon 206, 81). There are also some with everted, internally-bevelled rims and three vessels with everted grooved rims possibly designed to hold lids.

FIFTEENTH- AND SIXTEENTH-CENTURY POTTERY

The assemblage from Golden lane contained 40 sherds of imported late medieval pottery from France, Spain, Germany and the Netherlands. This pottery is discussed in detail below.

Table 4. Late medieval pottery from Golden Lane

Type	Sherds	MNV	MVR	Form	Date Range	Origin
Isabella *azul y morada*	1		1	plate	15th-16th	Spain
Saintonge polychrome	3		2	chafing dish	16th-17th	France
Tin-glazed earthenware	4		1	malling jug	16th	Anglo-Netherlands
Siegburg stoneware	2		1	*Schnelle*/tankard	16th	Germany
Frechen stoneware	18	1	7	bartmann jug, jugs/bottles	17th	Germany
Frechen/Cologne stoneware	7		2	bartmann jug, decorated jug	17th	Germany
Westerwald stoneware	5		2	chamber pot, possible tankard	17th	Germany
Total	**40**	1	**16**			

Spanish

Isabella *azul y morada* This type of tin-glazed earthenware was traded in Northwest Europe in the late fifteenth to mid-sixteenth centuries from Spain. This pottery type was formerly published as Isabella polychrome, but the term Isabella *azul y morada* is now preferred. It has a thick buff sandy fabric and a tin glaze typically decorated with purple and blue concentric lines (Hurst et al. 1986, 54); the example in this assemblage features a spiral pattern also (217:11).

French

Saintonge polychrome Later Saintonge polychrome was produced and traded from 1550 to 1650 (Hurst et al. 1986, 85–6). A single rim-fragment from the assemblage indicates the presence of a plate or serving dish with a yellow glaze. The assemblage contains two Saintonge polychrome vessels with pedestal bases, one of which has a frilled base and green glaze, while the other is glazed yellow and green. These base-fragments possibly represent chafing dishes, which were used to heat the contents of a second vessel which was balanced on its rim. Vessels of this type from southwest and central France had pedestal bases supporting a bowl which sometimes had handles and often had knobs on top (Hurst et al. 1986, 78).

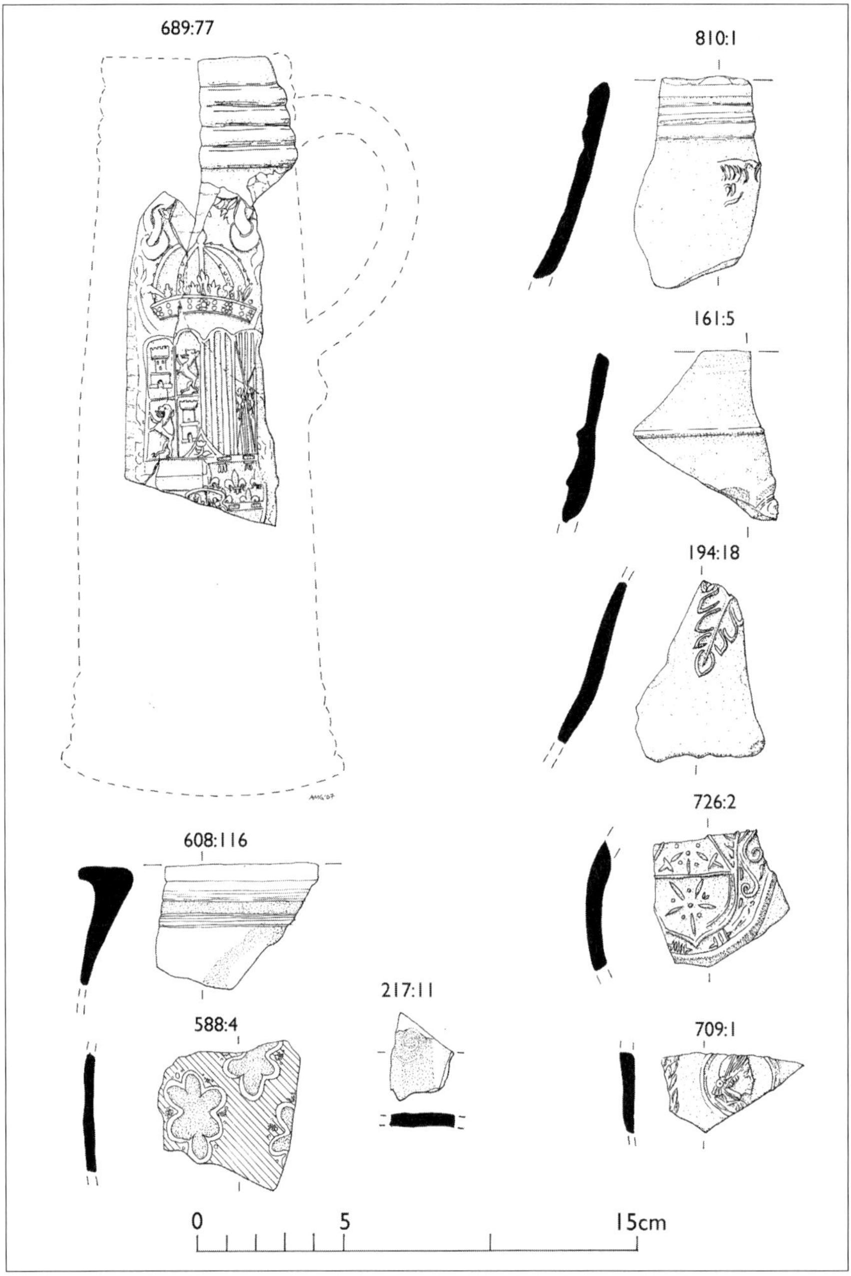

26 Late medieval imported pottery: Siegburg Stoneware Schnelle, body fragment (689:77); Westerwald, rim sherd (608:116) and body fragment (588:4); Frechen, rim fragment with Bartmann mask (810:1), body fragment with stamp/motif (726:2); Frechen/Cologne, rim fragment with Bartmann mask (161:5), body fragments with acanthus leaf motif (194:18), and with medallion with bust of man wearing a hat (709:1); Isabella azul y morada, body fragment with spiral pattern (217:11).

Anglo-Netherlands

Malling jug The assemblage contains a single example of a Malling jug that Hurst describes as 'the typical export jug of the second half of the sixteenth century', exported from the Low Countries and found widely on British sites, in Ireland and as far as Scandinavia (Hurst et al. 1986, 126). These wares have a fine buff fabric and are decorated with a mottled tin glaze outside in imitation of the German stoneware 'tiger' glaze (ibid). The assemblage contained a purple example achieved with the application of manganese powder and is a globular shape.

German

Siegburg Stoneware Siegburg is an abbey town on the river Sieg near Bonn in Germany, whose period of pottery production ranged from the twelfth to the seventeenth centuries. The fabric of this stoneware is light grey to white in colour, the finer wares of the sixteenth century unglazed while the coarser wares had a salt glaze (Hurst et al. 1986, 176). The assemblage from Golden Lane contains two fragments of *schnellen*, tall, ornate tankards, with mould-pressed decoration. One fragment is comprised of a cordoned rim above an armorial plaque. An almost identical tankard can be found in the Bernal collection in the British Museum and it appears that the fragments from Golden Lane represent one or possibly two such tankards. Gaimster describes the tankard as tapering slightly to the neck with cordons around the rim and base. The example in the British Museum was fitted with a pewter lid with baluster finial and twin-acorn thumb piece and also a pewter base mount, both of which were probably fitted in the nineteenth century to replace the original fittings (Gaimster et al. 1997, 181). One of the panels on the Golden Lane *schnelle* is identical to that on the Bernal *schnelle* described by Gaimster as for the King of Spain: 'Per fess in chief Castile and Aragon and Aragon-Sicily, Granada in point; in base quarterly impaling party Aragon and Aragon-Sicily, Granada in point; in base quarterly 1 Austria, 2 Valois Burgundy, 3 old Burgundy, 4 a lion, scocheon a lion impaling an eagle; Collar of Fleece' (Gaimster et al. 1997, 373). A similar *schnelle* fragment, also decorated with the Spanish coat of arms, was recovered from the Spanish Parade/Fish Market excavations in Galway and dated to the mid-1570s (Meenan 2004, 386). The presence of the Spanish and Imperial arms indicates the political allegiances of the potter and perhaps the groups within whose dominion they were located (ibid, 153).

Frechen Frechen was produced in a small town southwest of Cologne in a tradition of pottery production that spans the thirteenth to nineteenth centuries, with the earliest documentary references to stoneware makers, *Kannenbacker*, dating to 1544 and 1548. The fabric of this stoneware is a dark grey while the glaze is a rich brown with characteristic pitting caused by the salt glaze to produce a 'tiger glaze' effect (Gaimster et al. 1997, 208). This stoneware is very similar in appearance to that produced in nearby Cologne. Tall tankards of this type were imported into Ireland in the sixteenth century, while Bartmann jugs are more typical of the seventeenth century (Gahan and McCutcheon 1997, 346). The assemblage contains fragments of at least seven different jugs/bottles including a base-fragment with diagnostic concentric lines where a wire was used to remove the jug from the wheel (Hurst et al. 1986, 214). Decoration occurs in the form of a partial armorial medallion, which corresponds to that on a bottle from Westminster, England, housed in the Museum of London, and dated 1551–1700. The assemblage contains one rim-fragment from a Frechen bottle which bears the left eye of a Bartmann mask (810: 1) and fine rilling beneath the rim indicative of seventeenth-century products (Gahan and McCutcheon 1997, 346).

Westerwald Westerwald stoneware was produced in the Westerwald region east of the Rhine in Germany by multiple production centres from the sixteenth century. While the first reference to potting in the area dates to 1402, the variety, scale and quality of production improved in the late sixteenth century with the arrival of refugee potters from Siegburg and Raeren. Westerwald stoneware was traded across Europe and to the Far East, Africa and North America in the seventeenth and eighteenth centuries (Gaimster et al. 1986, 251) and is found mostly in seventeenth-century contexts in Ireland. The fabric is a light grey colour with coloured decoration in the form of cobalt blue and manganese purple and a salt glaze which gives Westerwald a characteristic orange-peel surface. The assemblage contains at least one chamber pot (608: 116) and fragments of smaller vessels. Decoration includes cobalt blue colouring of stamped heart and circle motifs with linear borders. The earliest form of decoration is applied stamped pads; one example in the Golden Lane assemblage is decorated in cobalt blue and manganese purple (588:4), which indicates that its production post-dates the late seventeenth century (Jennings et al. 1981, 123).

Frechen/Cologne Cologne stoneware has a dark grey fabric identical to that of Raeren with an overall even brown salt glaze; neither patchy like the Raeren products nor mottled like the later Frechen pottery (Hurst et al. 1986, 208). The assemblage contains six fragments of pottery with a slightly mottled (salt) though consistent, orange-brown glaze and a mid-grey fabric. The assemblage contains two fragments from a Bartmann jug; a plain rim-fragment with the eyes of the mask (161: 5) and a jug body-fragment with part of the beard (192: 8). Further decoration occurs as an acanthus leaf motif (194: 18) and a circular medallion with the bust of a man wearing a hat (709: 1).

POST-MEDIEVAL POTTERY: A SUMMARY

The post-medieval pottery assemblage from Golden Lane consists of 1,922 fragments of pottery, ranging in date from the fifteenth to the early twentieth century. The following table illustrates all the post-medieval pottery found in stratified contexts, arranged in groups according to date, place of origin and type. The post-medieval pottery is discussed in full in the final report (Doyle forthcoming) but is included here in summary to provide a balanced view of the ceramic assemblage from Golden Lane.

One interesting piece that merits a particular mention is a Montelupo olive jar. A large urn (902:1) was found in the basement of a house fronting onto Chancery Lane and was identified by Clare McCutcheon (pers. comm.) as an eighteenth-century olive jar imported from the Italian region of Montelupo. The urn measures 79cm in height with an internal rim-diameter of 23cm. The vessel has two lug handles attached to the shoulder of the jar. A possible maker's mark is painted below one of the handles as the initials 'CI'. The fabric is a buff to orange colour with an internal brown glaze and external painted cream slip pattern. The rim is painted with the slip and there are six vertical bands of decoration, consisting of two vertical lines running the length of the urn with a vertical wavy line between. The vessel was almost intact, with the main body surviving below ground, although the rim was broken in antiquity and traces of mortar at this point could indicate repair work or that it was incorporated into the floor of the house. The vessel has been fully conserved and restored. The vessel was used as a water cistern in the household basement, buried up to the neck so that only the rim remained above ground. It is one of only two found so far in Ireland; the other was found during excavations at James' Fort, Kinsale, although several have been found in Britain (McCutcheon 2002, 39). The James' Fort vessel was identified by Hurst and McCutcheon as an olive oil jar, possibly from Montelupo, Italy. It is noted that the vessel possibly represents more than evidence for the oil trade, as these vessels were also used on board British military ships to store water (McCutcheon 2002, 39). Writing about similar vessels found on mid-eighteenth century colonial sites in the United States, Hume mentions this possible function. He also says that they were used as water cisterns in the homes of 'peasants' in the West Indies and that six were used for the storage of soap powder in the Mount Vernon home of George Washington (Hume 1969, 143–4).

SIXTEENTH- TO TWENTIETH-CENTURY WARES FROM GOLDEN LANE

Table 5. Post-medieval pottery from Golden Lane

Type	Sherds	MNV	MVR	Form	Date Range	Origin
Black-glazed earthenware: fine	48	2	12	mugs, teapot, plates, dishes	16th–18th	Ireland/ England
North Devon gravel-free	73		12	cistern, 6 large storage jars, 2 small storage jars/ tankards, 1 pancheon, 1 pipkin, candlestick	17th	England
North Devon gravel-tempered	85	2	13	jug, cistern, storage jars, settling pan, chamber pots, pipkin,	17th	England
North Devon sgraffito	22		6	plates/dishes	17th	England
Lambeth white glazed tin-glazed earthenware	10	1	3	teacups, drug pot	17th	England
Manganese mottled ware	54		17	teacups, tankards, teapots	17th–18th	England
Slip coated red earthenware	17		3	dowl, pancheons	17th–18th	Irish/ English

→

Type	Sherds	MNV	MVR	Form	Date range	Origin
Slip trailed red earthenware	30		10	dish, bowl, plate	17th–18th	Irish/ English
Donyatt slipware: possible	3		2	dish, bowl	17th–18th	England
North Holland slipware	2		2	dish, bowl	17th–18th	Netherlands
Staffordshire-type slipware: possible	2		1	dish	17th–18th	England
Anglo-Netherlands tin-glazed earthenware	30		14	drug jar, dish, plates	17th–18th	Anglo-Netherlands
English tin-glazed earthenware	6		7	plates, dish	17th–18th	England
Montelupo olive urn	1	1	1	olive urn reused as cistern	18th	Italy
Porcelain	40		14	bowls, teacups, candlestick (?)	18th	England
Belfast tin-glazed earthenware	2		2	plates	18th	Ireland
Dublin tin-glazed earthenware	6		2	posset pot/ tea pot, plate	18th	Ireland
Nottingham stoneware	12		4	tankards	18th	England
Pearlware. Hand-painted floral under glaze	10		5	teacups, small bowls, large bowl	18th–19th	Ireland/ England
Pearlware: misc. decorated	17		14	teacups, saucers, plates, bowls	18th–19th	Ireland/ England
Pearlware: plain	71		18	teacup, conserve/ ointment jars, dinner plates, dishes, serving dishes, jug, sauce pots, possible chamber pot	18th–19th	Ireland/ England

→

Type	Sherds	MNV	MVR	Form	Date Range	Origin
Pearlware: shell edged ware	35		30	plates, dishes, charger, colander	18th–19th	Ireland/ England
Staffordshire Bristol slipware	26		12	candlestick, 2 plate/ dish, 4 teacups	18th–19th	England
Transfer printed ware: black	16		8	teacup, mugs, plates, saucer, ointment pot	18th–19th	Ireland/ England
Transfer printed ware: blue willow pattern	74		36	platters, serving dishes, plates, saucers, teacup, jug, small bowl	18th–19th	Ireland/ England
Transfer printed ware: brown	10		6	teacups, plate, saucer	18th–19th	Ireland/ England
Transfer printed ware: green	10		6	bowl, teacup, ointment pot	18th–19th	Ireland/ England
Transfer printed ware: purple	5		5	bowl, jug, saucer, teacup, plate	18th–19th	Ireland/ England
Transfer printed ware: red-pink	5		8	teacups, plate, bowls, saucer, ointment/ conserve pot	18th–19th	Ireland/ England
Transfer printed ware: blue	128		39	teacups, jugs, bowls, saucers, dishes, plates, serving dishes	18th–19th	Ireland/ England
Black glazed earthenware: purple fabric	104	2	11	storage jars, possible candlestick, chamber pot	18th–19th	Ireland/ England
Black glazed red earthenware: orange-purple fabric	155	8	20	pancheons, storage vessels, possible stool pots	18th–19th	Ireland/ England
Brown glazed red earthenware	293	2	22	cider bottle, storage pots, pancheons, pipkin	18th–19th	Ireland/ England
Creamware	247	49		egg cups, dinner plates, dishes, serving bowl, ointment/conserve jars, possible wash hand basin, chamber pots	18th–19th	Ireland/ England

→

Type	Sherds	MNV	MVR	Form	Date Range	Origin
Fulham stoneware	8		7	bottles	18th–19th	England
Glasgow stoneware	1		1	cider bottle	18th–19th	Scotland
Lambeth stoneware	22		6	bottles, jar, tankard	18th–19th	England
Misc. English stoneware	46		17	chamber pot, storage pots, ointment jar, cider bottle, jug, teapot, vase, teacup	18th–19th	Ireland/ England
Pearlware: spongeware	19	1	14	teacups, bowl, teapot, serving dish	18th–20th	England
Derbyshire stoneware	3		2	bottles	19th	Ireland/ England
Unglazed red earthenware	36	2	7	large and small flowerpots, flower pot holder	19th	Ireland/ England
Transfer printed ware: flow-blue	26	1	13	teacups, plates, dishes	19th	Ireland/ England
Lustreware	2		2	decorative bowls	19th–20th	England
Mocha ware	20		13	small bowls	19th–20th	England
Yellow ware	36		6	3 bowls, 2 cups, ointment jar	19th–20th	England
Drabware	3		3	plate, teacup, dish	19th–20th	England
Imitation Jasperware	8		2	teacup, bowls	18th–19th	England
North Devon white ware	3		3	dish, teacups	17th–18th	England
Total count	**1834**	**20**	**495**			

DISCUSSION

The medieval rectilinear enclosure A portion of the site was enclosed by two ditches, ditch 393 and 225; pottery from the latter is discussed here. The table below illustrates the pottery and date-range of the three fills of enclosure-ditch 225. The primary fill, 429, contains pottery that suggests an earliest date of thirteenth-fourteenth century for this deposit. The secondary fills contain pottery ranging in date from the twelfth-fourteenth century and also some post-medieval pottery that suggests they are intrusive finds. The upper backfill contains medieval pottery ranging in date from the twelfth-fourteenth century and also some post-medieval pottery. As the final fill it is not surprising that disturbance could occur at this level. This fill contained a coin (225: 6) that was issued in 1461, possibly in Dublin; it is a copper half farthing of Edward IV (Scully 2006). Ditch 225 also contained floor and roof tile, knife blades, nails and a stick-pin.

Table 6. Fills and pottery from Ditch 225

Enclosure-ditch 225	Context	Medieval pottery	Post-medieval	Date-range
Primary fill	429	Dublin-type ware, Leinster cooking ware, Dublin-type fineware		13th-14th C
	496	None		
	1336	None		
Secondary fill	493	Dublin-type coarseware, Leinster cooking ware, Dublin-type ware, Dublin-type fineware, SMGG, unidentified medieval	black glazed red earthenware	13th-14th C +post-medieval
	497	Dublin-type coarseware, Leinster cooking ware, Dublin-type ware, Dublin-type fineware, Dublin-type cooking ware, Saintonge mottled green glazed	North Devon gravel-free	12th-14th C + post-medieval
	1337	Dublin-type ware		
Upper backfill	226*	Southeast Wiltshire, Ham Green B, Dublin-type coarseware, Dublin-type ware, Dublin-type fineware, Saintonge mottled green glazed, Saintonge green glazed all-over, Merida-type	black glazed red earthenware	12th-14th C + post-medieval
	1338	Saintonge mottled green glazed		

Pit 1333 contained single fragments of Dublin-type ware and Dublin-type fineware pottery, dating to the thirteenth-fourteenth century. This pit fill, 1334, also contained a hand-bell (04E1030: 1334:1) that has been linked to the nearby church of St Michael le Pole (Scully 2006).

ACKNOWLEDGMENTS

The archaeological excavations at Golden Lane were technically challenging and complex. The success of completing the work on site goes in no small measure to the professionalism of the site crew. I am delighted to acknowledge their contribution. They were: Erica Strengbom, Lena Strid, Carina Eriksson, Steve McGlade, John Paul Ryan, Michelle O'Gara, Léan Ní Chléirigh, Niamh Doyle, Kevin McNerney, Colm McCavera, Neil Carlin, Britta Schnittger, Jenny Brittain, Rob Reynolds, Lorcan Harney, Deirdre Collins, Jack Whelan, Brian Drew, Sarah Tobin, Muirin O'Higgins, Kim Rice, Tiernan McGarry, Con Herriot and Ciara Reynolds; Goedetic survey work was undertaken by Liam Murphy and Eamon Briscoe; Thomas Cummins helped with the analysis of the site sections and importantly the site supervisors were Siobhán Scully (who was responsible for the small finds and who wrote the finds report), Johnny Monteith (who was the site excavation supervisor and also drafted a preliminary strategraphic text on the excavations) and Simon Dick (the senior site surveyor who also prepared and inked up the drawings for this article). The conservation was undertaken by Erica Devine, Claudia Koehler and Noël Siver of ArchCon Labs and the graphics and report production team in Margaret Gowen & Co. Ltd; Lindsay Rafter and Mario Sughi who prepared the images for publication; Matt O'Reilly, Gerry Sherman and Gerry O'Connor of J.J. Rhattigan & Co. who were always courteous and helpful.

I would like to acknowledge the role of Ruth Johnson and Mary McMahon in the Archaeological Office in Dublin City Council. I would like to record my thanks to Red Tobin for his helpful discussion on kilns, Penny Johnson for her insights into oats, Linzi Simpson and Kevin Weldon for their interest and help with the Viking LXXXV and the editor of this volume Seán Duffy for his patience.

BIBLIOGRAPHY

Barton, K.J. 1963 The medieval pottery kiln at Ham Green, Bristol. *Transactions of the Bristol and Gloucester Archaeological Society*, 82, 95–126.

Barton, K.J. 1965 Medieval pottery at Rouen. *Archaeological Journal* 122, 73–85.

Barton, K.J. 1988 The medieval pottery of Dublin. In G. Mac Niocaill and P.F. Wallace (eds), *Keimelia*, 271–324. Galway.

Biddle, M. 1990a *Object and economy in medieval Winchester*. Oxford.

Biddle, M. 1990b Tweezers. In Biddle 1990a, 690–2.

Biddle, M. 1990c Weights and measures. In Biddle 1990a, 908–928.

Biddle, M. and Hinton, D.A. 1990 Points. In Biddle 1990a, 581–589.

Biddle, M. and Smith, D. 1990 The Querns. In Biddle 1990a, 881–890.

Blake, H. and Davey, P. (eds) 1983 *Guidelines for the processing and publication of medieval pottery from excavations*. London.

Brenan, J. 1998 Furnishings. In G. Egan, *The medieval household: daily living c.1150–c.1450*. London.

Brooks, E.St J. (ed.) 1936 *Register of the Hospital of St John the Baptist without the New Gate, Dublin*. Dublin.

Clarke, H. 1983 The historical background to North Sea trade, *c*.1200–1500. In P. Davey and R. Hodges (eds) *Ceramics and trade. The production and distribution of later medieval pottery in north-west Europe*. Proceedings of the Medieval Pottery Research Group's annual conference at Hull, 1980. Sheffield.

Clarke, H.B. 1977 The topographical development of early medieval Dublin. *R.S.A.I. Journ*. 109, 33–47.

Clarke, H.B. 1978 *Dublin c.840–1540, the medieval town in the modern city*. 1st ed. Ordnance Survey. Dublin.

Clarke, H.B. 2002 *Dublin c.840–1540, the medieval town in the modern city*. 2nd ed. Royal Irish Academy. Dublin.

Clarke, H.B. 2002 *Dublin, part I, to 1610*. Irish Historic Towns Atlas, no. 11. Royal Irish Academy. Dublin.

Cleary, R.M., Hurley, M.F. and Shee Twohig, E. (eds) 1997 *Skiddy's Castle and Christ church, Cork: excavations 1974–77 by D.C. Twohig*. Cork.

Colgan, E. 2003 *For want of good money: the story of Ireland's coinage*. Bray.

Conway, M. 1999 *Director's first findings from excavations at Cabinteely*. Margaret Gowen & Co. Ltd. Dublin.

De Neergaard, M. 1987 The use of knives, shears, scissors and scabbards. In J. Cowgill, M. de Neergaard and N. Griffiths (eds), *Knives and scabbards. Medieval finds from excavations in London*, 51–61. Museum of London. London; this edn 2000, Boydell Press, Woodbridge.

Deroeux, D. and Dufournier, D. 1991 Réflexions sur la diffusion de la céramique *très décorée* d'origine française en Europe du Nord-Ouest, XIIIe-XIVe siècles. *Archaeologie Médiévale* 21, 163–77.

Doyle, N. 2004 'An analysis of Drogheda ware and its origins'. Unpublished MA thesis. University College Cork.

Doyle, N. (forthcoming) Medieval and post-medieval pottery. In E. O'Donovan, *Excavations at Golden Lane, Dublin*.

Draper, J. 1984 *Post-medieval pottery 1650–1800*. Shire Archaeology Series no. 40. Princes Risborough (England).

Dublin Archaeological Research Team 1981 *Preliminary report and recommendations on the site of St Michael le Pole and surrounding area*. Unpublished report lodged with the Office of Public Works. Dublin.

Dunning, G. The trade in medieval pottery around the North Sea. In J.G. Renaud (ed.) *Rotterdam Papers* 1, 35–58, Rotterdam.

Eames, E.S. and Fanning, T. 1988 *Irish medieval tiles*. Royal Irish Academy. Dublin.

Edwards, N. 1990 *The archaeology of early medieval Ireland*. London.

Egan, G. 1991a Buckles. In G. Egan and F. Pritchard (eds.), *Dress accessories: c.1150–c.1450*, 50–123. London.

Egan, G. 1991b Mounts. In G. Egan and F. Pritchard (eds.), *Dress accessories: c.1150–c.1450*, 162–246. London.

Egan, G. 1991c Lace chapes. In G. Egan and F. Pritchard (eds.), *Dress accessories: c.1150–c.1450*, 281–90. London

Egan, G. 1998 Security equipment. In G. Egan, *The medieval household: daily living c.1150–c.1450*. London.

Ellis, S.E. and Moore, D.T. 1990 The Hones. In Biddle 1990a, 868–81. Clarendon Press, Oxford.

Gahan, A. and McCutcheon, C. 1997 Medieval pottery. In Hurley et al. (eds) 1997, 285–336.

Gahan, A. and Walsh, C. 1997 Medieval pottery. In *Archaeological excavations at Patrick, Nicholas & Winetavern Streets, Dublin*. Dingle.

Gahan, A., McCutcheon, C. and Twohig, D.C. 1997 Medieval pottery. In R.M. Cleary, M.F. Hurley and E. Shee Twohig (eds), *Skiddy's Castle and Christchurch Cork: excavations 1974–77 by D.C. Twohig*, 108–29. Cork.
Gaimster, D. et al. 1997 *German stoneware 1200–1900: archaeology and cultural history*. British Museum Press. London.
Galloway, P. 1990 Combs of bone, antler and ivory. In Biddle 1990a, 665–78.
Goodall, I.H. 1990a Locks and keys. In Biddle 1990a, 1001–36.
Goodall, I.H. 1990b Knives. In Biddle 1990a, 835–60.
Gowen, M. 2001 Excavations at the site of the church and tower of St Michael le Pole, Dublin. In S. Duffy (ed.), *Medieval Dublin II*, 13–52. Dublin.
Graham-Campbell, J. 1998 The early Viking Age in the Irish Sea area. In H.B. Clarke, M. Ní Mhaonaigh, R. Ó Floinn (eds), *Ireland and Scandinavia in the early Viking Age*, 104–30. Dublin.
Groves, M. 1990 Silver and copper-alloy tacks. In Biddle 1990a, 1102–14.
Hayden, A. and Walsh, C. 1997 Small finds. In C. Walsh, *Archaeological excavations at Patrick, Nicholas & Winetavern Streets, Dublin*, 132–44. Dingle.
Hinton, D.A. 1990 Folded sheet strap ends. In Biddle 1990a, 505–6.
Hodges, G. 1978 A *Céramique Onctueuse* vessel from Dover. A Breton souvenir? *Medieval Archaeology* 22, 137–9.
Hurley, M.F. 1997 *Excavations at the North Gate Cork 1994*. Cork.
Hurley, M.F. 1997 Artefacts of skeletal material. In Hurley et al. (eds) 1997, 650–702.
Hurley, M.F. and McCutcheon, S.W.J. 1997 St Peter's church and graveyard. In Hurley et al. (eds) 1997, 190–227.
Hurley, M.F., Scully, O.M.B., and McCutcheon, S.W.J. (eds) 1997 *Late Viking Age and medieval Waterford: excavations, 1986–1992*. Waterford.
Hurst, J.G., Neal. D. S and van Beuningen, H.J.E. 1986 *Pottery produced and traded in north-west Europe, 1350–1650*. Rotterdam Papers VI. Rotterdam.
Janssen, H. 1983 Later medieval pottery trade in the Netherlands. In P. Davey and R. Hodges (eds), *Ceramics and trade*, 121–86. Sheffield.
Keene, S. 1990 Eyed weaving implements. In Biddle 1990a, 232–4.
Lawson, G. 1990 Pieces from stringed instruments. In Biddle 1990a, 711–18.
McCutcheon, C. 1994 Medieval pottery. In L. Simpson, *Excavations at Isolde's Tower, Dublin*. Dublin.
McCutcheon, C. 1995 Medieval pottery. In L. Simpson, *Excavations at Essex Street West, Dublin*. Dublin.
McCutcheon, C. 2000 Medieval pottery in Dublin: new names and some dates. In S. Duffy (ed.), *Medieval Dublin I*, 117–25. Dublin.
McCutcheon, C. 2003 Pottery. In R.M. Cleary and M.F. Hurley (eds), *Excavations in Cork City; 1984–2000*, 197–235. Cork.
McCutcheon, C. 2006 *Medieval Pottery from Wood Quay, Dublin: the 1974–6 Waterfront excavations.* Medieval Dublin Excavations 1962–81. Series B, 7. Royal Irish Academy. Dublin.
McEnery, J. and Refaussé, R. (eds) 2001 *Christ Church deeds*, Dublin.
MacGregor, A. 1985 *Bone, antler, ivory and horn: the technology of skeletal materials since the Roman period*. London and Sydney.
MacGregor, A., Mainman, A.J. and Rogers, N.S.H. 1999 *Craft, industry and everyday life: bone, antler, ivory and horn from Anglo-Scandinavian and medieval York*. Council for British Archaeology. York.
McMahon, M. 2002 Early medieval settlement and burial evidence outside the enclosed town: evidence from archaeological excavations at Bride Street, Dublin. *R.I.A. Proc.* 102C no. 4, 67–135.
Mainman, A.J. and Rogers, N.S.H. 2000 *Craft, Industry and Everyday Life: Finds from Anglo-Scandinavian York*. Council for British Archaeology, York.

Meenan, R. 1992 A survey of late medieval and post-medieval Iberian pottery from Ireland. In D. Gaimster and M. Redknap (eds), *Everyday and exotic pottery from Europe*, 186–93. Exeter.

Meenan, R. and McCutcheon, C. 1997 Post-medieval pottery. In Hurley et al. (eds) 1997, 338–55.

Meenan, R. et al. 2004 Pottery of the late medieval and post-medieval periods. In E. Fitzpatrick, M. O'Brien, and P. Walsh (eds), *Archaeological investigations in Galway City, 1987–1998*. Bray.

Monk, M. and Kelleher, E. 2006 An assessment of the archaeological evidence for Irish corn-drying kilns in the light of the results of archaeological and archaeobotanical studies. *Journal of Irish Archaeology*, XIV, 77–114.

MPRG 1998 *A guide to the classification of medieval ceramic forms*. London.

O'Brien, E. 2003 Burial practices in Ireland: first to seventh centuries AD. In J. Downes and A. Ritchie (eds), *Sea change: Orkney and Northern Europe in the later Iron Age AD 300–800*, 62–72, Balgavies, Scotland.

O'Donovan, E. 2005 There is an antiquarian in us all *Archaeology Ireland* 19, no. 3, 16–17.

O'Donovan, E. 2006 Mount Gamble, Townparks, Swords. In I. Bennett (ed.) *Excavations 2003: summary accounts of archaeological excavations in Ireland*, 181–3. Bray.

O'Floinn, R. 1988 Handmade medieval pottery In S.E. Ireland – Leinster cooking ware. In G. Mac Niocaill and P.F. Wallace (eds), *Keimelia. Studies in medieval archaeology and history in memory of Tom Delaney*. Galway.

Ó Floinn, R. 1998 The archaeology of the early Viking Age. In H.B Clarke, M. Ní Mhaonaigh and R. Ó Floinn (eds), *Ireland and Scandinavia in the early Viking Age*, 131–65. Dublin.

O'Rahilly, C. 1998 A classification of bronze stick-pins from the Dublin excavations 1962–1972. In C. Manning (ed.), *Dublin and beyond the Pale: studies in honour of Patrick Healy*, 23–33. Bray.

Ottaway, P. and Rogers, N. 2002 *Craft, industry and everyday life: finds from medieval York: the small finds*. Council for British Archaeology, York.

Papazian, C. 1989 The medieval pottery from the Dublin Castle excavations. Unpublished MA thesis, National University of Ireland.

Papazian, C. and Campbell, E. 1992 *Medieval pottery and roof tiles in Wales AD 1100–1600*, Medieval and Later Pottery in Wales 13, Cardiff.

Pritchard, F. 1991a Strap-ends. In G. Egan and F. Pritchard, *Dress accessories c.1150–c.1450*, 124–61. London.

Pritchard, F. 1991b Finger rings. In G. Egan and F. Pritchard, *Dress accessories c. 1150–c.1450*, 325–35. London.

Ronan, M.V. 1940 Lazar houses of St Lawrence and St Stephen in medieval Dublin. In J. Ryan (ed.), *Féilsgríbhinn Eóin Mhic Néill*, 480–9. Dublin.

Scully, O.M.B. 1997 Metal artefacts. In Hurley et al. (eds) 1997, 438–89.

Scully, S. 2006 Ferrous and non-ferrous metal artefacts In E. O'Donovan, *Excavations at Golden Lane, Dublin*. Forthcoming.

Simpson, L. 1997 Historical background to the Patrick Street excavation. In Walsh 1997.

Simpson, L. 2005 Viking warrior burials in Dublin: is this the *longphort*? In S. Duffy (ed.), *Medieval Dublin VI*, 11–62. Dublin.

Sweetman, D. 1984 Archaeological excavations at Shop St, Drogheda, County Louth. *R.I.A. Proc.* 84C.

Thomas, G. 2000 Anglo-Scandinavian metalwork from the Danelaw: exploring social and cultural interaction. In D.M. Hadley and J.D. Richards (eds), *Cultures in contact: Scandinavian settlement in England in the ninth and tenth centuries*, 237–55. Brepols, Belgium.

Vince, A. G. 1988 Early medieval English pottery in Viking Dublin. In Mac Niocaill and Wallace (eds) 1988, 254–70.

Vince, A.G. 1997 Petrological analysis of some medieval pottery from Waterford: medieval pottery. In Hurley et al. (eds) 1997, 337–8.

Wallace, P.F. 1984 A reappraisal of the archaeological significance of Wood Quay. In J. Bradley (ed.), *Viking Dublin exposed: the Wood Quay saga*, 112–133. Dublin.

Wallace, P.F. 1994 Anglo-Norman Dublin: continuity and change. In D. Ó Corráin (ed.), *Irish antiquity*, 247–66. Rpr. Dublin.

Whitehead, R. 2003 *Buckles 1250–1800*. Witham.

Wren, J. 2006 Medieval and post-medieval roof tiles. In McCutcheon 2006.

Websites:

www.wallacecollection.org/i_s/publications/mail_construction.htm The Construction and Metallurgy of Mail Armour in the Wallace Collection viewed 14/10/2004

APPENDIX: THE RADIOCARBON DATING RESULTS FROM GOLDEN LANE

The dates were processed by 14CHRONO Centre, Queen's University Belfast, 42 Fitzwilliam Street, Belfast BT9 6AX. Six archaeological features/burials were initially submitted from radiocarbon dating from the Golden Lane site (04E1030), and Table 1 presents a summary of the results. The dating program sought to establish dates for three archaeological features: the primary fill of corn-drying kiln (F1318), the basal fill of a well (F944) associated with lime production, and the lower fill of a domestic rubbish pit (F348). Additionally, three burials were selected for dating (Burial nos LXXXV, LXXXIII and CXXIX). LXXXV is an adult male buried with Viking-Age grave goods, LXXXIII is a male burial not accompanied by grave goods and interred in the 'Irish tradition' and burial CXXIX is a female burial, possibly associated with Viking-Age grave goods.

Table 1. Summary C14 dating results from Golden Lane

UB No.	Sample ID	Date	14C Age	±	$\delta^{13}C$	Material	treatment
UB-7074	04E1030:C1318:S7	12–9–06	941 BP	33	-28.0	wood	AAA
UB-7075	04E1030:C944:S50	12–9–06	1073 BP	34	-26.0	indet. cereals	Acid
UB-7079	04E1030:C348:S95	12–9–06	1108 BP	35	-25.0	charcoal	AAA
UB-7076	04E1030:LXXXV	29–9–06	1249 BP	32	-20.0	human bone	Collagen
UB-7077	04E1030:LXXXIII	29–9–06	1180 BP	31	-18.0	human bone	Collagen
UB-7078	04E1030:CXXIX	29–9–06	1247 BP	33	-20.0	human bone	Collagen

The well associated with lime production:
04E1030:C1318:S7, UB-7074
Radiocarbon Age BP 941 +/– 33

68.3% (1 sigma)	cal AD	1033–1052	0.211
		1080–1129	0.556
		1132–1153	0.233
95.4% (2 sigma)	cal AD	1022–1164	1.000

The corn-drying kiln:
04E1030:C944:S50, UB-7075
Radiocarbon Age BP 1073 +/– 34

68.3% (1 sigma)	cal AD	900–918	0.240
		965–1016	0.760
95.4% (2 sigma)	cal AD	894–928	0.250
		933–1020	0.750

The domestic refuse pit:
04E1030:C348:S95, UB-7079
Radiocarbon Age BP 1108 +/– 35

68.3% (1 sigma)	cal AD	895–926	0.413
		936–980	0.587
95.4% (2 sigma)	cal AD	830–837	0.006
		868–1018	0.994

LXXXV, an adult male buried with Viking-Age grave goods:
04E1030:LXXXV, UB-7076
Radiocarbon Age BP 1249 +/– 32

68.3 (1 sigma)	cal AD	688–754	0.720
		757–779	0.220
		794–801	0.060
95.4 (2 sigma)	cal AD	678–832	0.902
		836–869	0.098

LXXXIII is a male burial not accompanied by grave goods and interred in the 'Irish tradition':
04E1030:LXXXIII, UB-7077
Radiocarbon Age BP 1180 +/– 31

68.3 (1 sigma)	cal AD	781–790	0.098
		808–888	0.902
95.4 (2 sigma)	cal AD	772–900	0.896
		917–965	0.104

CXXIX is a female burial, possibly associated with Viking-Age grave goods:
04E1030:CXXIX, UB-7078
Radiocarbon Age BP 1247 +/– 33

68.3 (1 sigma)	cal AD	688–780	0.903
		792–805	0.097
95.4 (2 sigma)	cal AD	680–870	1.000

RADIOCARBON CALIBRATION PROGRAM CALIB REV 5.0.2. Copyright 1986–2005 M. Stuiver and P.J. Reimer. To be used in conjunction with: Stuiver, M., and Reimer, P.J. 1993, *Radiocarbon*, **35**, 215–30. Calibration data set: intcal04.14c # Reimer et al. 2004. % area enclosed cal AD age ranges relative area under probability distribution.

References for calibration datasets:
P.J. Reimer, M.G.L. Baillie, E. Bard, A. Bayliss, J.W. Beck, C. Bertrand, P.G. Blackwell, C.E. Buck, G. Burr, K.B. Cutler, P.E. Damon, R.L. Edwards, R.G. Fairbanks, M. Friedrich, T.P. Guilderson, K.A. Hughen, B. Kromer, F.G. McCormac, S. Manning, C. Bronk Ramsey, R.W. Reimer, S. Remmele, J.R. Southon, M. Stuiver, S. Talamo, F.W. Taylor, J. van der Plicht, and C.E. Weyhenmeyer (2004), *Radiocarbon* **46**, 1029–58.

Comments:
* This standard deviation (error) includes a lab error multiplier.
** 1 sigma = square root of (sample std. dev.^2 + curve std. dev.^2)
** 2 sigma = 2 x square root of (sample std. dev.^2 + curve std. dev.^2) where ^2 = quantity squared.
[ ] = calibrated range impinges on end of calibration data set
0* represents a 'negative' age BP
1955* or 1960* denote influence of nuclear testing C–14

NOTE: Cal. ages and ranges are rounded to the nearest year which may be too precise in many instances. Users are advised to round results to the nearest 10 years for samples with standard deviation in the radiocarbon age greater than 50 years.

Man, Ireland, and England: the English conquest of Ireland and Dublin-Manx relations[1]

R. ANDREW McDONALD

Sometime around the year 1200 an Irish bard sang the praises of the Manx sea-king Rögnvaldr (Reginald, Rag(h)nall) Guðrøðarson, who reigned from 1187 to 1226 and was slain in battle with his brother Óláfr at Tynwald in the Isle of Man in February 1229.[2] In his praise poem the bard elevated Rögnvaldr to the status of a super-viking, raiding, pillaging, killing (and engaging in that other memorable activity, rewarding poets): 'You will deal death from smooth-plained Man, slaughter by a great ship's host ... You'll hold a man back, and plunder, you'll burn a house and smash'. If the bard is to be believed, Ireland was a particular object of Rögnvaldr's attentions, and raids or attacks on Colptha's Strait (the lower reaches of the Boyne valley), Dublin, Tráigh Bhaile (Dundalk strand), and Aran are mentioned. 'You'll seek harbour behind Aran', the poet sings, 'while probing Ireland's cold shores'. More remarkably, perhaps, the poet intimated that Rögnvaldr might assume kingship in Ireland: 'You will get, Sadhbh's noble son, speech from the slab on Tara's side' – probably a reference to the famous Lia Fáil at Tara, which was said to cry out in recognition of the true high-king.[3] Finally, the poet rejoices in the expectation of Rögnvaldr conquering Dublin, and stakes a claim on his generosity when he succeeds: 'a house-site on coming to Dublin I ask beforehand, Raghnall'.[4]

Considering that Rögnvaldr belonged to a dynasty of Manx sea-kings with a history of Irish – and especially Dublin – connections, it would appear that

1 I am very grateful to Dr Seán Duffy and the Friends of Medieval Dublin for the invitation to participate in the 8th Annual Medieval Dublin Symposium in May 2006, and I would like to thank Dr Duffy for discussion of many aspects of this paper as well as my ongoing research. Many of the ideas presented in this paper are developed further in R.A. McDonald, *Manx kingship in its Irish Sea setting, 1187–1229: King Rögnvaldr and the Crovan dynasty* (Dublin, 2007). 2 *Cronica Regum Mannie et Insularum: Chronicles of the kings of Man and the Isles BL Cotton Julius Avii*, ed. and trans. G. Broderick (2nd ed. Douglas, 1995), fos. 40r–44v (hereafter *CRMI*); all subsequent references are to this edition, by folio number (e.g. fo. 44v), unless otherwise noted. 3 See E. FitzPatrick, *Royal inauguration in Gaelic Ireland, c.1100–1600: a cultural landscape study* (Woodbridge, 2004), 99–100, 102–4. 4 B. Ó Cuív, 'A poem in praise of Raghnall, king of Man', *Éigse* 8 (1956–7), 283–301; a more recent translation, lacking the critical apparatus of Ó Cuív, is *The triumph tree: Scotland's earliest poetry, AD 550–1350* ed. and trans. T.O. Clancy

the poet knew a thing or two about Irish and Manx history. On the other hand, however, the bard seems conveniently to ignore the fact that the political situation, not just in Ireland but also the whole Irish Sea basin, had been profoundly altered in recent memory by the coming of the English to Ireland in the late 1160s. Still, if the prospect of Rögnvaldr winning Dublin was farfetched by 1200, the notion that Manx rulers might still possess links with Ireland and Dublin was less so. In fact, the relations between Ireland and the Isle of Man in the Middle Ages are better studied for some periods than for others. While the close connections that existed in the eleventh and early twelfth centuries have been examined from a number of perspectives,[5] the period after about 1170 has received much less attention.[6] This paper concerns itself with the question of what impact the English conquest of Ireland made upon the Isle of Man, and upon the relations that the rulers of this tiny island maintained with Ireland. It concentrates upon the era of King Rögnvaldr, that is, the decades on either side of the year 1200, partly for the obvious reason that it was during his long reign that some of the more significant implications of the English conquest were worked out for the Isle of Man, but partly also for the less obvious reason that there survives a particularly rich and abundant trail of evidence that allows the problem to be developed in a fairly comprehensive manner (discussed further below).

* * *

The Isle of Man was well suited to play a role as a power centre for a medieval dynasty of sea-kings. Although small, Man is strategically positioned in the northern Irish Sea basin, almost precisely equidistant between St Bees Head in England and the mouth of Strangford Lough. The nearest landmass, Burrow Head in Scotland, lies only 30km to the north, and Anglesey in Wales is 80km to the south. In favourable weather all of these lands are visible from Snaefell, the highest peak on Man, and the island itself is visible from the surrounding landmasses. It is scarcely surprising that one medieval Welsh poet dubbed the Irish Sea 'Môr Manaw', 'the sea of Man', with the Isle of Man styled 'Midway island' by a modern historian.[7] Linked not only to those

(Edinburgh, 1998), 236–4. All references are to Ó Cuív's edition. 5 S. Duffy, 'Irishmen and Islesmen in the kingdoms of Dublin and Man, 1052–1171', *Ériu* 43 (1992), 93–133; B.T. Hudson, *Viking pirates and Christian princes: dynasty, religion, and empire in the north Atlantic* (Oxford, 2005). 6 But see S. Duffy, 'The Bruce brothers and the Irish Sea world, 1306–29', *Cambridge Medieval Celtic Studies* 21 (Summer 1991), 55–86, which is much more wide-ranging than the title suggests. 7 B. Jones, 'Gwriad's heritage: links between Wales and the Isle of Man in the early middle ages', *Transactions of the Honourable Society of Cymmrodorion*, n.s. [no volume] (1990), 30; N. Davies, *The Isles* (Oxford, 1999), 7 (map), 9. A. Moffat, *The sea-kingdoms: the history of Celtic Britain & Ireland* (London, 2002), 44–5, suggests that the name of the island itself is derived from the Gaelic root *meadhon*, 'middle'.

neighbouring lands but also to the North Atlantic and the Continent by the sea-road, the Isle of Man stood at a significant cultural crossroads.[8] In addition to its strategic position astride the western seaways, Man's abundant and fertile farmlands, plentiful natural resources, and numerous natural inlets and harbours made the island an economic as well as a strategic prize.[9]

The full potential of the Isle of Man as a power centre for a dynasty of sea-kings was realized about a century before the English conquest of Ireland, when a new era in the history of Man, the Isles, and indeed the Irish Sea opened with the arrival in Man of Guðrøðr Crovan and his entrenchment there in 1079. According to the *Cronica Regum Mannie et Insularum* (Chronicles of the Kings of Man and the Isles, or, for the sake of convenience, the Manx Chronicle) – our major source for the history of the Isle of Man in this period, composed in the second half of the thirteenth century[10] – Guðrøðr came to the Isle of Man after the battle of Stamford Bridge in 1066, in which he fought on the losing Norwegian side. Here, he was received by the king, Guðrøðr Sigtryggsson (possibly a kinsman) who died in 1070. The Manx Chronicle then relates how Guðrøðr invaded three times in 1079, ultimately defeating the Manx at the battle of Skyhill and establishing himself in the island as a conqueror.[11] Guðrøðr's identity remains slightly murky thanks to problems with the sources, but recent scholarship has linked him to the famous Óláfsson dynasty of Dublin, and he may have been a son of Ívarr Haraldsson who died in 1054.[12]

Guðrøðr died in 1095, when he succumbed to plague in Islay, and one of his most enduring accomplishments was as the founder of a vigorous line of sea-kings commonly referred to as the 'Crovan dynasty', who presided over something of a Golden Age in Man and the Isles until the death of the last Manx king, Magnús Óláfsson, in 1265. One significant characteristic of these

8 See e.g. M. Carver, 'The North Sea highway: cultural arena or political barrier', in J.M. Fladmark (ed.), *Sharing the earth: local identity in global culture* (London, 1995), 177–90. Seminal works in delineating the western seaways are: Sir C. Fox, *The personality of Britain* (4th ed. Cardiff, 1947); E.G. Bowen, *Britain and the western seaways* (London, 1972); idem, *Saints seaways and settlements in the Celtic lands* (2nd ed. Cardiff, 1977), and see now B. Cunliffe, *Facing the ocean: the Atlantic and its peoples* (Oxford 2000). On the place of the Isle of Man in Atlantic Britain see R.H. Kinvig, 'The Isle of Man and Atlantic Britain: a study in historical geography', *Transactions and Papers of the Institute of British Geographers* 25 (1958), 1–27. 9 See, inter alia, P.J. Davey, 'At the crossroads of power and cultural influence: Manx archaeology in the high middle ages', in P.J. Davey and D. Finlayson (eds), *Mannin Revisited: twelve essays on Manx culture and environment* (Edinburgh, 2002), 81–104; B.T. Hudson, 'The changing economy of the Irish Sea province', in B. Smith (ed.), *Britain and Ireland, 900–1300: insular responses to medieval European change* (Cambridge, 1999), 39–66; idem, *Viking Pirates*, passim. 10 Broderick, 'Introduction', *CRMI*, vii. 11 *CRMI*, fos. 32v–33v. 12 Hudson, *Viking pirates*, 171–2; S. Duffy, 'Emerging from the mist: Ireland and Man in the eleventh century', in Davey and Finlayson (eds), *Mannin revisited*, 55–6; Duffy regards Guðrøðr as a son or nephew of Ívarr Haraldsson. See also G. Broderick, 'Irish and Welsh strands in the genealogy of

kings was the strength of their Irish affiliations. Although frequently described as 'Norse','scandinavian', or 'Viking' kings of the Isle of Man, the argument can be made that the term 'Gaelic-Norse' is more appropriate in light of their strong links with Ireland.[13] Irish connections, in fact, were as old as the dynasty itself, since Guðrøðr Crovan hailed from Dublin, and in 1091 he even succeeded in briefly re-conquering it before being expelled in 1094.[14] Irish elements were also involved in the strife that characterized the years between Guðrøðr's death and the establishment of his son Óláfr in the kingship around 1113.[15] Óláfr's orientation may have lain more towards England and Galloway than Ireland, but political connections still existed: when he was assassinated in 1153 it was by his nephews who had, the Manx Chronicle says, been reared in Dublin.[16] Óláfr's son Guðrøðr may have provided ships for a naval attack on Connacht in 1154, and he also appears to have undertaken a brief and seemingly unsuccessful expedition to Dublin early in his reign, possibly around 1156.[17] Fifteen years later, in 1171, he sent thirty ships to assist in a counter-attack on the newly arrived English in Dublin – more on which below. The strength of Irish connections is also neatly reflected in the matrimonial politics of the Crovan dynasty: Óláfr's son Guðrøðr took at least one Irish concubine, Finnguala, whom he later canonically married, and he possibly had others, if, as the praise poem on Rögnvaldr states, Rögnvaldr's mother was named Sadhbh.[18] Finally, although the personal names of the dynasty are uniformly Scandinavian, the use of Gaelic bynames by some of the Manx kings is indicative not only of Irish connections but also of the blended cultural milieu in the Isles at this time.[19] The fact that a Scandinavian-speaking king of Man had his praises sung in Gaelic by an Irish bard is also suggestive of this mixed cultural environment; since the poem was almost certainly performed at his court, Rögnvaldr must have had a pretty good grasp of Gaelic – poets didn't work for free, and this one clearly expected a substantial reward for his masterpiece.

The 'coming of the English'[20] to Ireland in the last years of the 1160s and the subsequent conquest and colonization of much of Ireland have been

Guðrøðr Crovan', *Journal of the Manx Museum* 8:89 (1980), 32–8. **13** See e.g. B.R.S. Megaw, 'Norseman and native in the kingdom of the Isles: a re-assessment of the Manx evidence', in P. Davey (ed.), *Man and environment in the Isle of Man* (Oxford, 1978), 265–314 [hereafter 'Norseman']. **14** *CRMI*, fo. 33r.; *Annals of Inisfallen (MS Rawlinson B. 503)*, ed. and trans. S. Mac Airt (Dublin, 1951) 247 [hereafter *AI*]. **15** *CRMI*, fos. 33v–34r. **16** *CRMI*, fos. 36r –v. **17** *Annals of the kingdom of Ireland by the Four Masters*, ed. and trans. J. O'Donovan (7 vols Dublin 1856) ii, 1110–12 (s.a. 1154); *CRMI*, fos. 36v–37r. **18** *CRMI*, fos. 39v–40r; Ó Cuív, passim. **19** Megaw, 'Norseman', 276–8. The derivation of Guðrøðr *Crovan*'s by-name from Irish *cró-bán*, 'very pale', is suggested by A.O. Anderson (ed.), *Early sources of Scottish history, AD 500–1286* (2 vols Edinburgh, 1922; repr. Stamford, 1990), ii, 43 n 6, though compare Hudson, *Viking pirates*, 173; King Rögnvaldr had a son named Guðrøðr with the by-name *donn*, 'brown' or 'brown-haired': *CRMI*, fo. 44v. **20** Giraldus Cambrensis, *Opera*, ed. J.S. Brewer, J.F. Dimock, and Sir

described as 'the single most formative development in Irish secular affairs'.[21] This is not the place to rehearse the familiar story of the exiled Leinster king Diarmait Mac Murchada (d. 1171), his enlistment of English aid including Richard fitz Gilbert de Clare, lord of Pembroke and Striguil (d. 1176), better known as Strongbow, to recover his kingdom, and the subsequent involvement of the English king Henry II (r. 1154–89) as the conquest threatened to get out of hand.[22] But the English conquest of Ireland changed more than just the course of Irish history: it also resonated like a tidal wave through the Irish Sea basin and was of particular consequence for the rulers of the Isle of Man, whose Irish links, we have seen, were very significant.

On the one hand, the capture of Dublin by Diarmait and his English allies in late 1170 and the subsequent rebuff of counter-attacks by Ostmen and Irish forces in 1171 ended forever Ostman control of Dublin and its hinterland and severed the intermittent, century-old links with the town that the Manx kings had enjoyed. These facets are neatly encapsulated in the *Expugnatio Hibernica* of Giraldus Cambrensis, one of our most important, though not strictly contemporary, accounts of the English conquest written *c.*1189. Giraldus recounts how, after the fall of Dublin in 1170, many of the inhabitants led by their king, Áskell, 'went on board ship, taking their most precious belongings, and sailed off to the northern isles'.[23] Many probably never returned, although Áskell himself was back about six months later, around May Day 1171, at the head of a massive fleet to lead a sea-attack on Dublin; Giraldus relates his defeat and execution.[24] The significance of these events was not

G.F. Warner (8 vols London, 1861–91), v, 66 (*Topographia Hibernica*); the problem of terminology is reviewed by S. Duffy, *Ireland in the middle ages* (Dublin, 1997), 58–9. **21** S. Duffy, 'John and Ireland: the origins of England's Irish problem', in S.D. Church (ed.), *King John: new interpretations* (Woodbridge, 1999), 225. **22** The English conquest of Ireland has generated a considerable amount of historical literature; important modern studies are Duffy, *Ireland in the middle ages*, ch. 3–5; M.T. Flanagan, *Irish society, Anglo-Norman settlers, Angevin kingship: interactions in Ireland in the late twelfth century* (Oxford, 1989); F.J. Byrne, 'The trembling sod: Ireland in 1169', in A. Cosgrove (ed.), *New history of Ireland volume II: medieval Ireland, 1169–1534* (Oxford, 1987); R. Frame, *Colonial Ireland* (Dublin, 1981); and M. Dolley, *Anglo-Norman Ireland, c.1100–1318* (Dublin, 1972). An exemplary case study of English conquest and colonization in a specific region is B. Smith, *Colonisation and conquest in medieval Ireland: the English in Louth, 1170–1330* (Cambridge, 1999), while G.H. Orpen, *Ireland under the Normans 1169–1216* (4 vols, Oxford, 1911–20) remains a seminal work. **23** *Expugnatio Hibernica. The conquest of Ireland*, ed. and trans. A.B. Scott and F.X. Martin (Dublin, 1978), 68–9 [hereafter *Expugnatio*]. See also E. Purcell, 'The expulsion of the Ostmen, 1169–1171: the documentary evidence', *Peritia* 17–18 (2003–4), 276–94. **24** *Expugnatio*, 76–9. Both the *Expugnatio* of Giraldus and the late twelfth-century Anglo-Norman chronicle or *geste* (revised in the first half of the thirteenth century) usually known as 'The Song of Dermot and the Earl' recount the sea-attack on Dublin: *The deeds of the Normans in Ireland. La geste des Engleis en Yrlande. A new edition of the chronicle formerly known as The Song of Dermot and the Earl*, ed. E. Mullally (Dublin, 2002) [hereafter *Deeds*], ll. 2255–2492. The two accounts are in considerable agreement, but there are differences between them, the most significant of which is the

lost on the Manx king Guðrøðr Óláfsson, Rögnvaldr's father, who sent thirty galleys in support of the effort.[25] Giraldus, in relating these events, made the telling observation that 'Their fear of the threat of English domination, inspired by the successes of the English, made the men of the isles act all the more quickly'.[26] Giraldus's words are a potent reminder that the rise of English power in Ireland, on the left flank of the Manx sea-kings, represented a profound shift in the balance of power in the Irish Sea region, leaving the Manx kings to confront the reality of English might within sight to the east and west of the tiny Isle of Man. If the precedent of Hiberno-Manx relations in the eleventh and twelfth centuries was anything to go by, when Irish kings entertained ambitions in the Isles and when Manx kings entertained ambitions in Dublin,[27] the capture of Dublin by the English could lead to the extension of English power into the Irish Sea basin, a potentially threatening development for the Manx rulers. The English conquest of Ireland, which by 1171 was beginning to take on a look of permanence, was consequently, as Seán Duffy has perceptively remarked, 'looked on as a threat to the whole Irish Sea polity'.[28]

On the other hand, opportunities lost with the fall of Dublin to the English and the potential threat from the left flank might be offset with new ones presented by the English presence in Ireland; English advances did not in any event mean the complete severance of Manx ties with Ireland, merely a realignment. And this did not take long to occur. Notwithstanding his support for the foiled sea attack in 1171, within a decade – perhaps around 1180[29] – the Manx king Guðrøðr Óláfsson found a way to take advantage of the English presence when he married his daughter Affrica to John de Courcy, the conqueror of Ulster. The marriage represents a significant realignment of Manx interests in Ireland, and warrants closer examination.

* * *

John de Courcy's meteoric rise to prominence from relatively obscure origins has captivated both medieval and modern observers. Giraldus Cambrensis described him as one of the four great pillars in the English invasion, while his lightning conquest of Ulster in 1177 has been characterized by a modern scholar as 'one of the most extraordinary episodes in the Anglo-Norman invasion of Ireland'.[30] According to Giraldus, he set off from Dublin in

relationship of the naval attack to the unsuccessful siege of Dublin by Ruaidrí and his allies: in Giraldus the sea-attack precedes Ruaidrí's assault, but the *geste* has it follow: see *Expugnatio*, 304–5 note 106, where the chronology of Giraldus is preferred. Whichever sequence of events is accepted there is no doubt of Manx support for the attack. **25** *Expugnatio*, 78–9; Manx involvement mentioned in *Deeds*, ll. 2261, 2414. **26** *Expugnatio*, 78–9. **27** Good discussions of this phenomenon are Duffy, *Ireland in the middle ages*, 42–3 and 'Irishmen and Islesmen in the Isles'. **28** Duffy, 'Bruce brothers', 60. **29** *NHI*, *ii*, 116. **30** *Expugnatio*,

January 1177 with some twenty-two knights and three hundred others and invaded Ulaid (roughly modern Counties Antrim and Down), where various Irish kings struggled for supremacy. Within about six months he had overthrown an ancient Ulster dynasty and established himself in Downpatrick, from which he extended his sway over Ulaid by building castles, settling colonists, and establishing religious houses in a pattern well known to modern scholars.[31] By the mid-1180s de Courcy had reached the zenith of his career.[32] One crucial aspect of his lordship in Ulster was its maritime nature, which, in the words of Robin Frame, put him 'more readily in touch with south-western Scotland and the Isle of Man than with the south of Ireland'. One consequence of de Courcy's conquest, then, was that it brought with it involvement in the Irish Sea basin and ready-made contacts with the ruling dynasties in the southwest of Scotland and the Isle of Man.[33]

Such is the broad context for the marriage between Affrica of Man and John de Courcy. Historians, who have frequently commented upon the marriage, have tended to observe the ways in which it benefited de Courcy. G.H. Orpen, for example, regarded the marriage as one of the causes of de Courcy's success, arguing that it strengthened his position by securing his right flank and that it also gave him access to Manx resources.[34] Prime among those resources was, of course, the famous and formidable Manx fleet.[35] These aspects are difficult to dispute, particularly since, as things turned out, de Courcy did obtain support from his brother-in-law Rögnvaldr, although this occurred some twenty-five years later, in 1205. Like Orpen,[36] I would not rule out the possibility of earlier Manx assistance to de Courcy; but Irish aid may also have flowed to Rögnvaldr, who is said to have utilized Irish warriors for military operations in northern Scotland around 1200.[37] Less speculative is consideration of the marriage from the Manx perspective, and it has been suggested that de Courcy's decision to invade Ulaid was bound up with the involvement of the Isles in Irish affairs as much as it was with the Anglo-Norman invasion of Ireland. This is because the Manx kings had a long history of enmity with Ulaid,[38] while simultaneously being allied with the

180–1; S. Duffy, 'The first Ulster plantation: John de Courcy and the men of Cumbria', in T.B. Barry, R. Frame and K. Simms (eds), *Colony and frontier in medieval Ireland: essays presented to J.F. Lydon*, ed. (London, 1995), 1. **31** *Expugnatio*, 174–81; R. Bartlett, *The making of Europe: conquest, colonization and cultural change, 950–1350* (Princeton, 1993), 32–3 for de Courcy; see also T.E. McNeill, *Anglo-Norman Ulster: the history and archaeology of an Irish barony, 1177–1400* (Edinburgh, 1980), 3–20. **32** Good examinations of de Courcy's career are Orpen, *Normans*, ii, 5–23,109–18; Dolley, *Anglo-Norman Ireland*, 64–8, 91–103, 105–8; Frame, *Colonial Ireland*, 26–9; *NHI*, ii, 114–6 and 135–6; Duffy, 'The first Ulster plantation', passim. The quotation is from McNeill, *Anglo-Norman Ulster*, 6. **33** Frame, *Colonial Ireland*, 27–8, quotation at 27. **34** Orpen, *Normans*, ii, 18–19. **35** *NHI*, ii, 135; Dolley, *Anglo-Norman Ireland*, 87. **36** Orpen, *Normans*, ii, 19. **37** *Orkneyinga Saga*, ed. F. Guðmundsson (Reykjavík, 1965), 293 (ch. 110). **38** See F.J. Byrne, *Irish kings and high kings* (London, 1973), 109–10; Byrne

Meic Lochlainn of Cenél nEógain; and it will be remembered that King Guðrøðr Óláfsson, the father of Affrica and Rögnvaldr, had taken first as a concubine and later as an ecclesiastically sanctioned wife (in 1177) a daughter or grand-daughter of Mac Lochlainn. As Seán Duffy has aptly put it, 'Whatever de Courcy's own hopes and intentions, his intrusion into Ulaid was almost certainly used by the king of the Isles as a means of settling an old score'.[39]

For her part, Affrica Guðrøðarsdóttír deserves to be remembered as more than a mere matrimonial pawn on the chessboard of Irish Sea power-politics. She is significant in her own right as one of the few women – perhaps, in fact, the only woman – of the Crovan dynasty known to us as more than a mere name. Neither the date of her birth nor death is known, although she outlived her husband. De Courcy's charter of dower to Affrica survives (of considerable interest because of the survey of Ulster lands it contains), and in September 1219 the Irish justiciar was ordered to provide her with her widow's dower.[40] Affrica is, however, principally famous as the founder, in 1193, of the Cistercian Grey Abbey (Jugum Dei), on the Ards peninsula, a daughter of Holm Cultram in Cumberland; this house has been described as the 'most famous religious foundation dating from this era' in Ireland.[41] It was here, according to the *Manx chronicle*, that Affrica was buried, although the date of her death is not recorded.[42] Tradition relates that the stiff recumbent effigy of a woman in a tunic with her hands folded in prayer is hers, but the style of carving suggests a late thirteenth- or early fourteenth-century date; if this is Affrica, it must be a commemorative effigy made long after her death.[43] As a Manx princess and a sister of Rögnvaldr Guðrøðarsson who was wedded to the Anglo-Norman warrior John de Courcy, as well as a patroness of the reformed religious orders in Ireland, Affrica Guðrøðarsdóttír illustrates clearly some of the ways the Manx ruling élite came to terms with the

observes, 112, that the Ulaid kings were more inclined to seafaring than most of the Irish. 39 Duffy, 'Bruce brothers', 67–8. 40 J. Otway-Ruthven, 'Dower charter of John de Courcy's wife', *Ulster Journal of Archaeology* 12 (1949), 77–81; *Monumenta de Insula Manniae or a collection of national documents relating to the Isle of Man*, ed. and trans. J.R. Oliver, 3 vols (Douglas, 1860–2), vol. 2 [hereafter *Monumenta*] ii, 48 for order of 1219. Oliver's work provides ready access to many documents of Manx history, but some are misdated and others are omitted: see note 71 below. 41 *CRMI*, fo. 41r; A. Gwynn and R.N. Hadcock, *Medieval religious houses: Ireland* (Dublin, 1970, repr. 1988), 134; R. Stalley, *The Cistercian monasteries of Ireland: an account of the history, art and architecture of the white monks in Ireland from 1142 to 1540* (London, 1987); Archaeological Survey of Northern Ireland, *An archaeological survey of County Down* (Belfast, 1966), 275–8. Quotation from S. Duffy, 'Courcy [Courci], John de (d.1219?)', *Oxford Dictionary of National Biography*, Oxford University Press, 2004: http://www.oxforddnb.com/view/article/6443, accessed 15 December 2005. 42 *CRMI*, fo.41r. 43 J. Hunt, with assistance and contributions from P. Harbison, *Irish medieval figure sculpture, 1200–1600: a study of Irish tombs with notes on costume and armour* 2 vols (Dublin, 1974), i, 133–4 and ii, plate 22; Stalley, *Cistercian monasteries of Ireland*, 209–10, suggests an early fourteenth-century date.

profound political and social transformations taking place in the Irish Sea basin in the late twelfth and early thirteenth centuries.[44]

* * *

By the early years of the thirteenth century de Courcy's career was approaching its nadir; the reasons for his fall, however, remain unclear and problematic.[45] What is certain is that following a confused series of intrigues, raids, battles, and negotiations between 1201 and 1204, de Courcy was driven from Ireland by early 1205 and Ulster was awarded to Hugh de Lacy in early May of that year. Sometime in 1205 – whether before or after de Lacy's investiture in May is uncertain – de Courcy therefore rebelled and fled to the Isle of Man. Here is what the Manx Chronicle relates in its entry for 1205:

> In the year 1205 John de Courcy regained his strength and collected a massive force, and also took with him Reginald [i.e., Rögnvaldr] King of the Isles with about a hundred ships to Ulster. When they landed at the haven called Strangford they laid siege to the castle of Rath in a leisurely manner. However, Walter de Lacy arrived on the scene with a large army and put them to flight in great confusion.[46]

The episode is also recorded in the Annals of Loch Cé, which state that 'No good resulted from this expedition, however; but the country was destroyed and plundered; and they afterwards departed without obtaining power'.[47]

The castle called 'Rath' by the chronicle is almost certainly the fortress at Dundrum, the ruins of which include portions that probably date to the early years of the thirteenth century – ironically, perhaps constructed by de Courcy himself.[48] The castle, however, evidently withstood the assault. It is tempting, given the close geographical proximity, to connect the plundering mentioned in the annals with the praise-poem's reference to predatory activities around Dundalk, but so much is mere speculation. More certain is that for de Courcy the unsuccessful siege of Dundrum marked the end of his bid for restoration. As the Manx chronicler succinctly put it following the description of the failed attack, 'From that time on John de Courcy never recovered his estate'.[49] Indeed, his movements after this time are difficult to trace; it is certain that he was never restored to his lands in Ulster and lived out the rest of his life as a royal pensioner, virtually disappearing from history.[50]

44 For more on Affrica and her place in Irish Sea history see McDonald, *Manx kingship*, esp. 125–8. 45 *NHI*, ii, 135–6; see also Orpen, *Normans*, ii, 136–44. 46 *CRMI*, fo. 41r. 47 *Annals of Loch Cé*, ed. and trans. W.M. Hennessy (2 vols, London, 1871), i, 234–5 (s.a. 1205). 48 *NHI*, ii, 755 49 *CRMI*, fo.41r. 50 S. Duffy, 'Courcy [Courci], John de (d.1219?)', *Oxford Dictionary of National Biography*, Oxford University Press, 2004: http://www.oxforddnb.com/view/article/6443, accessed 15 December 2005.

Contrary to what might be expected, however, de Courcy's fall does not seem to have brought with it negative consequences for his brother-in-law and ally, the Manx king. In fact, it can be argued that Rögnvaldr's connections with de Courcy brought him new opportunities. For one thing, there can be little doubt that Rögnvaldr's relationship with John de Courcy and his involvement in Irish affairs and Anglo-Irish baronial politics led in turn to contacts with the English kings John (1199–1216) and Henry III (1216–72), and it is his relations with these kings that dominate the second half of his reign. Evidence for relations between the English and Manx rulers prior to about 1200 is sparse, although connections did exist. The Manx Chronicle, for example, relates that Óláfr, the son of Guðrøðr Crovan, was reared at the English court of Henry I (1100–35), and English financial documents show that Óláfr's son, Guðrøðr, received some financial assistance from Henry II whilst in exile in the late 1150s.[51] But these sporadic contacts were replaced, in Rögnvaldr's reign, by much more substantial and regular ones that can be traced from 1205 and that remained firmly in place until the end of the dynasty in 1265.

It may be no coincidence that the first evidence of contact between Rögnvaldr and John dates from the very same year that Rögnvaldr supported de Courcy in his bid for restoration.[52] On 8 February 1205, King John received Rögnvaldr under his protection: 'know that we have taken our beloved kinsman, Reginald, King of Man, under our keeping, protection, and defence, and all his lands and people. And we forbid any person to inflict injury or annoyance upon him or his, wherefore if any offence be committed against him, we will reckon the same done to ourself'.[53] One year later, John issued a safe conduct for Rögnvaldr to come to England for fifteen days at Easter in 1206.[54] On 28 April 1206, John ordered the sheriff of Lancaster to assign thirty marcates of land to Rögnvaldr, and English financial records

51 *CRMI*, fo. 35r; *The great rolls of the pipe for the second, third, and fourth years of the reign of King Henry II, A.D. 1155, 1156, 1157, 1158*, ed. J. Hunter (London, 1844), 155, 168 [hereafter *Pipe Rolls Henry II*]. 52 On the other hand, it is worth noting that the English records known as Letters Close and Letters Patent which contain most of the evidence for the relations between Manx and England rulers only commence in 1204 and 1201–2 respectively, and although it is likely that this represents the inception of these particular forms of record-keeping, the possibility of earlier connections and contacts that do not now survive in the record cannot be entirely ruled out. In other words, what appears to be the inception of diplomatic relations between Rögnvaldr and John may only represent the earliest surviving documented evidence. For further discussion of the nature of Letters Close and Patent see the introductions to *Rotuli litterarum clausarum in turri Londinensi asservati*, ed. T.D. Hardy, 2 vols (London, 1833–44) [hereafter *Rot. Lit. Claus.*] and *Rotuli litterarum patentium in turri Londinensi asservanti*, ed. T.D. Hardy, 2 vols (London, 1835) [hereafter *Rot. Lit. Pat.*]. 53 *Foedera: conventiones, literae et cujuscunque generis acta publica, inter reges Angliae et alios quosvis imperatores*, ed. T. Rymer (10 vols, Hagae Comitis, 1739–45), vol. i, pt i, 44 [hereafter Rymer, *Foedera*]; *Monumenta*, ii, 25. 54 Rymer, *Foedera*, i, pt. i, 44; *Monumenta*, ii, 26.

from 1205 to 1209 seem to show that the king's orders were indeed carried out.[55]

Remarkably, then, it would appear that far from being dragged down with de Courcy, Rögnvaldr actually benefited in the years after 1205: courted by King John, he was wooed with gifts of land and money and received the protection of the English king, beginning a longstanding relationship that saw him visit England on several occasions. Why should this have been so? Unquestionably King John, like de Courcy, recognized the strategic value of an ally in the Isle of Man for guarding the right flank of the English in Ireland. By cementing the friendship and goodwill of the Manx king, King John effectively removed the possibility of a threat from the Isle of Man and secured freedom of operation in the northern Irish Sea basin; he also acquired an ally with a formidable fleet of ships who was willing and able to patrol the Irish Sea and to guard the coasts of both England and Ireland (see further below).[56] Moreover, the evolving relationship between Rögnvaldr and John may also need to be considered within the context of the disintegrating relationship between John and Hugh de Lacy in Ulster: de Lacy found himself falling foul of John in the years between 1205 and 1210 and was driven out in 1210 as part of the famous Irish campaign in that year. Given the enmity that existed between de Courcy and de Lacy, Rögnvaldr may have represented a natural ally of the English king in any case.

The compiler of the Manx Chronicle, however, knew nothing of Rögnvaldr's contacts with the English king between 1205 and 1209. In its folios a single entry covers the years 1205 to 1210. It commences with the attack of de Courcy and Rögnvaldr on 'Rath' and concludes with this mention of King John's famous expedition to Ireland in 1210: 'The same year John King of England took a fleet of five hundred ships to Ireland, and he subjected the place to his sway. He then sent part of his army with a certain earl called Fuco to Man, where in a fortnight they laid waste almost the whole island. They took hostages from there and returned to their own country. Reginald and his nobles, however, were not in Man'.[57] It is tempting, given the arrangement in the Manx Chronicle, to read these events as cause-and-effect and to draw the conclusion that Rögnvaldr's support for de Courcy had earned him the wrath of King John,[58] but in reality, as the diplomatic contacts just discussed seem

55 *The Lancashire pipe rolls of 31 Henry I., A.D. 1130, and of the reigns of Henry II., A.D. 1155–1189; Richard I., A.D. 1189–1199; and King John, A.D. 1199–1216. The Latin text extended and notes added. also early Lancashire charters of the period from the reign of William Rufus to that of King John*, ed. W. Farrer (Liverpool, 1902), 199, 206 [hereafter *Lancashire Pipe Rolls*]; *Rot. Lit. Claus.*, i, 68; *Monumenta*, ii, 28. 56 For the military power of the Manx kings see R.A. McDonald, 'Dealing death from Man: Manx sea power in and around the Irish Sea, 1079–1265', in S. Duffy (ed.), *The world of the galloglass* (Dublin, 2007), 45–76. 57 *CRMI*, fos. 41r–v. 58 W.C. MacKenzie, *History of the Outer Hebrides (Lewis, Harris, North and South Uist, Benbecula, and Barra)* (Paisley, 1903, repr. Edinburgh, 1974), 31.

to show, the situation was much more complex than that and involved a complicated diplomatic, political and military situation that embraced not just Man, England and Ireland but that also, by the early years of the thirteenth century, had widened to embrace Norway as well.

King John's expedition to Ireland in 1210 has been widely discussed, although its implications for the Isle of Man remain largely unexplored. John's benevolence towards Rögnvaldr in the years between 1205 and 1207 makes it difficult to regard the ravaging of Man in 1210 as straightforward retribution for Rögnvaldr's role in the affairs of Ulster five years earlier. In fact, baronial politics may have played some role in these events. By 1210 not only the de Lacys but also the de Braose family had fallen foul of John in Ireland in circumstances that remain unclear, and one reason for John's famous Irish campaign was the taming of these noble families. Various sources relate the flight of William de Braose, his wife Matilda, and his family to Ireland in 1208, where the de Lacys harboured them. When John arrived in Ireland in June 1210, this was cause for Matilda and her sons to flee 'towards Scotland by sea', where they were subsequently captured in Galloway. The *Histoire des Ducs de Normandie*, an important and contemporary source from 1199 to 1220, records the vital detail that Matilda and William fled from Ireland to Scotland via the Isle of Man.[59] Perhaps, then, the ravaging of Man related in the Manx Chronicle is to be connected with these events. More difficult to say is whether the Manx king himself would have sanctioned the arrival of the de Braose refugees. In light of their affiliations with the de Lacys, the family responsible for driving John de Courcy out of Ulster in 1205, this seems unlikely, and might account for the short duration of their stay in Man. English financial records also show payment to Richard de Muroil for guarding the English king's supplies in the Isle of Man in 1210, suggesting that Man may have been used as a supply depot and further highlighting the strategic value of the island.[60]

There is also a Norwegian dimension to the events of 1210 – one that is not easy to discern, but that hinges upon references in Icelandic annals and two versions of the early thirteenth-century *Böglunga sögur* to a Norwegian military expedition to the Hebrides and Irish Sea in 1209–10 during a break in the ongoing Norwegian civil war. One objective of this expedition may have been a desire for plunder, but it may also have been connected with a reassertion of long-dormant Norwegian hegemony in the western oceans. One version of the saga records that the jointly-ruling Orkney earls were forced to

59 *Early sources*, ii, 387; various accounts of these events are conveniently collected here at 383–7. See also B.W. Holden, 'King John, the Braoses, and the Celtic Fringe, 1207–1216', *Albion* 33:1 (Spring 2001), 1–23. **60** *Rotuli de liberate ac de misis et praestitis, regnante Johanne*, ed. T.D. Hardy (London, 1844), 209; *Calendar of documents relating to Ireland preserved in Her Majesty's Public Record Office, London*, ed. H.S. Sweetman (5 vols,

pay tribute to the king of Norway, while another version relates, tellingly, how King Rögnvaldr and Godfrey (probably his son), both described as kings in the Hebrides and Man, also voyaged to Norway, paid tribute, and swore obedience.[61] The longer version of the saga (which survives only in a Danish translation of *c.*1600) provides important clues:

> Rögnvaldr, king of Möen in the Hebrides [*Konge aff Möen i Syderö*], and Godfrey, king over the island of Man [*Konge paa Manö*], had not for a long time given taxes to the kings in Norway. When the Norwegian vikings had now swarmed there about the island, and plundered and burned; and when the kings understood that there was peace made in Norway, they were afraid, and went to Norway, and reconciled themselves with King Ingi and Earl Hákon, and paid the tax that stood over; and swore them loyalty and obedience, and took their lands in fief of the king of Norway; and so went home again.[62]

Although the titles are confused, perhaps the result of (understandable) geographical bewilderment on the part of the saga-man, perhaps as a result of the transmission of the text of the saga, Rögnvaldr 'king of Möen in the Hebrides' is almost certainly Rögnvaldr Guðrøðarsson.[63] Godfrey is probably Rögnvaldr's son of that name who appears in the Manx Chronicle and who may have had authority over part of the Isles by the early thirteenth century.[64] Also of interest here is the reference to the tax [ON *skattr*] that had been owed for a long time and that was paid to the king of Norway. This has been interpreted this as a tribute or payment made by a vassal to a feudal superior, and there are indications that such tributes had been rendered sporadically by the Manx rulers to the Norwegian kings in the twelfth century.[65]

One problem with the testimony of the saga is that there is no corroborating evidence for either a voyage to Norway by Rögnvaldr or for an attack on Man in 1209/10. Neither seems beyond the bounds of possibility, however,

London, 1875–86) i, no. 407 [hereafter *CDI*]. **61** *Íslenzkir Annálar* in *Sturlunga saga*, ed. G. Vigfusson. 2 vols (Oxford, 1878), ii, 366, 367 (s.a. 1209, 1210); 'Böglunga Sögur', in *Konunga Sögur*, ed. G. Jónsson, 3 vols (Reykjavík, 1957), ii, 388–9; trans. in *Early sources*, ii, 378–81. **62** *Fornmanna Sögur*, ed. C.C. Rafn, 12 vols (Copenhagen, 1825–37), ix, 194; trans. *Early sources*, ii, 381. **63** E.J. Cowan, 'Norwegian sunset – Scottish dawn: Hakon IV and Alexander III', in N. Reid (ed.), *Scotland in the reign of Alexander III, 1249–1286* (Edinburgh, 1990), 112–13, suggests this might be Raghnall, son of Somerled, rather than Rögnvaldr Guðrøðarsson, although this does not seem likely to me. **64** *CRMI*, fos. 42v–43r; 44v. **65** A.O. Johnsen, 'The payments from the Hebrides and Isle of Man to the crown of Norway 1153–1263', *SHR* 48 (1969), 18–34; see also K. Helle, 'Norwegian consolidation and expansion during the reign of King Håkon Håkonsson', *Orkney Miscellany* 5 (Kirkwall, 1973), 7–16 at 9; and there is much of value on this topic in an Orkney context in S. Imsen, 'Earldom and kingdom: Orkney in the realm of Norway 1195–1379', in D.J. Waugh (ed.), *The faces of Orkney: stones, skalds and saints* (Edinburgh,

and the reference in the *Manx chronicle* to the absence of Rögnvaldr and his nobles in 1210 may be a veiled allusion to the Norwegian journey mentioned in the saga. Faced with what may have appeared as a dramatic resurgence of Norwegian hegemony, the likes of which had not been seen in over a century, Rögnvaldr may indeed have done as the saga states and journeyed to Norway. If so, this might have been the incentive for King John to launch a punitive expedition to the Isle of Man, since Rögnvaldr had, only a few years earlier, seemingly become a vassal of the English king. In essence, then, Rögnvaldr was experiencing a classic case of divided allegiances, something not uncommon among the rulers in the isles between Britain and Ireland in the thirteenth century and shared, for example, by the Hebridean chieftains who experienced the same problem with Scottish and Norwegian monarchs.[66] Whatever the case, it is difficult to avoid the conclusion that the year 1210 represented a watershed in the external relations of the Manx kingdom, signalling both the potential and the threat that faced the lords of a tiny island in the Irish Sea as the ambitions of northern superpowers waxed in the region.

* * *

Perhaps as a result of the events of 1210, the years 1210–15 saw Rögnvaldr move more perceptibly into an English orbit; English power, after all, remained closer to hand than Norwegian, and offered not only the potential for protection but also lucrative rewards. In a charter dated at Lambeth on 16 May 1212, Rögnvaldr announced, 'To all the faithful in Christ, who may inspect this present charter, Reginald, King of the Islands, greeting. Know that I have become liegeman of our lord, John, King of England, against all men, as long as I shall live, and that I have performed fealty, and oath to him'.[67] Three further documents, all with the same date, reveal some of the ramifications of Rögnvaldr's homage.[68] In the first, King John ordered that some of Rögnvaldr's people held in custody at Porchester and at Dover should be released, though the reasons for their incarceration are not disclosed.[69] A second document is more telling still. In it King John ordered his officials in Ireland to assist King Rögnvaldr against any 'wikini' – vikings – harassing him in his territories.[70] By a third document Rögnvaldr received a grant of a knight's fee in Carlingford:

2003), 65–80, esp. 77–8. **66** Johnsen, 'Payments', 18–34 at 24; also McDonald, *Kingdom*, ch. 4, and R. Power, 'Meeting in Norway: Norse-Gaelic relations in the kingdom of Man and the Isles, 1090–1270', *Saga Book* 29 (2005), 5–66. **67** Rymer, *Foedera*, i, pt. i, 51; *Rotuli chartarum in Turri londinensi asservati vol I pars I Ab anno MCXCIX ad annum MCCXVI*, ed. T.D. Hardy (London, 1837), 191 [hereafter *Rot. Chart*]; *Monumenta*, ii, 31–2. **68** Though dated by Oliver to 1213, these documents seem to me clearly belong to 1212: see note 71 below. **69** *Rot. Lit. Claus.*, i, 116; *Monumenta*, ii, 33. **70** *Rot. Lit. Pat.*, 92b; *Monumenta*, ii, 34.

> John, by the grace of God ... know that we have given, and by this our present charter confirmed to Reginald, King of Man, for his homage and service, one knight's fee in Ireland, at Karlingford, on the sea, in the province of Ulster ... together with one hundred measures of corn to be paid yearly at Drogheda, to have and to hold, to him and his heirs, of us and our heirs, for a service fee of one knight.[71]

Finally, on 3 January 1214, King John once again took Rögnvaldr under his protection, prohibiting his 'mariners of Ireland' from entering Manx territory, and demonstrating that he took his obligations seriously.[72]

The drawing of the Manx king into an English sphere of influence is evident in these documents, but several aspects of the relationship require elucidation. It has, for instance, been argued that Rögnvaldr was seeking an ally in the struggle with his brother Óláfr for the kingship that occupied much of Rögnvaldr's reign.[73] But since Óláfr was in Scottish custody between 1208 and late 1214,[74] this can hardly have been a foremost consideration. In fact, it seems much more likely that it was the Norwegian expedition of 1210 and the resurgence of Norwegian power that it symbolized that thrust Rögnvaldr into an English orbit.[75] This interpretation may be seen most tellingly in King John's command to his officials in Ireland to assist Rögnvaldr against the *wikini*, that is, vikings,[76] almost certainly a reference to Norwegian pirates and no doubt recalling the raiders who descended upon the Hebrides and Irish Sea in 1210. Whoever the *wikini* of the document were, it reveals clearly one of the benefits for Rögnvaldr of becoming a vassal of the English king. The relationship was a reciprocal one, however. Rögnvaldr, as this same document also emphasizes, was required to help keep the coasts of England and Ireland free from pirates. A clearer idea of what this might have entailed is gained from a similar commission awarded to Rögnvaldr's brother, rival, and eventual successor Óláfr in 1235. Óláfr was to guard, 'at his own cost, the coast of the sea of England towards Ireland, and towards the Isle of Man, and likewise the coast of the sea of Ireland towards England, and towards the aforesaid Isle of

71 *Rot. Chart.*, 186b. Oliver, *Monumenta*, ii, 35–6, misdated this to 1213. The regnal year 14 John encompassed 3 May 1212 to 22 May 1213, but the dating of the document to 1212 seems to be proven by the place-date of 16 May at Lambeth, identical with the others in the sequence discussed above. 72 *Rot. Lit. Pat.*, 108; *Monumenta*, ii, 37. 73 *CRMI*, fos. 41v–44v, deals with this feud; see R.A. McDonald, '"Disharmony between Reginald and Óláfr": The feud between the sons of Guðrøðr II and kin-strife in the kingdom of Man and the Isles, 1079–1265', in B.T. Hudson (ed.), *Household and familia in the medieval Atlantic region* (forthcoming). 74 *CRMI*, fo. 42r, says that Óláfr was imprisoned for seven years and was released upon the death of King William, which occurred in December 1214. 75 *Chronica regum Manniae et Insularum: the chronicle of Man and the Sudreys*, ed. and trans. P.A. Munch and Revd Dr. Goss (Douglas, 1874), 184 n. 31. 76 R.E. Latham, *Revised medieval Latin word-list from British and Irish sources* (London, 1965), 522; the translation 'villagers' offered in *CDI*, i, no. 429 makes no sense in this context.

Man, lest injury might happen to the aforesaid our lands of England and Ireland, by sea, upon these coasts, according to his ability'.[77]

The grant of Irish territory to the Manx ruler is significant for several reasons. In the first instance, it once again gave the Manx kings a territorial base in Ireland – something that had been enjoyed intermittently between 1079 and the 1150s – but with the difference that the focus shifted away from Dublin (by then under firm English control) and towards Ulster in the north. And the site itself was significant, since Carlingford, with its fine harbour, no doubt helped facilitate Manx patrols in the Irish Sea by giving Rögnvaldr and subsequent Manx kings a naval base in Ireland as well as in Man. Finally, this strategically significant fortified site had been the head of the de Lacy lordship. King John had seized Carlingford castle in July of 1210 and it was retained as a royal stronghold until 1226 when it was returned to Hugh de Lacy.[78] The award of a knight's fee in this vicinity to Rögnvaldr must therefore be fitted into the framework of the disintegration of de Lacy power in Ireland from 1210, and Rögnvaldr clearly had a role to play in this process. Given the enmity that existed between Rögnvaldr's brother-in-law John de Courcy and the de Lacys, the Manx king may have relished his acquisition of this particular piece of territory.

John's grant of lands at Carlingford to the king of Man and the Isles also needs to be considered against the broader backdrop of what McNeill described as the introduction of a 'second British element' to Ulster at around the same time, when grants were made along the north coast to the kindred of the powerful lords of Galloway in southwest Scotland.[79] In the most substantial of these, in 1212, Alan of Galloway (d. 1234) received a vast fief embracing all of north Co. Antrim from Larne to Coleraine as well as two cantreds across the Bann for the service of 140 knights' fees.[80] Rögnvaldr was, therefore, one of several external powers that established a presence in Ulster through English patronage in this period, and it is significant that the Manx king probably and the Galloway family certainly were active in military campaigns in Ulster and the Isles against political opponents of the English and Scottish kings between about 1212 and 1215.[81] Although there is no direct

77 *Foedera*, i, pt. i, 118; *Monumenta*, ii, 72–3. 78 Orpen, *Normans*, ii, 251–2. 79 McNeill, *Anglo-Norman Ulster*, 6; see also R. Oram, *The lordship of Galloway* (Edinburgh, 2000), 115–8; K.J. Stringer, 'Periphery and core in thirteenth-century Scotland: Alan, son of Roland, lord of Galloway and constable of Scotland', in A. Grant and K.J. Stringer (eds), *Medieval Scotland: crown, lordship and community* (Edinburgh, 1993), 82–113 at 85–8; J.R.H. Greeves, 'The Galloway lands in Ulster', *Transactions of the Dumfriesshire and Galloway Natural History & Antiquarian Society* 3rd ser. 36 (1957–8), 115–21. 80 *Calendar of documents relating to Scotland preserved in Her Majesty's Public Record Office, London*, ed. J. Bain et al., 5 vols (Edinburgh, 1881–1986), i, no. 573, dated May 1213 but shown by Stringer, 'Periphery and core', 86, to belong to 1212. 81 *AU*, ii, 252 (s.a. 1212), 256 (s.a. 1214); quotation from Stringer, 'Periphery and core', 88.

evidence of Rögnvaldr's involvement in these campaigns, given the maritime nature of the action involved it would scarcely be surprising if the Manx king, his fleets and his warriors had been involved – as at least one modern commentator thinks likely.[82] Whether that is the case or not, there can be little doubt that the tendrils of Anglo-Scottish Irish Sea diplomacy, which aimed at the pacification of turbulent, peripheral regions, had ensnared Rögnvaldr as well as the Galloways in the first years of the 1210s.

One aspect of the reign of King John that has exercised historians considerably in recent years is his relations with kings and princes in the Celtic parts of the British Isles. The loss of Normandy in 1204 meant that John was able to turn his attention to his Celtic neighbours in a way that his predecessors had not; as one scholar has remarked, 'No earlier king made himself so felt in the extremities of his realm as did King John'.[83] This is not the place to rehearse the evidence for this voluminous topic, which has been well explored elsewhere.[84] But it is worth noting that John had flexed his muscles in Scotland in 1209, Ireland in 1210, and Wales in 1211, and that in the years around 1210 Welsh, Scottish, and Irish rulers had all performed homage and fealty to him. Rögnvaldr's relationship with John therefore conforms to a well-established pattern of native rulers entering into increasingly well-defined relationships as vassals of the English monarch. At the same time, however, historians have seldom taken note of the Manx dimension to the topic. Ralph V. Turner's 1994 study of King John, for example, which considers the subject in an otherwise admirable and thorough discussion entitled 'John and the British Isles', makes no mention whatsoever of Rögnvaldr; the Manx ruler is also absent from R.R. Davies's 1990 pioneering study which took as its subject-matter the relations between England and its neighbours in the British Isles between 1100 and 1300 with particular reference to domination and subjugation.[85]

Rögnvaldr's relations with King John are important for a variety of reasons, not only because they form a largely neglected facet of the important subject of King John's relations with other rulers in the British Isles, but also for their political, military, and social ramifications. The late Professor Rees Davies pointed to the way in which diplomatic and political relations, usually

82 D. Brooke, *Wild men and holy places: St Ninian, Whithorn and the medieval realm of Galloway* (Edinburgh, 1994), 130. 83 W.L. Warren, *King John* (Berkeley, 1961, repr. 1978), 192. 84 Recently by D. Carpenter, *The struggle for mastery: Britain 1066–1284* (London, 2003), esp. ch. 9; see also Duffy, 'John and Ireland'; A.A.M. Duncan, 'John king of England and the kings of Scots'; and I. Williams, 'King John and Wales', in Church (ed.), *King John: new interpretations*, 221–45, 247–71, 273–87. 85 R.V. Turner, *King John* (Harlow, 1994), 135–46; R.R. Davies, *Domination and conquest: the experience of Ireland Scotland and Wales, 1100–1300* (Cambridge, 1990), esp. ch. 4; Rögnvaldr fares no better in Carpenter, *Struggle*, ch. 9. S. Painter, *The reign of King John* (Baltimore, 1949), 227, mentions the submission of the Manx king in passing.

involving, as in Rögnvaldr's case, visits to the English court, could lead to familiarity with contemporary trends in European culture: 'social visits were encouraged', writes Professor Davies, 'attention was lavished and flattery ladled in ample measure. By such means were men gradually attracted into the social orbit of the Normans and Angevins, to learn their manners and to ape their ways'.[86] One particularly fascinating by-product of the association of the Manx rulers from Rögnvaldr's time with the English kings John and Henry III was their increasing familiarity with the conventions of knighthood; there is no evidence that, despite holding a knight's fee, Rögnvaldr was actually knighted, but several of his successors in the later thirteenth century were certainly knighted by the English king,[87] showing one of the ways in which particular Continental or Anglo-Norman social and military conventions could be adopted by rulers on the political, if not geographical, margins of the British Isles.[88]

By the time of King John's death in 1216, a pattern of strong Manx links with England had been established that would endure down to the end of the Manx dynasty – the last Manx king, Magnús, was knighted by Henry III in 1256. As for Rögnvaldr, his English connection survived the death of King John, and although relations may have been strained for a short time after the succession of Henry III, a cordial tone was soon re-established, which endured through the 1220s.[89] Indeed, English support for Rögnvaldr forms an important component of the Manx war of the 1220s, as Rögnvaldr fought with his brother Óláfr for the prize of the Manx kingship – a prize that was eventually wrested from his grasp for good only with his death in 1229.[90]

* * *

The knighting of Manx rulers at the hands of English kings in the middle of the thirteenth century may at first glance appear far removed from the topic of the English conquest of Ireland and its impact upon Dublin-Manx relations. But this is precisely the point that emerges most forcefully from this investigation – namely, that the English presence in Ireland from the late 1160s had

86 Davies, *Domination*, 6. 87 *CRMI*, fos. 46r, 49r–49v for the knighting of Haraldr (d. 1248) and Magnús (d.1265) by Henry III; supported by documents in *Foedera*, I, i, 264; I, ii, 12. 88 The example could be multiplied many times over. The architecture of the new power-centre established in the Isle of Man around the end of the twelfth or beginning of the thirteenth century at Castle Rushen was almost certainly influenced by English models, possibly by way of Ireland: on Castle Rushen see P.J. Davey & A. Johnson, 'Medieval archaeology and architecture', in *NHIoM iii*, forthcoming; B.H. St J. O'Neil, 'Castle Rushen, Isle of Man', *Archaeologia* 94 (1951), 1–26; A. Rigby, *Castle Rushen: a historical and descriptive account* (1927); the subject is discussed in McDonald, *Manx kingship*. 89 *Rot. Lit. Claus*, i, 421, 564; ii, 139, 175. As late as April 1228 King Henry III of England was attempting to act as a peacemaker between the brothers: Rymer, *Foedera*, i, pt. i, 104. 90 *CRMI*, fos. 41v–44v details the struggle between the brothers.

implications that extended far beyond the coasts of Ireland and reverberated round the shores of the Irish Sea basin. The Manx kings, who were the most potent power in the islands between Britain and Ireland at the time, and who were also possessed of significant and longstanding links with Ireland, were inevitably and deeply affected by the English conquest. On the one hand, the English presence in Ireland brought an abrupt end to the old Dublin–Man axis of the eleventh and twelfth centuries as well as a very real danger of English domination in the Isles. But, on the other hand, thanks to the opportunism and, I would argue, a certain amount of cunning adaptation on the part of the Manx rulers (particularly Rögnvaldr), the challenges posed by an English presence on each flank were turned, in a remarkably short time, to new opportunities. Through the mutually beneficial marriage of a Manx princess to the English conqueror of Ulster, the Manx kings were led to political and social contacts with the English kings John and Henry III – contacts that not only proved lucrative in terms of gaining English patronage and protection, but that also resulted in a realignment of Manx interests in Ireland, from Dublin north to Ulster. Thus, while historians continue to debate the impact and significance of the English conquest upon Ireland from the late 1160s, examination of Hiberno-Manx relations in the decades following 1170 serves as a potent reminder that the English presence in Ireland sent shock waves resonating throughout the Irish Sea basin and profoundly altered the balance of power in the medieval British Isles. The kings of Man, who could have found themselves overwhelmed by this tidal surge of English might in the Irish Sea, managed to stay afloat – at least until they were eventually overwhelmed by another set of crises in the mid-1260s that brought about their subjugation to the Scots king in 1264 and, only a year later, with the death of Magnús in 1265, their extinction as a dynasty.[91]

91 *CRMI*, fo. 49v, records the death of Magnús at Castle Rushen on 24 November with surprisingly little comment as to the dynastic significance of the event; but compare *Continuatio Chronici Willelmi de Novoburgo ad annum 1298 (Annals of Furness)* in *Chronicles of the reigns of Stephen, Henry II, and Richard I*, ed. R. Howlett (4 vols, London, 1884–9), ii, 549, where Magnús's death is noted with the laconic comment that 'kings ceased to reign in Man'. A rebellion led by a son of Magnús in 1275 was quashed by the Scots: *CRMI*, fo. 50r.

The medieval city wall and the southern line of Dublin's defences: excavations at 14–16 Werburgh Street

LINZI SIMPSON

ABSTRACT

Recent investigations at a small site on the western side of Werburgh Street, Dublin 8, revealed a hitherto unknown section of the medieval city wall, which measures approximately 11m in length by 2.40m in height. A standing section was preserved as part of a 'Dutch Billy', a colloquial term for the redbrick houses built by the French and Flemish Protestant refuges who flocked into Dublin in the late seventeenth and early eighteenth centuries. On excavation, the foundations of the wall were found to be more expansive, extending on both sides in a stretch almost 11m long. Most importantly, the results of the excavation indicate that this new section can be identified as forming part of the Anglo-Norman rather than the Hiberno-Norse city wall circuit, confirming that there were two distinct and separate lines of defences, *c.*15m apart, at Werburgh Street, the first probably dating to between *c.*1100 and *c.*1125 and the second to sometime after 1170. The excavation also exposed the upper fill of the Anglo-Norman city moat at the southern end of the site.

INTRODUCTION

Nos 14–16 Werburgh Street represent a small but important site that straddles the line of the city defences, on the southern side of the city (figs 1, 2 and 3). The site is currently waste ground owned by Dublin City Council but there are proposals to develop the site sometime in the future. As a result, the brief of the archaeological investigations was to attempt to locate and identify any surviving remains pertaining to the defences, with a view to advising on a sensitive building-design layout. Two archaeological assessments were undertaken at the site and these established that, not only were foundations of the city wall surviving below ground level, but that a section survived within an existing stone wall, which until then had been presumed to be entirely eighteenth-century in date.

After a monitoring programme (1994) in the northeast corner of the site, the writer tentatively suggested that there were two walls in this location, a primary wall representing the Hiberno-Norse wall dating to between *c.*1100 and *c.*1125 and an Anglo-Norman rebuild dated to *c.*1170, which was sitting

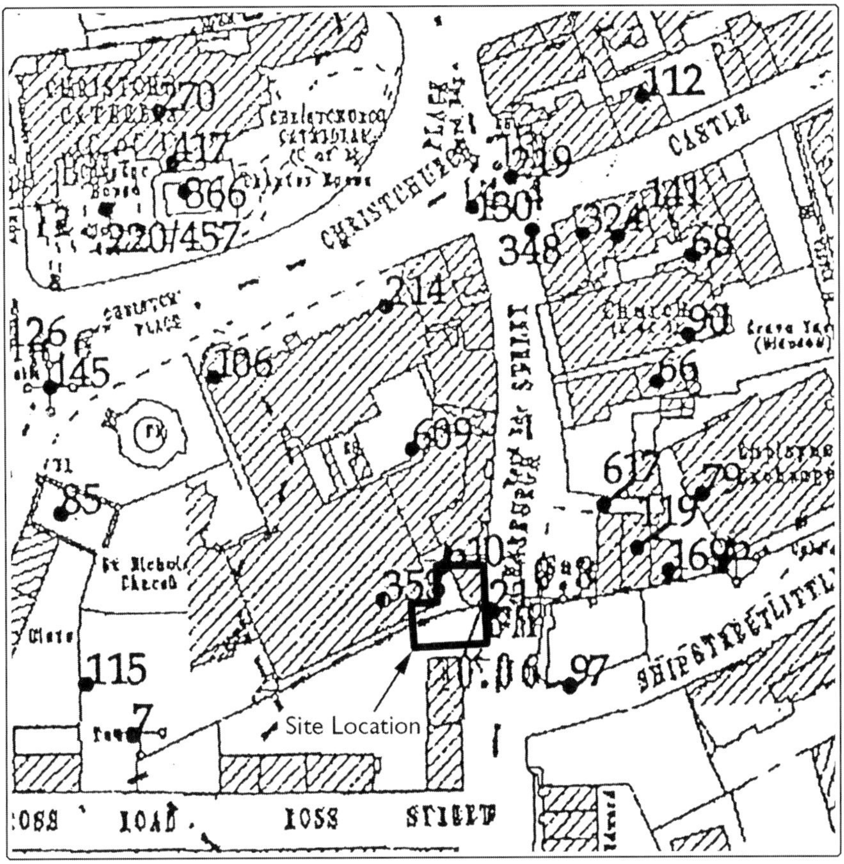

1 Site location

directly on top of it (see below). This conclusion was based on what appeared to be a change in the masonry at the base of this section of the wall, exposed during a piling operation. The western side of the site was assessed in 1998 (O'Rourke 1999: Licence no. 98E0081), and again by the writer in the following year, when two builds were again tentatively identified (Simpson 2000: Licence no. 99E0228) and dated similarly. However, the excavation under discussion clarified that the entire wall could be dated to the Anglo-Norman period. The excavation also located the remains, at foundation level, of a small domestic house (Building 1), probably dated to the late seventeenth/early eighteenth century, which was tacked onto the city wall, on the northern side. The excavation was carried out by the writer and Kevin Weldon in February 2000, under licence to the National Monuments and Architectural Protection Division, the Department of the Environment and Local Government (Licence no. 99E0228).

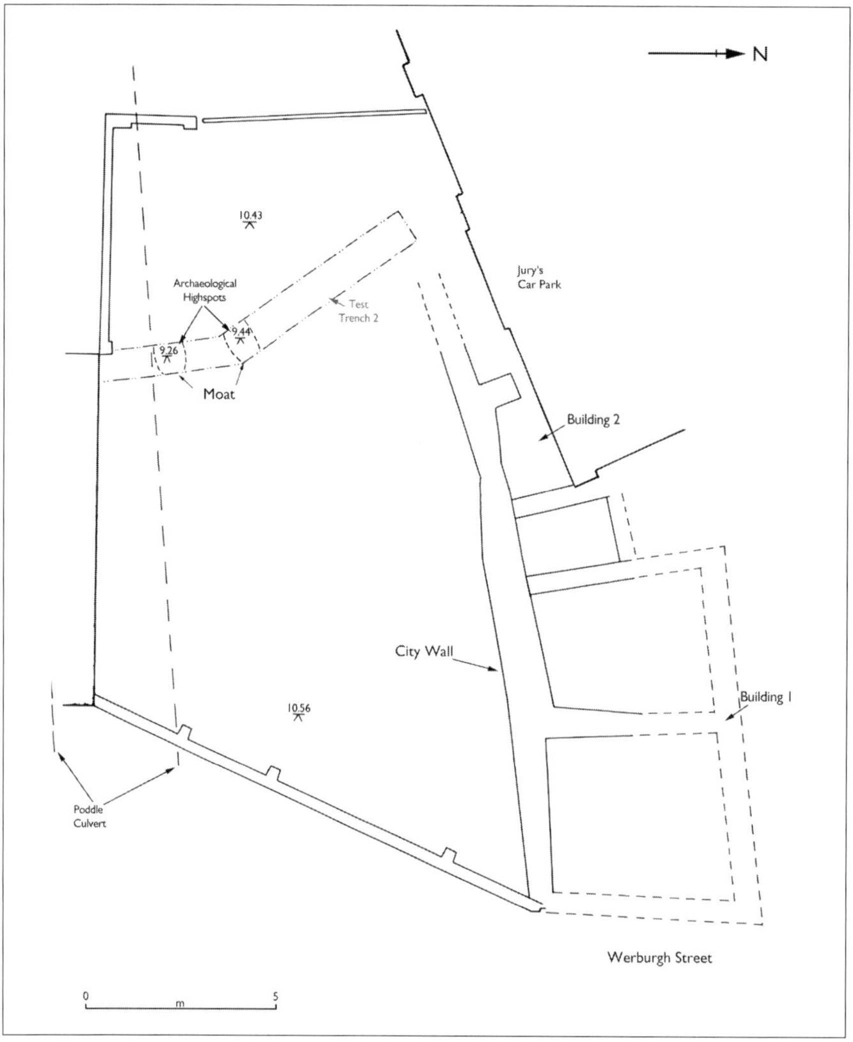

2 Detail of site location

HISTORICAL AND ARCHAEOLOGICAL BACKGROUND

The defences of Dublin

The city of Dublin was defended from an early date. Excavations in and around the city have revealed that, by the tenth century, the entire Viking-Age trading emporium was surrounded by a series of large earthen and clay banks, which were topped with strong palisade fences (Clarke 2002) (fig. 4). The banks were eventually replaced in the early twelfth century by a strong city

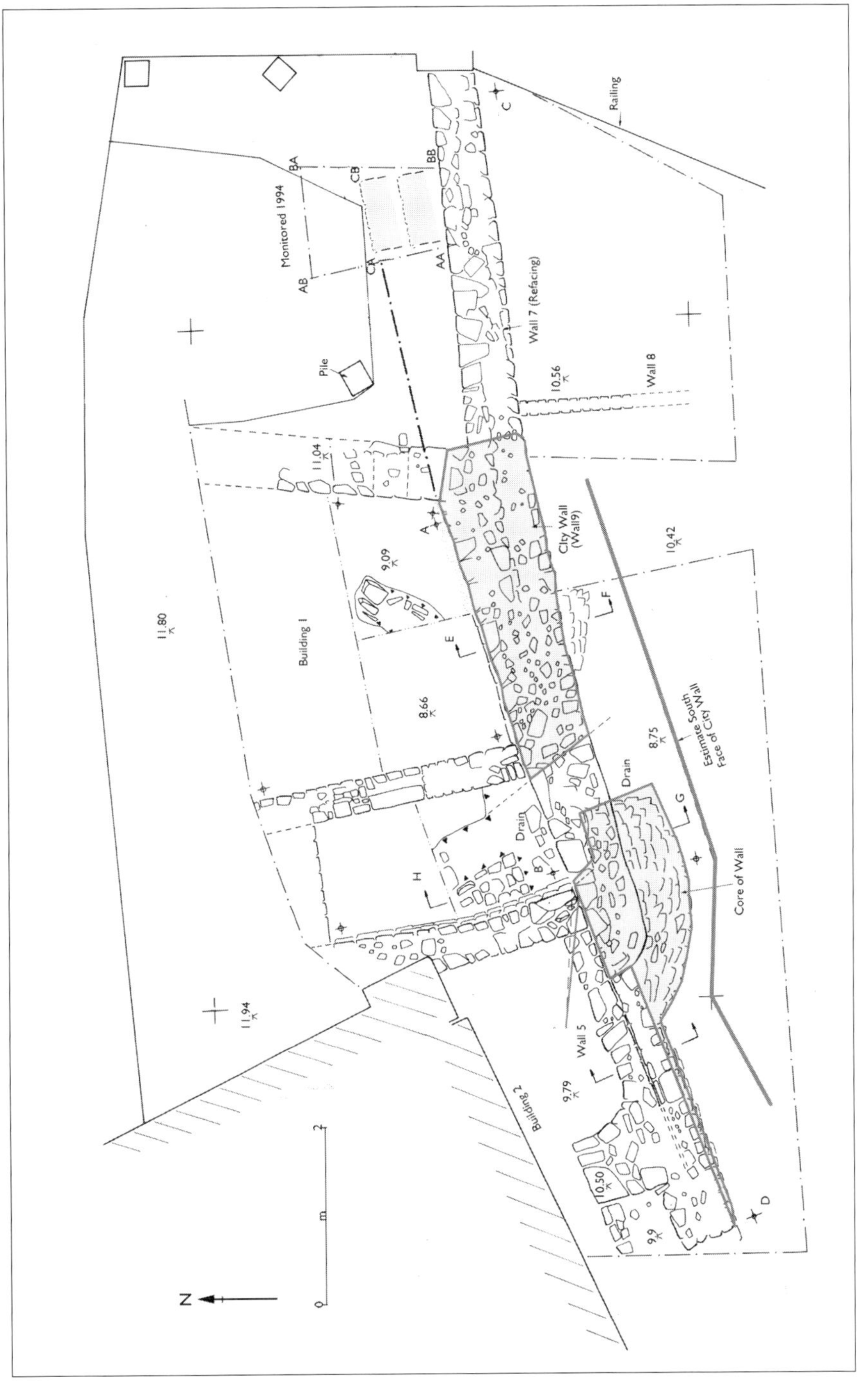

3 Excavated features

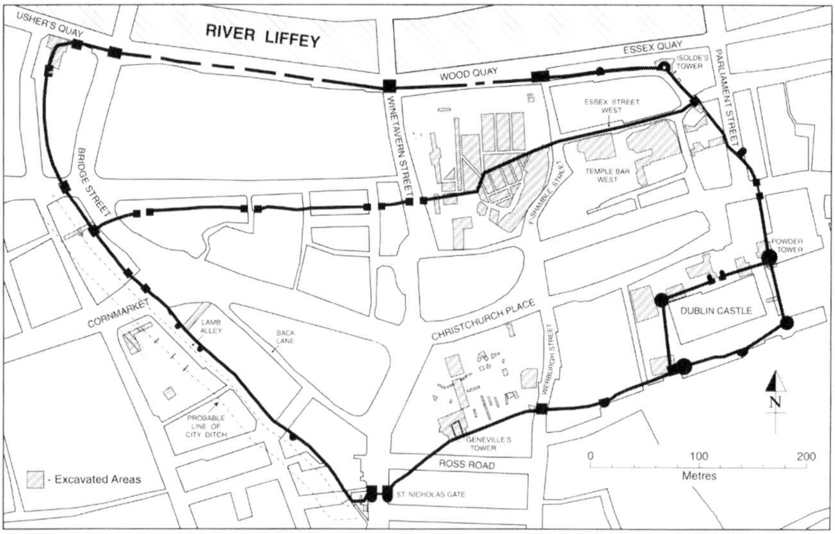

4 City wall circuit (after Walsh 2001)

wall, which completely enclosed the settlement and probably expanded the size of the defended area on the western side (Simpson 200a, 23–4). This city wall was substantially repaired and, in some places, rebuilt entirely in the late twelfth/early thirteenth century following Dublin's annexation by Anglo-Norman invaders. After considerable expansion of the port, the defended area was again extended on the northern side of the city when a new city wall was built in the mid- to late thirteenth century to protect the vulnerable quay area.

Sections of the various circuits still survive in the modern landscape, the best known at Cook Street, Wood Quay (within the Civic Offices), Isolde's Tower, Ship Street Little, Power's Square and Lamb Alley (Simpson 2006; Gowen 2004). Cook Street (*c.*1100–25) and Ship Street Little (*c.*1170), both aligned along important roads, represent significant stretches, which are generally intact, although the former has been much altered. Power's Square, however, is not as readily accessible or visible as it does not front onto a street and is hidden in various rear gardens.

The banks The banks enclosed an area which measured roughly 240m north-south by a similar width and encompassed the elevation of the landscape at Christchurch Place and Skinner's Row. A sequence of three or four successive banks, spanning a period running from the mid- to late tenth to the early twelfth century, have been identified through numerous excavations at various locations including Fishamble Street, Winetavern Street, Dublin Castle, Parliament Street and Werburgh Street (Simpson 200a, 27–8). The most relevant large-scale excavation to the site under discussion lay to the west, at Ross Road (1993), where Claire Walsh located a sequence of four clay banks culminating in a substantial embankment that finally measured at least 6m high by 4m in width (Walsh 2001, 88–127) (figs 5 and 6). The embankment survived almost in its entirety, displaying an evolution from a small bank, dated to the early tenth century, to a large defensive rampart, which was on an elevated site above the Poddle river. The original bed of the latter was also located during the excavation (ibid., 98). More significantly, Walsh also noted what may have been an even earlier bank located 10m to the north of her embankment, which was exposed during previous excavations by the National Museum of Ireland. This, she suggests, may have been the remnants of some sort of earthwork set on the slope above the Poddle which was possibly late ninth-century in date (ibid., 96)

A smaller but very important excavation was also carried out by Hayden in 1994, a short distance to the north of the site under discussion (at the entrance to what is now the Jury's Inn car-park; Hayden 2002, 44–68), within the medieval town (fig. 6). This, as expected, revealed a complicated sequence of Viking-Age domestic habitation levels, possibly dating, at the earliest levels, to the first quarter of the tenth century. A number of post-and-wattle houses were uncovered, which had associated fences, pathways and rubbish pits and these fronted onto and respected the line of present-day Werburgh Street, suggesting that this street was in existence by this date. Perhaps more importantly for this paper, Hayden also identified a section of the earthen embankment at the southern end of the site, which provides an anchor-point for the early town defences on this side.

Although the full footprint of the embankment was not within the excavation cutting, the clay bank that survived measured at least 3m wide by 750mm in height and had a slot trench, which held a palisade fence along the internal (i.e., northern) side. The structure was surprisingly early in the sequence of deposits at Werburgh Street and was dated by Hayden to the late ninth or early tenth century (Hayden 2002, 47, 66). This raised the possibility that it either represents a continuation of the early bank located during the National Museum excavations or that it forms part of the embankment located by Walsh. Either way, the defences on this side of the settlement appear to be early in the sequence.

The position of the embankment found by Hayden is very crucial to any study of the southern defences as, prior to this, they were presumed to follow the line of the surviving stretch of wall along Ship Street Little, to the east of the site under discussion. This route is also defined by the break in the slope (from north to south) in the existing topography, which is most marked just north of the junction of Werburgh Street and Ship Street Little. However, if Hayden's findings are correct this now indicates that the early line of the

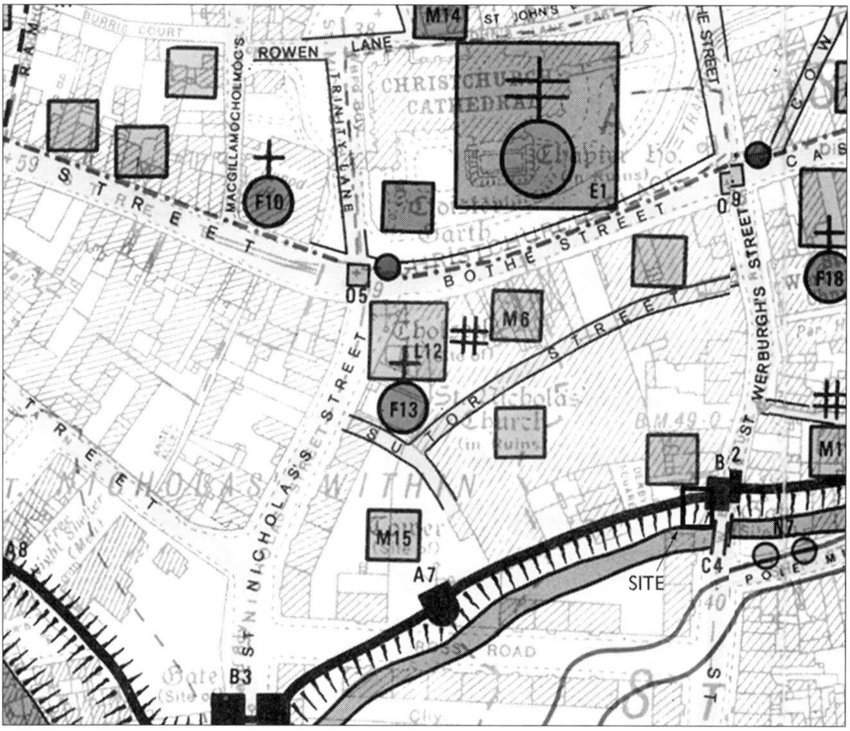

5 Detail of medieval Werburgh Street (Clarke 1978)

clay defences was set approximately 15m to the north, on a completely new alignment.

The Hiberno-Norse wall *c*.1100 The new position of the embankment found in Werburgh Street is also crucial in locating the next stage of defences at Dublin, which involved the construction of the first city wall, built between *c*.1100 and *c*.1125. The circuit of this wall has been well documented: the southern line was thought to be defined by Dublin Castle and Ship Street Little before continuing diagonally across Ross Road, just north of the junction of Bride Road and Patrick Street. The excavations at Ross Road, however, established that the early wall (*c*.1100–*c*.1125), which was cut into the earlier embankment, was actually set approximately 11m north of this line and that in this location both the wall circuits were entirely separate, although running parallel (Walsh 2001, 93) (fig. 6). The new wall route was also traced by Gowen and Hayden in a series of test-trenches as it extended eastwards (ibid.).

The identification of the section of the wall at 14–16 Werburgh Street as Anglo-Norman, rather than Hiberno-Norse as previously thought, also helps clarify the position of the early wall on this side. Although it was not located by Hayden at Werburgh Street, its position can now be reasonably estimated

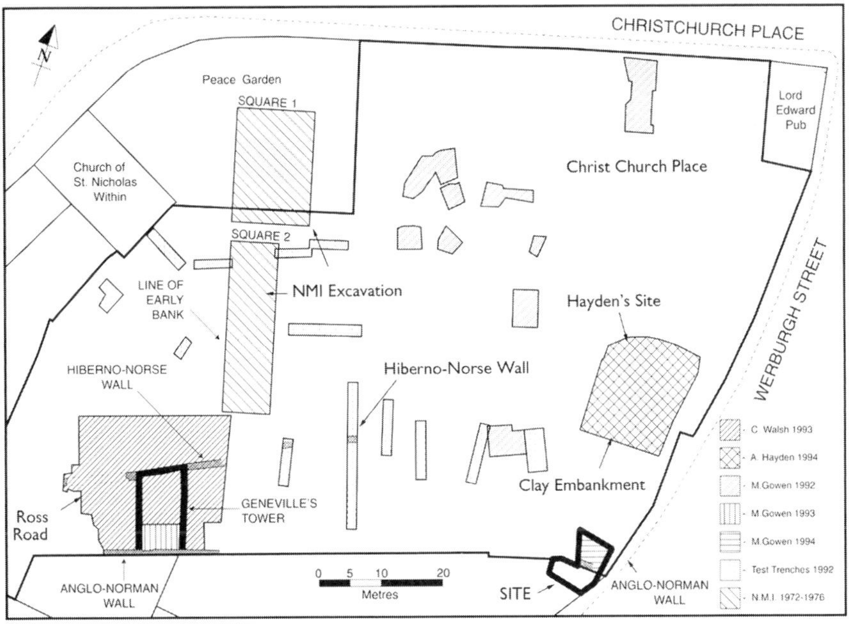

6 Southern defences (after Walsh 2001)

as just south of the site in question, cut into the southern flanks of the embankment, as at Ross Road. This suggests a distance of approximately 15m between both defences at this point (Halpin 2005, 111: figs 12 and 13). As the early wall was also presumed to follow the known route of the Ship Street Little alignment, this represents a major change in our current knowledge of the position of the early wall, and establishes, almost beyond doubt, that the Ship Street Little stretch is Anglo-Norman in date.

The new route of the early wall can be traced retrospectively in the cartographic sources for Dublin (figs 7, 8 and 9). Although Rocque's map, dated 1756, is out of scale and alignment for this area, once the route of the wall is known, it can be identified in various property boundaries and buildings and its route plotted. These alignments suggest that there was a distinctive northward bow or curve in this location and this was presumably related to the original course of the Poddle or some other topographical feature now gone. That the properties depicted by Rocque must preserve the alignment of the wall is clear from the succeeding Ordnance Survey maps (1847, 1866, 1892, 1911 and 1939) all of which record the distinctive line, crucially now anchored to the west by the known position of the wall at Ross Road.

The re-plotting of the route of the early wall also has implications for the continuation of the wall on the eastern side of Werburgh Street, towards Dublin Castle (figs 8 and 9). A corresponding (or continuation of the) wall

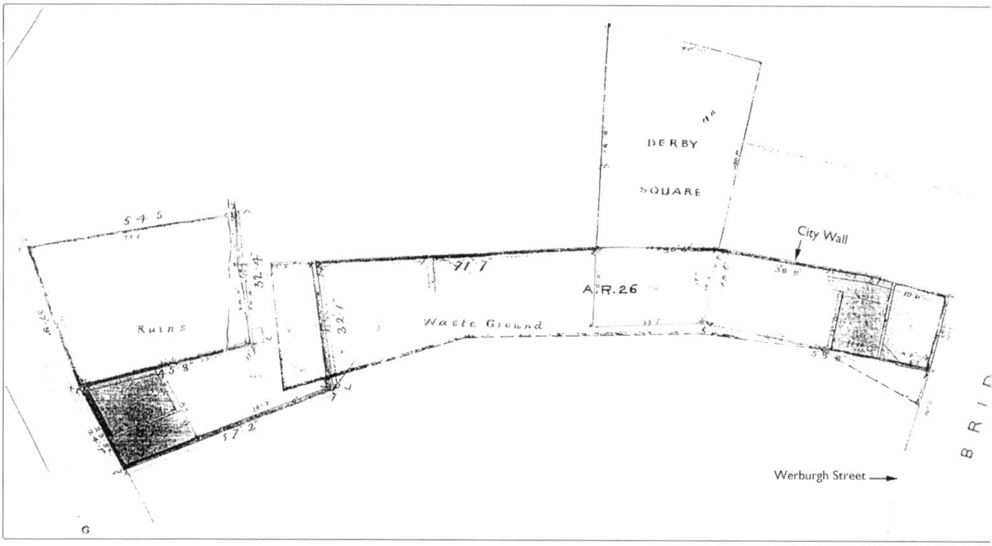

7 Dublin Corporation lease map (19th century)

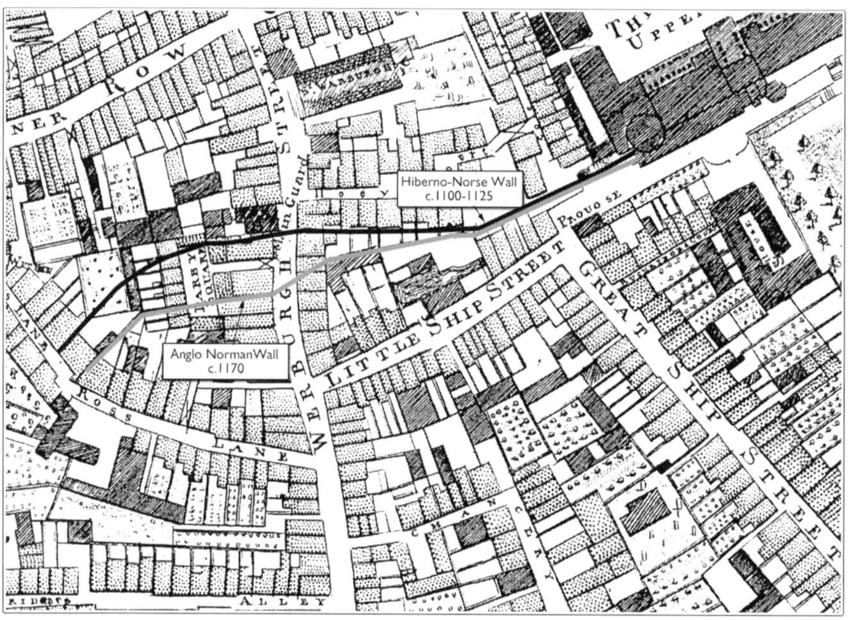

8 Rocque's map of Dublin, dated 1756

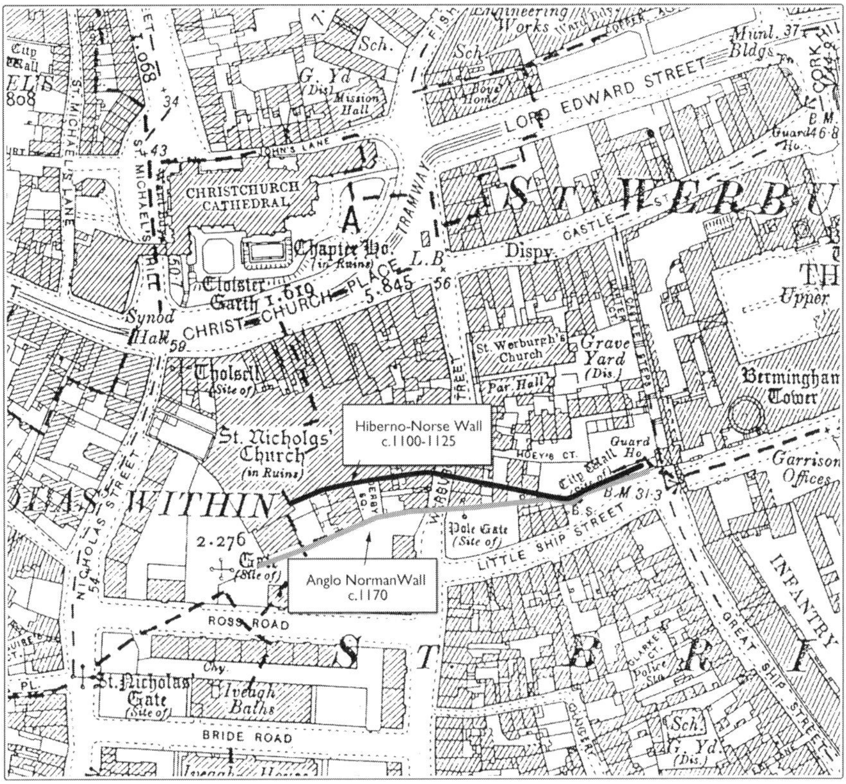

9 Ordnance Survey, dated 1911

alignment can be identified in Rocque (1756) on this side, marked by the rear (i.e., south) walls of the houses fronting onto Hoey's Court, which are orientated northwest/southeast. This diagonal property line is very distinctive and, most importantly, it converges with the Anglo-Norman stretch along Ship Street Little (in and around the bastion) before it reaches Dublin castle. This is very significant as large-scale excavations at Dublin Castle, the Anglo-Norman fortification in the southeast corner of the walled town, indicate that the site of the castle was originally within the Hiberno-Norse defended town and was possibly an earlier stronghold (Lynch and Manning, 2001). The discovery of what may be a Hiberno-Norse defensive ditch within the foundation of the square tower adjacent to Bermingham Tower (the southwest corner tower) establishes that the line of the early defences in this location was along the Ship Street Little alignment and not further north as at Werburgh Street (ibid., 182–3). That the later castle defined the southeast corner of the early settlement was also suggested by excavations within the Powder Tower (the northeast corner tower), which revealed the remains of a stone-faced bank which was also of Hiberno-Norse date (ibid.).

The Anglo-Norman wall and ditch When the Anglo-Normans took Dublin in 1170, they must have begun almost immediately to refortify the city defences, presumably because they themselves had breached them so easily when they attacked the city. While this was formerly thought to have consisted perhaps of only minor refurbishments, is now appears that an ambitious building programme was implemented, which involved replacing the city wall entirely on the southern side while possibly renovating the existing wall elsewhere, for example at Lamb Alley, on the western side of the city (Coughlan 2000, 209; see also Halpin 2005, 108–9). The works were long-running and costly and, on the southern side at Ross Road, involved an expansion of the city southwards of between 11m and 15m.

The Anglo-Normans also constructed a large defensive city ditch around their new acquisition, which measured between 18m and 20m in width and was up to 8m in depth (Simpson 200a, 43–4). As part of these works the river Poddle was pushed further south and was fed into the artificially-constructed ditch at Nicholas Street, where it created a water-filled moat protecting the southeast side of the city (Walsh 1997, 78–9). The ditch was probably augmented by an external (i.e., southern) embankment, as traces of such a structure were located further west at Nicholas Street (Walsh 1992; Hurley 1993).

The line of the Anglo-Norman wall, like the Hiberno-Norse wall, can be identified in the cartographic sources in the property boundaries and alignments of the area and this extends through the middle of the site, marking the parish boundary between St Brigit's and St Werburgh's (figs 8 and 9). As with the earlier circuit, the line depicted by Rocque (1756) is again somewhat distorted but this is righted in the succeeding Ordnance Survey maps. The wall is identifiable as the southern wall of a building (Building 1), which was not demolished until relatively recently. However, one of the curious facts is that the city wall must have been demolished to the west of the site by the late seventeenth century, as it extends through the southern end of Derby Square, which was laid out by this date (see below).

The 'Dutch Billy' house

The remains of a domestic house (Building 1) were found during the excavation, which would originally have fronted onto Werburgh Street and formed part of a passageway that led into a large square to the west of the site (figs 3 and 10). Derby Square was located to the rear of the properties fronting onto the western side of Werburgh Street and, according to M'Cready, was called after a pewterer called John Darby, churchwarden of St Werburgh's church in 1694 (M'Cready 1892, 29). Gilbert, however, records that John Darby was a 'Butterer' who is mentioned in an Inquisition of 1690 as owning land in the vicinity (Gilbert 1854–9, i, 45). The entire basement footprint of the building survived and this included the remains of a shared chimney-stack and triangular fireplace, which are usually associated with the

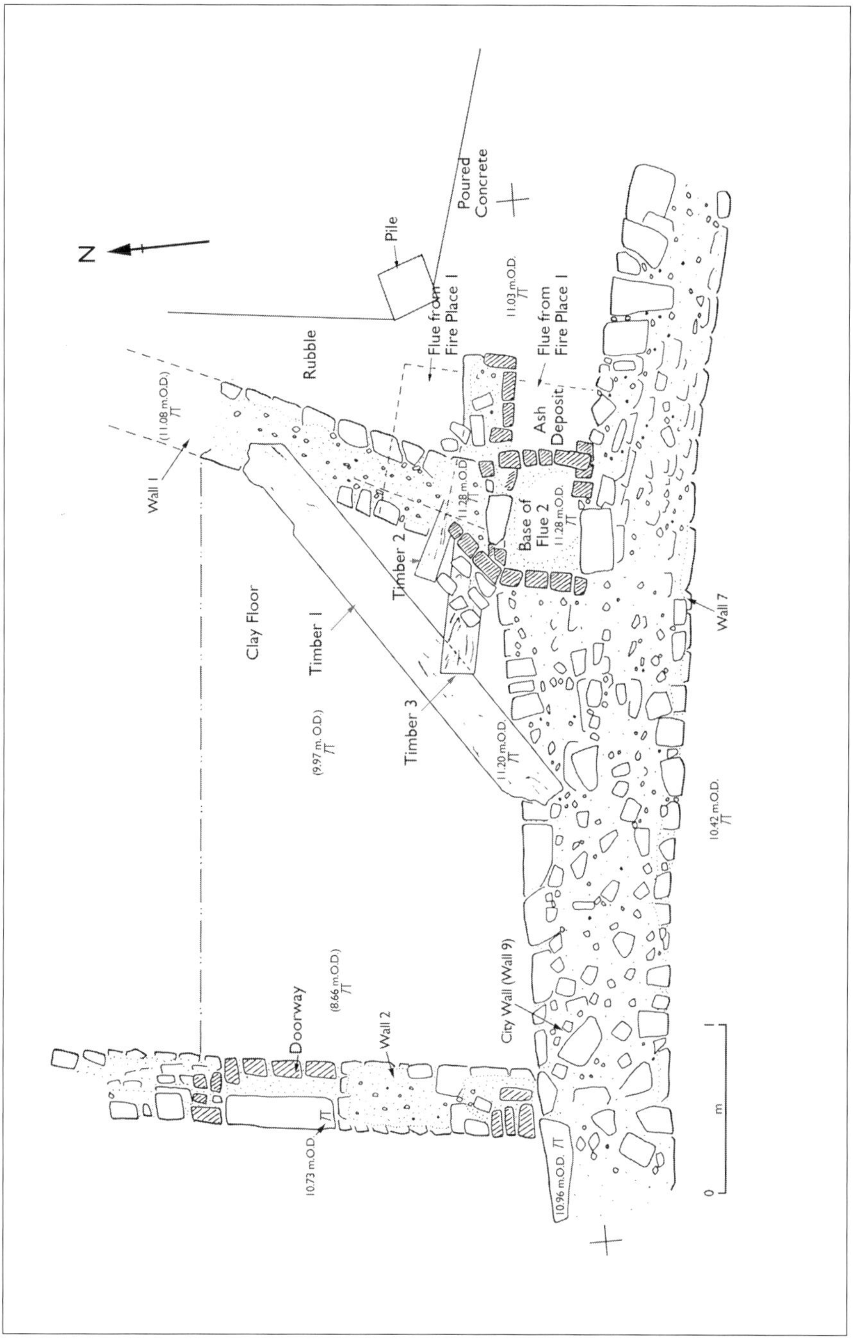

10 Plan of the 'Dutch Billy'

residences of French and Flemish refugees, built in the late seventeenth and early eighteenth centuries. A second structure (Building 2), also probably late seventeenth- or eighteenth-century in date, was identified at the western end of the site, tacked onto the city wall (fig. 3).

Both buildings formed part of the rebuilding programme at Dublin from the mid- to the late seventeenth century onwards during which many of the existing houses were demolished and replaced. The rebellion of 1641 followed quickly by the arrival of Cromwell's army in 1649 had resulted in the destruction of many of the surviving medieval buildings of Dublin, which were 'cage-work' houses, built around a timber frame that resembled a bird-cage. One of the last known examples was at the corner of Werburgh Street and Castle Street, which survived until it was demolished in 1812 (Craig 1980, 86). The Cromwellian armies were actively encouraged to demolish and plunder these buildings to the extent that, by the mid- to late seventeenth century, it was estimated that, after ten years of war, 'at least one half of the number of houses [were] pulled down and destroyed' (Walsh 1973, 60). The population was, of course, reduced and it has been estimated at less than nine thousand in the mid-seventeenth century, both inside and outside the walls. The low numbers suggest that a great number of houses in Dublin must have been derelict by this date (Craig 1980, 5).

The small population at Dublin meant that the city was facing long-term economic ruin and subsequently 'Protestants and Englishmen' were being actively sought to come and help rebuild Dublin (Walsh 1973, 61). The policy was generally successful and was followed by an influx in the 1650s and 1660s of French and Flemish Protestants refugees, including numerous Huguenots. The newcomers brought new building styles, predominantly terraced housing and they favoured brick as their building medium, their houses becoming known as 'Dutch Billys'. The earliest were small and cramped but, by the eighteenth century, they were larger, often three storeys in height with expanded attics or garrets. They usually had cruciform roof ridges and pronounced string-courses, the gables fronting onto the streets, which transformed the streetscape of Dublin. Their main advantage was economy, since they were cheaply built of rough materials and had shared party-walls and chimney-stacks. These central stacks, one of the main structural elements of the buildings, contained distinctive triangular fireplaces of brick, which also became known as 'Quaker fireplaces'.

PREVIOUS INVESTIGATIONS OF THE WALL

Monitoring programme 1994 As mentioned above, the first indication that the city wall survived in this location came when it was exposed as part of a monitoring programme in 1994 associated with a piling operation in the

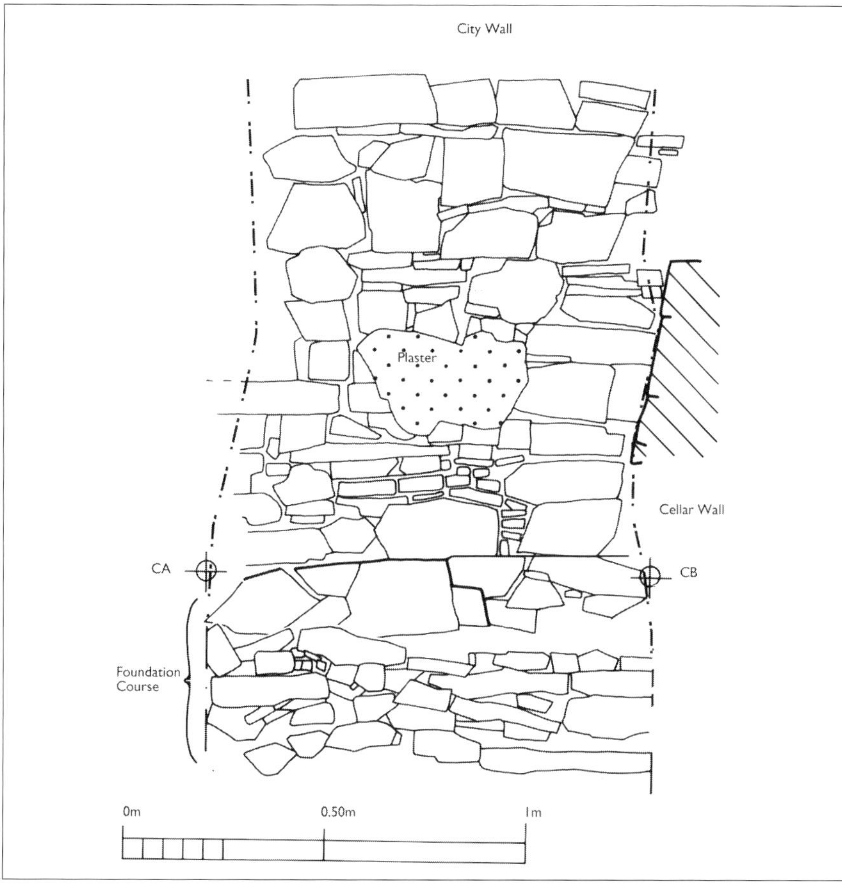

11 North-facing elevation of the city wall (1994)

northeast corner of the site, which was monitored by the writer (figs 11–13). The excavation was very small, the inner trench measuring 3m east-west by 2.50m wide, and access was restricted due to health and safety concerns (fig. 3). Only the northern face was exposed as the other side of the site was not available at the time. Despite this, two builds were identified in the southern face, one on top of the other. The upper build stood approximately nine courses high and was mortared with a bright orange, gritty, mortar. It was composed of large rectangular blocks that measured, on average, between 350mm and 400mm by 200mm and 250mm. However, while the face of the wall was flush, the coursing was not as regular as further west (see below), although rectangular limestone blocks were used in the interstices. The wall had also been plastered on the northern face in the post-medieval period. The foundations of the wall had been exposed also in the post-medieval period as a cut was visible in the western face, filled with rubble.

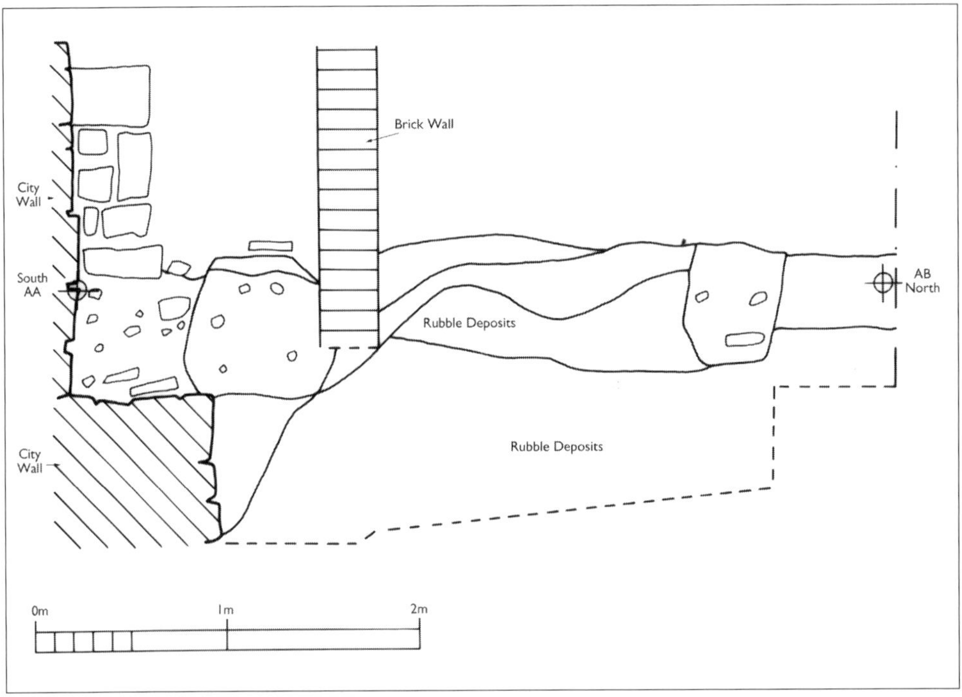

12 West-facing section of the city wall (1994)

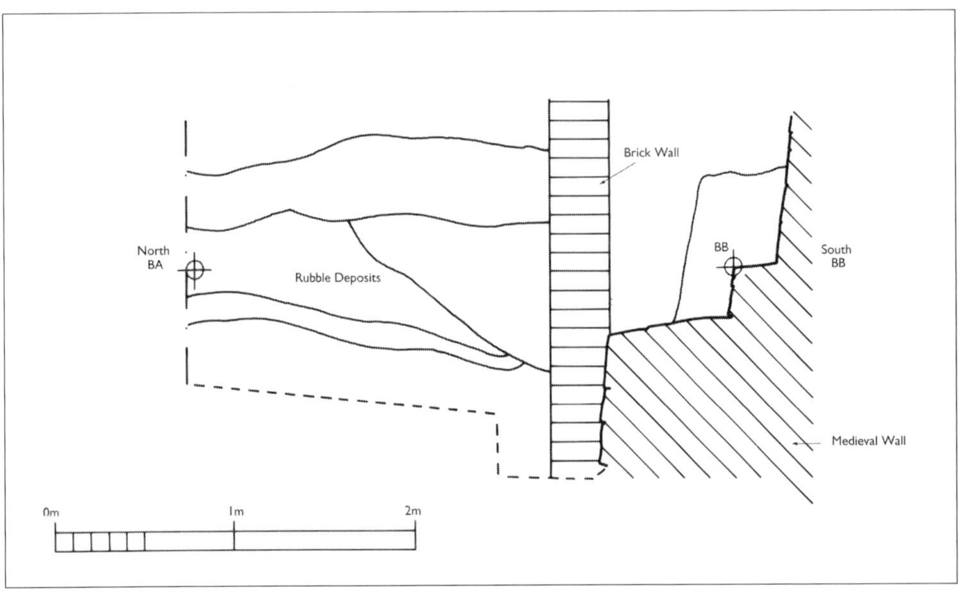

13 East-facing section of the city wall (1994)

Plate 1 The site from the west: note the line of the Ship Street Little wall

Plate 2 The site from the northwest

Plate 3 The triangular fireplace inserted into city wall, from the northwest

Plate 4 Overview of Dutch Billy: note city wall

Plate 5 City wall, from the west

Plate 6 City wall, northern face, from the north

Plate 7 City wall, northern face, detail of block work

Plate 8 City wall northern face: note offset

Plate 9 City wall, southern face: note exposed 'core'

Plate 10 New structure built up against city wall, from the northeast

The lower build of the wall was clearly inferior and, surprisingly, projected out approximately 1m from the base of the wall on the northern side. This section of the wall, which stood 800mm high, was composed of small, irregular-shaped rectangular limestone blocks measuring, on average, 300mm by 100mm, little mortar having been used in the construction. The coursing was also far less regular, especially at the eastern end, while there was a second projection or offset at the western end, between the interface of the two builds. There was no indication of the projecting offset, identified further west (see below).

Archaeological assessment 1998 This difference in the masonry was also identified in the second assessment (in 1998) of the site under discussion, which exposed a portion of what must represent the same wall, as it was positioned just a short distance to the west (Simpson 2000b). Two builds were also identified in this assessment but there was a difference: this section of the wall had a small projecting offset on the northern side rather than the 1m projection noted further east during the piling operation. Despite this, it is almost certainly the case that both sections of the wall are contemporary and can be dated to the late twelfth/early thirteenth century, the change in masonry being attributable to a distinctive non-mortared foundation course.

THE EXCAVATION

The small site is a derelict open space, which measures 12m east-west by 6m wide and was divided by a post-medieval wall, which was in a dangerous state (fig. 2). The Poddle culvert, dating from the eighteenth century, was located on the southern side of the site and the exact route was established prior to the assessment by an accurate internal geodetic survey. The brick structure was found to lie along the extreme southern boundary and the assessment established that the top of the culvert is positioned almost 3m below the present ground surface (at 8.05m OD). The aim of the investigation was to expose the extant section of the city wall but to keep actual excavation to a minimum.

The medieval wall

The excavations revealed that the remains of the city wall (F9) survived in a stretch that measured a total of 10.80m in length (east-west) and this included the above-ground section which was *c.*5m long by 500mm in height (figs 3 and 14). The northern face (within Building 1: see below) survived almost intact as did the clay deposits on which the wall was founded (fig. 15). On the southern side, however, these deposits did not survive and facing stones had been plundered when the wall was reduced in width in the seventeenth

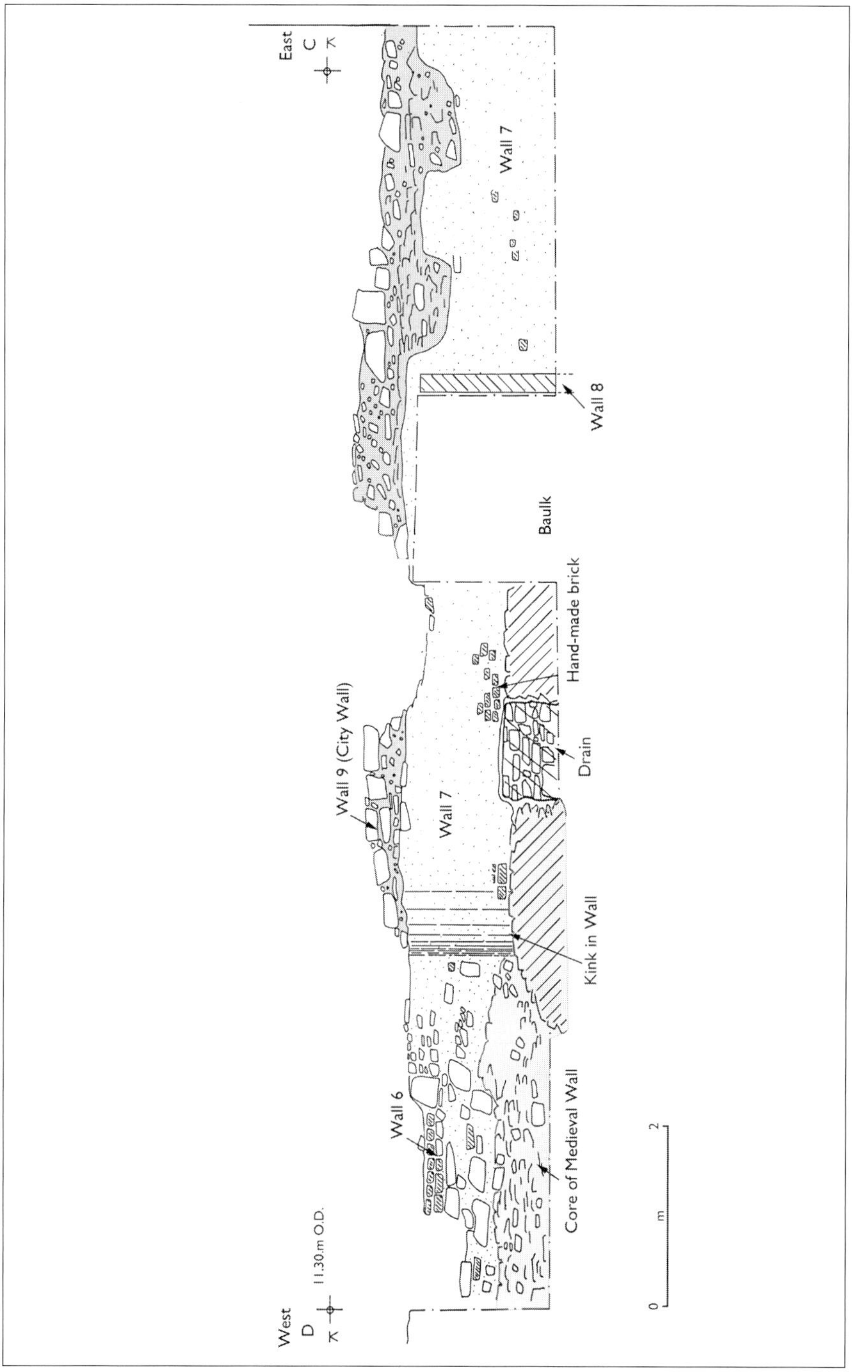

14 South-facing elevation of the city wall

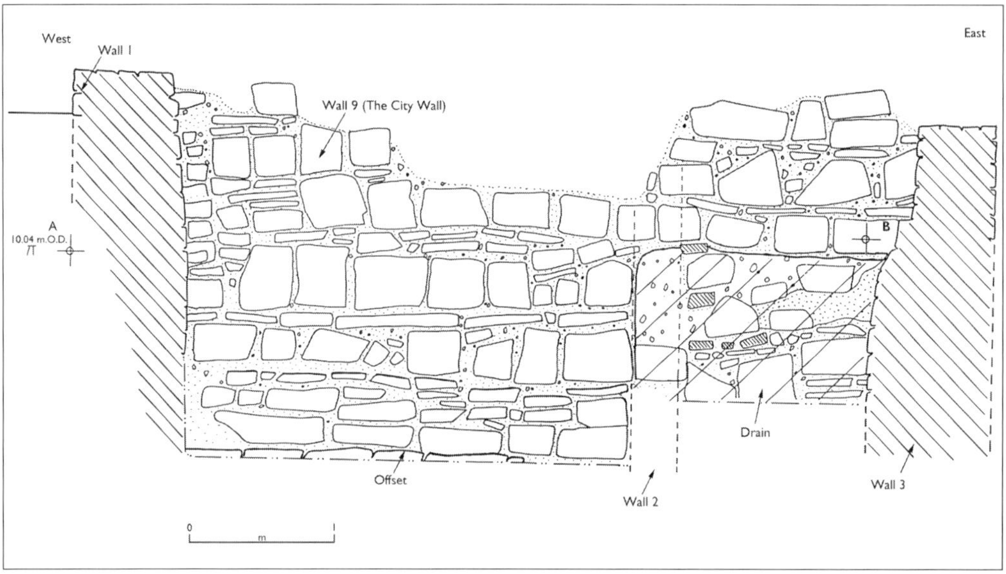

15 North-facing section through the city wall

century from approximately 1.70m to 1.10m. A new wall (F7), reusing the distinctive medieval blocks, was then constructed shortly afterwards up against the exposed core, and the wall was realigned southwards at the eastern end. However, below the new facing (F7) the original core of the wall still projected out at intervals, at foundation level.

A distinct turn or kink was noted in the wall at the western end, where it turned northwards, suggested by the exposed core section. As with the previous assessments, the foundation course which was 600mm in depth was represented in the northern face by a change in the masonry where it was within a foundation trench (see below). The very base on this side was marked by an offset.

The foundation trench The wall was constructed within a foundation trench (F3) which, on the northern side, measured 200mm in width, tapering towards the base of the wall (fig. 16). This was filled with a mortar-flecked dark green clay fill, which produced no datable finds, probably as only a very small section was excavated. However, the foundation trench was cut into a substantial dump of hard green clay (F2), which did produce datable finds, establishing that the wall could be dated to the Anglo-Norman period, i.e., from 1170 inwards. These finds included Dublin cooking-ware and Ham Green pottery, as well as metal slag, a glazed tile and a fragment of tuyeure.

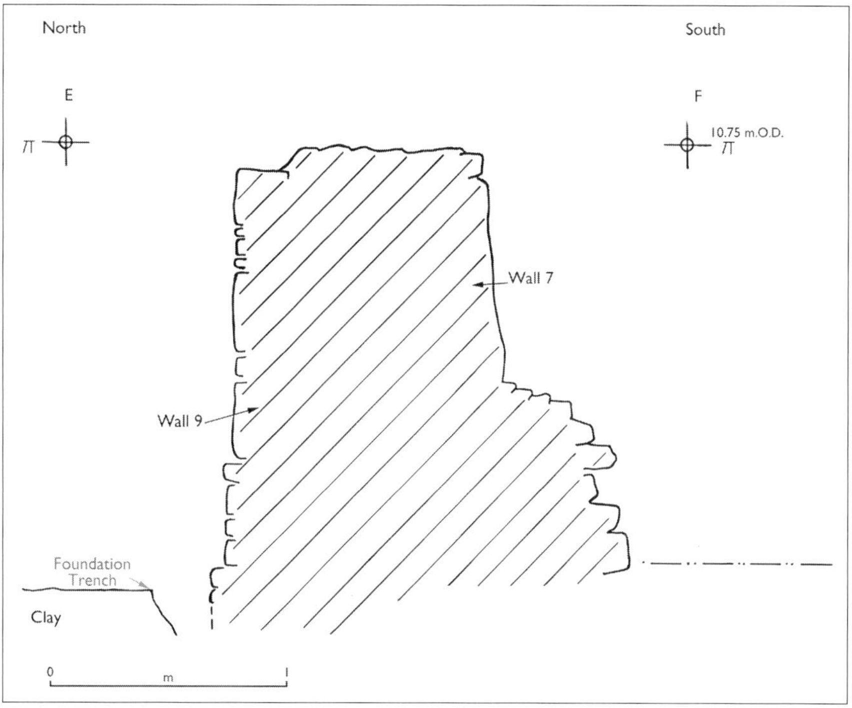

16 Profile through the city wall

The northern face The northern face of the wall is relatively intact and stands, as stated earlier, 2.40m in height composed of between seven and eight courses (figs 13–17). It is constructed from large distinctive limestone blocks measuring, on average, between 350mm by 300mm and 400mm by 300mm with small rectangular limestones filling the interstices. Distinct levelling courses could be identified between the main build, composed of long rectangular limestone flags. The mortar is a coarse lime, bright orange in colour and has a rough gritty texture. The foundation course, which extended for 600mm in depth, was built differently and the blocks used were long and rectangular, as opposed to square, measuring on average 400mm by 100mm. This side was also roughly faced, and an offset, 100mm in width, marks the base of the wall on this side.

The western end of the wall was breached to allow a drain to exit, which was associated with the domestic house (Building 1) (figs 3 and 14). The resultant opening measured approximately 1.20m square and was infilled or blocked up using a combination of limestone block and red-brick repair, all mortared with a light-grey lime mortar. Although the breach was neatly executed, it has rendered the wall very unstable in this location and, as a result, excavation there was limited.

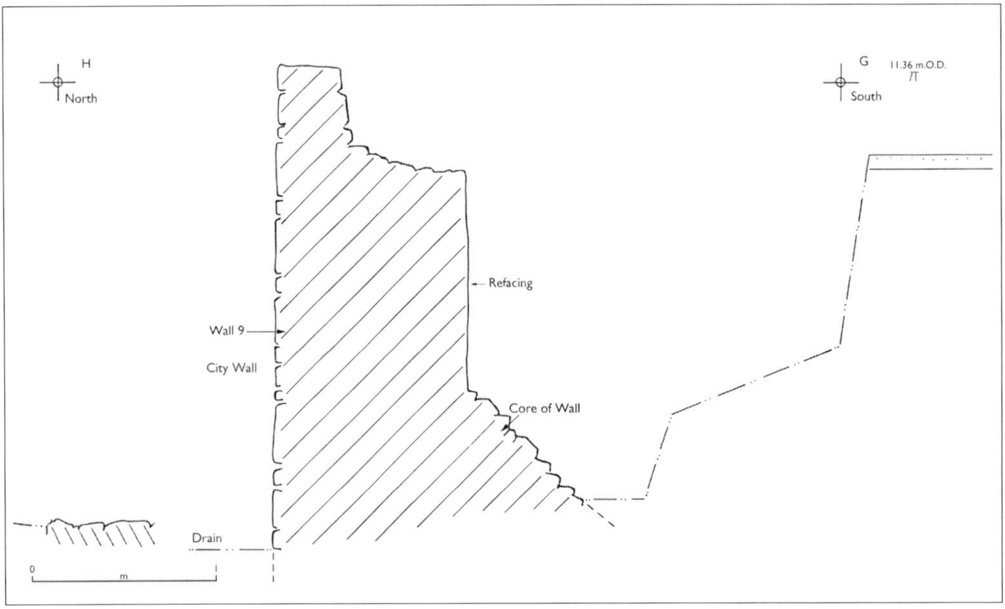

17 Profile through the city wall

The southern face Excavation on the damaged southern side of the wall was also limited because of the presence of the Poddle culvert, which ran east-west along the southern side of the site. However, the area was graded down and the wall core exposed to approximately 2.20m in depth. Although the medieval wall was mostly re-faced (Wall 7) details of the original medieval wall are still visible at foundation level. A slight batter at the eastern end suggests that there was originally an external (i.e., southern) batter and the core of the wall is visible in several locations at foundation level, allowing an estimation of the width of the wall. In the central area this core projects out for 400mm which, when added to the estimated width of an average facing block (approximately 500mm) gives a projected width of the wall of 1.70m at the base.

At the western end the medieval wall appears to kink northwards before extending westwards and this was suggested by the projecting core, 600mm in width, which still has the imprints of the facing stones. This turn appears real as it was mirrored in the facing Wall 7, which was deliberately rounded at this end.

The city ditch

The Anglo-Norman city ditch was known to border the city wall on the external side but, at the site under discussion, the Poddle culvert (which is active and could not be disturbed) extends through the known location. Despite this, several small patches of medieval soil were located at the western end of the site lying between 500mm and 1m below the present ground level (Trench 2). These layers did produce a large amount of medieval pottery/tiles and appear to represent the fill of the city ditch. However, there was no excavation in this area. On the eastern side of the site (fronting onto Werburgh Street), rubble deposits were found to be over 3m in depth, representing the remnants of demolished cellars.

The Dutch Billy: Building 1

A large timber was identified during the archaeological assessment, which had been inserted into the medieval wall at the eastern end and appeared to be structural in function. On excavation, this timber was found to be a massive beam, which supported a chimney-stack of a small pre-Georgian house or Dutch Billy. This dwelling, which originally fronted onto Werburgh Street, was tacked onto the northern side of the city wall, the wall itself forming the southern wall of the house, which survived until the work under discussion. It was oriented roughly east-west and measured originally 10m long by 6m wide. Only the western half was within the cutting and this consisted of a rear room, at basement level, with a small return or closet at the western end. The chimney-stack was in a central location and contained, at ground floor level, a triangular brick fireplace in both the front and rear room. However, the fireplace at basement level in the rear room was a simple ope through the main dividing wall, which was fed into the brick stack at ground-floor level.

CONCLUSIONS

Although the excavations at 14–16 Werburgh Street were very limited in size, important information was gleaned about the medieval defences of Dublin, which has the effect of completely altering our knowledge of the defences on this side of the city. Two separate building-lines can now be identified, the earlier of which has been completely lost, not only in the historical record but also in the existing landscape. The most crucial factor was the dating of the wall to the Anglo-Norman period rather than, as previously thought, the Hiberno-Norse period. This fact, in conjunction with the finding of the embankment by Hayden to the north of the site, suggests that two sets of wall formerly existed in this location, separated by a distance of approximately 15m. Thus the new section constructed in Ross Road extended at least as far as Werburgh Street and forms part of what must now be deemed a massive Anglo-Norman fortification programme which involved expansion of the southern side of the city by between 11m and 15m. The works did not just involve reclamation and the rebuilding of the existing wall. Thus the evidence from this excavation and from Ross Road indicates that, not only was the wall rebuilt but that the Poddle river was also pushed southwards and was then re-channelled to flood the new ditch, creating a city moat.

The charting of the route of the early wall and its possible identification in the cartographic sources also allows us to speculate about the continuation of the wall on the eastern side of Werburgh Street. A study of the property boundaries starting with Rocque (1756) suggests that the line of the early wall may be traced in the properties on the opposite side, which suggests a point of convergence somewhere close to the later bastion which still survives in the Ship Street Little wall-stretch. The information from Werburgh Street also indicates that it is most likely that the stretch of wall along Ship Street Little represents the Anglo-Norman wall rather than the earlier wall, which is not surprising given the general condition and height of the wall.

Most importantly of all perhaps, the excavation also alerts us to the possibility that sections of the medieval wall may still survive in the modern landscape, concealed within existing buildings, and that maximum care must be taken when demolition is proposed in the vicinity of the defences. It is certainly the case that the full location and current extent of the walled city of Dublin is still not known.

ACKNOWLEDGMENTS

The author would like to thank Kevin Weldon for his help on site and for providing the figures and photographs. Thanks are also due to Mario Sughi and Lindsay Delahunty for the graphics and to Margaret Gowen & Co. Ltd for supporting this publication.

BIBLIOGRAPHY

Clarke, H.B. 2002 *Dublin, part 1, to 1610*. Irish Historic Towns Atlas, no. 11. Royal Irish Academy. Dublin.

Clarke, H.B. 1978 *Dublin c.840–c.1540: the medieval town in the modern city*. Ordnance Survey, Dublin. Repr. Royal Irish Academy, 2002.

Craig, M. 1980 *Dublin, 1660–1860*. London.

Craig, M. 1989 *The architecture of Ireland from the earliest times to 1880*. London.

Coughlan T. 2000 The Anglo-Norman houses of Dublin: evidence from Back Lane. In S. Duffy (ed.), *Medieval Dublin I*, 203–34. Dublin.

Gilbert, J.T. 1854–9 *A history of Dublin*, 3 vols. Repr. 1972. Dublin.

Gowen, M. 2004 *Conservation plan: Dublin city wall and defences*. Dublin.

Halpin, A. 2005 Development phases in Hiberno-Norse Dublin: a tale of two cities. In S. Duffy (ed.), *Medieval Dublin VI*, 94–113. Dublin.

Hayden, A. 1995 Werburgh Street. In I. Bennett (ed.), *Excavations 1994: summary accounts of archaeological excavations in Ireland*. Bray.

Hayden A. 2002 The excavation of pre-Norman defences and houses at Werburgh Street, Dublin: a summary. In S. Duffy (ed.) *Medieval Dublin III*, 44–68. Dublin.

Hurley, F. 1993 Nicholas Street. In I. Bennett (ed.), *Excavations 1992*. Bray

Lynch, A. and Manning, C. 2001 Excavations at Dublin castle, 1985–7. In S. Duffy (ed.), *Medieval Dublin II*, 169–204. Dublin.

M'Cready, C.T. 1892 *Dublin Street names, dated and explained*. Repr. 1975. Dublin.

O'Rourke, D. 1999 Archaeological assessment at 15–16 Werburgh Street, Dublin 8. In I. Bennett (ed.), *Excavations 1998*. Bray.

Simpson L. 2000a Forty years a-digging. In S. Duffy (ed.), *Medieval Dublin I*, 11–68. Dublin.

Simpson L. 2000b Archaeological assessment at 14–16 Werburgh Street, Dublin 8, Phase 2. In I. Bennett (ed.), *Excavations 1999*. Bray.

Simpson L. 2006 *Dublin city walls and defences*. An Action of the Dublin City Heritage Plan. Dublin City Council. Dublin.

1992 Nicholas Street. In I. Bennett (ed.), *Excavations 1991*. Bray.

Walsh, C. 1997 *Archaeological excavations at Patrick, Nicholas and Winetavern Streets, Dublin*. Dingle.

Walsh, C. 2001 Dublin's southern town defences, ten to the fourteenth centuries: the evidence from Ross Road. In S. Duffy (ed.), *Medieval Dublin II*, 88–127. Dublin.

Walsh, P. 1973 Dutch Billys in the Liberties. In Elgy Gillespie (ed.), *The Liberties of Dublin. Its history, people, and future*, 56–74. E. & T. O'Brien, Dublin.

Dublin in the late-medieval Gaelic annals

BERNADETTE CUNNINGHAM

The historical annals in the Irish language compiled by professional Gaelic families are among the most important sources to survive relating to late-medieval Ireland. The scope of the Gaelic annals varies in terms of chronological and geographical coverage. In essence, they are regional annals and can be taken to represent the worldview of particular Gaelic lordships rather than of Ireland as a whole. The way in which Dublin is represented in the surviving late-medieval Irish annals has not previously been examined in detail. The evidence for perceptions of Dublin in four sets of late-medieval annals written in Irish in the sixteenth and seventeenth centuries, though drawing in part on older sources, will be considered here.

First, the evidence of three sets of annals that reached their extant form in the sixteenth century – the Annals of Ulster, AD432–1535, the Annals of Connacht, 1224–1544, and the Annals of Loch Cé, which span the years 1014–1590 (though with significant lacunae) – will be reviewed. These will be compared with perhaps the best-known Gaelic annals of all, the Annals of the Four Masters, compiled in Donegal in the mid-1630s. The Annals of the Four Masters cover the longest time span, from the biblical deluge down to the early seventeenth century,[1] and in contrast to the first three compilations, the Annals of the Four Masters offer an early seventeenth-century, rather than a sixteenth-century, perspective on the Irish past. For comparative purposes, the perspective of the Anglo-Irish annals, written mainly in Latin will be considered briefly, as will some non-annalistic sources in Irish. Key questions to be addressed will be whether the perspective of the Gaelic annalists differed from that of the Anglo-Irish annalists in their portrayal of Dublin, and whether perceptions had changed by the seventeenth century, as compared to the sixteenth.

The Irish annals are of course already well known to historians of medieval Dublin. They have been used to good effect in documenting aspects of the history of Dublin in the age of the Vikings.[2] Far less attention has been paid to what the annals record in relation to Dublin in later centuries. The essential point to be explored in this essay is how Dublin was perceived – by historians

1 Two major sets of annals that reached their current form in the seventeenth century, Chronicum Scotorum and the Annals of Clonmacnoise, are omitted from the present discussion because they end in 1150 and 1408 respectively. 2 See, for example, Howard Clarke, 'The bloodied eagle: the Vikings and the development of Dublin, 841–1014', *Irish*

in other parts of Ireland writing from a provincial perspective – in the centuries after Dublin/Áth Cliath had become established as an urban centre.

It is a relatively simple task to locate all the references to Dublin in the late-medieval Gaelic annals, because they are few in number. These references can be analyzed by date and by theme, so that a picture can be created of the nature of contact between Dublin and the provinces, the kind of role Dublin played in a wider Irish context, and how that role evolved over time.

Table 1. Themes relating to Dublin in the Annals of Ulster, 1301–1535

Theme	14th *c.*	15th *c.*	16th *c.* (to 1535 only)
Battle	1	0	1
Government	1	0	2
Visit	1	0	2
Imprisonment	0	1	0
Execution	2	2	0
Killing	0	1	0
Obituary	0	0	1
News	0	1	1
Other	1	0	0

Beginning with the references to Dublin in the Annals of Ulster,[3] summarized in Table 1, the first thing to be observed is the extremely small number of entries, and the apparent consistency over time. To read this table correctly, however, it should be noted that the sixteenth-century data covers just the first third of the century, since the Annals of Ulster end in 1535. Assuming that the data for the full century should be at least trebled, there is a hint there, even in the first part of the sixteenth century, of a quantitative shift in the number of occasions that Dublin is noticed by the Ulster annalist.

Table 1 categorizes the Dublin entries by theme. Over the three centuries under consideration, just two battles were recorded, entries that tell little enough about Dublin. Under 1355 the annalists record that 'Great defeat was inflicted by Ua Mórdha [O'More] on the Gaill Átha Cliath [Foreigners of Dublin], and twelve score were slain of them'.[4] Then, in 1510, there is a longer narrative of an expedition by Gerald, earl of Kildare, justiciar of

Sword, 18 (1991), pp 91–119. 3 W.M. Hennessy and B. MacCarthy (eds), *Annála Uladh: Annals of Ulster from the earliest times to the year 1541* (4 vols, Dublin, 1887–1901, reprint, Dublin, 1998), [hereinafter cited as *AU*]. Online editions of all the Gaelic and Anglo-Irish annals cited in this paper are accessible on the CELT (Corpus of Electronic Texts) website, www.ucc.ie/celt. 4 *AU*, 1355.5 (Citations from the annals include the year in question, together with the entry number assigned in the online edition as published on the CELT website, www.ucc.ie/celt).

Ireland, into Munster. A battle ensued near the river Shannon, in which the earl's forces included the Gaill and Gaeil of Munster in the front of the host and the Gaill of Meath and Dublin at the rear. The earl's forces were opposed by O'Brien and O'Donnell, and heavily defeated. Essentially, the story is told from the perspective of O'Donnell, and celebrates an O'Donnell success. That the earl of Kildare and 'Gaill Átha Cliath' are the losers is a matter for celebration. This perspective can be interpreted as evidence of a degree of hostility towards Dublin. However, two minor military encounters over a period of 235 years would seem to indicate that peace rather than hostility was the norm.

Entries in the Annals of Ulster that record cases of imprisonment and execution in Dublin provide a clearer picture of Dublin operating as a centre of control. In 1353 the annalist recorded that 'Gerodin Tyrrell was drawn *asunder* by the Saxons on the Green of Áth Cliath'.[5] Under the year 1366 it was recorded that 'Diarmait Red-hand Mac Murchadha [MacMurrough], arch-king of Leinster, was in long custody with the Foreigners of Áth Cliath, having been captured in treachery by the Black Knight and he was drawn *asunder* at the end by them – a deed the greatest [i.e., most dreadful] that was done in the end of time'.[6]

In the following century, the execution of the grandson of the earl of Kildare by Gaill Átha Cliath was recorded at the year 1431,[7] while the kidnapping of Edward Nugent, son of the baron of Delvin, in 1473 also ended with his execution in Dublin.[8] With the exception of Mac Morrough, the other executions all involved people of Anglo-Norman descent from within the Pale. Others experienced captivity, but escaped with their lives, and so it was recorded at the year 1412 that 'Aodh, son of Henry Ua Néill [O'Neill], escaped from Áth Cliath after being ten years in captivity there and brought many other captives with him'.[9] This was the only prisoner from outside the Pale specifically named as being held in captivity in Dublin in the Annals of Ulster between 1300 and 1535. The fact that he 'brought other captives with him' suggests that there were other inmates at Dublin Castle who did not merit being named. Nonetheless, the scant evidence hints that for those who lived beyond the Pale in this period, the likelihood of imprisonment in Dublin was remote.

This does not mean that there was no contact between the provinces and Dublin. The Ulster annalist recorded at the year 1302 the death of Donnchadh O'Flaherty, bishop of Killala, who died at Dunboyne, Co. Meath, en route to Dublin. The purpose of his journey is not recorded. By the early sixteenth century, there is evidence of increased political contact with Dublin, and the Annals of Ulster record two occasions when Hugh O'Donnell, head of the O'Donnells of Tyrconnell, travelled to Dublin to meet with government representatives there. The context of these visits was the ongoing hostility

5 *AU*, 1353.15. 6 *AU*, 1366.5. 7 *AU*, 1431.1. 8 *AU*, 1473.2. 9 *AU*, 1412.8.

between O'Donnell and O'Neill, and the purpose of the visits to Dublin was to negotiate peace under the auspices of the earl of Kildare. In 1516, only O'Donnell made the trip to Dublin, and it was recorded that he was treated honourably there by the King's council, and made friendly alliance with them.[10] On the second occasion, in 1525, both O'Neill and O'Donnell went to the council at Dublin, but the peace negotiations were unsuccessful. The annalists record that later in the same year 'a patched-up peace was made between them in the beginning of Harvest and a promise to abide as the earl of Kildare and Maghnus Ó Domhnaill [Manus O'Donnell] should say'.[11] That the peace was not made under the authority of the justiciar and council, but rather as a deal to be jointly overseen by the earl of Kildare and Manus O'Donnell, is an indication of just how little influence the Dublin administration had in Ulster at this time. In short, then, Dublin does not loom large in the political world of the Ulster annalists in the fourteenth and fifteenth centuries, though there is some slight hint of change in the early sixteenth century.

The Connacht annals present a broadly similar picture, and they cover a broadly similar time-span to the Annals of Ulster, coming to an end in the year 1544. The entries in the Annals of Connacht that make reference to Dublin total six for the fourteenth century, eight for the fifteenth century and four for the first half of the sixteenth century – not enough to be statistically significant, but yet sufficient to indicate that the annalists were at least aware of the existence of Dublin (Table 2).

Table 2. Themes relating to Dublin in the Annals of Connacht, 1301–1544

Theme	14th *c.*	15th *c.*	16th *c.* (to 1544 only)
Battle	2	3	0
Government	0	1	0
Visit	0	1	0
Imprisonment	0	1	0
Execution	3	0	0
Killing	0	0	0
Obituary	1	0	2
News	0	2	2

The early part of the Annals of Connacht shows a strong O'Connor bias, a fact that can be seen from the choice of 1224 as the year they commence. That was the year in which the great Cathal Croibhdhearg O'Connor died, and the annals open with his obituary. Three years later, in 1227, Aodh (Hugh) the

10 *AU*, 1516.11. 11 *AU*, 1525.1.

son of Cathal Croibhdhearg went to Dublin, having been summoned to attend 'a great court … held by the Galls of Ireland at Dublin'. However, it was noted that 'deceit and treachery was practised against him' and he had to be forcibly rescued by his followers and escorted back to his own territory. It is interesting that in retaliation for his treatment at Dublin he later attacked Athlone, killing the constable and plundering and burning the market there. The annalist concluded with the comment: 'now these things were of profit to the whole of Connacht, for he [Hugh] recovered his son and daughter and the hostages of Connacht and obtained peace for the whole province'.[12] The manner in which O'Connor retaliated against Athlone in revenge for his treatment at Dublin is an important indicator that, for those west of the Shannon, the castle at Athlone rather than Dublin was a more tangible and obvious symbol of English power.

Indeed, by the late sixteenth century, when the English administration in Dublin sought to extend its influence to the provinces in a systematic way, it did so by establishing provincial presidencies, and from 1569 the headquarters of the Connacht presidency was based at Athlone.[13] The building of the bridge at Athlone in 1567 was big news in Connacht in a way that developments in Dublin were not.[14] A permanent stone bridge at Athlone linked Connacht with the eastern part of the country in a highly visible and very practical way and opened up the western province to increased influence from the Dublin administration.

The remainder of the fourteenth-century entries in the Annals of Connacht essentially replicate those in the Annals of Ulster, with just one additional battle noted under the year 1355 where they mention, without descriptive detail, that 'the Galls of Dublin were defeated by the Leinster Gaels'.[15] In contrast, only two of the fifteenth-century entries in the Annals of Connacht have anything in common with the events concerning Dublin recorded in the Annals of Ulster.[16]

The Annals of Loch Cé, the final set of extant annals in the Irish language compiled during the sixteenth century, offer a very similar perspective on Dublin for the fourteenth century. Neither the Annals of Loch Cé nor the Annals of Connacht contain any references to Dublin for the first half of the fourteenth century. For the remainder of the century, the Loch Cé entries on Dublin are so similar to those found in the Connacht annals that it can be assumed that the compilers were using an almost identical source. The close parallel between these

12 A.M. Freeman (ed.), *Annála Connacht: the Annals of Connacht, AD 1224–1544* (Dublin, 1944, reprint, 1970) [hereinafter cited as AConn], s.a. 1227. 13 Bernadette Cunningham, 'Political and social change in the lordships of Clanricard and Thomond, 1577–1641' (MA Thesis, University College Galway, 1979), ch. 1. 14 W.M. Hennessy (ed.), *The Annals of Loch Cé: a chronicle of Irish affairs from AD 1014 to AD 1590* (2 vols, London, 1871) [hereinafter cited as *ALCé*], s.a. 1567; John O'Donovan (ed.), *Annals of the Kingdom of Ireland by the Four Masters* (7 vols, Dublin, 1851), (hereinafter cited as *AFM*), s.a. 1567.10. 15 *A.Conn*, 1355.9. 16 *A.Conn*, 1412.15, 1473.6.

annals is not sustained thereafter, however, and there are only two fifteenth-century entries relating to Dublin in the Annals of Loch Cé, as compared with eight in the Annals of Connacht. The picture changes even more substantially in the sixteenth-century section of the Annals of Loch Cé. These annals extend down to the year 1590 and contain significant new material not recorded elsewhere. Events in Dublin become much more consistently newsworthy for the Loch Cé annalist in the last quarter of the sixteenth century. Prior to that, references to Dublin were scant indeed (Table 3).

Table 3. Themes relating to Dublin in the Annals of Loch Cé, 1301–1590

Theme	**14th** *c.*	**15th** *c.*	**16th** *c.* (to 1590 only)
Battle	2	1	1
Government	0	0	4
Visit	0	0	1
Imprisonment	0	1	4
Execution	3	0	3
Killing	1	0	1
Obituary	1	0	2
News	0	0	3

It was recorded in 1513 that Gerald Fitzgerald, earl of Kildare, the justiciar of Ireland, died in Kildare and was buried in Christ Church cathedral in Dublin. In 1519 the annalists noted a great plague 'and a great number of the Foreigners of Áth Cliath died of this plague'.[17] In 1538 the general destruction of images and relics was noted, including the Bachall Íosa, 'which was in the town of Áth Cliath, working numerous prodigies and miracles in Érinn from the time of Saint Patrick to that date'.[18] These three events are clearly matters of broad general interest, news items that would have been disseminated countrywide and could well have come to the notice of an annalist who was not necessarily personally acquainted with events in Dublin. They do not document instances of interaction between Dublin and the regions, as such.

In contrast, most of the late sixteenth-century Dublin entries in the Annals of Loch Cé relate to the implications for the provinces of the workings of the Dublin government. Thus, in 1578 it was recorded that Dónal O'Connor Sligo and Brian MacDermott went to the 'great council' at Dublin, and remained there for five weeks. The annalist records that they 'received great honour from the council of Érinn, and they returned safely'.[19] What the Loch Cé annalist does not explicitly state here, but is known from internal evidence,

17 *ALCé*, 1519.2. 18 *ALCé*, 1538.6. 19 *ALCé*, 1578.6.

is that this entry was composed by none other than Brian MacDermott himself, one of the two local lords who had personally visited Dublin.[20] This annalist was not obtaining his references to Dublin at second hand; he had been there himself. In the circumstances, his lack of comment about Dublin is disappointing. He was only concerned to record the politically significant detail that he and O'Connor Sligo had been treated honourably by the Council. In the following year, 1579, the same annals recorded that an English administrator, Edward Fitton, treasurer of Ireland, died at Dublin on the last day of June. The annalist recorded that 'there came not of the Saxon Foreigners, for a long time, one more to be lamented than he, as regards nobility and dignity'.[21] At first glance, this seems an unusual obituary to be included in a set of Gaelic annals, which generally focussed on leaders from within Gaelic society, in the west and north of the country. But Sir Edward Fitton had not always been Dublin-based.[22] He had spent some eight years as president of the province of Connacht, from 1569 to 1577. During that time, he was generally based at Athlone, and may very well have been personally known to Brian MacDermott.

In addition to O'Connor Sligo and MacDermott, visits to Dublin by other representatives of Gaelic lordships are also recorded in the early 1580s. Thus, in 1582, it was recorded that Connor, son of Cormac O'Connor Faly got into a fight with Tadhg son of Giolla Phádraig O'Connor in Dublin, and that Connor was killed. In 1581 William O'Carroll was killed en route home from Dublin by members of the O'Connor Faly.[23] Precisely what business these people had in Dublin is not recorded.

Some who made the journey, there is no doubt, were reluctant visitors. In 1581 Brian Mac Giolla Phádraig died in prison in Dublin.[24] The well-known capture of Red Hugh O'Donnell along with the son of Mac Sweeney Fanad and O'Gallagher at Rathmullan, and their subsequent imprisonment in Dublin, is briefly recorded under the year 1587.[25] In the same year, the capture of four Munster men and their removal to Dublin on the instructions of the privy council is also recorded. In the following year, 1588, the capture of other prominent northern personalities, O'Doherty and O'Gallagher, and their removal to Dublin is noted. There were executions too. In 1581, 'eighteen heirs of the nobles of the Foreigners of Midhe [Meath] were put to death in Baile Átha Cliath, by the justiciar of Erinn'. In another case, in 1585, Alastair son of Sorley Boy Mac Donnell was killed along with twenty of his followers, and his head was taken to Dublin.[26] This was common practice.

20 On Brian MacDermott's annals see Bernadette Cunningham & Raymond Gillespie, *Stories from Gaelic Ireland: microhistories from the sixteenth-century Irish annals* (Dublin, 2003), pp 16–18. **21** *ALCé*, 1579.12. **22** *Oxford Dictionary of National Biography* (60 vols, London, 2004), 29, pp 749–50. **23** *ALCé*, 1582.29; 1581.14. **24** *ALCé*, 1581.23. **25** *ALCé*, 1587.26. **26** *ALCé*, 1581.33; 1585.28.

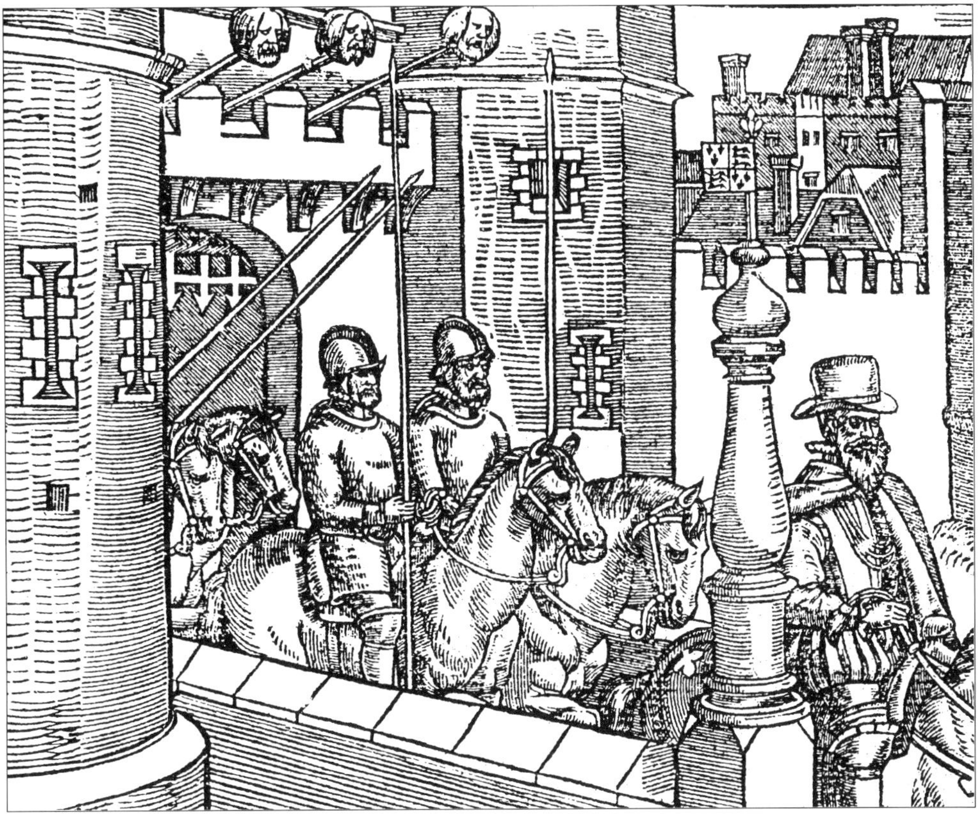

1 Lord Deputy Sidney riding out from Dublin Castle, as depicted in John Derricke's *Image of Ireland* (1581). Derricke draws attention to the heads of executed rebels above the gate, with the comment 'These trunckles heddes do playnly showe, eache rebeles fatall end, And what a haynous crime it is, the Queene for to offend'.

The heads of executed felons were regularly put on public display over the gates of Dublin Castle, as is graphically illustrated in John Derricke's image of the castle (fig. 1). The symbolism of the power of Lord Deputy Sidney riding out is not just denoted by the military personnel accompanying him, but also by the heads propped up above the walls.[27]

The growing power of the Dublin government in the last quarter of the sixteenth century was not just expressed in military terms. There were also the activities of the parliament, convened in 1585. This event was attended by the nobility from all parts of Ireland. The parliament is noted in a very cursory way by the Loch Cé annalist:

27 John Derricke, *The image of Ireland, with a discoverie of woodkarne* (London, 1581, rpr. Belfast, 1985), plate 6.

> The men of Erinn – such of them as were of any account – went to Baile Átha Cliath to an Act of Parliament. The son of O'Maelmhuaidh [O'Molloy], and Edmond Dorcha, son of Domhnall, son of Murchadh Mac Suibhne [MacSweeney], and several other persons, were hanged by this Act of Parliament. The nobles of Erinn came safely from that Council of Áth Cliath, without profit.[28]

The passage shows a very limited understanding on the part of the Loch Cé annalist of the proceedings of the Dublin parliament, but a pragmatic enough interest in the possible benefits to the Gaelic nobility. One might suppose that the annalist's information was obtained in very garbled form from some second- or third-hand source. Yet, that was not the case. The patron of the Annals of Loch Cé, Brian MacDermott, who as already noted wrote some of the late sixteenth-century entries in the manuscript in his own hand, had himself been a member of that 1585 Dublin parliament. He was accompanied there by other nobles from north Connacht including his brother-in-law O'Connor Sligo.[29] Thus, the annalist who provided a rather ill-informed record of what the parliament was about was not lacking in personal contacts who should have been familiar with its proceedings. It is not that the annalist did not have the contacts required to know the details of the Dublin parliament. Rather he judged it to be largely irrelevant to affairs in the MacDermott lordship and the surrounding lordships in north Connacht and southwest Ulster.

It seems clear therefore that the annalists were not simply recording every miscellaneous news item that came their way. Rather they were selecting what was important to them from the wide array of information available to them. Thus what is recorded – or omitted – in these annals about Dublin and events therein is a measure of perception, regarding the relevance of Dublin and events therein to the regions, rather than being a measure of what information about Dublin was available to the annalists. It is not that the sixteenth-century Gaelic annalists did not know much about Dublin; rather they judged that not much of what happened in Dublin had any relevance to them. In so far as Dublin is mentioned at all in the Gaelic annals, the entries normally relate to people from Gaelic lordships who happen to have dealings with Dublin, for good or ill, in the course of their careers.

There is something of a contrast between the Gaelic annals from the northwest and the late-medieval provincial annals from the province of Leinster in relation to how Dublin is represented. Friar Clyn's annals of life in Kilkenny in the early fourteenth century, James Grace's annals written a century later, and the annals of Thady Dowling which focus especially on the post-Norman period and extend as late as the year AD 1600, pay a little more

28 *ALCé*, 1585.11–12. **29** *AFM*, 1585.12.

attention to Dublin.[30] These Anglo-Irish annals sometimes include entries about people and events of specific Dublin interest, although the majority of these relate to archbishops of Dublin, and hence could be perceived as having a broader interest in that the archbishopric extended over a significant portion of mid-Leinster. On more specific topics, Thady Dowling includes references to a university for Dublin under the years 1318 and 1320, but this is still essentially presented in the context of the ecclesiastical career of Archbishop Alexander Bicknor.[31] Outside the ecclesiastical sphere, Dowling's annals contain a few scattered references to Dublin that occur in the context of military activity within the province of Leinster.[32] However, despite their relative proximity to Dublin in geographical terms, as compared with the Gaelic annals from the north and west, the references to Dublin would be very scant in Dowling's annals were it not for the prominence allowed to successive archbishops of Dublin. Thus, any contrast with the perspective of the Gaelic annals in relation to Dublin should not be overstated, and it may be best to regard all of the late-medieval annals, whether Gaelic and Anglo-Irish, and whether written in Latin or Irish, as essentially regional in focus.

The final question to be addressed here is whether the Gaelic annalists' perception of Dublin as largely irrelevant to the regions had changed by the early seventeenth century. In this context, the evidence of the Annals of the Four Masters, compiled in the 1630s, is the most important surviving source. It is known that the principal compiler, Mícheál Ó Cléirigh was a well-travelled man, having spent time in the Spanish Netherlands, joining the Franciscan order in Louvain. He returned to Ireland in 1626 and spent four years travelling to all parts of the country in search of manuscript sources for the lives of Irish saints. He personally visited Dublin on at least two occasions, and was acquainted with the friars who lived in Dublin. He made contact with the Catholic archbishop of the diocese of Dublin, as well as gaining access to the library of James Ussher at Drogheda.[33] In the light of this experience, what did Ó Cléirigh and his associates record about Dublin in their annals (see Table 4)?

30 Richard Butler (ed.), *The Annals of Ireland by Friar John Clyn and Tady Dowling* (Dublin 1848); Richard Butler (ed.), *Jacobi Grace, Kilkenniensis, Annales Hiberniae* (Dublin, 1847); see now, Bernadette Williams (ed.), *The Annals of Ireland by Friar John Clyn* (Dublin, 2007). 31 'Annales breves Hiberniae', pp 20–21, in Butler (ed.), *The Annals of Ireland*. 32 'Annales breves Hiberniae', s.a. 1312, 1398, 1401, 1534. 33 Brendan Jennings, *Michael Ó Cléirigh, chief of the Four Masters and his associates* (Dublin, 1936), pp 55, 61–2.

Table 4. Themes relating to Dublin in the Annals of the Four Masters, 1301–1600

Theme	14th *c.*	15th *c.*	16th *c.*
Battle	1	5	1
Government	0	1	14
Visit	0	1	1
Imprisonment	0	4	15
Execution	1	2	5
Killing	1	0	0
Obituary	1	0	3
News	0	5	3
Other	1	0	0

For the fourteenth century, they recorded almost nothing that was not to be found in several of the earlier annals discussed above. For that entire century, the Four Masters have only two entries that mention Dublin that are not found in the other Gaelic annals: a reference to the arrival of King Richard II at Waterford and his proceeding from there to Dublin in 1394, and the death of Camchluana O'Dougan, slain at Dublin by the people of the king of England in the same year.[34]

For the fifteenth century, the Four Masters have a total of eighteen entries that mention Dublin as compared with seven in the Annals of Ulster, and eight in the Annals of Connacht. Of these eighteen entries in the Annals of the Four Masters, fourteen have no equivalent entry in either the Annals of Ulster or the Annals of Connacht. Thus, it certainly seems that the Four Masters had more information about events in Leinster than the earlier annals, though their source for this information remains unidentified. The extant Anglo-Irish annals by Grace and Dowling were not their source. Three of the entries open with the formula 'An army was led by the English of Dublin …'; 'The English of Dublin and Meath made an incursion into the country of the O'Byrnes …'; 'An army was led by the English of Meath and Leinster into Offaly …'. These episodes are not stories of Dublin successes, however: one ends with an obituary of an Englishman, and the other two stories are the prelude to descriptions of retaliation by the O'Byrnes and O'Connor Faly respectively.[35] An episode in 1453 against O'Neill of Clandeboy, involving the fleet of Dublin against a Welsh fleet as well as various east Ulster chiefs, was more successful.[36]

As elsewhere in the annals, Dublin features in several of the fifteenth-century entries in the Annals of the Four Masters as a place of imprisonment

34 *AFM*, 1394.1; 1394.14. These entries are not found in the extant Latin annals of Grace and Dowling. 35 *AFM*, 1408.2; 1442.15; 1466.13. 36 *AFM*, 1453.7.

of Gaelic chiefs.[37] High-profile prisoners included O'Neill, Eoghan O'Neill, Neachtan O'Donnell, the son of O'Neill of Clandeboy, MacQuillan, Mac Donnell Gallóglach, and O'Mellan in 1425, and Manus O'Donnell and his son in 1434. Dublin was still the place to display heads as trophies, too, as happened in 1452 when the head of Fearghal Ruadh Óg Mageoghegan was taken to Dublin by the sons of the baron of Delvin, for exhibition, as the annalists record. However, the Four Masters also note that the head was afterwards brought back to be buried with the body at Durrow Choluim Cille.[38] Appropriate burial was something the Four Masters would have considered important.

Very occasionally, the Four Masters recorded specific information about Dublin. In 1492, as part of a longer military narrative it is mentioned that 'the street of the Sheep in Dublin [modern Ship Street] was burned by the Lord Justice'.[39] The most revealing entry of all, perhaps, is the record of plague in 1439. It was recorded that

> The plague raged virulently in Dublin, so that three thousand persons, both male and female, large and small, died of it, from the beginning of Spring to the end of the month of May. Donnchadh, the son of O'Dowda, i.e. the son of Tadhg; Conor, the son of Dónal, son of Cormac MacDonagh, and his wife, the daughter of Tadhg MacDonagh; the Vicar of Imleach Íseal; Donnchadh son of Tomaltach O'Beollain; Edmond Burke, the son of Mac William of Clanrickard, and heir to the lordship of Clanricard, all died of the plague.[40]

In this entry the named people are not Dubliners. Most are from west of the Shannon, so the question arises as to why they are mentioned in a Dublin context. Did they contract the plague because they had visited Dublin themselves? It is possible, but far from certain. If the impact of the plague extended beyond the confines of the city then the entry is simply another example of the annalist focussing on prominent Connacht personalities, because it was they rather than Dubliners who were of primary interest to the annalists.

The sixteenth-century events recorded in the Annals of the Four Masters indicate that Dublin was beginning to have a greater relevance to the annalists. The Four Masters record two occasions when Manus O'Donnell visited Dublin, in 1526 as part of a military expedition, and in 1543 to attend before the council. In both instances peace negotiations evidently involved arbi-

37 *AFM*, 1425.3; 1431.24; 1434,7. 38 *AFM*, 1452.19; the same episode is also recorded in an older source, the so-called 'Annals of Lecan': John O'Donovan (ed.), 'The annals of Ireland from the year 1443 to 1468 translated from the Irish by Dudley Firbisse, or as he is more usually called, Duald Mac Firbis, for Sir James Ware in the year 1666', in *Miscellany of the Irish Archaeological Society*, 1 (Dublin, 1846), p. 235. 39 *AFM*, 1492.25. 40 *AFM*,

tration in which both Manus O'Donnell and English officials had a role, evidence of the gradual extension of the jurisdiction of the Dublin government in the provinces.[41] Leaders of Gaelic lordships were becoming a regular sight on the streets of Dublin, by the mid-sixteenth century, or at least their presence at the viceregal court was no longer unusual. In 1550, it was recorded that Anthony St Leger was reappointed as lord justice, 'and a great number of the Irish chieftains went to meet him at the great court at Dublin'.[42] In 1564 the Four Masters recorded that Calbhach O'Donnell and Tarlach O'Boyle 'repaired to Dublin to the lord justice, to confer with him; O'Donnell received great honour and respect from him'.[43] Despite the occurrence of these peaceful transactions, on the basis of the entries in the annals, it appears that cases of imprisonment, and indeed execution, continued to outnumber instances of welcome, honour and respect, by a considerable margin.

There is a curious discrepancy in respect of one such execution. Under the year 1574, the Four Masters provided a description of an occasion where hospitality was shown by Brian son of Feilim Bacach O'Neill to the earl of Essex and his entourage, the ultimate outcome of which was a massacre of Brian's supporters by Essex. The entry then proceeds to state that Brian mac Fheilim, together with his wife and brother, were sent to Dublin, 'where they were cut in quarters'.[44] This account appears to be inaccurate in several respects. The annalists mistakenly describe Essex as the lord justice, an office he did not hold at that time, but more significantly, their reference to Dublin as the place of execution may also be an error. An entry in the corporation book of Carrickfergus for the month of June 1575 records the death of Brian in a very different way: 'In this same month Sir Brian McPhellime and Rowry Ogg McQuillin were executed in this Towne [Carrickfergus]'.[45] There is no mention of Dublin. The very different, if inaccurate, account offered of this event by the Four Masters in the 1630s is instructive. From their seventeenth-century perspective, and relying on what may be presumed to be oral sources, Dublin is presented by the Four Masters as the place where summary justice is administered. Given the contradictory nature of the evidence, the inclusion of a reference to Dublin in this instance should probably be read as evidence of a perception among the annalists – or their contemporary informants – that Dublin had a role in such matters, rather than taking the entry at face value as an accurate record of actual events.

The Four Masters appear to be on surer ground in their description of the 1585 parliament, which was convened at Dublin, but it is worth looking at their entries on the parliament in some detail. Under the year 1585, they record that:

1439.16. 41 *AFM*, 1525.4; 1543.5. 42 *AFM*, 1550.6. 43 *AFM*, 1564.2. 44 *AFM*, 1574.4. 45 Public Record Office of Northern Ireland, T 707, p. 11. I owe this reference to Raymond Gillespie.

> A proclamation of parliament was issued to the men of Ireland, commanding their chiefs to assemble in Dublin precisely on May-day, for the greater part of the people of Ireland were at this time obedient to their sovereign; and, accordingly, they all at that summons did meet in Dublin face to face.[46]

The Four Masters had a rather clearer sense of the workings of the 1585 parliament than did the Loch Cé annalist, and well they might. First, they had the benefit of hindsight and familiarity with later parliaments in 1613–15 and 1634–5 respectively. Secondly, the man credited by Mícheál Ó Cléirigh with being patron of the Annals of the Four Masters, was Fearghal O'Gara, a member of the 1634–5 parliament, which was in progress while the Annals of the Four Masters were being compiled. They had earlier had sponsorship from Tarlach MacCoghlan and Brian Maguire, two other members of that same parliament, so that there is no doubt but that these annalists were personally acquainted with their own contemporary MPs.[47] In the circumstances, they recorded remarkably little about the 1585 parliament. Again it would appear that its proceedings were of little relevance to their worldview.

Under the year 1586 they simply observed: 'The parliament of Dublin was finished this year; and the most remarkable Act passed in it [was one by which] the inheritance of the earl of Kildare [recte Desmond] was annexed to the crown of England'.[48] Several details of this comment are interesting. First, they confused the earl of Kildare with the earl of Desmond – it was Desmond's lands that were confiscated, which suggests again that they may have been relying on an oral source. Secondly, it suggests that they knew little enough about either Desmond or Kildare. Thirdly, they referred to the parliament as the 'parliament of Dublin', rather than the 'Irish parliament'. They did not have a sense of the parliament being representative of Ireland as a whole; their perspective was more local and they were inclined to identify the parliament with the city in which it took place.

* * *

The present discussion of perceptions of Dublin has concentrated on the evidence of four sets of late-medieval Irish annals; but it may be appropriate to conclude by mentioning an important early seventeenth-century Irish text which was a source for the Annals of the Four Masters, and which has Dublin as the backdrop for its opening narrative. The narrative is Lughaidh Ó Cléirigh's biography of Red Hugh O'Donnell. It tells the story of a ship being

46 *AFM*, 1585.8. 47 For the socio-political world of these patrons see Breandán Ó Buachalla, 'Annála Ríoghachta Éireann is Foras feasa ar Éirinn: an comhthéacs comhaimseartha', *Studia Hibernica*, nos 22–3 (1982–3), pp 59–105. 48 *AFM*, 1586.12.

fitted out at Dublin 'with a murderous odious crew', sailing out past the sheltered harbour of Dublin ('cuan Duibhlinne') into the deep sea and sailing past Howth to head northward to Lough Swilly where Red Hugh and his companion were captured and taken back to Dublin to be imprisoned in a strong stone castle. There is a clear image of Dublin Castle not just as a place of oppression but as a place of alienation, where Red Hugh learned the ideology of hostility to the Dublin government from other inmates. It may have been alien, but it was not entirely unfamiliar, because at the time of his escape, one of those who assisted Red Hugh was Tarlach Buidhe O'Hagan. He was described by Ó Cléirigh as 'one of Aodh O'Neill's own people, and he spoke the language of the foreigners and knew them and was acquainted with them, for he was in attendance on the Earl O'Neill whenever he came on business to the city of Dublin'.[49] So, while Dublin was a hostile place politically, it was not an unfamiliar place, and the political elite from all parts of the country regularly visited there in the late sixteenth century. Thus, in the same narrative it was recorded of Donnchadh O'Brien, earl of Thomond, that 'his voice and influence were powerful among the English of Dublin'.[50] Few could match the influence of O'Brien, however, and the more general perception appears to have been of Dublin as a hostile place from which summary justice was administered.

While the evidence of bardic poetry of this period is beyond the scope of the present essay it may be noted in passing that in the late 1570s one poetic composition by the Munster Franciscan priest Eoghan Ó Dubhthaigh included a specific reference to the court at Dublin Castle as symbolic of a place of hostility and rough justice.

> 's ar mháthair Airdrí[ogh] na ndúl,
> ríoghan úr dárab oighre Dia –
> ní fhuighe acht dorn ar a dúid,
> istigh i gcúirt Átha Cliath.
>
> The mother of the High-king of the elements,
> young queen who had God for heir,
> would receive only a slap on the face
> in Dublin Castle.[51]

Earlier in the same poem, it emerged that the geographical extent of Ó Dubhthaigh's conceptual world clearly encompassed Dublin. East and west of the river Suir, he had searched, and even as far as Dublin, in a futile search for a man better than God:

49 Paul Walsh (ed.), *Beatha Aodha Ruaidh Uí Dhomhnaill* (2 vols, ITS, London, 1948–57), i, p. 26. 50 Walsh (ed.), *Beatha Aodha Ruaidh*, i, p. 196. 51 Cuthbert Mhág Craith (ed.),

'S ní mó fuaras ó Shiuir soior
-is féch a bhfoil go hÁth Cliath;
is air do chuirfinn mo gheall
mac máthar is fearr ná Dia.

Neither did I find, east of the Suir
a man superior to God.
And I wager, neither is there such a one
among all the people up to Dublin.[52]

That Dublin should feature in this way in provincial Irish poetry of the late sixteenth century should not be regarded as in any way remarkable. Some level of awareness of Dublin as a power centre and a focal point was nothing new. Long before the establishment of the Viking town, four of the five main roadways in the country led to Dublin. The fifth, from Connacht, led to Drogheda. The site had a commanding position, a safe harbour, and a system of overland communication. It is generally agreed that from the late eleventh century, as Howard Clarke has observed, Dublin was regarded by contemporaries, both native and foreign, as the 'key power centre' in the country,[53] while James Lydon has noted that through the middle ages Dublin Castle was the symbol of royal power in Ireland, and the principal place in Ireland for detaining high-profile prisoners.[54]

This undoubtedly continued to be the case, and in the course of the sixteenth century the effectiveness of the Tudor administration in the Irish provinces was greatly increased. Yet Dublin in the late-medieval Irish annals is a rather elusive entity, and if we were to rely solely on the view from the provinces we would know very little indeed about it. The annals are important, however, as an indicator of how Dublin was perceived by those who lived outside it. Whatever Dubliners may have thought of themselves and their city, the evidence of the regional annals suggests that most people could get by, most of the time, knowing little about Dublin, and the annalists from professional families of Gaelic historians made little effort to make them better informed.

Dán na mBráthar Mionúr (2 vols, Dublin, 1967–80), poem 27, stanza 26. **52** Mhág Craith (ed.), *Dán na mBráthar Mionúr,* poem 27, stanzas 2–3. **53** H.B. Clarke, *Dublin, part 1, to 1610*, Irish Historic Towns Atlas, No. 11 (Dublin, 2002), p. 1. **54** James Lydon, 'Dublin Castle in the middle ages', in Seán Duffy (ed.), *Medieval Dublin III* (Dublin, 2002), pp 120–4.

The annals and chronicles of medieval Dublin: an overview

ALAN J. FLETCHER

Why is a city prompted to produce annals and chronicles? The answer is complex, partly because the question of the city itself is complex. Medieval Dublin, no less than any other medieval European city, comprised a collaboration of social institutions with vested interests; and as is the nature of things, sometimes that collaboration was harmonious, sometimes fraught and difficult. Certain of medieval Dublin's institutions found time to preside over the production of sets of annals and chronicles which, while they issued normally as a by-product of the institution's primary activities, were nevertheless a significant by-product, one uniquely placed to reveal how the matter they recorded impinged on the institution or interest under whose aegis it had been chosen for memorialization.

Indeed, one of their chief functions, something that they can all be considered to have had in common no matter how generically diverse they were among themselves, lay in their more or less explicit support for their sponsor. When that sponsor was an institution, they helped it to articulate the extent of its power and negotiate the terms of its legitimate authority vis-à-vis those other institutions and vested interests with which it found itself obliged to coexist, and sometimes, whether for better or for worse, to compete; indeed, those other institutions might be just as likely to keep annals and chronicles of their own and to derive similar benefits from the keeping of them. When that sponsor was an individual, they helped to insert him, if not indeed also by proxy the institution by which he was in turn sponsored, into the wider scheme of things.

Thus the root activity of all annal and chronicle keeping might be thought to inhere in acts of historical memorialization that were also, to more immediately practical effect, acts of consolidation, whether personal, institutional, or social.[1] And often, accompanying whatever interest of intrinsic historical

1 Giraldus Cambrensis expressed his reason for writing history thus: 'posteritati consulens, inclita nostri temporis acta sub silencio perire non permisi' ('taking thought for posterity, I have not allowed the noble deeds of our time to perish through silence'; A.B. Scott and F.X. Martin (eds), *Expugnatio Hibernica: the Conquest of Ireland by Giraldus Cambrensis* (Dublin, 1978), p. 8, lines 108–9). While his explanation may be a literary topos, it may also gesture, despite its conventionality, towards a similar desire for consolidation: in 'posterity', Giraldus imagined the future existence of his social order, continuing in its currently

actuality the matter recorded may have for us today, may be the interest of the way in which that matter was selected, aspected and perceived. That is, agendas of selection, bias and prejudice in the shaping of annals and chronicles have themselves an historical tale to tell that it is profitable to listen to, rather than merely to identify as so much chaff before discarding and passing on to some privileged actual historical grain. That is, selection, bias, and prejudice are the condition of our annals and chronicles, to be savoured for the histories that they too express, rather than spurned.

As well as producing annals and chronicles of this indigenous sort, supportive of their sponsors, whether institutional or individual, by implicitly defining and thus asserting the parameters of their jurisdiction within the wider order, a city is likely to become an adoptive home to migrant sets of annals and chronicles. These, though originating elsewhere, might find their way into cities and into the libraries of city-based annal and chronicle consumers. Also, by virtue of the fact that cities are likely to be epicentres for important events, they may loom large in the consciousness of visitors to them, some of whom in Dublin's case produced what might be called the 'extraneous' annals and chronicles of the city.

I wish in this essay to illustrate by selected examples the taxonomy outlined in the opening paragraphs. The examples will afford an overview both of what was produced in the annal and chronicle line by the various constituencies of medieval Dublin, and also of what became available in that line within the city. I will also try to keep in mind what this annalling and chronicling production and consumption may tell us about the part played by annals and chronicles in the construction of medieval Dublin's sense of its corporate identity. It may be convenient to begin by glancing at the second species of annal and chronicle just identified, ones of the 'extraneous' sort, because they have a prominent representative from a very early date in Dublin's history, a man whose work weighed heavily upon subsequent writers, even if many of them repudiated his stance.

II

Probably the most famous early historian of medieval Dublin was its incidental historian. Giraldus Cambrensis declared that his purpose in the *Expugnatio Hibernica* (1189) was to record recent events in Ireland. Since Dublin was the stage of many of them, Dublin would necessarily feature prominently in his work, more prominently than in his earlier *Topographia*

recognized form, its continuity partly ensured by its having the benefit of a record of 'noble deeds' to hand and in which were exemplified precisely those values that had held, and would continue to hold, that social order together.

Hibernie (1186–7), which had chiefly devoted itself to the history of Ireland in remoter times.[2] Even if only incidental to the declared aims of his works, Dublin's presence preoccupied Giraldus; he even betrayed his awareness of how a focus on the city might serve to keep his narrative on track and help fulfil its aims: as he announced at one point in the *Expugnatio*, *Dubliniam de cetero revertamur* ('for the rest, let's get back to Dublin').[3]

Although the legacy of Giraldus to later Dublin-based annalists and chroniclers was substantial, the most conspicuous effects of that legacy are seen only in the early-modern period.[4] There are, of course, occasional notable exceptions. Copies of Giraldus's work evidently circulated in late medieval Dublin where they were available for plundering. For example, *c.*1300 someone entered into the *Liber Niger* or Black Book of Christ Church, a manuscript that will be revisited later, a passage that he had found in Giraldus concerning the *Bachall Íosa* (traditionally the staff of St Patrick that had come to Dublin from Armagh and that provided Holy Trinity priory with one of its most famous relics).[5] This entry suggests that the priory either owned or had access to a copy of Giraldus's *Topographia*, whose matter was available for exploitation by the man who made the entry.[6] Or again, and this time in the late fourteenth century, the compiler (whose work will be revisited later) of the annals associated with Thomas Case had access to a formidable

2 On Giraldus's life, see H.C.G. Matthew and B. Harrison (eds), *Oxford dictionary of national biography*, 60 vols (Oxford, 2004), xxi, 925–8. The work of Giraldus, along with the early-thirteenth-century poetic *Song of Dermot and the Earl* (see G.H. Orpen (ed.), *The Song of Dermot and the Earl: An Old French poem from the Carew Manuscript No. 596 in the Archiepiscopal Palace in Lambeth Library* (Oxford, 1892)), comprise the most important historical evidence for events of the late twelfth-century in Ireland. 3 Scott and Martin (eds), *Expugnatio Hibernica*, p. 180, line 28; the prologue to the *Expugnatio* also expresses Giraldus's sense of the difficulty that attended the structuring of chronicle narrative. 4 To cite but one salient case from the beginning of the early-modern period, the compiler (or compilers) of the Book of Howth were heavily dependent on him; its contents are transcribed and calendared in J.S. Brewer and William Bullen (eds), *Calendar of the Carew manuscripts, preserved in the Archiepiscopal Library at Lambeth*, 6 vols (London, 1867–73), v. 5 Dublin, Representative Church Body Library, MS C/6/11, fol. 150v col. b; the fundamental study of this manuscript is by Aubrey Gwynn, 'Some unpublished texts from the Black Book of Christ Church, Dublin', *Analecta Hibernica* 16 (1946), 281–337. See also Colmán Ó Clabaigh, 'The Liber Niger of Christ Church cathedral, Dublin', in R. Gillespie and R. Refaussé (eds), *The medieval manuscripts of Christ Church cathedral, Dublin* (Dublin, 2006), pp 60–80. 6 Compare J.S. Brewer, James Dimock, and George F. Warner (eds), *Giraldi Cambrensis opera*, 8 vols, Rolls Series (London, 1861–91), v, 179 (Distinctio III, capitulum 33, of the *Topographia*). The hand of this entry may be that of Henry la Warre (on whom see further below), since aspects of its letter formation compare closely with those of the marginalia plausibly argued by Gwynn, 'Black Book of Christ Church', to be by la Warre that were entered on fols 201v, 202v, and 203r–v. The same identification is perhaps also to be made for the hand that entered the note about the foundation history of Christ Church on fol. 160 col. b. This note is almost certainly in the hand of the man who entered the fol. 150v col. b note on the *Bachall Íosa* (and who may thus in turn be la Warre, if Gwynn's suggestion is correct).

array of imported and native annal and chronicle compilations, and drew even more heavily on Giraldus's *Expugnatio*.[7]

Nevertheless, the flowering of the influence of Giraldus upon indigenous Dublin historiography belongs to a later period. No other subsequent late medieval visitors to Dublin who chose to record their experiences left such a legacy. For example, Sir Henry Chrysted did not, who, while not an annalist or chronicler by trade, reported to the chronicler Jean Froissart events in Dublin in the later fourteenth century that Froissart wrote up in his *Chroniques*; nor did Jean Creton, a member of the entourage of Richard II who composed a metrical French account of the king's second Irish visit in 1399.[8] Both these late fourteenth-century visitors evidently knew Dublin, but their observations of historical events happening in the city can be mentioned in passing and solely for the sake of comprehensiveness. What they had to say was not reworked, to my knowledge, in subsequent, indigenously-produced Dublin annals and chronicles. Instead, these subsequent works depended in the main on other annal and chronicle compilations, most of which were anonymous, rather than on the personally and idiosyncratically coloured accounts of visitors.

III

It is time now to turn to these mainly anonymous endeavours, for they comprise the more interesting and complex aspect of this overview. I will consider them under two broad headings: those produced under ecclesiastical auspices, and those under civic ones. In the ecclesiastically-produced annals and chronicles, Dublin city and its workings tend not to feature as topics in their own right; the city is present simply as a locus of events. A more productive quarry in which to prospect for emerging concepts of civic identity, and where civic concerns are most conspicuously memorialized, is in the Dublin Chronicle and a series of texts to which it gives rise.[9] Amongst Dublin's indigenously-produced annals and chronicles, this latter group is qualitatively different in this regard. But for the moment we remain with the annals and chronicles that were ecclesiastically superintended.

7 Also used by him were the chronicle of Roger of Hoveden, the *Historia Anglorum* of Henry of Huntingdon, the *Gesta Pontificium* of William of Malmesbury, the *Expugnatio Hibernica* of Giraldus Cambrensis (this text prominently drawn on for annals from 1170 onwards), the *Polychronicon* of Ranulph Higden, and yet other hagiographical materials and materials relating to Irish monastic orders. The are printed in J.T. Gilbert (ed.), *Chartularies of St. Mary's abbey Dublin: with the register of its house at Dunbrody, and annals of Ireland*, Rolls Series, 2 vols (London, 1884), ii, pp 241–86. 8 Henry Chrysted, an English knight captured while in the service of the earl of Ormond, married a daughter of his captor, learned Irish, and was employed for his linguistic skill as an intermediary by Richard II. For Creton's account, see John Webb (ed. and trans.), 'Histoire du roy

The tradition of keeping annals and chronicles within medieval Dublin was to some extent an imported one and driven by the momentum of deference to old custom. If an institution had already nurtured annal and chronicle keeping, it would be likely to continue so to do as a means of maintaining its institutional ethos when transplanted to a new context, especially when that new context was a colonial one with attendant colonial anxieties that the keeping of annals and chronicles might in its own way help to alleviate. Some of medieval Dublin's most influential indigenous annals and chronicles began life as English imports which were then further developed and customized according to the circumstances of their new Irish environment. As might be expected, a characteristic of these imported cases is the way in which their earliest entries either exclusively or chiefly concern non-Irish matter.

An outstanding group of instances is provided in the *Liber Niger* or Black Book of Christ Church, a manuscript whose core probably came to Dublin as an English import with its owner late in the 1290s and around which subsequent material chiefly of Irish and local concern coagulated.[10] Amongst its various contents the manuscript includes what it calls a *cronica*, a record of English historical events from 1066 to 1291 that a colophon declares to have been written in the church of St Paul in London on the feast of Pentecost (6 June) in 1294.[11] Since the handwriting of the *cronica* dates palæographically to the end of the thirteenth century, it may even be that of the St Paul's annalist himself, rather than simply that of a contemporary copyist of his work. This *cronica* was then supplemented by a short series of marginalia, added in a different, though near contemporary, hand of *c.*1300.[12] Most of them record matter of Irish and local interest, the earliest among them dating to 9 December 1294, some six months, therefore, after the *cronica* was said to have been written in London, and the latest dating to 1301, the year in which is noted the outbreak of a fire in Dublin that burnt St Werburgh's church and the greater part of the city.

Aubrey Gwynn marshalled a persuasive argument that these marginalia were entered by the Augustinian canon Henry la Warre, originally of Bristol, and elected prior of Holy Trinity, Dublin, on 31 January 1301. Since the note about the *Bachall Íosa* on fol. 150v col. b and another about the foundation history of Holy Trinity on fol. 160 col. b seem to be in the same hand, these notes may have been entered by la Warre too. He had evidently been resident

d'Angleterre Richard', *Archaeologia* 20 (1824). 9 See further on these in the present volume, Raymond Gillespie, 'Dubliners view themselves: the Dublin City Chronicle', pp 213–27. 10 Gwynn, 'Black Book of Christ Church'. 11 Dublin, Representative Church Body Library, MS C/6/11, fol. 202 col b; the name of the writer of the *cronica* has been carefully expunged. 12 Dublin, Representative Church Body Library, MS C/6/11, fol. 201v upper margin, fol. 202v upper and lower margins, fol. 203 lower margin, and fol. 203v lower margin.

in Dublin at Holy Trinity in the years immediately preceding his election. While in England, then, la Warre somehow acquired the St Paul's London *cronica*, essentially English in focus, and subsequently brought it with him, not long after it had been written, to Dublin, where he supplemented it with material that reflected his new Irish circumstances. Gwynn's description of la Warre's marginalia as constituting a *continuation* of his imported chronicle is doubtful because the marginalia are not systematic enough so to qualify, nor added consecutively after the last entry, but randomly and without regard to serial chronological order. Yet, this very fact of informality might be scrutinized and pressed further to reveal la Warre's attitude to what he was doing and also to the *cronica* that he was doing it to.

Evidently, this was the section of his substantial book that drew la Warre's attention when he was minded to enter material of an annalistic sort. In it he had many other folios available on which he could have made his annalistic entries, yet he chose to do so here: the pre-existing *cronica* made a natural catchment area for his own entries, and just a few folios further on there would be found another set of annals that will be considered here shortly and which, along with the St Paul's London *cronica*, constituted what was in effect a gravitational nucleus of annal and chronicle material in this particular portion of the book. Nevertheless, the sheer informality in the arrangement of la Warre's annalistic entries also argues for his more strictly pragmatic approach to the annal and chronicle genre, one that paid little heed, on this occasion at least, to observing any of the niceties of its formal literary conventions or format.

Possibly the difference between la Warre's interest as manifest in the casual manner in which his entries were made and the interest manifest in the more formal manner of their destination, the *cronica* proper, most nearly resembles the difference that distinguishes the keeping of diary memoranda from the maintenance of an official, serial history: both activities may be thought of as overlapping but not fully commensurate; both record history, but one pragmatically, with the implications that pragmaticism entails, and the other formally, with its implications of a different order. Indeed, la Warre's choice of destination for his marginalia does more than merely betray a regard, simultaneously respectful yet utilitarian, for the chronicle and annal genre; it also implicitly reveals a man weaving together into one seamless alignment the concerns of two different geographies and their respective political interests. La Warre had become part of Dublin now, and his incorporation *into* Dublin reflects also the terms of his incorporation *of* Dublin. That is, the process of incorporation flowed both ways. So there is a cultural suturing going on in the *Liber Niger*, seen here in la Warre's manner of adopting his adoptive city, so to speak.

The manuscript's annalistic sections are places in which this two-way process is to be seen occurring. One imagines that if some subsequent Irish scribe were to come along and make a copy of the *Liber Niger*'s *cronica* with la Warre's marginal additions, he would have tidied the additions into the main body of his newly copied *cronica* text, and would have produced as a result a composite document in which the la Warre ingredient simply added to the general blend. It would then conceivably have become an ingredient difficult enough to distinguish in its own right, especially if that Irish scribe chose to add further Irish material on his own account. This sort of scenario, the steady elision into one cumulative document of contributions from different contributors each with their own particular interests and outlook, seems paradigmatic of how annals and chronicles were perpetuated in medieval Dublin, and indeed in medieval Ireland generally: as their texts circulated, they attracted layer upon layer of textual strata, these layers being instructive in themselves to the historian or textual archaeologist (provided, that is, that they are not so utterly assimilated into the cumulative document that their original circumstances of compilation lie beyond retrieval). Yet, even if the attempts at textual excavation yield imperfect or inconclusive results, there is no substitute for trying to dig through the various textual layers in order to uncover buried histories about the circumstances and processes of chronicle compilation.

The essential consolidating function of the annal/chronicle genre that was spoken of in general terms at the beginning of this essay, and indeed the comparable function of cognate genres like la Warre's marginal additions, is multiply witnessed in the *Liber Niger*, and for that reason it offers an especially valuable entrée to the general topic of annal and chronicle keeping in medieval Dublin. The *Liber Niger* can be viewed as a radar screen, as it were, of this activity as it was registering in one of the city's chief cultural and political institutions, Holy Trinity priory, between *c.*1300 and the early years of the sixteenth century.

Henry la Warre's Dublin additions to the London *cronica* are not the only blip on that radar screen. It was mentioned earlier that a second, briefer, annal/chronicle compilation is to be found a few further folios on from the *cronica* that helps generate a small gravitational nucleus in this section of the manuscript of annalling and chronicling activity. This second set of annals, entered in a different hand of the early fourteenth century, and of which only the first folio is extant, also calls for comment.[13] Originally, there existed two further folios that continued this set of annals. These were subsequently cut away. As much of the annals as is extant runs from Christ's Incarnation to the

13 Dublin, Representative Church Body Library, MS C/6/11, fol. 202. Gwynn, 'Black Book of Christ Church', seems to suggest that this second chronicle was la Warre's holograph copy, but this cannot be so, because its hand bears no comparison with that of the marginalia more plausibly attributed to him (nor indeed to that of the notes on fols 150v col. b and 160 col. b that also seem to be in the same hand; see footnote 6 above).

year 1168, but there are clear indications that entries extended at least to *c.*1300 before the excision occurred. Gwynn called these annals the 'Anglo-Irish Annals of Christ Church', although I prefer simply to call them the Black Book Annals, since what we have in them is a set of annals in Latin that were probably both compiled and copied under the aegis of Holy Trinity priory *c.*1300. Thus their compilation coincides exactly with la Warre's priorate. It may even owe something to his encouragement. The Black Book Annals were worked up partly out of an earlier set of annals imported from somewhere in England, though as Bernadette Williams has clearly demonstrated, this was not from the Benedictine abbey of Winchcombe in Gloucestershire, the provenance initially proposed by Robin Flower and seconded by Aubrey Gwynn.[14]

Interestingly, much of the matter of the Black Book Annals also appears recycled in another set of indigenous Dublin annals, those associated with Thomas Case, this time compiled late in the fourteenth century and often but probably incorrectly linked with the Cistercian monastery of St Mary's.[15] These so-called Annals of St Mary's, however, contain in addition some local Dublin entries for the years 1074, 1084–5, and 1095 (that is, entries which coincide with the archiepiscopates of Patrick, Dublin's second bishop, and of Donngus, Dublin's third) which cannot be traced to any known source. On the basis of their appearance, Gwynn inferred the former existence of what he called the 'First Dublin Chronicle', a chronicle or set of annals inaugurated, one imagines, at Holy Trinity priory in the last quarter of the eleventh century, and that was available for amalgamation with the annals imported from England some while after their arrival in Dublin.[16] Perhaps there existed indeed such a 'First Dublin Chronicle', but it is equally possible to imagine a situation similar to la Warre's also arising much earlier, in the late eleventh century. That is, annals imported into Dublin may have come to acquire late eleventh-century annotations or marginalia of local Irish interest. Therefore, nothing so formal as a 'First Dublin Chronicle' need necessarily have existed at all.

14 Robin Flower, 'Manuscripts of Irish Interest in the British Museum', *Analecta Hibernica* 2 (1931), 292–340; see pp 317–29. For a convincing challenge to Flower's conclusions, see Bernadette I. Williams, 'The Latin Franciscan Anglo-Irish annals of medieval Ireland' (unpublished PhD thesis, University of Dublin, 1991). 15 Extant only in Dublin, Trinity College, MS 175. In his description of this manuscript, Marvin L. Colker, *Trinity College Library Dublin: catalogue of the mediaeval and renaissance Latin manuscripts*, introduction by William O'Sullivan, 2 vols (Aldershot and Brookfield, Vermont, 1991), I, 330–37, considers the copy of the so-called Annals of St Mary's as a holograph of the scribe Thomas Case, written in 1427, but conceivably the script could date to around the middle of the fifteenth century on palæographic grounds, and if so prove MS 175 a slightly later copy of the Case original. The compilation of the so-called Annals of St Mary's was dated by Gwynn, 'Black Book of Christ Church', to *c.*1230–40, with further compilation happening in the late fourteenth century. 16 The compilation circumstances are in fact even more complex, with evidence of some Cistercian input into

Another set of indigenous Dublin annals produced beyond the walls of Holy Trinity, are those generally known as the Chronicle of Pembridge, almost certainly from the John de Pembridge who was prior of the Dominican convent of St Saviour, Dublin, intermittently from at least 1329 until *c.*1343.[17] His annals are continued from the year 1347 (at which point the manuscript declares 'Hic finitur chronica Pembrigii') to 1370 by another Dominican, possibly a friar of Trim.[18] This time, then, we may be dealing with a set of annals that migrated out of Dublin where they were originally compiled to Trim where they were continued. Whatever the truth of that,[19] Pembridge compiled his annals from pre-existing materials, and added to them further material on his own initiative.

Thus a pattern can be perceived in medieval Dublin already, a full century or more before that pattern would repeat itself in la Warre, of annal or chronicle importation, compounded subsequently with local amplification, perhaps fully-fledged annal continuation, witnessed within the *Liber Niger* of Holy Trinity priory.[20] A collateral implication of this would seem to be that an annalling and chronicling mentality comparable to la Warre's was already at large in the priory when he joined it in the late thirteenth century. At the end of her thesis on the chronicling activity of the friars of the Anglo-Irish communities of medieval Ireland, Williams poses the question, rhetorically, of whether the friars produced annals 'because it was the custom to do so?'[21] The resounding answer to that rhetorical question must be, yes, they surely did. Nor was that custom exclusively mendicant, for it has parallels outside the mendicant orders. What was happening among the Augustinian canons of Holy Trinity priory, for example, certainly seems in part to have been a function of custom.

the imported annals, alongside the input from the 'First Dublin Chronicle'. **17** Bernadette A. Williams, 'Pembridge, John (*fl.* 1347)', *Oxford dictionary of national biography*, Oxford University Press, Sept 2004; online edn, Jan. 2008 [http://www.oxforddnb.com/view/article/21825, accessed 12 Feb 2008]; eadem, 'The Dominican annals of Dublin', in Seán Duffy (ed.), *Medieval Dublin II* (Dublin, 2001), 142–68. Dr Williams is currently preparing a new edition of these important annals. **18** A medieval copy of the Chronicle of Pembridge is available in Dublin, Trinity College, MS 583, fols 1–34; its Dominican continuation from 1348 to 1370 runs from fols 34v–7. The palæography of this copy of the chronicle dates to the middle of the fifteenth century. The Chronicle of Pembridge found its way into other annal compilations and later copies, as, for example, in Dublin, Trinity College, MS 584, a transcription made by Philip Flattisbury in 1517 for Gerald FitzGerald, ninth earl of Kildare (On Flattisbury, see the entry in Matthew and Harrison, *Oxford dictionary of national biography*, xx, 1.) **19** It is interesting that the final entry has the obits of two Meath barons, Simon Fleming of Slane and John Cusack of Colmolyn, but also of John Taylour, formerly mayor of Dublin, 'vir dives et potens in pecuniis'. **20** One imagines that, had the *cronica* with la Warre's marginalia provided the exemplar for some subsequent copy, the copyist might have tidied the marginalia into the main text of his copy. **21** Williams, 'Latin Franciscan Anglo-Irish annals', p. 372.

At Holy Trinity, we have seen this custom being observed from at least the late eleventh century to the early fourteenth, and a further instance may be cited to illustrate its longevity at least into the early years of the fifteenth century, for it gives further credence to the proposition that an annalling and chronicling mentality prevailed in the late-medieval priory. Another prior, possibly James de Redenesse, is likely to have been the person responsible for entering memoranda, many of which are annalistic in nature, onto the fly- and endleaves of the de Derby Psalter in the opening years of the fifteenth century. This Psalter is the most opulent manuscript book to have survived from the priory's archives. By choosing to enter annalistic memoranda there, Prior de Redenesse ensured as nearly as human provision could contrive that they would be preserved to posterity. Moreover, the esteem of annalling and chronicling per se, over and above the intrinsic interest of the matter memorialized, again seems reflected in de Redenesse's activity, just as it was in la Warre's.[22]

Esteem for old custom in the recording of annals and chronicles therefore had an even longer pedigree at Holy Trinity than it did among the friars studied by Bernadette Williams. Indeed, in all principal departments of the church in medieval Dublin (that is, amongst the church's regulars, its mendicants, and its seculars), annal and chronicle keeping found a natural habitat.

For the sake of completeness in this overview, the place occupied by the last group, the seculars of Dublin, needs consideration. Their activity can be approached both obliquely and also directly. First, obliquely, in that they can be seen either owning, or copying, annals and chronicles that had originated in other clerical departments, those departments sometimes even being lodged beyond the Pale and in relatively remote places. Thus the so-called Annals of Multyfarnham, for example, which were principally the compilation *c.*1272 of a Franciscan friar, Stephen de Exonia, who was active in Connacht, are extant in a manuscript that, according to an inscription of ownership, passed from its previous mendicant owner, a certain Frater John Knock, into the possession of a secular, John Hothum, rector of Cloghran.[23] The inscription in the manuscript that records this transmission is entered in a hand that Marvin Colker, in his catalogue of the medieval Latin manuscripts of Trinity College, Dublin, dated to the fifteenth century.[24] However, there is reason to doubt this date. The hand is an informal Anglicana cursive without the least trace of influence

22 On the de Derby Psalter, see most recently Alan J. Fletcher, 'The de Derby Psalter of Christ Church Cathedral, Dublin', in Gillespie and Refaussé, *Medieval manuscripts of Christ Church cathedral*, pp 81–102. 23 Dublin, Trinity College, MS 347. MS 347 is a typical small-format mendicant anthology, most of whose scribes were active *c.*1300; Alan J. Fletcher, 'Preaching in late-medieval Ireland: the English and the Latin tradition', in Alan J. Fletcher and Raymond Gillespie (eds), *Irish preaching, 700–1700* (Dublin, 2001), pp 56–80 (see pp 66–9). 24 Colker, *Mediaeval and renaissance Latin manuscripts*, i, 710–40; see p. 739 for his dating of the inscription of ownership which appears at the foot of fol. 1.

from Secretary script, and its general aspect conforms with scripts in vogue around the middle of the fourteenth century.[25] But in addition, it may be possible to identify who this John Hothum was. The name is not especially common in Dublin records.[26] There was, however, a John Hothum, canon of St Patrick's Cathedral, who was active in the early part of the fourteenth century,[27] and he may well be the individual of this name who was a senior royal administrator under Edward I and Edward II, on whose behalf he undertook more than one important mission to Ireland, for which he was rewarded with the bishopric of Ely in 1316.[28] The palæography of the inscription would be compatible with his date. But in addition, the inscription says that Hothum was rector of Cloghran. Cloghran, some few miles to the north of Dublin, was part of the rich prebend of Swords which returned funds directly to the St Patrick's cathedral economy. Thus there seems little doubt that not so very long after John de Exonia compiled these annals in a friary in the west, they migrated east into the Pale, where they also became available outside their original mendicant context to a secular cleric – indeed, to a member of the chapter of St Patrick's Cathedral. This case history amounts to another interesting instance of annal and chronicle consumption in medieval Dublin of sets of annals that have migrated into it.

Or again, the so-called Annals of St Mary's Dublin, which as was seen were a compilation finally coming together in the late fourteenth century, are now extant in a manuscript of the following century which was copied not by a member of an order but by a secular, another man whose name survives. In fact, the actual date is known on which he finished his copying. On 25 May 1427, one Thomas Case, a clerk of the church of St Werburgh, copied what he called his *Cronica* and what today is commonly (if misleadingly perhaps) referred to as the Annals of St Mary's.[29]

25 Compare Malcolm B. Parkes, *English cursive book hands, 1250–1500*, repr. with minor revisions (London, 1979), Plate 1 (ii). **26** Similarity of name suggests prima facie that he may have been a relative of William de Hothum OP, archbishop of Dublin, 1297–8 (Another William de Hothum, also like John a canon of St Patrick's Cathedral, is on record between 1303 and 1306). **27** He is on record as a canon of St Patrick's Cathedral between 1306 and 1313. He appears in the *Dignitas Decani* of the cathedral as a co-signatory to the initiative of the canons in 1306 to be vigilant on behalf of the cathedral's temporalities (N.B. White (ed.), *The 'Dignitas Decani' of St Patrick's Cathedral Dublin*, with an introduction by Aubrey Gwynn (Dublin, 1957), p. 82). The inscription of ownership is found at the foot of fol. 1. **28** For whom, see M.C. Buck, 'Hotham, John (*d.* 1337)', *Oxford dictionary of national biography*, Oxford University Press, Sept 2004; online edn, Jan 2008 [http://www.oxforddnb.com/view/article/13851, accessed 13 Feb. 2008]. **29** Dublin, Trinity College, MS 175, fols 2v–13v; Case's colophon is at the bottom of fol. 13v; see footnote 15 above for suggestions about the date of this copy. Some word has been erased after the word *Cronica*, but too thoroughly for ultraviolet light to reveal what it may have been. These annals are edited by Gilbert, *Chartularies*, ii, 241–86. Again there may be some institutional link between the *Cronica* and Holy Trinity priory by virtue of the fact that there is some evidence of commerce between the priory and St Werburgh's clerical personnel, certainly by the early sixteenth century, and possibly earlier; see Raymond

These two instances offer examples of what has been termed here oblique witness either to Dublin seculars simply encountering annals or even transmitting them.[30] Further, they provide additional incidental evidence of the investment in annal and chronicle keeping that the surviving evidence suggests pervaded medieval Dublin's entire ecclesiastical community. For a direct witness to palpable authorship and compilation of annals by a secular cleric we need only turn to the person of Henry Marlborough. Marlborough belonged to an old Dublin family whose name in the city is first on record from 1219.[31] He was rector of Killadoon, Dublin diocese, in 1398, vicar of Balscaddan in 1412, and vicar of Donabate in 1413. He died either in 1421 or in some year shortly thereafter.[32] Thus he was a contemporary of Thomas Case, the secular cleric and copyist of the 'Annals of St Mary's'. Unlike Case, however, Marlborough may be unequivocally thought to have taken responsibility for compiling and also personally contributing to what he called his *Cronica excerpta de medulla diversorum* (his 'Chronicle extracted from the marrow of various men'), and which he apparently began writing in 1406.

Marlborough's marrowbone chronicle provides an informative snapshot of a chronicler at work.[33] While he owed a major debt to earlier writers, as his title indeed suggests (and the famous chronicling monk of Chester, Ranulf Higden, is explicitly invoked as one of them), much in it was nevertheless his own composition.[34] It contains a cluster of what might be described as chronicle topics, whose inclusion was possibly dictated as much by convention as it may have been by personal preoccupation. If there is a personal element, perhaps it inheres in the particular choices that Marlborough made from a conventional menu of chronicle topics. Thus his annals record events like the deaths of famous men (sometimes giving the circumstances of those deaths), archiepiscopal consecrations and other high-ranking spiritual and temporal

Gillespie, 'The coming of reform, 1500–58', in Kenneth Milne (ed.), *Christ Church cathedral, Dublin: a history* (Dublin, 2000), pp 155 and 157. The family name of Case or (Casse) is prominent in Dublin civic records of the sixteenth century. **30** How much, if anything, Thomas Case added to the so-called Annals of St Mary's on his own initiative is impossible to tell. **31** See the entry on Marlborough in Matthew and Harrison, *Oxford dictionary of national biography*, xxxvi, 717–18. **32** On 12 May, in whichever year it was, according to the Book of Obits and Martyrology. **33** I have consulted the two known early manuscripts of his chronicle that contain the Irish entries excerpted as an appendix: Troyes, Bibliothèque Municipale, MS 1316, and London, British Library, MS Cotton Vitellius E. v. The Troyes manuscript is the earlier, being a late-fifteenth-century copy on parchment; its script suggests that it was written by a continental scribe. The London manuscript is later, a mid-sixteenth-century copy on paper; its script belongs to these islands. While I have preferred in general to follow the Troyes manuscript, since it ends imperfect at the entries for 1420, the two entries for 1421 referred to in this essay have necessarily been consulted in the London manuscript. **34** Gearóid Mac Niocaill, *The medieval Irish annals*, Medieval Irish History Series 3 (Dublin, 1975), p. 39, also points out that Marlborough had access to some of the sources used by Pembridge and of those associated with Case for the thirteenth century.

appointments, and Irish military campaigns and meetings of parliament. All this is standard chronicle fare, even down to recording the building or collapse of Dublin bridges.[35] Sometimes, like other Dublin-based chroniclers, he glances at events happening in England.[36] Yet in places a more arguably personal note emerges in the context of these conventional chronicle topics. For example, while reporting the death of an archbishop might be routine for many a chronicler, Marlborough's obituary for Thomas Cranley, archbishop of Dublin (†25 May 1417) is also turned in terms that suggest personal acquaintance.[37] A less edifying personal note, an interest in church gossip, may have been struck in his account *s.a.* 1421 of the citation of Richard Ó hÉidigheáin (O'Hedian), archbishop of Cashel, by John Geese, bishop of Waterford and Lismore, on thirty charges, including a charge that Archbishop Ó hÉidigheáin had stolen a ring from an image of St Patrick to give to his concubine.[38]

Although Marlborough knew Dublin well, as with other Dublin-based ecclesiastical chroniclers before him, the city featured only incidentally in his writing. Nevertheless, what we do see emerging in his writing more noticeably relative to the writing of his predecessors is an awareness of the city as represented in the persons of its civic officers.[39] For example, under 1419, the death of a former mayor, Edmund Berle, is noted, with his burial at the Black Friars, and, under 1421, the death of another former mayor, Geoffrey Gallane, with his burial at the same place.[40] A particularly good example of this awareness shows in Marlborough's record of events in 1402, when the mayor of Dublin, John Drake, led a hosting of the citizens of Dublin against the O'Byrnes of the Wicklow mountains.[41] This particular battle near Bray

35 For natural disasters and plagues, compare Gilbert, *Chartularies*, ii, 317 (*s.a.* 1271); for civic calamities like the burning of Dublin and the campanile of Holy Trinity priory, compare Gilbert, *Chartularies*, ii, 319 (*s.a.* 1283). An emphasis on battle and warfare is a common chronicle preoccupation (compare famously in this respect Geoffrey of Monmouth's *Historia regum Britanniae* of *c.*1136–8). Amongst records of meetings of parliament, compare those in Kilkenny and Westminster, Gilbert, *Chartularies*, ii, 294–5 (*s.a.* 1309–10). Episcopal consecrations are often noted in the annals preserved in the manuscript by Thomas Case. 36 He is known to have travelled to England, though in the Irish context, his recording of some English matter may have been a convention in itself, over and above its being prompted by personal acquaintance. 37 Troyes, Bibliothèque Municipale, MS 1316, fol. 52v. The praise of Cranley, by Marlborough's standards, is fulsome (he was a 'vir largus et elemosinarius, magnus clericus, doctor sacre theologie, egregius predicator … sibi diceretur speciosus forma pre filijs hominum', 'a generous man and an alms-giver, a great cleric, a doctor of sacred theology, an outstanding preacher … of whom it might be said that he was in form fairer than the sons of men …'). 38 London, British Library, MS Cotton Vitellius E. v, fol. 147r–v. 39 There are, of course, occasional exceptions; compare the entry in the Case MS (*s.a.* 1370) when the death of John Taylor, former mayor and a 'vir dives et potens in pecuniis' ('a rich man, and one with financial muscle') is noted (Gilbert, *Chartularies*, ii, 398). 40 See Troyes, Bibliothèque Municipale, MS 1316, fol. 53 for Berle; see London, British Library, MS Cotton Vitellius E. v, fol. 147r–v, for Gallane. Berle was mayor in 1382–3, and Gallane mayor in 1396–7. 41 The

may have come to loom large in the civic consciousness, for although the habit of tallying the slain was itself a convention of chronicle writing – Marlborough gives the tally of the O'Byrne slain as 493 – another ecclesiastical contemporary of his, probably James de Redenesse, prior of Holy Trinity, who also chronicled the event, gave an alternative tally of 487.[42] What may be a little less conventional is the stress placed by both chroniclers on the civic component in this episode.

The city of Dublin, then, present by proxy in the persons of its prominent civic office holders, starts to become somewhat more noticeable in Dublin's ecclesiastically-sponsored annals and chronicles from the late fourteenth century: *c.*1400 makes a convenient date from which to begin charting the emergence, at least in documentary record, of this sort of civic awareness amongst Dublin's ecclesiastically-based chroniclers. And this may not be fortuitous, for it seems to be the fifteenth century that saw the evolution of the final category of annal and chronicle keeping that calls for attention here.

IV

As stated at the outset, the memorializing city is a complex organism whose rationales for memorialization may be correspondingly complex. So far, I have given an overview of the annals and chronicles produced within the principal departments of the church in medieval Dublin. These ecclesiastically-sponsored texts tend to cannibalize each other extensively, and in doing so they bridge different religious orders. They also bridge geographical divides: they immigrate into the city, where they become part of the city's evolving annal and chronicle tradition, and also emigrate out of it, taking that tradition elsewhere.[43] In respect of its ecclesiastically-sponsored annals and chronicles, Dublin is more fittingly regarded as a hub of annalling and chronicling activity than as an historiographical topic in its own right. However, from *c.*1400, notices of civic officers in ecclesiastical annals gain ground, and through them we witness a capacity evolving for conceiving the city of Dublin as a constituency of specifically secular civic forces and processes.

recording of hostings against the Irish has, of course, a longer history (for example, one is recorded *s.a.* 1309 in Gilbert, *Chartularies*, ii, 294), but it becomes more conspicuous from the fifteenth century on. 42 For Marlborough's tally, see Troyes, Bibliothèque Municipale, MS 1316, fol. 50v (the copy of the entry in London, British Library, MS Cotton Vitellius E. v, fol. 145v, concurs). For the de Redenesse tally, see Oxford, Bodleian Library, MS Rawlinson G. 185 (commonly known as the de Derby Psalter; on this manuscript, see Fletcher, footnote 20 above. The de Redenesse tally was misread by G.J. Hand, 'The psalter of Christ Church, Dublin (Bodleian MS Rawlinson G. 185)', *Reportorium Novum*, 1 (1955–6), 311–22; see p. 318. 43 The fact that much of the matter of the Black Book Annals, copied under the aegis of the Augustinian canons, appears in at least two other annal collections, demonstrates that there was some circulation and

This capacity is seen in its most developed form in the second species of annal or chronicle that falls within the remit of this overview. This species seems to have been a fifteenth-century development, and it evolves not out of an ecclesiastical institution but a lay one.[44] The earliest extant recension of a document that, for want of any title of its own, may appropriately be referred to as the Dublin Chronicle, exists in rotular form in Dublin, Trinity College, MS 543/2/14, and one of its most salient features, perhaps one so self-evident as to cause it to go unremarked, is its composition not in hieratic Latin, the language of the chronicles discussed hitherto, but in common English.[45] This civic chronicle is akin to one that evolved contemporaneously in London, a city with which Dublin often compared itself during this period.[46] Further, the Dublin Chronicle shares certain formal traits with the London Chronicle that suggest that it was not a coincidentally parallel chronicle tradition but one that at some level was genetically related: the four essential components of each Dublin Chronicle annal (the year in Arabic numerals, a statement of who the mayor was, the regnal year, and the two bailiffs in that year) are matched in the London Chronicle, though not necessarily in the same sequential order.[47]

While the fundamental function of the Dublin Chronicle could certainly be regarded as resembling that of the church-sponsored ones to the extent that they were all consolidatory undertakings, unlike them, the Dublin Chronicle, in its earliest extant recension, admits no obviously discernible cross-over of content from any other annal compilation, and certainly not from any that was ecclesiastically sponsored.[48] Thus it seems, at least in its

exchange of annal/chronicle material between Dublin's various religious congregations and houses. This is hardly surprising when there are many precedents for similar circulation and exchange from much earlier times elsewhere in Europe. 44 Even though, as already noted, ecclesiastically-sponsored annals and chronicles seem to begin paying noticeable attention to civic office holders from *c.*1400. 45 I will edit this chronicle, with a commentary, in a forthcoming publication. 46 Mary-Rose McLaren, *The London chronicles of the fifteenth century: a revolution in English writing* (Cambridge, 2002). There is some evidence that civic chronicles of this species were kept in other walled towns of medieval and early-modern Ireland. Drogheda, for example, maintained such a set of annals that seem to have begun each annal with a statement of the year, the mayor for that year, and then either recording, or not, as the case may be, some historical matter related to that year. This compares with the practice of the Dublin Chronicle. The Drogheda annals, however, survive only in the form of a late-seventeenth-century transcript by Sir James Ware in Oxford, Bodleian Library, MS Rawlinson B. 484 (see Diarmuid Mac Iomhair, 'Two old Drogheda chronicles', *Journal of the County Louth Archaeological and Historical Society* 15 (1961), 88–95). 47 Also, of course, in the London Chronicle it is the mayor and *sheriffs* who are named. Sometimes in the Dublin Chronicle, a simple statement of who the mayor and bailiffs were in a year constitutes the entire substance of the annal entry; certain of the Drogheda annals seem to have been similar in this regard (unless the Ware transcript was not minded to reproduce them fully and is thus misrepresentative). 48 The version of the Dublin Chronicle in Dublin, Trinity College, MS 591, by contrast, is a compilation targeted at a different kind of readership; see below, Gillespie, 'Dubliners

earliest extant recension, that this was a more self-contained, even hermetically-sealed, civic enterprise, whose similarities with other annal genres and materials, where they exist, exist solely at the level of form rather than of content. The Dublin Chronicle therefore represents a further variation on the theme of medieval Dublin's annal and chronicle keeping traditions such as have been illustrated so far: its emphasis falls much more squarely upon civic events likely to impact on the civic weal, particularly that of the merchant classes who at this date were the city's chief administrators.[49] Hostings against hostile neighbouring Irish septs constitute one of the important threads in this repertoire of civic-centred themes: notices of them occur in 1513, 1516, 1517, 1519, 1521, 1523, 1530, and 1533 (the roll ends imperfect with a notice of Robert Shillyngford's mayoralty in 1534–5, but gives no further content for his year of office).[50] The codicological form of the Dublin Chronicle in MS 543/2/14 is rotular, and this circumstance may suggest the social context that it originally served. Rotular form is more characteristic of official than of private consultative use, the latter being more normally served by the codex. Consequently, MS 543/2/14 conceivably represents a former official Tholsel document copied, its palæography suggests, around the middle of the sixteenth century.

If in fact originally a Tholsel-sponsored document, the Dublin Chronicle might be regarded as having served a significant and special function among the various muniments generated by the Dublin Civic Assembly; this function seems to have been less administrative – the function of much of the rest of the Tholsel archive – than 'ceremonial'.[51] The Dublin Chronicle is a barometer of the sort of events considered important for stocking the civic memory with. As such its value, in addition simply to recording events – perhaps indeed co-equivalent with that value – lay in its reification of a particular civic mentality. Hence it was 'ceremonial' both in the sense that one of its thematic preoccupations is with historical occasions on which civic ceremony was to the fore, and also in the sense that it was itself a 'ceremonial' object or muniment.

It might, of course, be said also of those Tholsel muniments that served more immediately practical ends, as executive records and similar instruments, that they were 'ceremonial' too, for they equally formed part of the very panoply of civic process, part of the civic authority's very fabric. But this

view themselves', pp 213–27. **49** Colm Lennon, *The lords of Dublin in the age of reformation* (Dublin, 1989). **50** There is also a reference to the Battle of Knockdoe, County Galway, in 1504 (though imperfectly legible due to ink loss). The hosting of 1513 is imperfectly legible in MS 543/2/14, but is recoverable by collation of the extant text with that of the version of the Dublin Chronicle preserved in Dublin, Trinity College, MS 591. This latter manuscript also notes a hosting against O'More in 1522 that is not mentioned in MS 543/2/14. **51** Ceremonial in two senses: first, it is preoccupied with ceremonial events; and second, it becomes itself a ceremonial artefact by virtue of its inclusion in the official civic archive.

function could be doubly claimed in the case of the Dublin Chronicle, both intrinsically in its content and extrinsically as a document in rotular form. Collateral testimony to how civic authority might be felt to inhere even in objects (amongst which the Tholsel documents must necessarily be included) and places, let alone in actual office-holding persons, is plain in the bylaw that ruled that insulting the mayor in the Tholsel constituted a worse offence than insulting him in the street: since the Tholsel muniments were integral to a building whose very precincts this bylaw legislation rendered sacrosanct, those muniments, no less than the building hosting them, were equally a site in which the city's sense of identity and civic dignity might be convened, focused and projected in a unique way. However, while all the civic muniments, among which the Dublin Chronicle may have begun its life and originally have been housed, may be thought to have had something of a quasi-totemic force attaching to them, the Dublin Chronicle constellated that force.

The more precise terms of this cultural work whereby a sense of civic identity was convened, focused and projected are discernible in the characteristic emphases and perspectives recurrent in the Dublin Chronicle, and among whose entries, as already noted, occasions of civic ceremony and pageantry feature prominently. It may be that, if we wish to understand better Dublin's sense of civic identity in the late-medieval period and to trace its emergence, the workings of the Tholsel and their ancillary documentation afford a promising point of departure. The Tholsel's muniments supported those to whom it fell to manage the general civic process, and an inevitable by-product of that management was the articulation of a sense of civic identity: the procedures of executive office in any age often become performable litanies of power; indeed, they may be actively dimensioned as such. The very act of participation in those dimensionings confers a sense of identity. When also dressed in the appealing public guise of ceremony and pageantry, then that identity was given a communally accessible form: what hitherto might have existed as a disembodied concept now received a physical palpability. This strategy could only but profit the city by helping its citizens assimilate through ostensible examples the consensual value system by which the city was held together. The archives supported this social enterprise of civic consolidation in the first instance purely administratively.

But civic identity and those distinctive social roles which bodied it forth (membership of trades guilds, for example, or of the aldermanic class) were performable entities, capable of being incarnated in various regular colourful symbolic and ceremonial civic practices: even office holders of the lowest rank might be expected to wear distinctive livery as occasion prescribed, or to participate from time to time in various profile civic rituals. By performing citizenship, these high-visibility practices implicitly addressed the issue of what it meant to be a late-medieval or early-modern Dubliner. The Dublin

Chronicle may itself be locatable within this continuum of performative civic identity. And it seems that it is within these terms that another of the Dublin Chronicle's thematic centres of interest, its record of religious plays, may best be understood. On the face of it, annalling play productions may appear an idiosyncratic choice of topic among all those other weightier matters of state that caught the chronicler's attention; not, however, if those productions were commemorated precisely for a special leaven of their own they were able to add the general, overarching project of articulating civic identity.[52]

VI

Our overview of the annals and chronicles of medieval Dublin has taken us from a church-sponsored keeping of history in Latin, where Dublin was not so much an historiographical topic as a place of historiographical facilitation, to a lay-sponsored keeping of history in English. In this vernacular history, 'the people are the city', as Shakespeare might have put it (the people who ultimately counted in Dublin's case being its civic patriciate, many of whom were of the merchant class). We have traced in Dublin in the fifteenth century the emergence of a lay appetite for history, an obvious corollary of which was the appearance of vernacular annal and chronicle material. But this lay appetite was also for a history largely emancipated from the preoccupations of the Latin, church-sponsored annals and chronicles that had hitherto held sway. It might be all very well, of course, for the lay upper classes to acquire and read annals and chronicles of the church-sponsored sort, and this seems on occasion to have happened. For example, William Preston, second Viscount Gormanston (†21 September 1532), owned, and presumably found opportunity to read, the fifteenth-century copy of a set of medieval Latin annals (ending in the year 1370) preserved in Oxford, Bodleian Library, MS Laud misc. 526.[53] But as a member of the laity Preston was exceptional. A holder of various high offices, including that of Lord Justice from 13 April 1515, he would have been conversant with Latin and the textual products of Latinate culture. Those members of the Dublin laity less educationally accomplished, but who, being sufficiently close to the social milieu of men like Preston to gain occasional insight into its workings may have wished to emulate the access they saw there to written history, cultivated an analogous annal and chronicle tradition, though now one responsive chiefly to issues of local civic

52 On the social function of plays and civic ceremonial in late-medieval and early-modern Dublin, see Alan J. Fletcher, *Drama, performance, and polity in pre-Cromwellian Ireland* (Cork, 2000). 53 Gilbert, *Chartularies*, ii, 398, for the colophon that reads 'Iste liber constat Domino Willelmo Preston', and discussed ibid., ii, p. cxv. Compare also the copying of Dublin, Trinity College, MS 584 for Gerald FitzGerald, ninth earl of Kildare, referred to in footnote 18 above.

moment. In the details of this responsiveness may be traced important aspects of the civic consciousness of Dublin as this was emerging in the late-medieval and early-modern period.

Dublin on the eve of the Reformation, then, was a city in which a spectrum of annal and chronicle varieties was to be seen. The most famous sixteenth-century historiographer of Dublin is probably Richard Stanihurst, a man whose works have attracted sustained scholarly attention.[54] In the light of the present overview, it might be stressed in connection with Stanihurst, special though his achievement was, that it had grown out of precedents set by a number of such annalists and chroniclers of the kind surveyed here.[55] Their works were circulating in Dublin, and, in some cases, were coming to celebrate Dublin as a topic of interest per se, even if by a somewhat incidental route; that is, they were conceived in the first place as part of a larger enterprise intrinsic to which was the promotion of the city's sense of its civic identity. Stanihurst, undisputably unique, could nonetheless never be said to have sprung entire and fully armed from the head of the Renaissance.

54 See pre-eminently Colm Lennon, *Richard Stanihurst the Dubliner: a biography* (Dublin, 1981), pp 106–16. 55 As Lennon noted, *Stanihurst the Dubliner*, p. 110, the historian Edmund Campion, Richard Stanihurst's mentor, had received 'written monuments' from James Stanihurst, Richard's father, that helped Campion when he came to write his own history, especially from the year 1513 onwards. May a Dublin Chronicle have been among these 'monuments'? James Stanihurst had, after all, been city recorder (Lennon, *Stanihurst the Dubliner*, pp 19–20), and therefore well placed to come by such material as the Dublin Chronicle contains.

Dubliners view themselves: the Dublin City chronicles

RAYMOND GILLESPIE

Understanding how Dubliners viewed themselves in the late fifteenth and sixteenth centuries is a complicated task. In part the problem stems from the sort of records they created and chose to preserve for later historians to read. Undoubtedly, the most important body of material for this period is the assembly rolls, beginning in 1447 and continuing, with a few lacunae, into the modern period. Keeping such documents marked a new departure for the corporation of Dublin since before this the city archives comprised mainly of deeds and charters.[1] The assembly rolls recorded in fine detail the internal workings of urban government, including the dispensing of urban office and patronage, but tell us little of the mentality of the governed. Contemporary narrative histories would be more helpful in elucidating how Dubliners saw their city and the values that underpinned urban life but none survive before that written by Richard Stanihurst in 1577.

The sort of evidence that would help us to see into the lives of Dubliners in the later medieval period are the oral traditions and the detail of everyday chatter that, for the most part, has not been preserved because of its oral form. In the later middle ages Dubliners told stories about the buildings and people in their city's past and invented legends to explain to themselves and to each other how the city came to be as it was. In doing so they conveyed the meaning of and their expectations of urban life. The tale of Richard Mutton, the first mayor of the city and his building of the Tholsel, is one example of this genre which has survived because it was preserved in a later history.[2] Another story with similar functions, recorded by Richard Stanihurst, is that of the thirteenth-century archbishop of Dublin, Henry of London, who acquired the nickname 'Scorch Willein, that is burn bill, because he required to peruse the writings of his tenants, colourably pretending to learn the kind of each man's several tenure, and burnt the same before their faces, causing them either to renew their takings or hold them at will'.[3] This has all the

1 Mary Clark, 'People, places and parchment: the medieval archives of Dublin city', in Seán Duffy (ed.), *Medieval Dublin III* (Dublin, 2002), pp 140–50. 2 Raymond Gillespie, 'Robert Ware's telling tale: a medieval Dublin story and its significance', in Seán Duffy (ed.), *Medieval Dublin V* (Dublin, 2004), pp 291–301. 3 Liam Miller and Eileen Power

hallmarks of an oral story later written down. It serves a number of functions. First, it was a good story which accounted for a nickname. Secondly, it explained why those who lived on the archbishop's estates in the sixteenth century held their land by the then rather unusual tenure of copyhold, which had no deed and was common only on church and crown land, rather than the more usual leasehold.[4] Finally, in a world that was only beginning to become accustomed to the importance of the written word over the spoken agreement the story served as a cautionary tale of the importance of keeping deeds safe.

Despite these problems with sources one body of material that has the potential to reveal something of the way in which the inhabitants of Dublin saw their city is the city chronicles. City chronicles became increasingly common in the late fifteenth century. Vernacular London chronicles began to be kept from 1414 and Bristol began keeping such a chronicle from about 1440. However, most of the English town chronicles belong to the sixteenth century.[5] Such town chronicles, the creation of someone involved in or close to urban administration, are easily recognizable since they use mayoral years as their primary means of dating rather than regnal or calendar years. This may suggest that the origins of town chronicles lie in a simple mayoral list to which compilers over time added notes of significant events occurring under each mayoralty. In many cases the compiler was the town clerk and his additions evolved into a chronicle or set of annals for the town. It seems that officials in some Irish towns emulated this English practice. Drogheda, for instance, seems to have kept a chronicle with contemporary entries from about 1470, possibly linked to the granting of a new charter of the town in 1469. The chronicle, as it survives in Sir James Ware's transcript of the 1660s, begins in the twelfth century, although much of the earlier material seems to have been compiled in the fifteenth century. The contemporary entries in the Drogheda chronicle record local events such as the building of the market cross, the construction of the bridge at Drogheda, and the building of churches.[6]

I

Undoubtedly the most complete urban chronicle for Dublin is that in Trinity College Dublin [hereafter TCD], MS 591, fos 1–24, which contains an

(eds), *Holinshed's Irish chronicle* (Mountrath, 1979), p. 195–6. The story also appears in the sixteenth-century Book of Howth written near Dublin, see *Calendar of the Carew manuscripts: Book of Howth* (London, 1871), p. 122. 4 Raymond Gillespie, 'Small worlds: settlement and society in the royal manors of sixteenth-century Dublin', in H.B. Clarke, Jacinta Prunty and Mark Hennessy (eds), *Surveying Ireland's past* (Dublin, 2004), pp 199–203. 5 Antonia Gransden, *Historical writing in England II: c.1307 to the early sixteenth century* (London, 1982), pp 227–48. 6 Bodleian Library, Oxford [hereafter Bodl.], Rawlinson MS 484, fo. 67. Printed as Diarmuid Mac Íomhair (ed.), 'Two old

unbroken chronicle of the city from 1408 to 1576. This can be described as the 'long Dublin chronicle'. The text is in English and all in one hand, although there is one slightly later addition in another hand on fo. 20. There is no indication in the manuscript of the name of the scribe but there is good reason to believe that it was made in Dublin. The scribe was also the copyist of parts of TCD MS 593, which contains extracts from the sixteenth-century manuscript known as the Book of Howth. From internal evidence the Book of Howth was compiled *c.*1570 in north Dublin but by 1600, at least, it was in Dublin Castle.[7] It seems therefore reasonable to conclude that the scribe was at work in Dublin where his main manuscripts were located. By the early seventeenth century TCD MS 591, together with TCD MS 593, was in the hands of Archbishop James Ussher. He lent the city chronicle to his friend Sir James Ware who made a copy of it with the heading 'Register of the mayors … with other memorable observations' which is now British Library [hereafter BL], Additional MS 4791, fos 133–144v.[8] In turn J.T. Gilbert had a copy made of this manuscript in the nineteenth century which is now Dublin City Libraries, Gilbert MS 45.

What is clear is that the 'long Dublin chronicle' is a composite text. The diplomatic form, and particular the forms of dating, suggest that it is an amalgam of at least three earlier works. From the beginning of the chronicle to 1557 each year is dated in the form: calendar year in Roman numerals, regnal year and finally mayor and shrieval year. Up to this point there is also an original foliation which stops here. For 1558 the date is in the form: calendar year, mayor and shrieval year, and regnal year. From 1559 until 1572 regnal years are omitted, suggesting a different source was being used. From 1572 the form of dating changes again, reverting to: calendar year, regnal year and mayor and shrieval year. Unlike the first form of dating the calendar year is given in arabic numerals. It seems likely that the scribe compiled his text from at least three sources (though in fact probably more): one or more up to 1558, a second from 1559 to 1572 and a third from 1572 to the end of the text.

Nowhere in the text does the scribe describe his sources but it is possible to reconstruct some of them. From 1572 until the end of the text the entries may be near contemporary or possibly written from memory. Prior to this the 'long Dublin chronicle' is based on a shorter version complied in the 1560s, the original of which does not survive. There is, however, a copy of the text in TCD MS 591, fos 21–23v, written by a different hand to the 'long Dublin chronicle' proper but bound in the same manuscript. This copy of the 'short

Drogheda chronicles', in *Journal of the County Louth Archaeological & Historical Society*, 15, no. 1 (1961), pp 89–91. For more Ware notes from this see TCD, MS 6404, ff 148–8v.
7 *Cal. Carew: Book of Howth*, p. 375. 8 This appears in Ware's 1648 catalogue of his books as 'Regestum Praetorum sive Majorum civitas Dublin. Anglice. ab anno Dom. 1406. usq; ad annum 1574 cum additis notis historicis': William O'Sullivan, 'A finding list of Sir

Dublin chronicle' was made after the longer form had been written, since the scribe of the shorter work added a few lines in the margin of the completed long city chronicle. By the time this 'short Dublin chronicle' of the 1560s was copied the exemplar was clearly in some confusion. Entries in the copy are left unfinished, presumably because the scribe could not read them since the manuscript was damaged. Moreover, the chronological arrangement of the entries is erratic, again presumably because the text from which he was working was in some disorder. Whether this short chronicle is an official city chronicle compiled in the recorder's office or whether it is a private history, written by a citizen of Dublin, or even the product of one of the guilds, is not immediately clear. There are long narrative passages unlike the normal chronicle form and the detail accorded to mercantile affairs suggests it may have originated with a Dublin merchant. There is only one possible hint as to authorship. The 'short Dublin chronicle' contains a long and detailed account of the funeral of Mayor Robert Cusack, who died in office in September 1564 and was buried with full civic honours.[9] This does not occur in any other known source. It may be that the chronicler was a relative of Cusack concerned to preserve a piece of family history or that he had access to a family history of the Cusacks, the possible existence of which is discussed below. Whoever the author was his background seems to be a mercantile one.

The earliest, and longest, part of the 'long Dublin chronicle', that dealing with the period before 1558, is more complex. It is clearly an amalgam of sources and what may be some later commentary. The entry for 1462 that 'this year the most excellent science of printing first began in Almane [Germany] at the city of Marburgh' does suggest the addition of someone who understood the later impact of printing. While the 'long' chronicle begins in 1408, there are no entries relating to Ireland until 1469 when it records the beheading of the earl of Desmond and his two sons. It is possible that the period from 1408 to 1469 is a later composition based on English materials. It is not possible to identify the source but there are indications that it may have been a London chronicle. From 1435 to 1521 there are entries in the 'long Dublin chronicle' about what appear to be local events in London. For example, in 1435 the freezing of the River Thames is noted, in 1442 the burning of St Paul's steeple, Cade's rebellion in 1449, the prosecution of bakers in London in 1478 for making underweight bread, the price of herrings at London in 1494, the blowing down of the weathercock at St Paul's in 1504 and Charles V's visit in 1521. Such detailed local accounts suggest that a London chronicle was being used to enhance the fifteenth-century entries in the Dublin manuscript. London chronicles of the fifteenth century were certainly available in sixteenth-century Dublin. John Bale's London chronicle was

James Ware's manuscripts', in *R.I.A. Proc.*, 97, sect. C (1997), p. 93. 9 TCD, MS 591, fo. 26.

probably in Dublin by that date.[10] However, this cannot be the source since it stops in 1461, but other similar works were probably also in Dublin.

From 1469 there appear to have been new materials on which the 'long' chronicler could draw. At least some of these had an Irish provenance. It is impossible to know what this material was. The author may even have had access to official city records. It is not improbable that someone not part of the civic administration could have had access to the corporation records. Certainly by the early seventeenth century these were widely scattered. In 1605 the council complained that 'sundrie rolls and ancient muniments or records are dispersed in sundrie … hands by an unknown course which breedeth not a little hurt to this city' and in 1610 the 'diverse charters, books, rolls and muniments belonging to this city are come into the hands of certain of the citizens by some sinister means and [are] by them detained'.[11] Given what is known about the record-keeping practices of central government in the sixteenth century this is unlikely to have been a recent development.[12]

One hint that the chronicler had access to some form of official account of the city's history is the list of mayors that he used. Before 1448 the list of mayors around which the chronicle was constructed is very inaccurate indeed. Of the forty-one years from 1408 to 1448 the chronicler only managed to assign mayors correctly to eleven years, suggesting that he was working from a very defective source indeed. Moreover, it is not that the chronicler was using a list which got out of synchronism, since the names offered for mayors in some years do not appear on any mayoralty lists at all. After 1448 it is still difficult to synchronize the chronicler's list with a modern one. However, the names of the mayors are usually relatively correct after 1448, although in absolute terms the chronology may be up to four years adrift. By the middle of the fifteenth century the mismatch between the chronicler's mayoral list and the actual one is rarely more than one year and by the 1520s the two lists have few differences.

The dramatic change in the accuracy of the list after 1448 is almost certainly due to the use of the official assembly rolls, which begin in 1447. It is possible that the chronicler did not have direct access to the assembly rolls but rather a mayoral list compiled from them, perhaps without dates attached to mayoral terms. This would explain the problem that the chronicler seems to have had in assigning mayors to dates. That the chronicler had access to at least some official sources is also suggested by the considerable overlap in content between the official civic chronicle (the details of which will be discussed below) and the 'long' and 'short' chronicles. This overlap varied

10 Mary-Rose McLaren, *The London chronicle of the fifteenth century* (Cambridge, 2002), pp 106–7. **11** J.T. and Lady Gilbert, *Calendar of ancient records of Dublin* (19 vols, Dublin, 1889–1944), ii, pp 452, 510. **12** Herbert Wood, 'The public records of Ireland before and after 1922', in *Transactions of the Royal Historical Society*, 4th ser, 13 (1930), pp 17–25.

over time. For instance there is considerable overlap between the 'civic' chronicle of the early sixteenth century in TCD MS 543/2/14 and the 'long Dublin chronicle'. There is much less overlap between that 'long chronicle' and another text that appears to comprise fragments of the official, civic, Dublin chronicle of the 1550s, now preserved in BL Add. MS 4822, fos 43–5. This may indicate that the author of the 'long Dublin chronicle' had access to only parts of the city's archives, possibly for the late fifteenth and early sixteenth centuries rather than for the period closer to his own day.

The compiler of the 'long' chronicle nowhere gives his name but it is clear that he was writing in Dublin. It may be that he was a merchant since on several occasions he records the price of wheat, malt and (once) grey mullet in the city, although these are usually given for poor years, so it may simply be a more general preoccupation with harvests.[13] Again he only notes the issuing of very few proclamations, most of which relate to the coinage which may suggest a mercantile background.[14] One hint of the world in which the chronicler moved is the fact that of the eleven names that he managed to assign to the correct mayoral years before 1488 seven relate to Thomas Cusack. Cusack appears incorrectly in the list on two other occasions. The chronicler seems therefore to have some knowledge of the Cusack family, as the author of the 'short Dublin chronicle' apparently did, or he may have used a family history. It is not known whether Dublin families wrote such histories, but in Kilkenny the Langton family did, as did the Sexton family in Limerick.[15] It may be that the Cusack family had such a history which recorded a tradition of mayoral years for the family. In either case the chronicler was probably from or linked to the Cusack family, which would place him at the core of the Dublin mercantile elite. Another piece of evidence hinting at authorship may be an apparently personal note under 1524 that the wife of Christopher Ussher died that year.[16] Ussher was not mayor or bailiff in that year and the chronicler does not record anywhere else the deaths of ordinary citizens. This may suggest that the compiler was a member of the Ussher family or a friend of that family. It may be significant that TCD MS 591 was owned by James Ussher, archbishop of Armagh, in the early seventeenth century, although he was not a direct descendant of Christopher. Whether the links of the author lie with the Ussher or Cusack families is not clear but, at least, his mercantile origins seem to be demonstrable.

In contrast to what seems to be a chronicle tradition based on private efforts represented by the 'long' and 'short' Dublin chronicles there are a number of surviving fragments of what seem to be earlier, probably contemporary civic chronicles of Dublin. In the seventeenth century Sir James Ware

13 TCD MS 591, fos 7, 15, 16v, 17, 19v. 14 TCD MS 591, fos 20, 21. 15 J.G.A. Prim (ed.), 'Memorials of the family of Langton', in *R.S.A.I. Journ.*, 8 (1864–6), pp 85–108; National Library of Ireland, MS 12123. 16 TCD MS 591, fo. 10v although this also appears in TCD, MS543/2/14 under 1523.

transcribed a text 'ex 2 rot[ulorum] Praetor[u]m Dublin' into one of his notebooks.[17] This transcript contains chronicle entries for 1469, 1478, 1480 and 1488 retelling the execution of the earl of Desmond and his two sons, a great flood on St Margaret's Day, a campaign against the O'Mores and the crowning of Lambert Simnel in Christ Church cathedral. The reference to a second roll suggests the original work may have extended back some time, possibly as far as 1408, which is the commencement date of the 'long Dublin chronicle', but since Ware did not leave a copy of or extracts from any earlier roll it must be presumed that it was already lost by the seventeenth century. Ware's note, together with the dating of the entries by mayoral years, confirms this as an official Dublin chronicle, kept in the mayor's office and Ware certainly made notes from the Chain Book of Dublin which suggests he worked in the city archives.[18] The compiler of the 'long Dublin chronicle' probably knew of this or a similar manuscript, although the dating forms are not the same and the later chronicler omitted the crowning of the 'young king' at Christ Church on Whitsun, although he included all the other entries. This early chronicle was clearly known in the late sixteenth century since a list of Dublin mayors in TCD MS 456, fos 29v–31 which ends in 1594 includes the entry recording the coronation of Simnel in the same words as used in Ware's text.

A possible second fragment of the official civic chronicle is contained in a roll which is now TCD MS 543/2/14. This is written on the dorse of a vellum roll and on the recto is a list of mayors and bailiffs.[19] The chronicle is arranged by mayoral year and the mayoral years agree with those in the assembly rolls (unlike in the 'long Dublin chronicle'), suggesting an official product. The hand is an early sixteenth-century one but the chronicle may be rather later than that which records the civic officers. The chronicle extends from 1504 to 1534 although some of the earliest entries are damaged and it may originally have begun in the 1490s. The early entries are short, confined to notes of events such as the performance of a play on the Passion of Christ at Hoggen Green in 1506 and a great flood in 1510. Later entries tend to be longer and more expansive, dealing in some detail with the hostings by the mayor and citizens with the lord deputy against the Irish.

What may be a third fragment of the official civic chronicle is contained in three sheets of vellum preserved among Sir James Ware's papers in BL Add. MS 4822, fos 43–5, which contains entries dated by the Dublin mayoral year for 1553–5 in what appears to be a contemporary hand. In their present form there is no evidence that they once formed a roll but they have been heavily

17 Bodl., Rawlinson B 484, fo. 35v. 18 BL, Add. MS 4791, fo. 149. 19 For a description of the manuscript see Alan J. Fletcher, *Drama and the performing arts in pre-Cromwellian Ireland: sources and documents from the earliest times until c.1642* (Cambridge, 2001), p. 82. Prof. Fletcher is preparing an edition of this text.

trimmed and it is not impossible that they did so. One piece of evidence that these fragments had an official provenance is that on the verso of two of the leaves are lists of names. Seventeen appear on fo. 43v and twenty on fo. 44v, fo. 45v being blank. There is no indication of what these names represent but all are those of prominent Dublin families. Two of those who became aldermen in 1553, John Challoner and John Spensfield, appear on the list for that year.[20] However five of those admitted as aldermen in 1554 do not appear on the list for that year so this does not provide an explanation for the making of the lists. The most likely possibility is that these are the freemen admitted in those years, perhaps with some aldermen, since the later careers of many of those mentioned on the roll would suggest that they became freemen about this time. The Dublin freemen's rolls for these years are missing, so it is not possible to confirm this supposition.

On the basis of the manuscripts, therefore, it is possible to distinguish two strands of chronicle-writing within Dublin in the late fifteenth and early sixteenth centuries. First, there is a family of manuscripts which seem to have emanated from the offices of the city government itself. This comprises material in Bodl. MS Rawlinson B 484, fo. 35v, TCD MS 543/2/14 and BL Add. MS 4822, fos 43–5. It is not possible to be sure about the relationship of these manuscripts since there are no points at which they overlap and so provide points for comparison. However they contain sufficient features to be able to regard them as a family of manuscripts. Two, at least, were originally in roll form and the two original survivals are on vellum. They all show a preoccupation with the city itself. Secondly, there is the 'long Dublin chronicle' (TCD MS 591, fos 1–24) which appears to be a transcript, probably with some near contemporary additions, of an existing work. As discussed above, this seems to have been not an official record of the city's history but to have been compiled by a resident of Dublin, possibly a merchant. Its compiler probably had access to the late fifteenth- and early sixteenth-century chronicles of the city, although its entries for the 1550s bear little resemblance to the material in what may be the official chronicle in BL Add. MS 4822. It incorporates most, though not all, of this earlier material. Whether there were other chronicles kept in Dublin outside the civic offices is a difficult question to answer but there probably were. The 'short Dublin chronicle' (copied in TCD MS 591, fos 21–23v) is probably another chronicle of merchant origin. Again in TCD MS 456 there is a list of mayors that concludes in 1594, and agrees with the assembly rolls, and there are a few chronicle entries under mayoral years which do not appear in the same form in any of the fragments discussed above. For example in 1534 this list notes 'in that year was a great war and rebellion [against] the king in Ireland and the city of Dublin besieged by Thomas Fitzgerald but by the help of God preserved and not taken'.[21]

20 Dublin City Archives, MR/35, p. 106. **21** TCD MS 456, fo. 30.

This is a much longer entry with more circumstantial detail for this event than is found in any of the surviving chronicles. Whether this was inserted by the compiler of the list in the 1590s or whether he was working from a now lost chronicle is not possible to say but there is a strong possibility that the latter was the case. If this is true then the two chronicles in TCD MS 591 may only be the tip of the iceberg of an unofficial chronicle tradition in sixteenth-century Dublin.

II

While it is possible to discern on the basis of the manuscript tradition various strands of chronicle-writing within Dublin it is worth stressing the features they had in common. First, they are all in the vernacular rather than the customary Latin of the earlier chronicle tradition. This reflects the growing use of English in the city, a development also confirmed by the fact that although the city assembly rolls were kept in a mixture of Latin and English from 1447 they were written exclusively in English from 1452 onwards. Secondly, they were not simply written about the city but in it, by its inhabitants. Thus in 1525 the 'long Dublin chronicle' noted 'this year the franchises of this city was ridden' or in 1566 the chronicler observed 'there landed at Howth Sir Peter Carew and came to here, Dublin'.[22] Thirdly, the provenance of these chronicles was neither the traditional monastic or clerical world, or that of the learned classes who compiled the Gaelic Irish annals. Rather they reflect a new tradition of secular writing about history, and particular the local history of the city. As such they provide evidence of a new departure in the contemporary understanding of Dublin. In particular the 'long Dublin chronicle' is roughly contemporary with Richard Stanihurst's history of the city written in the early 1570s, although different in form and preoccupations. This may indicate a wider interest in civic matters at this point than has previously been apparent.

This development of the writing of civic history by the inhabitants of the city deserves attention because it represents a new way in which civic identity and power was articulated. Chronicle-writing was not a random activity. Chronicles were texts where power was declared or invoked and where issues of importance in society were defined and contested. They validated a civic culture and justified its rituals as well as communicating these to contemporaries. Hence the chronicles recorded, for instance, the riding of the franchises of Dublin in the same way as the Chain Book of the city did in the seventeenth century.[23] Again the noting of the performances of plays at Hoggen Green was intended to perpetuate a city tradition of urban drama,

22 TCD MS 591, fos 10v, 25. 23 *Anc. rec. Dub.*, i, pp 264–5.

also reflected in the Corpus Christi procession recorded in the Chain Book, as well as recording a special event. In making these entries the city chroniclers were attempting to translate what they knew of the city into memorable and brief stories by which these universal ideas could be made useable in everyday life. To do this they had to know about events, select those that had particular meaning and translate that into writing in a city where writing was still a relatively restricted art. In organizing this material the city chroniclers had no Irish guidelines since this genre of historical writing was a new development there although they did have English models which could be emulated.[24]

It is possible to understand something of how these chroniclers went about this task. Like the manuscript tradition the results fall into two groups. First, there is the official civic chronicle, of which the most extensive fragment is TCD MS 543/2/14. This official record is preoccupied by the internal workings of the city. There are a few entries about events elsewhere, most significantly the death of Henry VII in 1509. However, it is local events, including the playing of the Passion on Hoggen Green in 1506, floods in 1510 and 1523, an earthquake in 1534 and a dispute among merchants in 1531, that mainly concerned the chronicler. In particular, events that link the city with the wider world, such as hostings against the O'Tooles and the arrival and departure of lords deputy and commissioners, are to the fore in the latter part of this chronicle.

Secondly, there is the 'long Dublin chronicle' which is of much wider scope than the official record but still betrays very similar preoccupations. In the first part of the chronicle, material has been extracted from other works to contextualize the history of the city. Significant events in the Wars of the Roses, such as battles, are reported, as are diplomatic dealings with France and the hanging of Sir John Oldcastle in 1418. This locating of Irish events in a wider, British context was not unusual for the late fifteenth century. The annals compiled by Thady Dowling, chancellor of Leighlin, about 1600 (although working from earlier materials) contain a number of references to developments in fifteenth-century England such as royal marriages and the evolving politics of war in the Wars of the Roses.[25] Given the interconnections between English and Irish events such comments should not surprise us.

What is, perhaps, more important is the use of a London chronicle, as discussed above, as a way of filling out the fifteenth century in the 'long Dublin chronicle'. The use of London as a context within which to present developments in Dublin was probably not accidental. There were certainly linkages between Dublin and London although relations were not always cordial. In 1538 the Dublin merchants refused their London counterparts the

24 For many of these issues see McLaren, *The London chronicle*. 25 'Annales breves Hiberniae', in Richard Butler (ed.), *The annals of Ireland by Friar John Clyn and Thady Dowling* (Dublin, 1849), pp 28–31.

right to trade in Dublin, as they had done some fifty years earlier, and further disputes erupted in 1546, although the issues involved are not clear.[26] However, in the sixteenth century some Dubliners at least saw the city as being comparable to London. Some in Dublin viewed elements of their city in relation to their London equivalent. In the 1530s the citizens of Dublin told the English administration that their cathedral, Christ Church, 'stands in a high place as St Paul's does in London'.[27] In the 1570s Richard Stanihurst, for instance, stressed the city's loyalty, 'manners and civility', arguing that it was superior to all other Irish towns 'and therefore it is commonly called the Irish or young London' and that the hospitality of the city was superior to other towns, saving London.[28] However Dublin also had a strong sense of its own identity. Thus while Dublin corporation ordered the standards to be used for weights and measures from London it also decreed that Dublin measures would be twice those of London.[29] Despite these reservations, such contexualization of the doings of Dublin in relation to London was clearly meant to send messages to readers of the chronicle, emphasizing the role of the city as a capital and exhibiting all the metropolitan virtues evident in London and enunciated by Stanihurst for Dublin.

Important as this contextualization was it was not the main aim of the chronicle. From the 1530s, when presumably information became more freely available, Irish entries predominate in the chronicle. Moreover the chronicler indicated the Irish content of earlier entries by drawing a small shamrock in the margin to draw attention to them. After 1550 he abandoned this practice since it was no longer necessary to indicate specifically Irish entries as almost all the entries were of Irish relevance. The preoccupation of these later years in the 'long Dublin chronicle' is with two inter-related themes: the comings and goings of lords deputy and the campaigns of the deputies against the Irish, especially the O'Tooles, O'Neills and the O'Carrolls.

The movements of lords deputy were clearly important to the Dublin chroniclers as were various sets of commissioners sent from England to Ireland. The city as viceregal court and capital clearly gave it status and demonstrated its position as the principal city in Ireland and in that sense the interest in the movement of lords deputy parallels the fascination of the London chroniclers with the formal processions of the monarch there.[30] Describing the parliament of 1542, after which Henry VIII was proclaimed

26 The National Archives: Public Record Office, London, SP60/7/26; Dublin City Archives, MR/35, p. 50. 27 *State papers, Henry VIII* (11 vols, London, 1869–85), iii, pp 130–1. 28 Miller and Power (eds), *Holinshed's Irish chronicle*, pp 39, 44–5. 29 Dublin City Archives, MR/35, p. 121; *Anc. rec. Dub.*, ii, p. 55. 30 For the concern of the London chronicles with royal processions see Mary-Rose McLaren, 'The aims and interests of the London chroniclers of the fifteenth century', in Dorothy Clayton, Richard Davies and Peter McNiven (eds), *Trade, devotion and governance: papers in later medieval history* (Stroud, 1994), pp 159, 163–71.

king of Ireland, the Dublin chronicler noted the city's role in the proceedings since the mayor bore the mace on horseback before the lord deputy to the parliament, in which the representatives of Dublin took their seats.[31] The treatment of the newly arrived deputies was of some importance.[32] Under 1539 the chronicler recorded the arrival of commissioners with Lord Deputy St Leger and a dinner was given for them by the mayor, Walter Tyrell, 'in his house'. This was clearly thought of as of some significance since the chronicler included a very detailed account of the seating plan and the role of the mayor in the proceedings.[33] Again, banquets given to lords deputy in the Tholsel were a common feature of early sixteenth-century life in Dublin, as were presents of wine given to viceroys by the corporation.[34] Again banquets were a feature of the payment by the corporation for entertainment by players and others in the city.[35]

This sort of hospitality clearly reflected an attribute of Dublin commented on by Stanihurst: the hospitality of the city. Stanihurst drew attention to 'the hospitality of the mayor and sheriffs … that soothly, London forepriced, a very few officers under the crown in England keep so great a port', and he offered a number of examples of this hospitality among the mayors.[36] The same theme was touched on under 1573 when the earl of Desmond was imprisoned but the mayor of Dublin said 'he [the earl] should have meat, diet and lodging, but he [the mayor] would take charge of him'.[37] Clearly men of standing, whatever their offenses, were felt to be charges on the hospitality of the city. Such episodes gave voice to Dubliners' perception of their city as a place of hospitality, which Stanihurst held to be not only a civic but a religious duty and a mark of civility.[38]

The entry of the lord deputy was not always celebrated by feasts. Under 1521, for instance, the chronicler noted the arrival of the earl of Surrey, recently appointed as lord deputy, at Wood Quay. He went to the castle after which 'the mayor and aldermen with the commonality went unto the castle and so went before him unto Christ Church and so back again unto the castle'.[39] Again when the earl of Ossory arrived as lord deputy in the city in 1528 he was accompanied by the 'mayor and his company' who accompanied him to Kilmainham, dined and departed.[40] There were subtle distinctions to be made here. The lord deputy was clearly entitled to full civic honours but in 1542 when the lord deputy's wife came to the city she was accompanied to

31 TCD MS 591, fo. 14v; Dublin City Archives, MR/35, pp 28, 146. 32 For the ritual of viceregal entrances see Fletcher, *Drama, performance and polity in pre-Cromwellian Ireland* (Cork, 2000), pp 153–8. 33 TCD MS 591, fos 13–13v. 34 Dublin City Archives, MR/35, pp 16, 17, 28, 34, 54, 55, 57, 58, 87, 93, 121, 150. 35 TCD MS 591, fos 18v, 25. 36 Miller and Power, *Holinshed's Irish chronicle*, pp 40–42. 37 TCD MS 591, fo. 24. 38 For the link between hospitality and civility in an urban context, see Felicity Heal, *Hospitality in early modern England* (Oxford, 1990), pp 300–51. 39 TCD MS 591, fo. 9v. 40 TCD MS 591, fo. 11v.

Kilmainham through the city only by the bailiffs without the mayor.[41] Again when the lord deputy did not pass through the city he was not accorded the presence of the mayor. According to the chronicler, in 1566, when Lord Justice Fitzwilliam arrived in Ireland be did not pass through the city but went to Kilmainham by way of St Mary's abbey escorted only by the sheriffs.[42] However, in another longer version of this event in another chronicle the sheriffs met him outside the city and accompanied by trumpeters he went to Hoggen Green where he was met by the mayor and aldermen who escorted him through the city.[43]

Clearly the Dublin chronicler altered his story to make a particular point about the role of mayor. Such subtle distinctions gave the city an opportunity to articulate a sense of its political importance. As the apex of the civic pyramid the mayor was supreme within the city, the guardian of the rights set out in the royal charter. Thus when the lord deputy entered the city it was the role of the mayor to accompany him to demonstrate civic rights and the loyalty of the city. Other dignitaries might be accorded the honour of being met by sheriffs but not the mayor himself and the mayor would not stray out of the jurisdiction of the city, even if the lord deputy was involved. Such entrances were given added effect by contrasting them with those of other visitors to the city. Recording the attempt by Silken Thomas to take the city by force in September 1534 the chronicle noted that the earl 'with a strong company rode through the city and out by Dames gate over the ford to St Mary's Abbey'.[44] The procession could well have been a viceregal one, especially since Silken Thomas had been lord deputy until June, but since it was not accompanied by the mayor it emphasized the rebellious nature of the gathering. It was a sort of anti-procession.

The second theme which preoccupied the chronicler was the campaigns of the lords deputy against the Irish. He frequently recorded the appointment and swearing in of lords deputy as well as their comings and goings on military campaigns. At one level this was a matter of self-preservation. The O'Tooles, in particular, were close enough to Dublin to inflict damage by raiding and hence campaigns against them were of defensive importance to the city. Raising one's own force also preserved the city's independence and prevented royal soldiers being billeted there, which not only cost the city money but also introduced a group of men outside mayoral authority into Dublin.[45] At another level the campaigns against the Irish served to demonstrate the loyalty of the city to the lord deputy and to set up an opposition between the order and loyalty of the city and the disorder and disloyalty of the Irish. This was highlighted by the context of the city's involvement in the hostings. As part of the lord deputy's force the city under the mayor provided a group of men, as

41 TCD MS 591, fo. 15. 42 TCD MS 591, fo. 22v. 43 TCD MS 591, fos 22–22v. 44 TCD MS 591, fo. 12v. 45 Dublin City Archives, MR/35, p. 175.

had been the tradition in the late middle ages. In 1495, for instance, the summer assembly in the city had to be cancelled because the mayor and council were on expedition with the lord deputy. In the early sixteenth century the mayor and corporation subvented the lord deputy's campaigns against the Irish, although this resulted in later disputes about the cost and how it was to be proportioned.[46] Thus in 1522 the chronicler noted the 'lord deputy went upon O'More and took the mayor and company of the city with him'. In 1524 the mayor went hosting with the earl of Kildare against O'More, and in 1540 the mayor and lord deputy went against O'Neill.[47]

The process of raising this troop was important. According to the 'long chronicle', on one occasion in October 1566 the mayor was commanded to accompany the lord deputy on campaign to Drogheda. It was then the mayor who caused a proclamation to be made that the force should muster on Oxmantown Green so that the force became the mayor's force.[48] Such action demonstrated the power of the mayor within the city, over which the lord deputy clearly did not have the authority to raise troops. Equally it demonstrated the willingness of the mayor to support the government in its campaigns against the disloyal and disorderly Irish. Such military activity provided concrete examples which gave substance to Stanihurst's claims that the city was not inferior to any other in Ireland 'in martial chivalry'. This was demonstrated by the chronicler by recording the various honours bestowed on the mayor by the lord deputy in return for his military services. Thus under 1505 he noted 'this year [the] mayor went to the battle of Knockdoe with the lord deputy and on return [he] gave him [the] order of the garter'. In 1515 the head of one of the O'Tooles was sent to the mayor 'for a present'.[49] The outcome of these hostings was mixed and the chronicler records them whether they succeeded or failed, but never does he record campaigns against the Irish in which the city was not involved. It was clearly the city's participation in such campaigns that demonstrated its loyalty and valour and hence gave tangible meaning to such abstract virtues.

III

The fragmentary Dublin chronicles that survive from the late fifteenth and early sixteenth centuries provide evidence of a new tradition of historical writing in Dublin. As in contemporary London a practice of chronicle-writing evolved. The earliest examples seem to have been generated within the civic administration itself, probably in the recorder's office. Only fragments of

46 *Anc. rec. Dub.*, i, pp 381, 483; ii, pp 4, 67; Dublin City Archives, MR/35, pp 10, 13, 14, 15, 16, 17, 21. 47 TCD MS 591, fos 10, 14. 48 TCD MS 591, fo. 22v. In a longer form in TCD MS 591, fo. 28v. 49 TCD MS 591, fos 7v, 9.

this official chronicle have survived. Rather later than this there is evidence of chronicle-writing by inhabitants of the city. Fragments of one and a more complete version of another have survived in TCD MS 591. This, together with Stanihurst's writings about the city in the 1570s, marks a new awareness of the meaning of living in Dublin. As new departures they had to create ways of organizing events into written history and thereby to articulate civic values at this point. The official civic chronicle and the unofficial private ones both had remarkably similar interests in the things they chose to record for posterity. Both focused on stories of the doings of the viceroys and the military campaigns of the mayor and the citizens that gave concrete expression to a rather inward-looking sense of the city as a bastion of civility and upholder of traditional values of hospitality and valour in ways perceived to be comparable to London. As such these civic chronicles provide a unique perspective into the concerns of the late-medieval inhabitants of the city of Dublin and their hopes and fears as a result of the political, social and economic changes of the sixteenth century.

Excavations within the manor of Merrion Castle, Dublin

CHRISTINE BAKER

The following is an account of the excavation of a medieval settlement site revealed within an extensive development of the former lands of the Sisters of Charity, Merrion Road, Dublin 4 (fig. 1). Located on high ground which swept down to the strand, the excavation site was situated south of open fields and a river, immediately south of the site of Merrion Castle (DU023–001–4). The southern limit of the excavation site, and indeed the development, partially equates with Bellvue Avenue which corresponds with the former parliamentary boundary of the city of Dublin, now the city limits, south of which is the site of Merrion Churchyard (DU023–053). Prior to excavation, the site had been subject to an archaeological assessment (Humphrey 2002) resulting in the identification of archaeological features across the site including 'undated ditches'. A dedicated topsoil-strip concentrated on an identified area of archaeological potential contiguous to the southern limit of the site at Bellvue Avenue. The excavation programme was carried out under licence (04E0272) and took place over a six-week period in April–May 2004.

HISTORICAL AND ARCHAEOLOGICAL BACKGROUND

Historical context

Historical references centre on Merrion Castle but, as the excavation site was located within the manorial lands of the castle, such references reflect its immediate physical context. The lands around Merrion (Meriyonge or Muryong) were granted in 1173 by Strongbow to Walter de Ridelsford, the well-known English lord of Bray (who also held lands in Cos Kildare and Galway) (MacShamhráin 1994, 196). Merrion seems to have been held in conjunction with the manor of Thorncastle, which consisted of the lands between Merrion and Blackrock. De Ridlesford is recorded as granting in 1238 to one Frambold Fitz Boydekym of Tristeldermoth (Castledermot, Co. Kildare) a carucate of land in Dounabroc (Donnybrook). Of interest is the description of the lands and its holders, which gives an insight to the environs of Merrion at this period. The land subject to the grant was described as

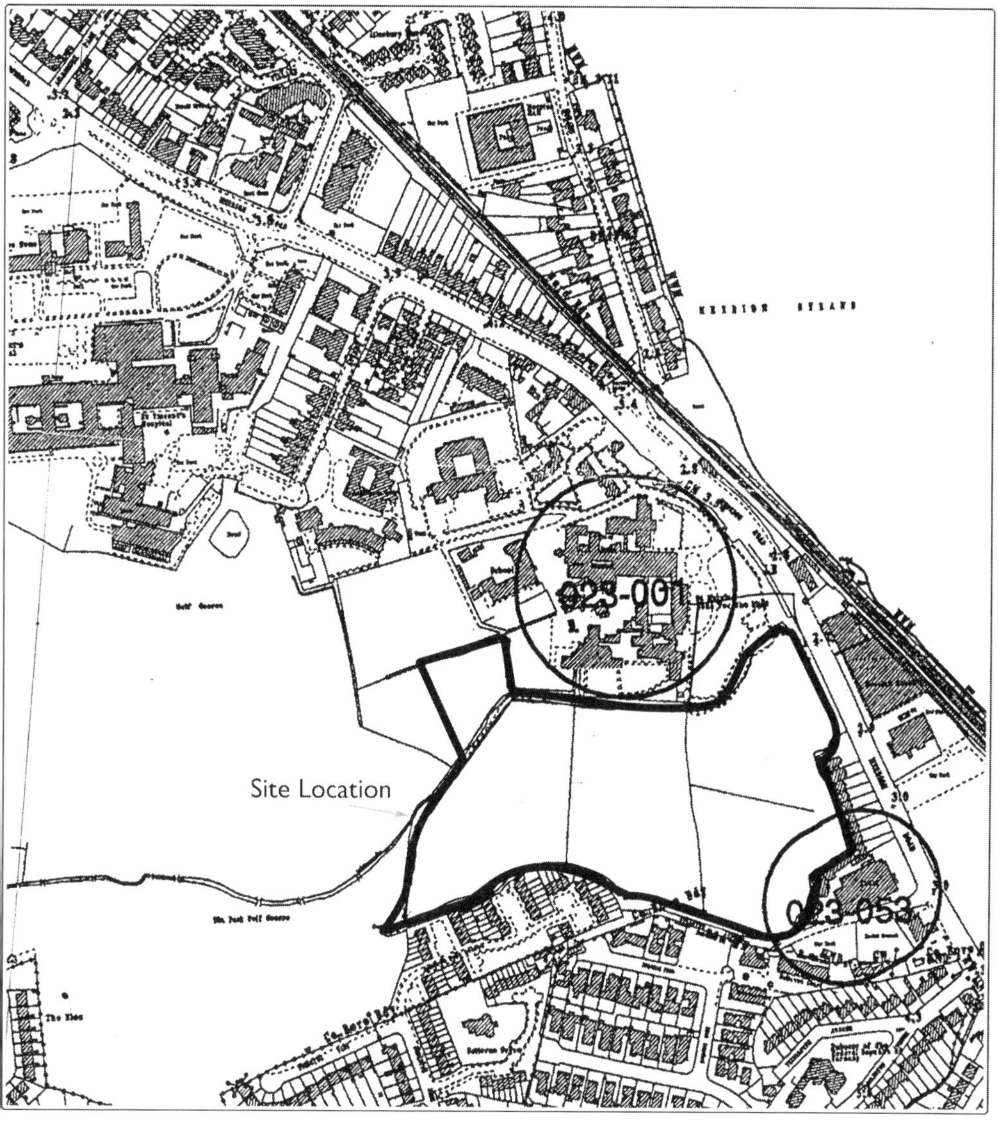

1 Site location map

near the highway from Dublin to Thorncastle, extending from the Dodder bridge along the highway to the grantor's meadow called Manemanagan and on the other side according to the boundary between Henry de Vernoil and William Taleboth … any deficiency made up on the other side of the road between his land and the burgage lands of the citizens: rent, a mark (McEnery and Refaussé 2001, 128, no. 490).

By the late thirteenth century the lands had passed to Christiana de Marisco, a minor, who was closely associated with Eleanor of Provence, the widow of King Henry III (d. 1272), and accompanied her abroad. In June 1306 a writ regarding 1½ carucates of land, rent and a fishery at Thorncastle was submitted by Walter le Deveneis, who

> prayed the King to grant him wreck of the sea when any occurred, the pools on the sea coast and the 'escheats' which might happen to be found on the sand there with other advantages and profits, to wit, from the rivulet called Glaslower to the river Dodder running to Karna as Christiana de Marisco and her ancestors were wont to enjoy and have of old.

An inquisition was then held on 9 February 1307 wherein it was said that

> Christiana de Marisco who held that … belonging to the land of Thorncastle, to wit, from the rivulet called Clarade running to the sea near the boundaries of the land of the city of Dublin towards the west to the south Lake and thence towards the sea … towards the east. And they say that no other person ought to have right of or receive any profit there unless by licence of Christiana or her ancestors (Sweetman 1886, 160, no. 547).

Christiana never married and it seems likely that she entered a convent with Eleanor of Provence. She eventually exchanged her lands in Ireland for property in England.

Merrion and Thorncastle subsequently became the property of William le Deveneis, remembrancer of the exchequer of Ireland. The lands then passed to Walter de Islip and, in about 1320, to Robert de Nottingham, then mayor of Dublin. After his death, they passed to Thomas Bagod (a quo Baggotrath Castle and modern Baggot Street, etc.), through his marriage to Nottingham's widow. Thomas Bagod held the lands of Thorncastle and Merrion until his death. The lands then passed to John de Bathe and, in 1366, from him to Sir John Cruise, the owner of the adjacent estate of Stillorgan. It was under the terms of the lease that 'if within the 12 years the lessor shall construct or repair any buildings, houses or ditches he shall be entitled to retain the lands until his expenses be recovered' (Pembroke and Montgomery 1891, 19, no. 51). The building of the castle (and Merrion Chapel) is attributed to Cruise who is described as 'of Merrion' (Ball 1900, 313).

The need for the erection of a castle at this time was paramount. The O'Byrnes and O'Tooles still desired vengeance for their expulsion from their territories of Ofelan and Omurthy (extending from modern Co. Kildare eastwards) by de Ridelsford in the late twelfth century. With impetus from unrest of the kind familiarly associated with the Bruce invasion and its aftermath, the frequency of raids on the lands at Merrion was such that Cruise was allowed hold his property free for life. Similarly in 1435 Philip Fitzwilliam petitioned the King for a remission in rent that he might rebuild the tenant village (Booterstown) and also erect a fortified castle to replace the Castle (Thorncastle) destroyed by the Irish (Donnelly 1977, 86). The grant for the latter, dated 6 October 1446, is recorded as

> King Henry ... remits the rent of Thornecastell during the life of Philip, considering that Philip began to build a fortilace in Ballybothir [Booterstown] on parcel of lands of Thornecastell, pardons arrears of rent and any debts due to James Fitzwilliam father of Philip (Pembroke and Montgomery 1891, 47, no. 160).

From Sir John Cruise, the lands of Merrion and Thorncastle passed to the Fitzwilliam family. The first of the Fitzwilliams to be resident on these lands was James, who was married to a daughter of Sir John Cruise. At the end of the fifteenth century, Merrion became the property of another branch of the Fitzwilliams, seated at Dundrum. The Fitzwilliam (a quo, for example, Fitzwilliam Square) holdings stretched from the Dublin Mountains to the middle of the river Liffey.

In 1519 Richard Fitzwilliam leased Merrion to one 'Oon Albanaghleche', the details of which reflect some of the life of the estate:

> leases all messuages and lands in Meryyong Co. Dublin with the franchise of the city of Dublin. To hold during the life of John White, John Reade, Thomas Blake and James Bran or for 40 years if they do not live so long; and lessee shall render the customs of herrings and other fish they happen upon the sea and strand of Meryong yearly. Whenever the lessor returns from England he shall be at liberty to re-enter the premises' (Pembroke and Montgomery 1891, 62, no. 208).

The Fitzwilliams played a highly visible part in political life. Richard Fitzwilliam bore the title of gentleman of the bedchamber to Henry VIII while his grandson Thomas was knighted, represented County Dublin in parliament for almost twenty-five years and was vice-treasurer of Ireland. During Thomas Fitzwilliam's residence at Merrion Castle, Sir Henry Sidney made his entrance as Lord Deputy into Dublin from there (Ball 1900, 313). However, the family was not beyond the rule of law. In 1564 it was recorded that from the

> Mayor, sheriffs, commonalty and citizens of Dublin to Thomas Fitzwilliam of Meryong controversy moved between the parties concerning two congers by Meryong ... Fitzwilliam grants to Mayor etc.

> the said sea water, arm or cutt of the sea that runneth to Meryong … and all the rights that may by reason of the same water and also anchorage and all rights of that kind on the land or shore above the value of 40s. … right reserved to the public to pass to the water by land and to use the strand or shore to haul nets (Pembroke and Montgomery 1891, 80, no. 243).

In 1595, his grandson (also) Thomas Fitzwilliam acceded to the estate and in 1629 was created Baron Fitzwilliam of Thorncastle and Viscount Fitzwilliam of Merrion. He is recorded as one of the most prominent lords of the Pale to offer his services during the rebellion of 1641 (Ball 1900, 313). However the castle was occupied to its detriment by a garrison of King Charles I's forces during the war. The Civil Survey 1654–6 records the 'Moyety of Meriyong by estimate one ploughland', that is, 'fourscore acres 20:00:00 meadow, 060:00:00 arable and 0 pasture', held by the 'Lord of Meriyong, Irish Papist' and valued by 'ye Jury at forty poundes and by us at seaventy poundes'. Interestingly, 'the proprietor was possest of ye p'missess as his inheritance and did Mortgage ye same to Richard Earle of Corke, five or six yeares before ye Rebellion'. Merrion Castle itself was described as an 'Old decayed Castle with a large Bawne, valued by the Jury at 200 poundes' while 'the p'misses are a Manor and kept Court Leet and Court Baron, the tithes belong to ye Colledge of Dublin [i.e., Trinity College]' (Simington 1950, 259).

The castle remained occupied and was gradually altered by subsequent occupants. After the Restoration, Charles II bestowed the title of earl of Tyrconnell on Oliver Fitzwilliam. The earl added to and restored Merrion Castle and it was assessed as being a house with sixteen hearths, which would place it as one of the largest houses in County Dublin. On the second floor of the castle, the family coat of arms was engraved in stone. It was noted that Oliver Fitzwilliam was granted liberty to demolish bulwarks of a fort on the estate (Humphrey 2002, 2). The earl died in the castle in 1667 and was succeeded by his brother William who occupied Merrion Castle as his country residence. The Fitzwilliams owned brickfields to the north of the castle and developed Merrion Square, Fitzwilliam Square and most of what is now called 'Dublin 4' (Pearson 2001).

Meanwhile construction began in 1711 of Mount Merrion House by Richard, fifth Viscount Fitzwilliam, due to the poor state of Merrion Castle. The castle fell into such a decayed state that *Walsh's Impartial News Letter* of 16 May of that year referred to 'an account from Merian that a parcel of these outlandish Marramounts which are called Mountain Rats who are now here grown very common … walk in droves and do a great deal of mischief'. After supposedly having devoured a woman and nurse-child in Merrion the inhabitants 'killed several which are as big as Katts and rabbits' (Joyce 1912, 31).

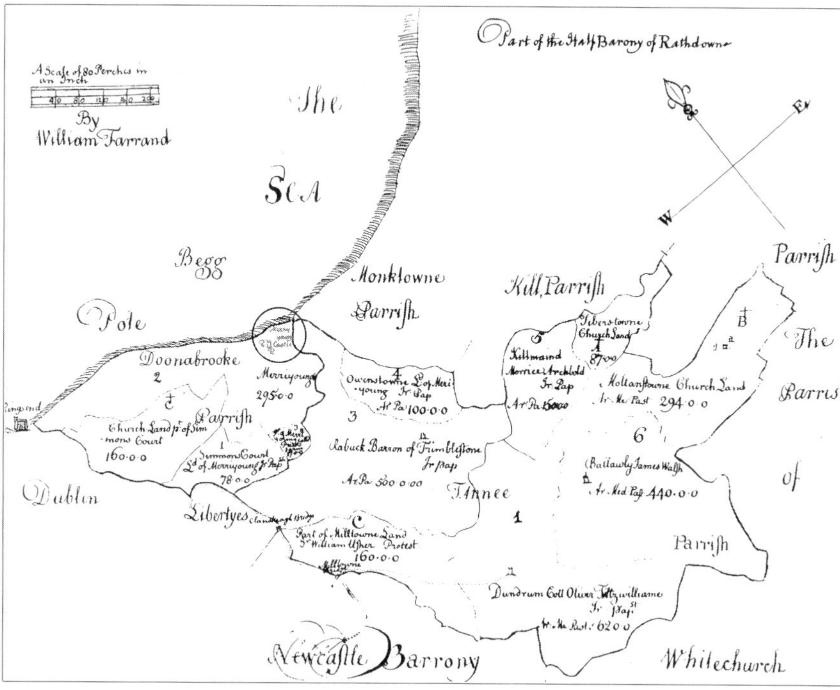

2 Down Survey map, 1655–7

In 1866, the site was acquired by the Irish Sisters of Charity and a convent and home for the blind was constructed there. After the First World War, the Pembroke estate began to be sold off and in the 1930s, the large-scale construction of suburban housing around Mount Merrion began. The site of Merrion Castle is now occupied by St Mary's Hospital for the Blind, at Merrion Gates. Whatever vestiges of the castle survived the demolition of the 1780s would have been completely obliterated during the subsequent building of the convent and hospital.

Archaeological context

No recorded monuments are located within the limits of the development area. However, the castle site, immediately north of the development area, formed a complex of four recorded monuments: tower house site, dwelling site, armorial stone head and a stone head (DU023:001). Only the latter two components are still evident on the site, the structural remains having been previously demolished.

Cartographic analysis

One of the earliest cartographic references is the Down Survey Map of 1655–7 by William Farrand which depicts 'Merryiyoung' Castle surrounded

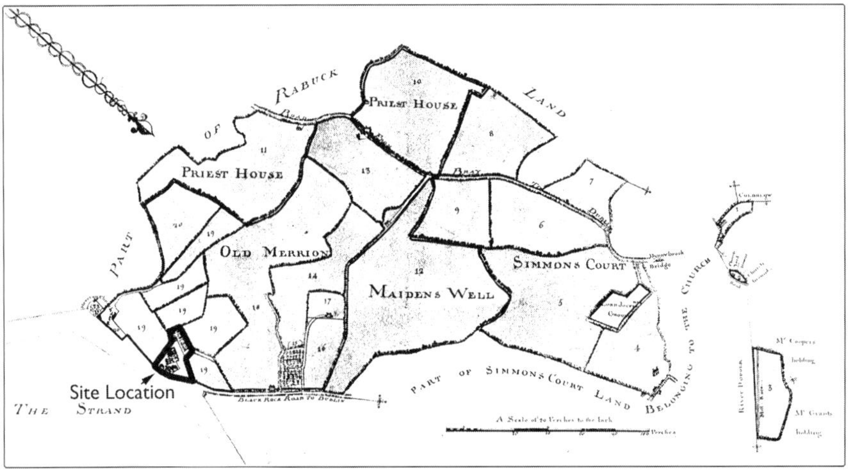

3 Barker's map, 1762

with trees (fig. 2). Rocque's map of 1760 depicts the castle as three buildings north of a rivulet. At a distance to the south is the 'Burying Place'. The space in-between, which correlates with the site of development, is under pasture. It is bounded to the south by a laneway, an intersection of which forms the western boundary. The former laneway no doubt corresponds with Churchyard Lane.

A map of 'Old Merrion and Simmonscourt' surveyed in 1762 by Jonathon Barker was beautifully reproduced at a scale of 20 perches to the inch (fig. 3). The map depicts Merrion Castle in detail. It is shown with a double-fronted crenellated façade out of which a roofed house juts, all of which front northwest. The castle environs are defined by a bawn wall with what appear as large haycocks between the castle and the road to Dublin. To the north and west of the castle is an outbuilding and kitchen gardens. Merrion graveyard is depicted beyond the southern boundary of 'Old Merrion' with 'Part of Rabuck'. Opposite it is a single building (the church perhaps?). What is outstanding about this map is that it depicts the field divisions. To the south of the castle are three outer fields, which are delineated by tree-lines on east-west axes with two larger fields abutting the castle grounds. This is the area which corresponded with the development under discussion here.

Beranger's 1766 sketch shows Merrion Castle as being four to five storeys in height with good fenestration, which Cooper described as 'ornamented with limestone casements 'suggesting a sixteenth-century date' (fig. 5). Whereas the castle is difficult to distinguish on Taylor's map of 1816, Church Laneway is more pronounced. It was formerly an 'ancient route via Donnybrook bridge or ford that preceded it emerged at the Rock Road at Old Merrion Churchyard. It also seems to have been the route taken by the Dublin

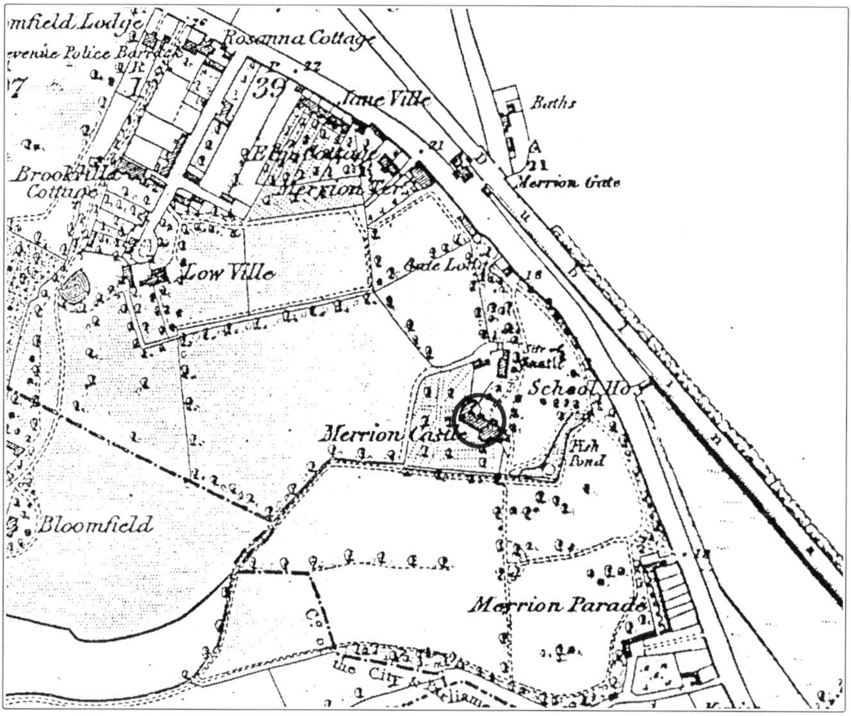

4 Ordnance Survey map, 1844

5 Beranger's Merrion Castle, 1766

Corporation in former times on the occasions of the annual ceremony of riding the franchises or boundaries of their municipal boundaries' (Joyce 1912, 27).

Duncan's map of 1821 records Merrion Castle as extant (rather than 'site of'). The rivulet that delineates the northern limit is clearly visible and tree-lined at its eastern end. Church Laneway to the south of the site is also distinct, as is the terrace of houses that constitute Merrion Parade. The area within the development site as a whole is blank except for the presence of two structures to the southeast corner corresponding to the area of excavation.

The Ordnance Survey maps of 1844 (fig. 4), 1866, 1869 and 1879 record the demesne development throughout the nineteenth century. A north-south field division is common to all of the plans and correlates with the extant hedge-line. However, it appears to have constituted a pathway that extended from the footbridge at Merrion Castle, west of a fishpond, to the southern perimeter pathway. It also provided access to a well (uncovered during the monitoring programme: 04E0167). An east-west pathway/land-division is in evidence on the 1869 and 1871 editions, but the bulk of the site appears to have been under grassland.

Previous work

A series of archaeological assessments was carried out on or adjacent to the development site from 2000, including at the site of Merrion Castle (Tobin, 00E0886) which did not yield any features or artefacts of archaeological significance. Two assessments were carried out at the rear of the Tara Towers Hotel between the excavation site and Merrion churchyard (Baker, 03E1407 (ext.)), neither of which yielded anything of archaeological significance. The excavation site itself was the subject of a test-excavation programme which revealed a low density of archaeological features (Humphreys: 02E1260). This was complimented by an archaeological survey of the stream-bed that forms the northern limit of the site (Kieran: 02D079) which revealed two possible bridge foundation-plinths. Finally, a monitoring programme (04E0167) was undertaken on the development site in February 2004. This revealed that the subsoil within the eastern low-lying limit of the site consisted of sand terminating in an extensive bank of water-rolled stone and gravel in a sand-matrix, which indicated that the shoreline in this area was once much further west. Not only must this have been reclaimed but the frequent identification of drainage trenches points to an area prone to flooding and its subsequent management. There was, however, little to indicate when such reclamation would have taken place. No revetments were identified and any deposits in this area relate to 'dump' episodes of the nineteenth century. Archaeological deposits were limited to those that resulted in the excavation (Baker 2004).

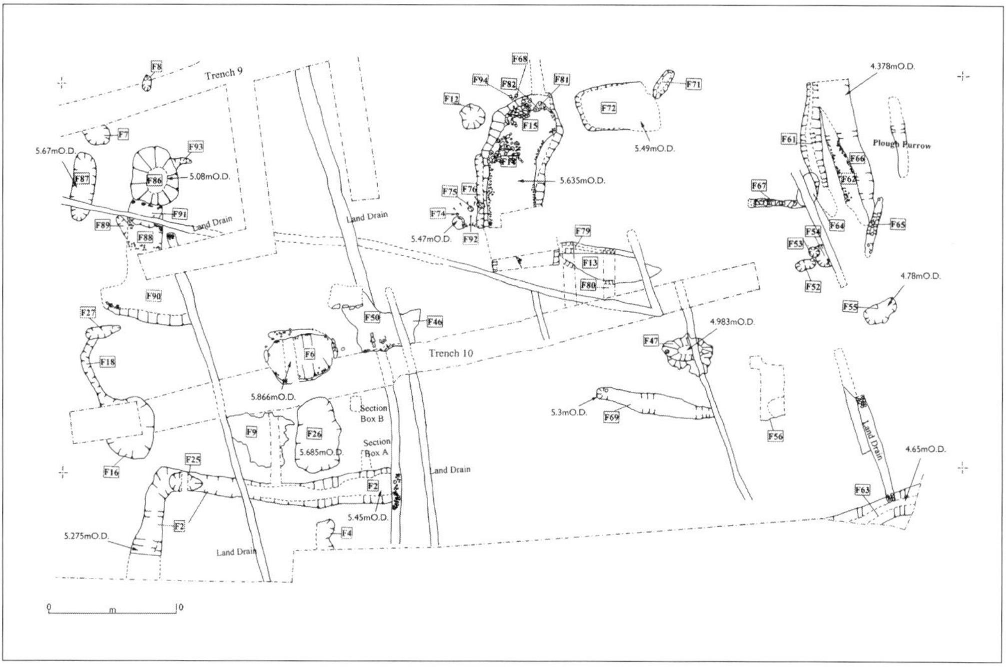

6 Post-excavation plan

Location and stratigraphy

The site of the development consisted of approximately 14.5 acres under rough pasture. The excavation site was located on an east-west ridge of high ground (average 7m O.D.) on the southern side of the site, which dropped relatively sharply to low-lying flat ground (average 3.80m O.D.) that has been shown to be subject to flooding. An area of approximately 40m NS by 70m EW was topsoil stripped under archaeological supervision, within which the archaeological remains were dispersed on the flat top of the ridge and were not encompassed by any delineating features. Former land-usage had severely truncated the features, which were identified *c.*30m below the existing ground level. Also identified were the test trenches formerly excavated by Humphreys (02E1260). A grid, laid out at 10m intervals, measured 60m EW by 30m NS (Grid Squares 1–18). Medieval pottery was recovered from the topsoil and site clearance and definition, and was bagged according to grid to record a preliminary spatial layout. The stratigraphy was relatively homogenous across the site and consisted of dark brown clayey topsoil which overlay a light yellow/orange-brown plough-soil, which varied in depth reflecting the topography. It was also mixed with pockets of grey/blue marl and had small stone, shell and occasional post-medieval pottery-inclusions. The subsoil consisted of a stony yellow/grey natural clay.

THE EXCAVATION

In total, ninety-four distinct features were identified, the majority of which were cut into subsoil (fig. 6). There was little cohesion in the pattern of layout of the features excavated. However, three spatially distinct concentrations of activity were identified, although these may not be representative of function or chronology of use but rather represent patterns of truncation and survival. Similarly, the lack of an extensive stratigraphy means that features cannot be phased, and therefore the features are described in terms of morphology rather than their location or phasing. They can be divided on that basis into pits, post-holes/stake-holes, surfaces, gullies/ditches/drains and archaeological deposits/layers.

Pits A total of twenty-eight pits were identified, distributed throughout the site. The majority were sub-circular in plan and ranged from 0.04m to 0.50m in depth, reflecting the truncated nature of the site. The pits measured from 0.54m to 0.65m in diameter, the exception being two curvilinear pits (F14, F15) that extended for 14.50m. The pits were filled with variations of dark grey silty clay, some exhibiting evidence of heat (F47, F53) and charcoal inclusions (F3, F71) or metalling at the base (F88, F90). A relatively homogenous artefact-range was recovered from these pits dominated by medieval pottery and iron nails. However two pits produced lithic evidence. A tertiary flint flake was recovered (F27) and a secondary flint flake along with pottery, and slag (F52). Although these pits no doubt had a variety of functions and uses, none were immediately apparent. Two pits, however, warrant further discussion.

Located centrally, F6 consisted of a sub-rectilinear pit (5.70m EW x 4.20m NS, 0.42m d.), originally identified as an extensive charcoal-rich spread. The basal fill consisted of a metalled surface, comprised of small stones (<0.06m dim) set in a heat-affected grey orange matrix which did not extend to the edge of the feature. Directly over it was a large dump of stones (0.25m–0.35m), which extended 2m north-south and 4.6m east-west (fig. 7, pl. 1). These angular and rounded stones were overlain by light brown and yellow silty clays. A total of twelve stake-holes were located primarily to the east and north of the feature, both within and beyond the line of the cut, possibly indicating a superstructure. Medieval pottery and distinctive iron clench-bolts were recovered from this feature. A sample from F6 was subject to radiocarbon dating. The result was a C14 date of 636 +/- 30yr BP (UB-6306 (AMS), which when calibrated resulted in a date-range (at 2 sigma) of AD 1277–1397.

Located to the northwest of the site, an oval pit (F86) was orientated north-south (4.60m NS x 3.50m EW, 0.50m d.). The eastern portion of the

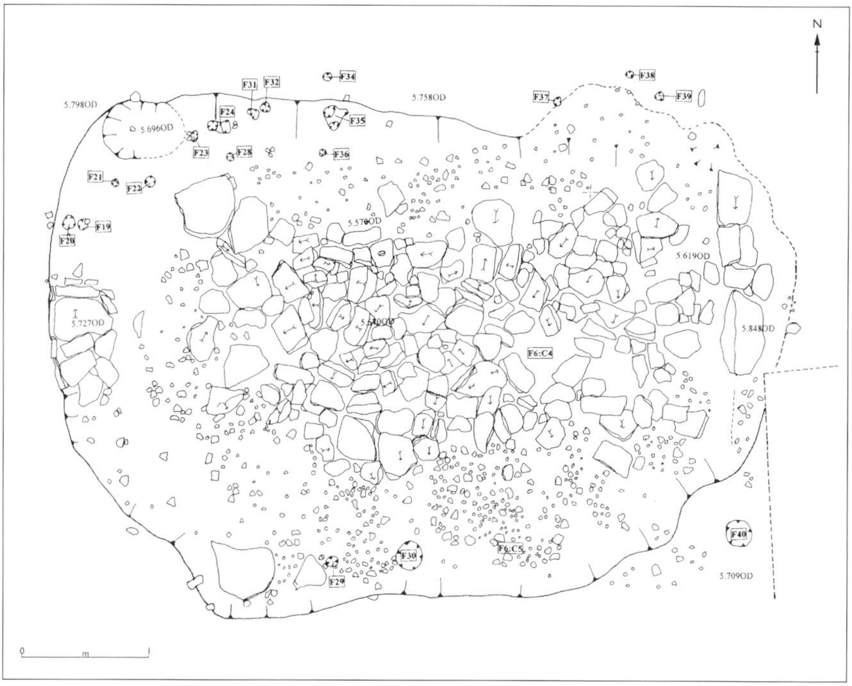

7 Pit F6, mid-excavation

Plate 1 F6, mid-excavation, facing east

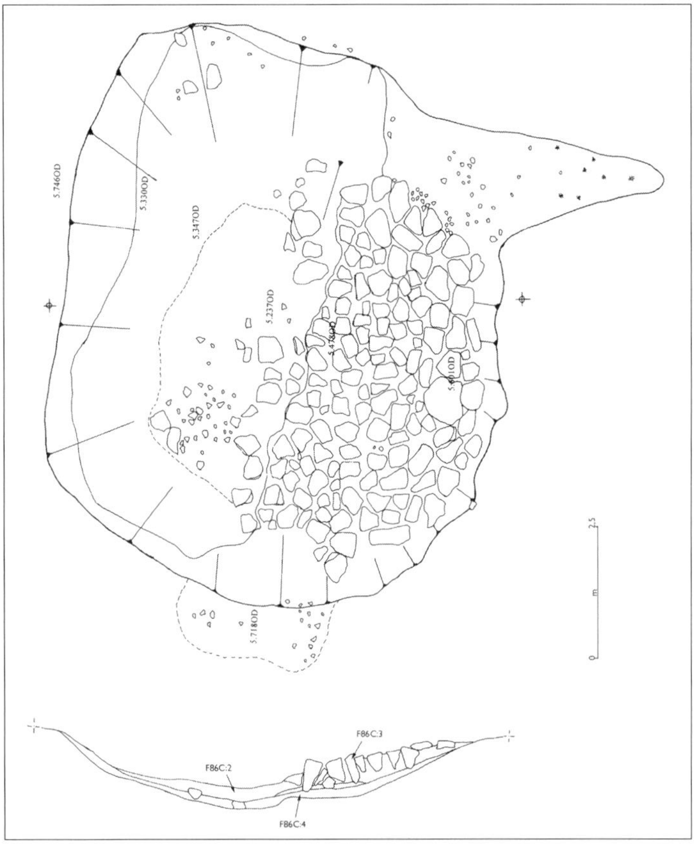

8 Pit F86, mid-excavation

feature was characterized by large set cobbles (2.80m NS x 1.50m EW), which sloped down from the eastern limit of the feature, and consisted of large rounded cobbles up to 0.20m in diameter, which were carefully set upright in a light grey brown silty clay with coarse sea-sand inclusions, to form a sloping surface (fig. 8, pls 2, 3). This surface abutted dark grey silty clays with inclusions of shell, charcoal, and animal-bone. An iron shears (04E272:86:3), a possible lead weight (04E272:86:4), and sherds of medieval pottery were recovered from this feature. A sample from F86 was subject to radiocarbon dating. The result was a C14 date of 517 +/- 29yr BP (UB-6307 (AMS), which when calibrated resulted in a date-range (at 2 sigma) of AD 1328–1438.

Ditches/gullies/drains A total of ten linear features were distributed across the site, none forming a delineating function. The majority were linear in plan and ranged from 2.58m to 11m in length, 0.50m to 2.50m in width and from 0.12m to 0.85m in depth. Primarily for drainage, a range of artefacts including medieval pottery, slag and iron nails were recovered from these features.

Plate 2 F86, mid-excavation, facing west

Plate 3 F86, mid-excavation, facing north

Surfaces A total of four surfaces were identified, all of which were truncated and some of which overlay ditches and gullies. The surfaces were irregular and measured from 2.20m to 9.90m in diameter and from 0.04m to 0.10m in thickness. Constructed of closely set gravel from 0.02m to 0.06m in diameter, the surfaces were interspersed with medieval pottery. A single heavily utilized tertiary flint flake (04E272:51:7) which may possibly be a small late Mesolithic Bann flake was also recovered from one of the surfaces (F51) (see Appendix III below).

Deposits and layers There were a number of deposits irregular in plan, which were dispersed throughout the site. A total of eighteen distinct deposits or layers were identified and ranged from 0.50m–7.50m in diameter and from 0.06m to 0.30m in depth. A range of artefacts, including pottery, slag and nails, were recovered reflecting the assemblage of the rest of the site. Outstanding, however, was a flint arrowhead (04E272:5:9); it was identified as a complete retouched tertiary barbed and tanged arrowhead of Green's Sutton type (b), a classic Beaker (Early Bronze Age) type (see Appendix III).

DISCUSSION

Form and function

The layout of the excavation site at Merrion Road was not cohesive (fig. 6). There are no identifiable structures or even a distinctly recognizable spatial pattern in the dispersion of features. The site was heavily truncated by agricultural activity, drainage systems and even previous archaeological investigations. Thus the stratigraphic relationships were limited. The main foci of activity were at the western and eastern limits of the site, which was defined by its topography, that is, a high ridge sloping down to the north and east. Of particular interest are pits (F6, F86) both of which, while different in form, appear to have been modified to fulfil particular functions. Both were in proximity to areas/surfaces of metalling which may have formed a base for the functions carried out at the pits. F6 was characterized by an infill of large stones which is not without parallels. At the medieval occupation-related site of Ballynageragh, Co. Cork a roughly crescent-shaped depression (4.60m x 1.20m) was excavated. It had a maximum depth of 0.50m and comprised a large dump of angular stones (0.30m–0.50m diam.) overlain by a deposit of black, burnt soil. The pit edge was characterized by oxidized colouration and three groups of post-/stake-holes were revealed along an alignment inside the southern edge of the depression. Identification of charcoal yielded fragments of ash, alder, holly and oak (Gowen 1988, 137).

In comparison F6 was sub-rectangular (5.70m EW x 4.20m NS) in plan and had a maximum depth of 0.50m. The large angular stone (0.35m diam.)

fill was overlain by black charcoal-rich soil, the pit base had oxidized colouration and there were stake-holes along the northern limit of the feature. Charcoal identification yielded fragments of ash, alder, hazel, oak, blackthorn and cherry. Similarly, at the rural medieval settlement site of Tullykane, Co. Meath excavation of a shallow pit (4.50m NS x 3m EW) revealed a fill of large angular stones overlain by charcoal-rich material. It was located in proximity to a metalled surface (Baker forthcoming).

While morphologically similar, the pits from the above sites have not been easily interpreted. For instance Ballynageragh may 'represent a dumping of stones with the burning of agricultural waste' (Gowen 1988, 137). A quarter of a rotary quernstone was recovered from the pit at Ballynageragh, a possible whetstone and fragments of Dublin type fineware from that at Tullykane, while over 300 sherds of 'Leinster cooking ware', carpentry nails, two awls, a lock and hasp, and eight clench bolts were recovered from F6. It had been hoped that macro plant analysis may indicate a specific function for F6. Two samples from the fills of F6 were analyzed for plant remains. The upper fill (F6:c1) contained large frequencies of cereal grains (>50), predominantly wheat and small amounts of grass, pulse and weed seeds. However the lower fill from the same pit had only five cereal grains. It has been suggested that the most likely explanation for the presence of seed would be that a burnt crop had been cleared out after burning and thrown away as waste (Johnston 2004). Given the evidence combined with that from comparable sites it appears that F6 may have functioned as a barn or the site of grain-processing activity.

Based on its morphology pit F86 also appears to have served a specific if not immediately apparent function. The large set cobbles form a stable surface that slopes down into the pit. Two samples were analyzed for plant remains from the primary fill of F86. Both samples contained cereal grains that were exclusively identified as what was interpreted as representing one charred crop that was discarded after burning. Also included were weed seeds of the dock family and a large number of sedge seeds. The latter are indicative of crops grown in damp rather than well-drained fields (Johnston 2004).

The recovery of horse bones, a lead weight and shears indicates multiple processing functions, which may include the rendering of horse carcasses and sheep shearing.

The western activity consisted mainly of drainage activity and a metal processing area. Intercutting pits (F52, F53, and F54) which contained slag were the primary evidence for both *in situ* burning and metal processing on-site. The northern focus of activity consists of a large shallow pit (F15), associated metalled surface (F13) and various pits (F11, F12, F72) and spreads (F83, F84). The metalled surface (F13) was abutted by drains (F79, F80) on either side, indicating contemporary activity, which was cut to the west by the pit F15. Except for a processing element no obvious function can be attributed to this group of features.

Artefacts and samples

Pottery (see Appendix I) The most abundant artefact recovered from the site was pottery. In total, 7917 sherds were collected, the majority (99%) being Leinster cooking ware (1.33% of which was decorated). A total of 19% of the pottery was uncontexted, retrieved from the plough-zone or the preliminary clean-back of the site. The uncontexted pottery was assigned as far as possible by grid squares, providing a preliminary spatial analysis. Allowing for factors such as disparate depths of plough-soil, previous disturbance, etc., the majority of uncontexted pottery was retrieved from the very western quadrants of the site (i.e., Grids 1, 2 and 13) and the very eastern (i.e., Grids 6 and 12). These grids correspond with areas of intense activity, exemplified by the number of features contained within them. The pottery was directly associated with 50% of the features.

Metal (see Appendix II) A total of 151 metal artefacts were recovered from the site, the majority of which are iron. Spatially, the uncontexted metal artefacts reflect the distribution of the pottery, i.e., the very eastern and very western quadrants of the site. Definite identifications have been made, although no artefact type is exclusive to one feature or layer, indicating a range of functions carried out in the same place. The predominant metal artefact is iron nails which have been divided into horseshoe nails (12), square-headed nails (9) or carpentry nails (54). The horseshoe nails can be assigned to the Museum of London typology as Type 3 and Type 4, which date to the thirteenth-fourteenth century. The carpentry nails which have been assigned to either type, and Type B of Ford and Walsh's typology, have a date-range from the thirteenth to sixteenth century. A total of eleven awls/punches were recovered. These artefacts were generally used for leatherworking. However, the majority of the iron artefacts appear to be tools used in construction or carpentry, including U-shaped staples (7), which would have been used as fastenings in structures or furniture, possible auger bits (2), cutting tools (2), a timber dog, straps (6) and bars (3). In addition, six possible blade fragments were identified and an iron shears was recovered from pit F86. A total of seven clench-bolts were recovered from F6. These distinctive bolts were used not only in boat-construction but in doors as the roves, perforated iron plates, prevented them from pulling through wood.

A total of five artefacts of copper alloy were recovered; all are of a more personal nature than the iron objects, and include a possible buckle, rumbler bell and finger ring. In general the chronological assignation of the metal artefacts tends to correlate with that of the pottery.

Flint (see Appendix III) A total of seven worked flint fragments were recovered, all but two directly associated with features. Analysis by Conor Brady has identified two flints of particular note, a single barbed and tanged arrowhead (04E272:5:9) and a heavily utilized tertiary flint flake (04E272:51:7). The former can be assigned to Green's typology as a Sutton 'type b' which is Beaker in date while the latter is possibly a Late Mesolithic Bann flake. There are two explanations for the presence of prehistoric flint on an essentially medieval site. The first is that the flint artefacts were reused after rediscovery in the medieval period and the second is that the artefacts are residual in secondary contexts. Given that the two artefacts of greatest antiquity were recovered from metalled surfaces and in association with medieval pottery it appears likely that they were subject to reuse upon rediscovery. That several other flints were also directly associated with a variety of features may indicate a similar reuse, while it is likely that the uncontexted flints are residual.

Animal bone (see Appendix IV) The animal-bone assemblage consisted of 1779 fragments, that weighed 27kg and was directly associated with 71 features. Cattle, sheep/goat, pig and horse are well represented, with some fragments of dog, cat, bird and fish. An analysis of the animal bone by Jonny Geber indicates that cattle were the dominant species. However, the fragments were derived from meat-poor parts of the body and, combined with evidence that the age of slaughter was 2–3 years old, it is concluded that cattle were held for meat not milk and slaughtered, but probably not consumed, on-site.

In contrast the evidence for sheep/goat points to their primary function being for milk and wool production, although the animals were slaughtered after 2–3 years of age. Pigs compare with cattle in the overrepresentation of meat-poor parts but results based on meat weight show a relatively high percentage of possible pig consumption. Also the majority of pigs were slaughtered between 1–2.5 years, the period where they reach maximum size.

Horse bones were directly associated with 15 features and were predominantly present in the westernmost grids. Similarly there is a definite correlation between the distribution of horseshoe nails and horse bones.

Charcoal (see Appendix V) Two samples were submitted for charcoal analysis, one each from pits F6 and F86. According to Lorna O'Donnell the charcoal level from both pits was low. However, wild/bird cherry, blackthorn, oak, ash, alder and hazel were identified, the alder being most prolific. Assuming the wood identified from the samples was not transported onto site, the wood identification infers both the presence of nearby wetlands and a dry-land environment (that could support trees such as ash, oak and hazel), which would tally with the site topography. The growth pattern of the hazel indicates coppicing, which may be a result of woodland management. The profile of the wood identified is similar to that of a number of sites within medieval Dublin where the woods of preferred use were ash and hazel. However the identified charcoal cannot be associated with any particular function.

Environmental samples (see Appendix VI) A total of 11 samples were taken as most of the features were truncated leaving the depth of undisturbed soil negligible in many cases. Hence the majority of samples were taken from pits and did not seem to have a very high organic content. Primary processing was undertaken by Thomas Cummins and analysis of the carbonized plant-remains was carried out by Penny Johnston. To summarize, the plant remains from medieval deposits excavated at Merrion Road, Dublin were identified as being predominantly from wheat, probably the free-threshing variety of bread wheat. The results indicate that these crop-remains were burnt either as they were being prepared for storage, or in some cases the deposit may represent a stored crop that had to be burned in order to control an infestation of stored product pests such as the grain weevil. There are parallel medieval rural sites around Dublin where crop assemblages suggest a crop economy predominantly focused on the production of wheat and the assemblage from Merrion Road conforms to this established picture.

Economy and diet

The manorial system introduced by the Anglo-Normans generated a cash economy, which was fuelled by a substantial expansion in the production and export of grain (McCormick and Murphy 1997, 199). This must be borne in mind when drawing conclusions from the animal-bone evidence at Merrion Road. As analyzed by Geber the bone assemblage profile consisted of cattle (the dominant species), sheep/goat, pig with horse, dog, cat, bird, hare and fish.

Cattle, at Merrion Road, the majority of which were between two and three years when slaughtered, were held primarily for the production of meat. In general, cattle bones form a large component of both urban and rural settlements. Results from urban excavations show an age/slaughter profile of 70%–85%, being older than *c.*2 years at time of slaughter, indicating that producers found it more profitable to send semi-mature or fully grown beasts to the Dublin market (McCormick and Murphy 1997, 200). In terms of comparable profiles, the average proportions of cattle bones in Britain are similar in towns and higher-status rural sites, but lower in ordinary rural settlements (Grant 1988, 155). The meat/weight statistics from the Merrion Road site are suggestive of cattle being the main source of meat, which would correlate with urban results.

Sheep were an important 'cash crop' in the Anglo-Norman economy because of the value of wool, which was one of the most important exports from Ireland. Not only that, but sheep dung was of a higher quality than that of some other animals, an important consideration in view of the demand for grain export. The evidence from Merrion Road indicates that the sheep were kept primarily for wool or milk production, a conclusion confirmed by the recovery of iron shears (04E272:86:3) from the site.

Pig are a specialized-meat animal and were commonly used for the provisioning of military garrisons (McCormick and Murphy 1997, 204). The intensive production of pig peaked in the twelfth and thirteenth centuries (more than at any other time since the Bronze Age), which coincided with the intensification of land use for grain production (Grant 1988, 159). In Britain pigs were particularly important at castles and monastic sites, which is indicative of a high-status economy allowing for spare/waste food on which to feed them (Grant 1988, 158). The faunal evidence for the castles of Dundrum, Trim and Maynooth indicates the presence of neonatal pig bones, which may be suggestive of the rearing of pigs within the lord's household (Murray 2000, 10). In contrast there is no such evidence for pig rearing at Merrion Road.

Horses, from the twelfth century on, were increasingly used to provide traction and would have been well-represented on high-status/manorial sites where they would have been kept for riding, hunting and for use in warfare. The eating of horseflesh had been entirely forbidden in a proscription issued by Pope Gregory III in 732 AD (Grant 1988, 174); however, in times of famine, this is thought to have been set aside. Some of the horse-bones recovered from Merrion Road did show chop- and cut-marks. In addition, the metal artefacts include horseshoe nails, and a rumbler bell that may have come from a horse harness. It is likely that the horses, which may have been used for traction, were rendered to provide hides, glue, horsehair, etc., after their demise.

Domestic animals such as dogs and cats form part of all assemblages whether urban or rural. The partial remains of at least two adult dogs and cats were recovered from Merrion Road. In addition there was indirect evidence for the presence of dogs in the form of gnaw-marks on cattle, pig and horse bones. Cats were used as a source of pelts but the lack of cut-marks may infer that they were kept as ratters and mousers.

The remainder of the faunal assemblage, including domestic fowl, duck, pigeon, hare and fish, are elements common to low- to middle-status sites. Eggs and poultry were almost a rural 'currency', mentioned as rents or pittances, as well as being an importance source of protein in the diet of those of lower status. The small number of the remainder of species recovered indicates that they were not integral to the diet of the occupants of the site. Fragments of fish may indicate the consumption of salmon on-site. However, at this period the rights to fish salmon were very tightly controlled, as evidenced by the historical records for the manor of Merrion. Most features, and the topsoil, contained marine molluscs. Cockles predominated while razor shells, scallops and occasional oyster shell were frequently encountered. Given the proximity to the sea, the commonality of marine molluscs on both low- and high-status sites during the medieval period, and their popularity as a food source, it is not unusual that they were recorded at Merrion Road.

The profile of the faunal assemblage at Merrion Road is not indicative of any particular social strata. It is comparable in some aspects to urban, rural and manorial sites of the period. The evidence primarily indicates on-site slaughter, which does not automatically infer on-site consumption. The high incidence of bones representing the meat-poor parts of cattle and pigs may indicate the processing of the prime joints which could have been cured and consumed elsewhere, most obviously at nearby Merrion Castle. The management of sheep appears to have taken place at the site, reflecting the significance of their contribution to the Anglo-Norman economy.

The evidence from Johnston's analysis of the carbonized plant-remains indicated the handling of cereal crops: both processing and storage was common at Merrion Road. Identification of the crop-remains indicates that the predominant crop was wheat, probably mostly bread wheat. Bread wheat was considered high-status in the early historic period and it was the staple cereal crop in areas of Anglo-Norman control. As its name suggests, it was used to make bread, and in both Ireland and Scotland during this period bread was considered a luxury food eaten by the rich, although historical records indicate that wheat was the standard food crop in the area of the Pale in the middle ages (Nicholls 2003, 133).

The evidence for the cereal and weeds suggests that winnowing and threshing had already been carried out by the time they were charred. Much of the chaff would have been removed from the crops during these first stages of processing, and indeed there were very few chaff fragments found. The suggestion that infestation necessitated widespread crop-burning is a strong possibility, as some of the grains showed possible signs of insect bore-holes. Stored products such as grain are liable to infestation by insects. When this occurs, the entire store will frequently be destroyed by fire in order to contain the infestation. Several medieval sites in the vicinity of Dublin where carbonized plant-remains were examined by Johnston were used as comparisons for the Merrion Road material. The profile suggests that Merrion Road conforms to the general picture of arable agriculture being predominantly wheat crops in the areas around Dublin during the medieval period.

Crop rotation, using legumes as one of the rotations, appears to have been common practice in England by the fourteenth century (Campbell 1995), and the recovery of small amounts of legumes among cereal remains in some of the samples from Merrion Road may indicate that this was also carried on in Ireland at this period if these legume seeds were remnants of crops from previous harvests that were self-sown in the field while the cereal crop was grown. The plant remains, combined with the evidence from the faunal assemblage, point to intense wheat-production taking place at or near Merrion. This would tie in with the substantial expansion in the production and export of grain during the thirteenth century.

Manorial Dublin

The excavation site at Merrion Road formed part of the demesne lands of Merrion Castle or Old Merrion (as it was named on the eighteenth-century maps) and as such it would have been part of the manorial settlement. The siting of the castle, north of the stream and presumably near the seashore was characteristic of castles of the thirteenth century, many of which were built on relatively low-lying ground next to water. In contrast, the excavation site was situated on high ground and, although also close to the shoreline, was located at the periphery of the manorial lands. There was also (as in many castles of this period) a frontier aspect to the siting of the castle at Merrion. By the seventeenth century the demesne lands of Old Merrion were bordered by 'part of Rabuck' to the south, 'Priesthouse' to the west, and 'Maiden's Well' to the north. However, in the preceding period the sea formed the eastern boundary while the southern limit of the lands comprised the boundary of the Liberties of Dublin (the Dublin city boundary). The excavated site was located immediately adjacent to the limit of the franchise and almost opposite the graveyard of Merrion, confirming its peripheral nature.

In terms of socio-political status, Merrion Castle and its environs fell within very narrow parameters. Perhaps in contrast to the decades immediately following the Anglo-Norman arrival, the thirteenth century was characterized by consolidation interrupted only at a local level. It was a period of stability within the baronial lordships allowing for the establishment of fixed boundaries in the form of cantreds, manors and parishes (McNeill 1997, 81). This was reflected in the manors granted, and the castles constructed, within the colony and the subsequent economic expansion. It was during this period that Ireland became an exporter of grain on a significant scale such that Edward I was able to use this surplus to supply his armies in Scotland and Gascony (Lydon 1972, 89–90). However, by the end of the thirteenth century the European-wide economic boom began to falter leading to a slackening in demand for Irish produce. This was combined with political upheaval, for example, the Bruce invasion of the early fourteenth century, deteriorating weather conditions, increasingly frequent famines and the eventual onset of the Black Death in the mid-fourteenth century. It is against this backdrop that the site excavated at Merrion Road was occupied.

From *c.*1290 the relationship between the local Irish and the Anglo-Normans began to deteriorate. William le Deveneis who held the neighbouring manor of Thorncastle, and subsequently Merrion, was also in possession of Glencree (in modern Co. Wicklow). In a petition to the crown he set forth that his tenants had fled and his lands had to be given up as useless. Incursions by the inhabitants continued into the period of ownership of John Cruise and were of such frequency that Cruise was allowed hold his property free for life (Ball, 1903, 22). The material assemblage recovered from the site at Merrion

Road points to a low-status occupation dating to the late thirteenth/ fourteenth centuries, a period when the manor of Merrion was held by, among others, Christiana de Marisco, companion to the dowager Queen of England, William le Deveneis, remembrancer of the exchequer of Ireland, and Robert de Nottingham, sometime mayor of Dublin.

The faunal assemblages indicate the processing or preparation of food-stuffs reflective of a low- to medium-status diet comparable to that of any rural settlement site of that period. Although there is emphasis in many of the historical records on the fish pools along the coast there is little evidence other than seashells for the processing or consumption of fish at the site. Although it is likely that the excavated site land linked to the tenants of Merrion, it is worth exploring the differing perceptions of wealth. In the thirteenth and fourteenth centuries, Merrion and adjoining Thorncastle were in the hands of a minor and subject to absenteeism, famine, frequent raids and plague. Although it seems that the fisheries associated with the land were a source of income, sufficient enough to be the subject of petition to the crown, it is likely that the value of Merrion was much less in practical terms. During this period both the material and faunal assemblages are comparable to those found within the manors of Nangor and Dundrum Castles. The source of income from these manors was principally agriculture with all its vagaries and, given the unstable conditions of the period, politically, socially, economically and meteorologically, it is likely that the manor of Merrion constituted little more than a glorified farmstead until the latter half of the fourteenth century.

CONCLUSIONS

Monitoring of topsoil removal within the 13-acre development site at Merrion Road resulted in the identification of medieval occupation of the high ridge to the south of the site. Subsequent archaeological excavation revealed a site comprised mainly of pits, gullies, ditches and metalled surfaces. The material assemblage was dominated by pottery, datable from the late twelfth to mid-fourteenth centuries while radiocarbon dates indicate occupation of the site from the late thirteenth to the early fifteenth century. Combined with the lack of structures and the evidence for rendering rather than consumption, in advance of complete analysis of the evidence the excavation-site can be interpreted as a working/processing area, located at the periphery of the manor of Merrion.

APPENDIX I: THE MEDIEVAL POTTERY

by *Clare McCutcheon*

Introduction

A total of 7968 sherds of medieval pottery were presented for study. Following some reassembly within and between features this was reduced to 7917 sherds of which 7901 (99.80%) are of 'Leinster cooking ware'. Sherd links were established between the ditch (F2) and the spread (F5) overlying the metalled surface (F9).

Dating Samples from two pits (F6 and F86) produced C14 date-ranges of 1277–1397 and 1328–1438 respectively. No coins were recovered and there is no record of any samples suitable for dendrochronology. The dating of the pottery falls within the established dating based on stratigraphic and other information on other sites in Dublin and along the southeast. While Leinster cooking ware has a date-range from the later twelfth to the mid-fourteenth centuries, the presence of a small quantity of 'Dublin-type fineware' indicates a date from the later thirteenth to the early fourteenth century and this is not incompatible with the C14 dates listed above.

Methodology The sherds were identified visually, in the case of this assemblage consisting almost entirely of 'Leinster cooking ware'. The detailed information is listed in Table 1, beginning with the quantity of sherds in each fabric type. The minimum number of vessels, an objective number, is based on the quantity of rim/handle junctions (23) in the case of the jugs and the shallow bowls (2), and on the complete bung-holes (14), in the case of the cisterns. Cooking pots are not at all easy to quantify but a minimum number represented can be estimated based on the different rim-sections present.

Database The sherds have been identified visually and the identifications have been entered on a database table (Access format) as per the requirements of the National Museum of Ireland.

Discussion The terminology of Leinster cooking ware as 'traditionally associated with low-status occupation' needs to be addressed firstly. It is always tempting to judge archaeological materials in the light of current fashions and trends but this has the effect of devaluing materials or vessels that have been the choice of a considerable number of people over a long period of time. Even the rapid changes of the last decade or more, that have led to the purchase of ready-made over home-cooked meals, have diminished our abilities to see the potential for many vessels. For example, what is the use of a dripping dish to catch the fats and meat juices for potential gravy if you are of a generation that thinks that making gravy only consists of a powder mixed with boiling water! The Leinster cooking ware vessels were fabricated from clays chosen specifically for their particular properties and fashioned into vessels for a number of purposes. The use of words and phrases, therefore, such as simple, native, primitive, coarse, low-status, roughly made, poorly fired, lacking in decoration, and so on, are too loaded with negative judgement to be suitable for use in describing vessels that were actually functional, useful, suitable for their purpose, readily available, locally made, reasonably priced and widely used for a period of some 200 years. Use of the carelessly chosen term 'a simple pulled spout', for example, is to misunderstand the complexity of the potters' craft, however lowly that craft may have been viewed. There is nothing simple about a pulled spout, as a poorly manipulated rim can be cracked or badly distorted if it is not carefully carried out. In contrast, the applied spouts so characteristic of Saintonge mottled green-glazed and Ham Green B jugs allow for other dangers, with poorly applied spouts and inadequate pouring holes cut out, both leading to a jug that actually functions less well than that without a spout or with a 'simple' pulled spout.

Having said all that, it is also true to say that pottery in general was not highly valued in the medieval period. In a period with little disposable income and less small coin circulating, the investment in the production and distribution of vessels was not to be undertaken lightly and a secure market was essential to repay the time and talents invested. Even imported pottery, so highly regarded in modern times, failed to register in the customs dues of the time, being grouped together with many other small items that were of so little value that it was deemed unnecessary to quantify or charge for them by name. There is a misunderstanding that imported pottery was traded into Ireland, for example, when in fact it most likely came in as an advertising-ploy along with the wines of the time. The very large percentage of Saintonge green-glazed ware in thirteenth-century Cork, up to 60% (McCutcheon 2003, 211) should not be taken as proof of the more sophisticated tastes in that city in comparison to Dublin where only 15% of the glazed wares were French (McCutcheon 2006, fig. 9). It is simply a case of better access by sea to the city centre, reduction in the double-handling of breakable material and the safer environs of the city in which to produce pottery.

The absence of pottery-making in Ireland extended for some 1000 years from later Bronze Age to the Late Viking age i.e., the eighth century BC to the ninth century AD. Ireland had not been settled by the Romans in the Iron Age and so had not acquired the custom of everyday usage of pottery. Pottery was not unknown in Ireland, as evidenced by the small quantities of imported B-ware and E-ware during the fifth to eight centuries but the alternatives of wood, leather and metal more than adequately fulfilled the requirements of the people (Ryan 1973). The presence of vikings in the ninth and tenth centuries, largely of Norwegian origin, did not affect this situation as they too were aceramic. Later tenth- and eleventh-century levels in Dublin, Waterford and Cork have produced unglazed wares from southeast England and some glazed wares from eastern England and the continent, primarily France and Belgium. The first locally made wares in Ireland are the ninth-century 'souterrain ware' of the northeast (Ivens 2001) and mid-twelfth century Leinster cooking ware of the east and southeast (Ó Floinn 1988). The official arrival of the Anglo-Normans in the latter part of the twelfth century saw the production, into an open market, of glazed wares based on the familiar prototypes from Bristol. The Dublin Guild Merchant Roll indicates at least 40 names directly associated with pottery- and tile-making in the city from *c.*1190–1265 (Connolly and Martin 1992). The documentary, stratigraphic and stylistic evidence indicates that glazed pottery was made in Dublin from *c.*1180 onwards (McCutcheon 2006). The increasing amount of medieval pottery from excavations in Kilkenny also indicates a locally-made glazed ware in production from the late twelfth century (McCutcheon forthcoming (a)). Kilkenny shares with Dublin the limited access by river to the centre of the city while, in contrast, access to the centre of Waterford and Cork by seagoing vessels was very straightforward and therefore there was not the same pressure on local pottery production.

Leinster cooking ware was originally defined by Raghnall O Floinn in 1976 and then published in 1988. The many large-scale urban and rural excavations in recent years have contributed greatly to our knowledge of the materials used at the time. The quantity of pottery from Carrickmines Castle is a case in point. Presumably this is not seen as a low-status site, yet 70% of the *c.*26700 sherds of medieval pottery recovered is Leinster cooking ware with only 0.2% French glazed wares (McCutcheon in preparation (a)). Likewise, the assemblage from Dundrum Castle contained some 70% Leinster cooking ware in an assemblage of *c.*3000 sherds with 0.46% of French glazed ware (McCutcheon in press). The material and faunal assemblage at Nangor Castle is compared with that from Merrion Castle (12.9), and here too a large percentage of the pottery (37%) consisted of Leinster cooking ware (McCutcheon 2001). With the Merrion Road site, these four castle sites, all within a radius of *c.*5 miles or 8 km, would have provided excellent markets for the local production of Leinster cooking ware.

A further comment is necessary also on the actual term 'Leinster cooking ware', which itself is loaded with functional overtones. The term was chosen for this unglazed ware, as the majority of the vessels excavated at the time of writing were cooking vessels (Ó Floinn 1988), but more recent excavations, including the present one at Merrion Road, have substantially increased the relative quantity of other vessels such as jugs, platters and lamps. It must be made clear that many of the vessels made in this fabric were never used for cooking, although they could take heat from a fire. It is worth commenting here also on part of the definition given in the MPRG Classification of Medieval Ceramic Forms. The jar form is frequently called a cooking pot, a term which has a specific functional implication. While it is undoubtedly true that many of these vessels were used for cooking, a simple utilitarian form might also have been used for a multitude of other functions, which could have changed during the life of the vessel. The term 'jar', therefore, is recommended in order to avoid possibly spurious functional connotations and the term 'cooking pot' should be used only for vessels that show evidence for cooking in the form of sooting and burnt residues (MPRG 1998, 4.1).

Table 1. Medieval pottery, Merrion Road, Dublin (04E0272).

Fabric type	Sherds	MNV	MVR	Form	Date
Leinster cooking ware	7901	39	107	platter, *c.*50 cooking pots, *c.*40 jugs, 14 cisterns, 2 shallow bowls, lamp	L12th –14th
Dublin-type ware	8	-	1	Jug	13th
Dublin-type fineware	8	-	1	Jug	L13th–14th
Total	**7917**	**39**	**109**		

Leinster cooking ware

Leinster cooking ware is the single most widespread medieval pottery type in Leinster (Ó Floinn 1988, 340). The ware is very distinctive, containing as it does visible silver-coloured mica platelets and white quartz stones along with feldspar. The choice of clay, while appearing coarse and crude, is actually an excellent one to withstand the

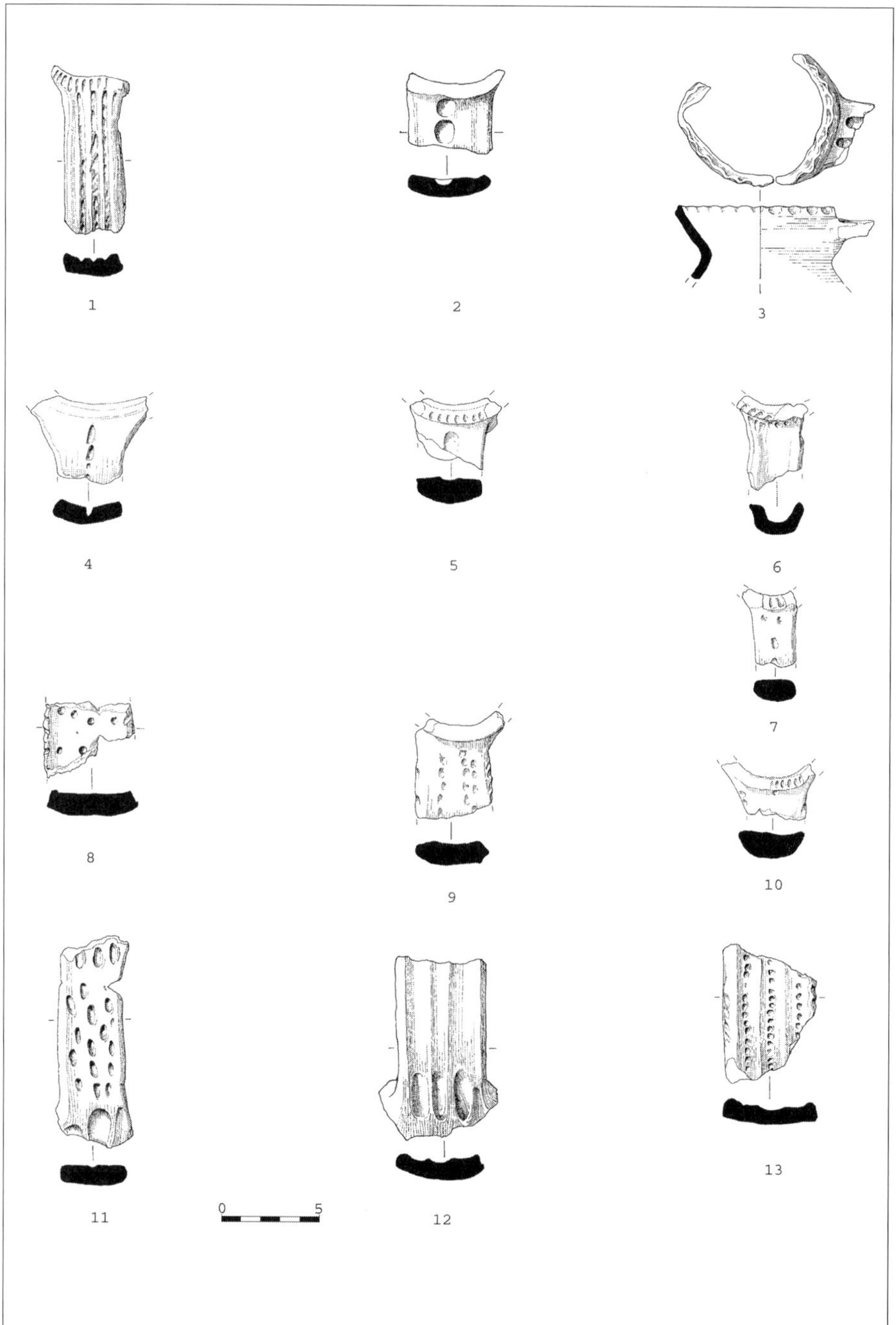

9 Pottery

contraction and expansion of temperature variations. The characteristic sand-gritted bases are present on all vessels, including the jugs and cisterns. Of particular interest is the number of cisterns and jugs present along with the more standard cooking pots.

Jugs A minimum of 23 jugs are present in the assemblage with at least another 20 represented. There was a variety of widths in the strap handles with narrow (28–34mm), medium (42–55) and wide (65–80mm) fragments found. It is difficult to be certain but it appears that the small quantity of body decoration was confined to the cooking pots (below). Decoration on the jugs was present, however, on both rims and handles. Twenty-seven medium handle-fragments and four wide handle-fragments were undecorated. Many of the wider decorated handles appear to have been decorated in bands of three, either fingered lines (fig. 9.12), fingering and stabbing (fig.9.13) or stabbing alone (fig. 9.11). The narrow handles generally had a single line of stabbing (fig. 9.2, 5, 7, 10). Two of the handles were set at the top of the rim (fig. 9.1, 4) but the more common fixture was below the rim (fig. 9.2, 3, 5–7, 9, 10). There does not appear to have been any correlation between decoration on the rim and on the handle, i.e., a plain rim with a decorated handle (fig.9.2) and vice versa (fig.9.6).

Cooking pots A large number of jars used for cooking were recovered throughout the site. These are in the standard form of medieval jars with ovoid bodies, rounded or sagging bases and everted or flared rims. Occasionally the hand moulding of the vessel is very clear as with a rim and two bases illustrated (fig. 10.2, 15, 16). As noted, the bases are sand-marked or sand-gritted and often have a slight kick where the wall of the vessel meets the base (fig. 10.14, 16). Many of the rims were undecorated (fig. 10.1, 7–12) but some of the decorated ones have also been illustrated. Several of the rims were pinched on the inside, some continuously (fig. 10.5) and some in groups (fig. 10.4). Occasionally the shoulder or upper body was also decorated (fig. 10.6). The shell motif on this vessel was also noted on a detached sherd (fig. 11.5.) but was not necessarily from this same jar. Other jars were pinched around the outside of the rim (fig. 10.3). The very straight-sided rim (fig. 10.2), with light pinching on the outside, may be from a bowl rather than a jar, with a possible base such as that illustrated at fig. 10.13. There is evidence for sooting on the exterior so this vessel may also have been used for cooking.

Decorated bodies Forty-seven body sherds were decorated with a variety of motifs. The most common of these (27 sherds) consisted of applied straight pinched lines (fig. 11.1), although some were on small fragments and may have been part of a larger design. Four sherds appeared to have a circular motif in these applied pinched lines with a fifth sherd carrying a complete circle (fig. 11.3). Five of the sherds were decorated with a shell motif, possibly a small cockle-shell, one of the sherds large enough to show two marks (fig.11.5). Six sherds had applied knobs (fig.11.4) while another had an applied flattened pellet. This form of decoration is often found on the glazed wares that were further decorated with quartering and seeds. The final three sherds had applied thumbed strips, again reflecting the decoration so characteristic of Saintonge green-glazed ware, although in this case smaller in scale (fig.11.2).

Bung-hole jar or cistern These vessels start out as a rounded jar form, in shape very similar to the cooking pots (above). It is the addition of the component part, i.e., the bung-hole, which identifies the function of this particular jar, although the profile of

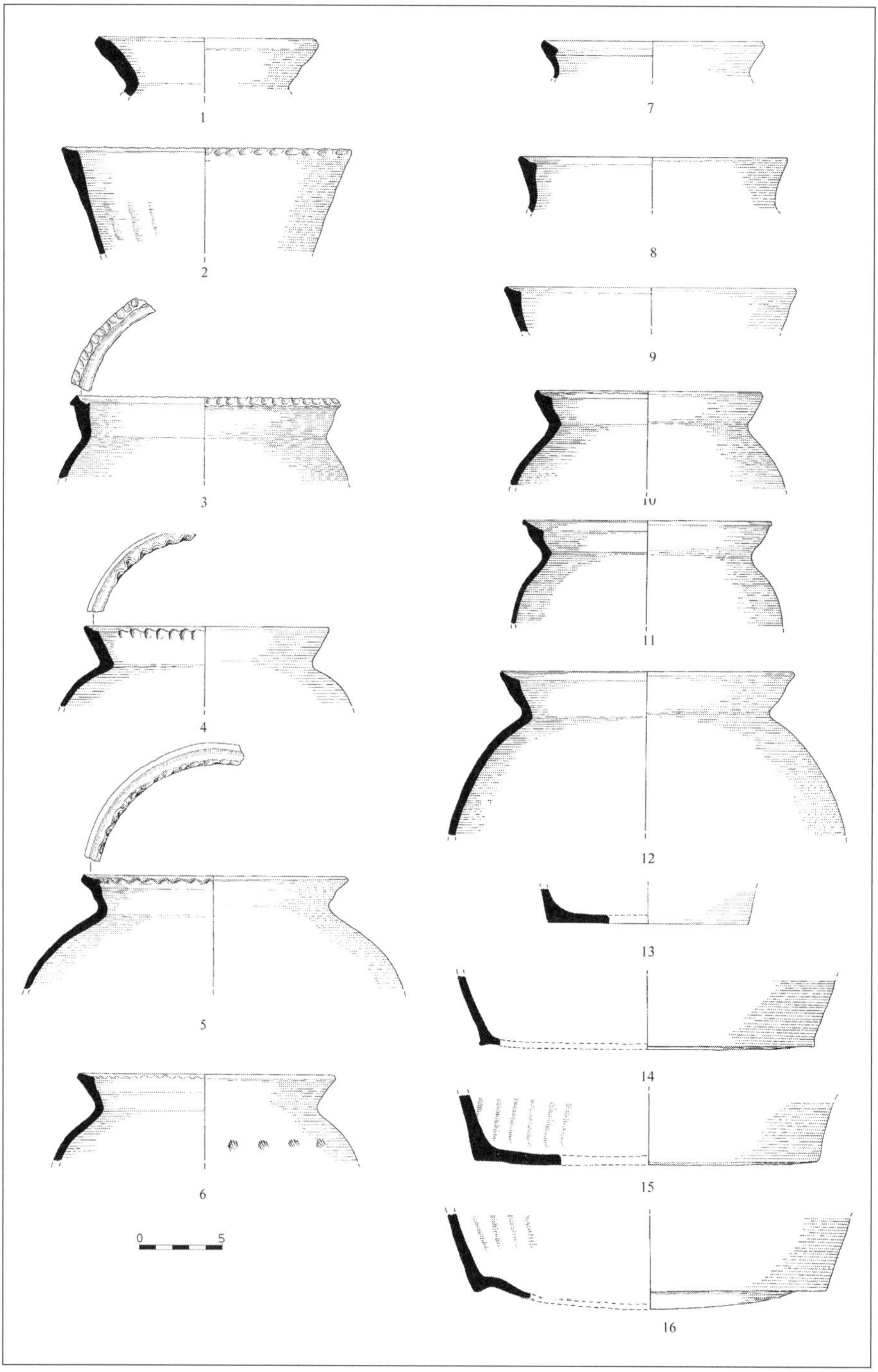

10 Pottery

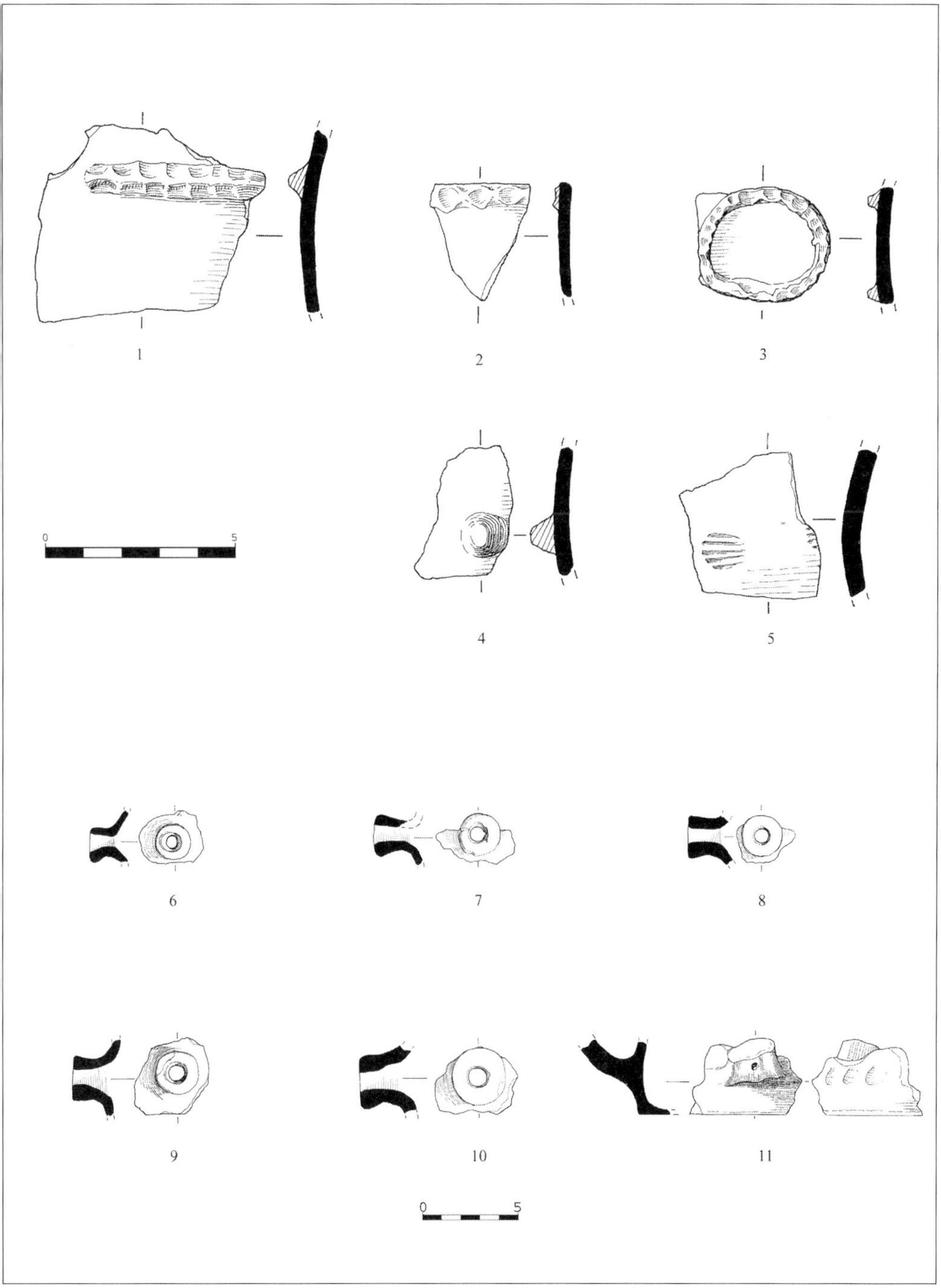

11 Pottery

the vessel is identical to the vessel commonly referred to as cooking pot. It is rare to recover a complete profile but one such from Carrickmines Castle (McCutcheon in preparation (a)) allows for some comment. It may be that the softly flaring rim is characteristic of those jars modified as bung-hole jars or cisterns. It would be foolhardy to make such a definite claim, however, based on a single example, and it would be wiser to suggest only that the two may be found together. Given these defining characteristics, therefore, these vessels should be described as rounded bung-hole jars, also called cisterns. While the bung-hole can also be made as a hole in the vessel wall, the bung-hole jars or cisterns in Leinster cooking ware all appear to be a circular knob or disc of clay applied to the exterior of the vessel wall. These vary in profile and five of the complete bungs have been illustrated here to show the variety from small, to large flat, to almost bottleneck type, with rounded tops.

Shallow bowls At least three shallow bowls with handles are represented in the assemblage. These may have been used for sauces. One piece shows the decorated handle attached close to the base but the rim is not present (fig. 3.11). Two other sherds (11:77 and 55:200) provide full profiles, the former measuring a height of 49mm, the latter 40mm.

Platter Fragments of a single platter were recovered. These are recognizable from their thickness, with characteristic sand-marked underside and smoothed surface. These were often made as flat slabs, similar to an oval bread board (Hurley 1987, 94, fig. 17.6), but low edges are also known (Foley 1989, fig. 24; McCutcheon in preparation (a)).

Dish Several sherds from dishes were found, similar in thickness to the platters but with a definite wall for use as a container rather than simply a flat surface.

Lamp Leinster cooking ware lamps were made as single cressets, based on a stone prototype 'which is of foreign inspiration' (Moore 1997, 432). The form is of a Class 1 type 'and their principal characteristic is that they have no distinguishable stem; their profiles curve gently in a concave fashion from top to bottom' (Moore 1984, 101). The sherds from lamps in Leinster cooking ware are often only recognizable by the smooth outer surface and by the very low-fired crumbly inner material. Often what survives is only a series of low-fired undiagnostic sherds, almost prehistoric in appearance (McCutcheon forthcoming (b)). As with the stone lamps of the period, where the basal hollow was voided in order to lessen the weight (Moore 1997, 433), the pottery lamps may have been similarly voided in order to aid with firing. Fragments of a lamp were recovered in features 61 and 62 and from topsoil in Grids 1 and 18. In addition, a sherd from a lamp was modified as a face, with two eyes stabbed into the clay (15:11).

Dublin-type wares

The designation of a fabric with the suffix '-type' is recommended pottery practice to indicate that a ware has been consistently found in a particular area while evidence for a production centre or kiln has not yet been discovered (Blake and Davey 1983, 39–40). The general term London-type, for example, has been adopted to describe wares that share general traditions and clay sources (Pearce et al. 1985, 2). A fuller discussion of the names of the Dublin-type wares has been detailed elsewhere (McCutcheon 2000, 120–3; 2006) and only a general outline is included in this report.

The relative dating of the Dublin-type wares has been developed as a result of consistent recovery in the stratigraphic levels of the Dublin excavations, and the absolute dating is developing by the association of imported wares, and the dating information from coins and dendrochronology. To date no pottery production site has been found in Dublin along Crocker Street at the west of the medieval city. Pottery wasters have been recovered at excavations in the Iveagh Markets to the south of the medieval wall (McCutcheon in preparation (b)) and ridge-tile production, in clay similar to Dublin-type coarseware, has been recovered at the Cornmarket (Wren forthcoming).

Dublin-type ware This is a less coarse micaceous fabric, the vessels are generally wheel-thrown, and the production and use appears to date broadly from the early thirteenth to the early fourteenth century (McCutcheon 2000, 122). The single strap-handle sherd was decorated with a single incised line.

Dublin-type fineware This is a fine, clean fabric, the vessels are wheel-thrown and the use appears to date from the later thirteenth century onwards (ibid.). Only eight sherds were recovered representing a single jug.

APPENDIX II: METALS CATALOGUE

by *Christine Baker*

Introduction

A total of 145 metal finds were recovered from the site on the Merrion Road. They reflect a myriad of uses including woodworking, ironworking and horseshoeing. The predominant find type (58%) was nails which indicated both carpentry and horse-shoeing. Where datable, the artefacts appear to fall into a date-range of thirteenth-fourteenth century which is directly comparable to that of the pottery. The majority of the artefacts were of iron and associated with features.

Horse- or ox-shoe nails Using the Museum of London typology (Clark 1995) two distinct types of horseshoe nails were identified. The first is associated with the use of Type 3 horseshoes and combines a rectangular expanding head with ears. The shaft exhibits a distinctive bend at its terminal. Known as double clenching it is the result of fastening the shoe whereby the point of the nails are bent over and hammered back. There are also examples (not in this assemblage) whereby the tip has been twisted into a spiral, which may have allowed the tightening of a nail (Clark 1995, 87). They are dated to the thirteenth-fourteenth centuries. The second identified type are nails with a square or rectangular head. Associated with Type 4 horseshoes the shank of the nail is rectangular in section and tapers to a chisel edge. They are dated predominantly to the fourteenth century, perhaps extending into the fifteenth century (Clark 1995, 88). A total of 12 horseshoe nails were recovered.

Carpentry nails Using the typology developed by Ford and Walsh (in Walsh 1997, 140–42), the majority of the nails fit into the Type A and Type B categories: Type A (circular, oval or square-shaped flat head and the shank of the nail can be either rectangular or square in section); Type B (circular, oval or sub-rectangular domed head, with a square or rectangular sectioned shank). Nails of these types can be dated to the thirteenth to sixteenth centuries, and were generally wrought and used in carpentry. In all 54 nails were recovered.

Awls and punches A total of 11 awls/punches were recovered from the Merrion Road site. Used for piercing stitching-holes or holes for attachments in leather. They are frequently found on medieval urban sites, in Dublin, Waterford and Cork and were used throughout the medieval period (Cleary et al. 2003, 266).

Clench bolts and roves Clench bolts which were driven through wood were held in place by the use of roves, small perforated iron plates to prevent them pulling through the wood. The most common type of rove is lozenge-shaped which were used not only in boat construction but also on doors. There are eight clench bolts were recovered from the site; of these six are complete, and two have roves remaining. They were all recovered from a single feature (F6) and all are of similar size and shape, having one globular-shaped terminal and one lozenge rove terminal.

Staples A total of six U-shaped staples, one possible staple and two possible wall-hooks were recovered from the Merrion Road site. Staples were used as fastenings, either in structural work or in furniture. U-shaped staples could have held fittings such as chains or hasps or have supported rings and handles on doors, etc. Merrion Road staples are all U-shaped with tapering arms, and were probably used to secure fastenings to wood. Wall-hooks are all-purpose hooks of varying sizes with tapering shanks, which were driven into timber or masonry joints (Biddle 1990, 328).

Blades A total of six possible blade-fragments of knives were recovered. The fragments appear to conform to knives of the period, which were made from a single piece of metal, single-edged, triangular in section with a tapered protruding tang (Scully 1997, 165). None of the fragments recovered include a tang, which would allow for a closer typological assignment. The size, intimated by the fragments, indicates domestic use.

Tools A number of tools which can be attributed to the functions of daily life have been recovered. At least four (augers, cutting tools) were used in woodworking, another four are part of building ironwork, while the shears infers sheep-shearing. Wood was the principal building material and used for a wide range of implements and vessels of domestic and industrial use. As the conditions for the preservation of wood did not prevail on the site, it is the associated metalwork that provides indication of its use.

Timber dogs Rectangular staples with pointed, down-turned ends which were used for securing logs to the frame over a sawing pit, and for holding heavy timbers in position when used as shores to buildings (Biddle 1990, 328).

Shears In use since the Iron Age, shears were in use at least until the fifteenth century. The majority are made of iron and were in common use, mainly for shearing sheep throughout the medieval period. The shears recovered from Merrion Road are so heavily accreted that anything other than basic form is difficult to distinguish. Simple forms such as those recovered from the urban sites of Cork have been dated to before the development of a more elaborate form in the fourteenth century (Cleary et al. 1997, 175).

Locks/keys Keys can be divided into barrel padlock keys and those for mounted locks. The former, depending on their size, were used for securing chests, caskets, etc., and doors, and shutters in buildings. The Merrion Road key cannot be definitively assigned to a typology as the loop of the key is missing, and the bit has been heavily corroded.

Hasp The hasp was recovered from the same feature as the key (F6) and is more than likely the frame which correlates to the key.

Bars These are bars of metal which may have been used for weights.

Copper alloy A total of five artefacts of copper alloy were recovered from Merrion Road, of a disparate nature. All have been submitted for conservation.

Buckles In general, buckles of smaller dimensions were used as dress accessories unlike the larger examples, which were used in horse harness, girdles and saddlebags. They were utilized in clothing, shoes and belts and were often decorated.

Rumbler bells Spherical rumbler bells in copper alloy, brass and tin become common in the late thirteenth century. Produced from four components; a suspension loop cut from sheeting, a hollow body made of two halves, leaving a flanged seam line and a round iron pea. Recovered from thirteenth-fifteenth-century deposits in London their use as dress accessories was limited to jesters, acrobats, pilgrims and priests. There was little to distinguish the rumbler bells attached to pet collars and horse harness, which were made in profusion (Egan and Pritchard 1990, 336–41).

Finger ring Medieval finger rings are wide and varied in form, and over 200 rings can be designated Irish in origin although the majority are uncontexted. Plain hoop rings can be assigned to the typology developed by Baker as Class 10a, thirty seven of which are contained within the corpus of the National Museum. They are exceedingly difficult to date.

APPENDIX III: LITHIC ANALYSIS

by *Conor Brady*

Introduction

The assemblage under discussion comprises of a total of eight pieces, all of which are flint. All pieces were measured, weighed and an objective standardized colour determination was made using Munsell Soil Colour Charts.

Raw Material Pebble flint appears to be the only type of flint used for knapping in this assemblage and the total weight of flint represented is 34.94g. Flint occurs naturally in chalk and has a range of colours from grey to black and caramel brown. The cortex or outer skin on a nodule of fresh or chalk flint is usually soft and white, or chalky. During times of glaciation, flint was extracted and transported by ice sheets to non-flint bearing areas where it was deposited as a constituent of the general glacial drift (Jackson 1991, 34; see also Woodman 1987). Once deposited, the colour of the material tends to be altered by the absorption of minerals from the local soil and colours vary widely, ranging from shades of grey, to cream, through to brown (Dillon 1997, 33). Due to the abrasion and erosion experienced during transportation, any cortex remaining is generally textured or smooth in character rather than being chalky. The size of nodules and pebbles found in glacial drift tends to be much smaller than nodules from *in-situ* chalk deposits because of the stresses to which the nodules were subject during transportation.

The individual pieces in this assemblage are small: the largest piece is a complete tertiary flake (04E272:51:7) measuring 52mm while the next largest piece is an incomplete retouched flake (04E272:52:29) with a maximum length of 35mm which, judging by the texture of its cortex surface, probably derives from a local glacial-till source. It was possible to record the colour of all artefacts in the assemblage as none was very heavily patinated. There was a range of colours present suggesting a glacial-till origin for most, if not all, of the artefacts. All but one of the finds were shades of brown or yellowish brown and the remaining piece was light grey. While grey flint is sometimes taken as an indicator of a possible *in-situ* chalk origin for flint, this is not automatically the case as grey flint is frequently found in glacial-till assemblages.

Five of the pieces from the assemblage had at least some cortex still adhering. Analysis of the texture of cortex on these pieces supports the idea of a glacial-till origin for the flint with all cortical pieces having either a smooth or textured cortex. Just two pieces were patinated. One was interesting in that it indicated the curation of an already deposited artefact. This is the incomplete retouched flake (04E272:52:29) already mentioned above. The piece is incomplete and the surface of the break is not patinated, indicating that the breakage took place sometime after its original deposition. The retouched portion of the flake edge was also unpatinated, indicating recovery and modification of the artefact at some time in the past. This points to at least two phases of lithic use on the site.

Technology The finds in each assemblage have been grouped according to their place in the production cycle. This method attempts to identify the behaviours involved in the production and maintenance of the assemblage (after Peterson 1990; Dillon 1997).

Finds from the *Selection of Material* category represent the initial collection and testing of raw material for knapping. The *Production of Tools* involves the production of cores and associated waste flakes. *Discarded Material* includes flakes that show no signs of having been utilized and are by-products of the production of usable flakes and tool blanks. The *Unmodified Tools* category includes all flakes that show signs of having been utilized, i.e., they display visible traces of edge damage. The assignation of pieces to either of these two categories is based solely on a visual inspection of the edges of each piece. It is possible that for some activities the wear patterns produced are not discernible to the naked eye. It is also possible that some of the edge damage assumed to have been caused by the use of a tool was, in fact, caused by post-depositional processes. Notwithstanding these limitations, the figures derived do give a useful impression of the proportion of utilized to unutilized flakes and the process is worthwhile. The *Modified Tools* category accounts for all formal tools that have been modified or retouched, i.e., the systematic removal of tiny flakes from the edge of a flake to create a tool of a particular form, a sharp edge, a steep edge suitable for scraping or for blunting an edge in order to facilitate hafting. Diagnostic pieces will normally belong to this category as flakes are sometimes modified according to culturally prescribed templates which tend to vary over time. *Miscellanea* forms the final category in the analysis and includes waste pieces. While it is possible that waste is produced at any one of the preceding stages, it not assignable to any particular category because it does not occur in forms that can be associated with one or other of the categories. Items of other materials that do not fit into the preceding scheme are also included here.

Bipolar or scalar reduction is a method which allows the knapping of smaller material that it is not possible to reduce using the more conventional hand-held knapping methods. It involves wedging a small pebble securely between two stones while it rests on top of an anvil stone and hammering directly down on top of it in order to split it. This technique is less predictable and controlled than normal knapping. A number of the flakes in the present assemblage display the characteristics of having been struck using the bipolar technique–crushing at both ends of the flake as if it had been struck simultaneously from both ends. Use of this technique was represented by just one artefact, a bipolar flake (04E272:42).

Table 1. Lithic assemblage, Merrion Road

	no.	%
Selection of material	0	0
Production of tools	0	0
Discarded pieces		
Unutilized flake	2	25%
Unmodified tools		
Utilized flake	1	12.5%
Modified Tools		
Barbed and tanged arrowhead	1	
Retouched flake	3	
Retouched bipolar flake	1	62.5%
Miscellaneous	0	0
Total		100%

Chronology The only chronologically diagnostic artefact in the assemblage is the barbed and tanged arrowhead (04E272:5:9) which was found in Feature 5. This is an example of Green's Sutton type (b) arrowhead (1980, 117; fig. 45, p. 122) with barbs present but unshaped rather than pointed. It is accepted that these arrowheads are a classic constituent of the 'Beaker Package' and similar contexted examples are known from Knowth and the Newgrange Beaker settlement (Eogan 1984, 274, fig. 99, 273; Dillon 1997, 251; Lehane 1983, fig. 64, 151, Table XVI, 152). However, this was the only flint find from the feature and whether or not it can be taken as being associated with the other flint finds is not known. The heavily patinated piece (04E272:52:29) points to a phase of activity far predating that represented by the barbed and tanged arrowhead.

Conclusion Although these finds came from features identified as medieval because of the presence of medieval pottery, it is considered highly unlikely that the artefacts described here were produced during the medieval period. The artefacts are very few in number, there are no concentrations which might indicate an activity area, and no contexted evidence of *in-situ* production of lithic artefacts was identified. Lithic finds have been previously noted as being relatively common on early medieval and medieval sites (Edwards 1990) but no specific work has been carried out on this question in Ireland. While it is entirely possible that flint artefacts were produced or reused after rediscovery during medieval times, in the absence of clear evidence of medieval flintworking, it is more likely that artefacts are residual and in secondary contexts, having been disturbed from their original places of deposition by medieval activity.

Catalogue

04E272:2:5 A complete utilized secondary flint flake. The platform is cortical and soft hammer percussion was used. The cortex is smooth and brown in colour and *c.*1.5mm thick. The flint is translucent and brownish yellow in colour. The flake has a hinge termination and there is a splinter off the left hand side on the dorsal face (L: 21mm; W: 18mm; Th: 7mm; Wt: 2.65g: Munsell No: 10YR 6/8).

04E272:5:9 A complete retouched tertiary flint barbed and tanged arrowhead, Green's Sutton type (b) (1980 117; fig. 45, p. 122). The platform is reworked and the type of percussion used is unclear. There is bifacial invasive retouch along all sides. The flint is translucent and light yellowish brown in colour. One tang is missing so the piece does not present a normal symmetrical profile. The break surface appears to have been reworked but it is possible that this is an original feature of the piece representing an attempt to overcome a knapping error (L: 22mm; W: 19mm; Th: 4mm; Wt: 1.5g: Munsell No: 10YR 6/4).

04E272:18:4 An incomplete retouched secondary flint flake with the proximal missing. The platform is missing and soft hammer percussion was used. There is abrupt retouch along the top of right hand side on the ventral surface. The cortex is textured and brown in colour and *c.*2mm thick. The flint is opaque and light brown in colour (L: 22mm; W: 19mm; Th: 4mm; Wt: 2.35g: Munsell No: 7.5YR6/3).

04E272:27:3 An incomplete crudely retouched tertiary flint flake with the edges missing. The platform is missing and the type of percussion used is unclear. There is abrupt retouch along the distal end on the ventral surface. The flint is translucent and strong brown in colour. The edges on the piece appear to be rolled (L: 13mm; W: 19mm; Th: 7mm; Wt: 1.95g: Munsell No: 7.5YR 5/6).

04E272:51:7 A complete heavily utilized tertiary flint flake. The piece has a brown patina. The platform is prepared and hard hammer percussion was used. The flint is opaque and strong brown in colour. The flake has prominent bulb and a prominent dorsal ridge and the point of percussion is clearly visible. It is possible that this piece is a small Late Mesolithic Bann flake (L: 52mm; W: 22mm; Th: 10mm; Wt: 8.52g: Plat W: 14mm; Plat D: 8mm: Munsell No: 7.5YR 5/8).

04E272:52:29 An incomplete retouched secondary flint flake with the proximal. The piece has a very heavy pre retouch and break patina. The platform is missing and the type of percussion used is unclear. There is abrupt retouch along the distal end on the dorsal surface. The cortex is smooth and cream in colour and *c.*1mm thick. The flint is opaque and yellowish brown in colour. There is an iron-oxide accretion on the piece (L: 35mm; W: 30mm; Th: 11mm; Wt: 12.8g: Munsell No: 10YR 5/6).

04E272:42 An incomplete retouched secondary flint bipolar flake with the distal missing. The platform is crushed and the type of percussion used is unclear. There is invasive retouch along one side. The cortex is smooth and light brown in colour and *c.*1mm thick. The flint is translucent and very pale brown in colour (L: 19mm; W: 22mm; Th: 6mm; Wt: 2.6g: Munsell No: 10YR 7/4).

04E272:43 A complete unutilized secondary flint flake. The platform is crushed/ incomplete and soft hammer percussion was used. The cortex is smooth and cream in colour and *c.*1mm thick. The flint is translucent and light grey in colour. There is a bipolar splinter missing off right hand side (L: 26mm; W: 21mm; Th: 5mm; Wt: 2.57g: Munsell No: 10YR 7/2).

APPENDIX IV: OSTEOLOGICAL REPORT ON THE ANIMAL BONES

by *Jonny Gerber*

Introduction

An osteological analysis was conducted on the animal-bone assemblage that was found during the archaeological excavation at Merrion Road in Dublin. The excavation took place over a six-week period in April-May 2004 for McNamara and Company under licence (04E0272) by Christine Baker at Margaret Gowen and Co. Ltd. The site is part of a manorial/castle system and has been preliminarily dated to 1250–1350 AD. The total assemblage consists of 1,779 fragments at a weight of 27446.27g, which gives a mean fragment weight of 15.43g. About 91% of the weight and 67% of the fragments could be identified to either species or bone element.

Methodology

The bone fragments have been identified to species, bone elements and then to the side of the animal's body. It was usually possible to assign a category of mammal based on size of a fragment if it did not have any specific species-indicating characteristics. These categories were large mammal, which primarily would be cow or horse, and medium mammal, which would be sheep, goat or pig. The fragments have been counted and weighed with 0.01g accuracy. Measurements were taken using a digital calliper with 0.01mm accuracy. For intra-comparative analysis, the amount of total fragments (NISP =Number of Identified Specimens) has been counted and minimum number of individuals (MNI) has been calculated based on recording of the zones used by Serjeantson (1996). Side and sex characteristics were also taken into consideration when the total minimum number of individuals was estimated. To distinguish between sheep and goat, the methods by Boessneck (1969) and Prummel and Frisch (1986) were used. Bird bones have been identified with help by the descriptions by Cohen (1996). Measurements were taken according to von den Driesch (1976) and the withers' heights of dog and sheep were calculated by using the formulas in Harcourt (1974) and Teichert (1975). When possible, the animals were aged by using the time schedule of epiphyseal closure according to Habermehl (1975). Age at time of slaughter has also been estimated from the dental attrition by using the method developed by Grant (1982), and then converted to years by Benecke (1988 in Vretemark 1997: tab. 6.).The animal-bone data from Merrion Road has been compared with the thirteenth- to fifteenth-century layers from Maynooth Castle in Co. Kildare (Murray 2000). It has also been compared with the contemporary urban materials from the thirteenth- to fourteenth-century layers from Charlotte's Quay in Limerick (McCormick 1984), the twelfth- to fourteenth-century layers from Patrick Street in Dublin (McCormick and Murphy 1997), the medieval layers from George's

Street in Dublin and the thirteenth- to fourteenth-century period from Hammond Lane, also in Dublin (Strid forthcoming a; b). Additionally, the animal-bone assemblage from Tullykane medieval rural settlement, dated to 1250–1300/1350 AD, has been included in one comparison (Butler [2001] 2002).

Results

In total, 67 features contained bones of animal origin. The largest assemblage was found in features 2 and 56. Since all contexts are believed to be contemporary, and due to the rather limited sample, the bones will be considered as one entity in the discussion. The meat-providing animals make up the majority of the material. Cattle are the dominant species according to NISP and weight, and sheep/goat according to MNI. Pig is also rather common in the material, and horse is relatively well-represented. Only a few fragments of dog, cat, bird and fish were identified.

Cattle (*Bos taurus*) Bones from cattle were present in 57 contexts. The fragments derived mainly from the skull and other meat-poor body parts (definition according to Vretemark 1997: fig 13.). Butcher marks were present primarily at the proximal and distal ends of the long bones, on the wrist bones and ankle bones, on the vertebrae and at the angles and temporal joints of the mandibles. Shallow transverse cut-marks were usually present on the rib fragments. Gnaw-marks, probably caused by a dog, were present on two astragali, one humerus and a phalanx. Four pelvis fragments could be sexed to three cows and one bull. The age at slaughter based on epiphyseal fusion could be determined from 39 bones, and the results indicate that the majority were between 2–3 years old when slaughtered. The conclusion is the same on the dental wear of the mandibular teeth; however this could only be estimated on two specimens. The age profile suggests that the animals were primarily held for meat and not milk. This is also indicated by the fact that bones from calves were not identified in the material, which can suggest that no cattle rearing occurred on the site (see McCormick 1984).

Not enough measurements could be taken to ensure that a mean value could be statistically significant. However, the data corresponds to the other contemporary assemblages (Table 1). The only evident difference is the distal breadth of the metatarsals in the Merrion Road material, but this is based on only one measurement. It is also evident that the proximal and distal breadth of the metacarpals and metatarsals at Maynooth Castle is considerably smaller compared the other contemporary materials.

Table 1. Mean value of osteometrics on cattle bones in Merrion Road and contemporary assemblages

Measurement	Merrion Road	Maynooth Castle	Patrick Street	Hammond Lane
Radius Bp	73.52 (n: 1)	71.85 (n: 2)	71.9 (n: 13)	73.4 (n: 11)
Mc Bp	48.48 (n: 2)	42.3 (n: 16)	51.3 (n: 26)	51.7 (n: 2)
Mc Bd	49.81 (n: 1)	49.2 (n: 18)	53.1 (n: 20)	54.8 (n: 21)
Tibia Bd	54.8 (n: 8)	56.1 (n: 7)		
Calcaneus GL	121.5 (n: 14)	119.4 (n: 5)		
Mt Bp	40.22 (n: 1)	42.3 (n: 17)	41.7 (n: 20)	
Mt Bd	56.15 (n: 1)	44.1 (n: 17)	48.0 (n: 24)	49.2 (n: 18)

Sheep/Goat (*Ovis aries* and *Capra hircus*) Bones from sheep/goat were present in 36 contexts. A total of 25 bone fragments could be identified as sheep and none as goat. Cranial fragments were well represented, but also meat-rich body parts such as legs and the torso. Butcher-marks were only present on a mandible, a humerus, a radius and a pelvis fragment. Shallow transverse cut-marks were present on a fragment of a lumbar vertebra, a rib, a humerus, a metacarpal and a tibia. A pubic bone from a sheep and a radius from a sheep/goat showed evidence of animal gnawing, probably caused by a dog. Three pelvis fragments and one fragment of an atlas could be sexed to three ewes and one ram. The animals were primarily slaughtered after 2–3 years of age, which could indicate that the primary function of the animals was for milk or wool production. From the dental wear it could be determined that three animals were slaughtered between 2–4 years of age and two animals at between 4–6 years of age.

It was possible to calculate the withers height from two fragments. A radius gave the height of 63.52cm. The measurement of a calcaneus gave the height 79.88cm. There is an obvious difference between the heights of these two individuals, but since they are only two measurements from two different bones, the significance cannot be proven. A general comparison with contemporary sites regarding the osteometric shows that the size of the sheep/goats from Merrion Road does not differ much from the other materials (Table 2).

Table 2. Mean value of osteometrics on sheep/goat bones in Merrion Road and contemporary assemblages

Measurement	Merrion Road	Maynooth Castle	Patrick Street	Hammond Lane
Radius GL	131.8 (n: 13)	150.7 (n: 2)		
Radius Bp	27.69 (n: 1)	27.3 (n: 13)	28.9 (n: 8)	
Mc Bp	19.82 (n: 3)	21.8 (n: 18)	21.4 (n: 8)	
Mc Bd	24.1 (n: 19)	23.5 (n: 9)		
Mc GL	122.0 (n: 19)	115.3 (n: 7)		
Mc SD	13.7 (n: 18)	12.5 (n: 8)		
Tibia Bp	35.9 (n: 17)	34.0 (n: 1)		
Tibia Bd	23.88 (n: 5)	23.2 (n: 21)	23.2 (n: 10)	
Mt Bp	20.13 (n: 1)	19.5 (n: 2)	18.7 (n: 14)	18.2 (n: 6)
Mt Bd	22.4 (n: 2)	22.4 (n: 14)	23.0 (n: 6)	
Mt GL	133.1 (n: 1)	130.2 (n: 14)	125 (n: 6)	
Mt SD	10.83 (n: 3)	11.2 (n: 1)	11.8 (n: 14)	10.7 (n: 6)

One left radius displayed pathological changes of the bone. Enthesophytic bone was present at the lateral part of the proximal metaphysis and there was osteophytic growth at the margins of the articular surface. Sclerotic bone was present on the anterior aspect of the lesion. It could be a result of either an infection or possibly osteochondroma, which is a benign tumour that affects bone during the fusion of the epiphysises.

Pig (*Sus domesticus*) Pig bones were present in 37 contexts. The over-representation of meat-poor body parts was more evident in this case compared with the cattle and sheep/goat assemblages. Chop-marks were present at the neck of two scapulae and the proximal ends of two humeri. There were gnawing-marks from dog present on one calcaneus. Sexing of the animals was carried out using the canine teeth. They showed a clear over-representation of boars. This fact might reflect a selection where boars were slaughtered at a later stage since they would have yielded more meat than sows. The result can, however, not be regarded as significant since the total number of teeth available are rather few. From the epiphyseal fusion of the bones and the wear of the teeth, it could be determined that a clear majority of the animals were slaughtered between 1–2? years of age, which is the period when they would have reached their maximum size. There is no clear evidence that any animal was spared for breeding purposes. The few measurements that were taken indicate no obvious difference in the size of the pigs between the different contemporary materials (Table 3.).

Table 3. Mean value of osteometrics on pig bones in Merrion Road and other contemporary assemblages

Measurement	Merrion Road	Maynooth Castle	Patrick Street	Hammond Lane
Humerus Bt	29.05 (n: 1)	29.8 (n: 3)	28.9 (n: 4)	
Radius Bp	26.97 (n: 1)	25.8 (n: 23)	25.7 (n: 11)	25.8 (n: 7)
Pelvis LAR	28.0 (n: 10)	30.0 (n: 1)		
Tibia Bp	41.4 (n: 3)			
Tibia Bd	27.46 (n: 1)	26.4 (n: 15)	26.8 (n: 6)	31.6 (n: 3)

No bones indicative of wild boar were found in the material, but a possible presence of wild boar cannot be discounted.

Horse (*Equus caballus*) Horse bones were present in 23 contexts. In this case, there was no over-representation of either meat-poor or meat-rich body parts. Horsemeat would usually not have been eaten since it is a taboo proclaimed by the church (Egardt 1962: 82 in Vretemark 1997: 144). However, a chop-mark was present through the medial condyle of a humerus, and six shallow transverse cuts were present on the medial side of a metatarsal. This could possibly suggest that the horse bones are waste from a tannery production. One metatarsal of horse had considerable dog gnaw-marks on it. This suggests that the horse carcasses were not buried directly after the slaughter, which is expected if there was no use of the body.

Dog (*Canis familiaris*) Dog bones were present in 10 contexts. In all, there were 15 bone fragments deriving from at least two adult animals. From one of them, the teeth in a mandible were considerately worn down, which either suggests that the bones come from a very old animal or that the attrition reflects a behaviour pattern for that specific individual.

Cat (*Felis domesticus*) Only parts of a right humerus and a right femur identified as cat were found in the material. The epiphyseal fusion on both elements was complete which indicate that they came from adult animals.

Bird (*Aves* sp.) Three bird species were identified in nine contexts. Nine fragments from at least three individuals derived from fowl *(Gallus gallus)*. One tarso-metatarsus and an ulna derived from a duck *(Anas sp.)*. One humerus and one femur were identified as pigeon *(Columba sp.)*.

Hare (*Leporidae* sp.) A fragment from a right pelvis and another from a left femur were identified. The bones derived from adult animals and were found in two contexts.

Fish (*Pisces* sp.) A dental bone and two other fragments of the skull from fish, possibly salmon, were identified in two contexts.

Discussion

The quantitative relation between the three meat-producing animal groups is presented in fig. 1, according to NISP, weight and MNI. The chart is a good example of the difficulties of quantifications in animal osteology. In both the NISP and weight categories, there is an evident majority of cattle represented. On a MNI basis, more than 50% is represented by sheep/goat. This reflects the fact that those animals are smaller than cattle, and therefore the bones would be less exposed to fragmentation. There is also a difference in the representation of sheep between the NISP and weight categories. This, again, is probably due to the physical size of the animal, which means that there might be more traits indicating sheep or goat present on a fragment of the same size as any unidentified fragment from a larger animal.

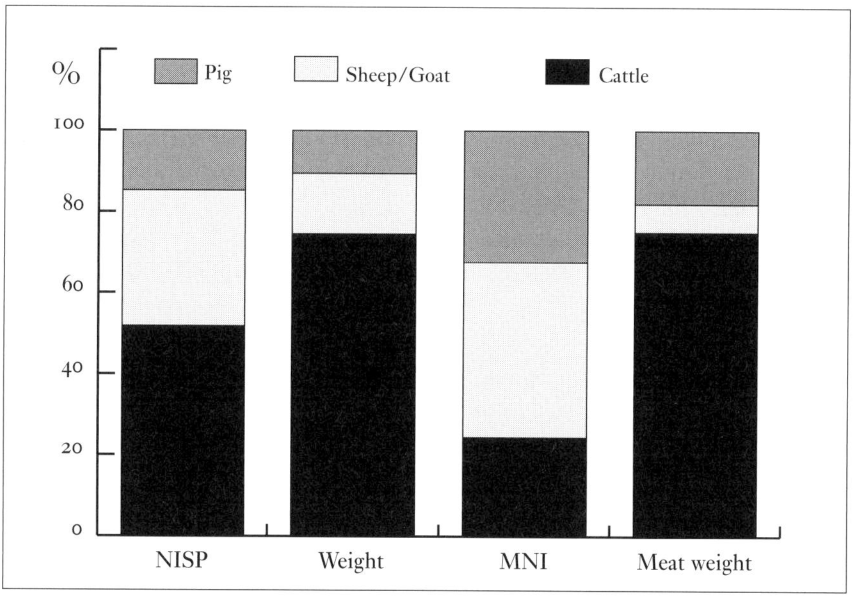

1 The quantitative relation between the meat-providing domesticates

The bones of the skull, the carpal and tarsal bones, the metacarpals and metatarsals and phalanges belong to the meat-poor parts of the bodies. Since there was a clear over-representation of those parts in all the meat-providing animals, it seems likely that the bone material from Merrion Road is primarily slaughter waste. The result can, however, in relation to the horse bones indicate that there was tannery activity at the site, but the quantitative limitation of the material does not allow for any definitive conclusions.

Table 11. Relation between NISP on bone fragments from meat-rich and meat-poor segments of the animal bodies of the meat-providing animals

	Cattle		Sheep/Goat		Pig	
	NISP	%NISP	NISP	%NISP	NISP	%NISP
Meat-rich	160	35%	117	40%	42	33%
Meat-poor	294	65%	176	60%	87	67%
Total	**454**	**100%**	**293**	**100%**	**129**	**100%**

The meat weight has been estimated by multiplying the MNI value with the assumptions on live animal weight that have been suggested by McCormick and Murphy (1997: 200). The relation between the meat-providing animals based on meat weight gives a completely different result (fig. 1; Table 4). It is now suggestive of Merrion Road that cattle were the main source of meat, followed by pig. This is indicative of an urban habitation since sheep/goats could not be reared within the town (McCormick and Murphy 1997: 199).

Table 4. The relation between the meat-providing animals in meat weight

	MNI	Assumed live animal weight	Meat weight	% Meat weight
Cattle	9	450 kg	4 050 kg	75%
Sheep/goat	16	23 kg	368 kg	7%
Pig	12	80 kg	960 kg	18%

In comparison with the other contemporary materials, the closest correlation based on MNI is Maynooth Castle. Based on NISP, there is a better correlation between Merrion Road and the other sites but not with Maynooth Castle. By comparing meat weights, it is clear that sheep/goat and pig had a considerable greater importance at Merrion Road and Maynooth Castle compared to the other sites. A relatively high percentage of pig compared to sheep/goat is usually indicative of an urban settlement, and since most comparative sites are urban, it is difficult to place Merrion Road, which would have been in a rural location, in context. There could be an easy explanation, e.g., that the household at Merrion Road generally preferred pork. A more easily argued explanation is the structure of the empirical data itself. There were many pig canine teeth present in the Merrion Road material, from which is easy to calculate MNI. The amount of osteological data is also related to the overall condition of the bone material. A more likely explanation though is that the household at Merrion Road had living habits that were similar to the urban population of Dublin, probably because of the socio-economical function of the manor/castle.

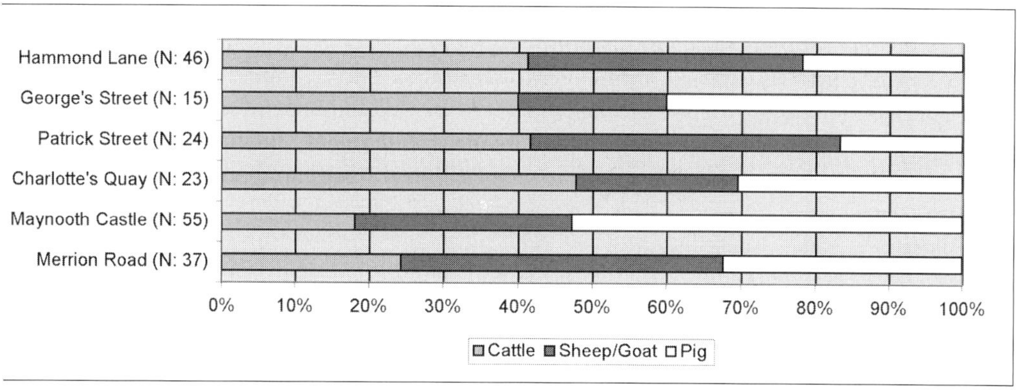

2 Relative percentage of the meat-providing mammals in MNI

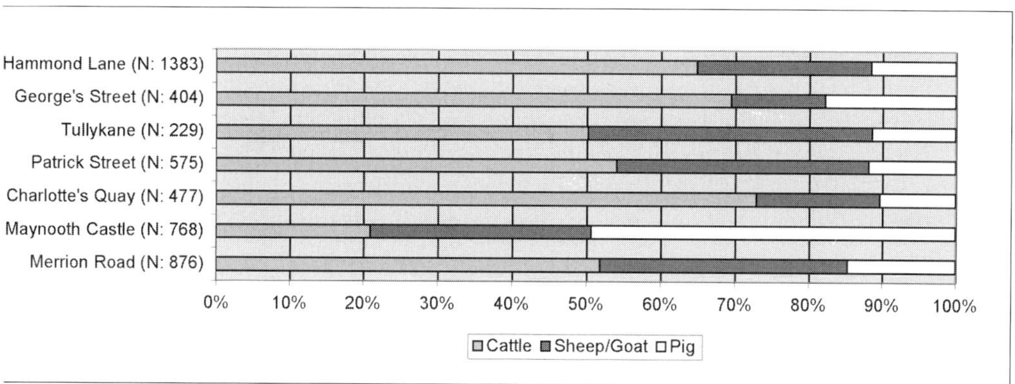

3 NISP percentage of the meat-providing mammals

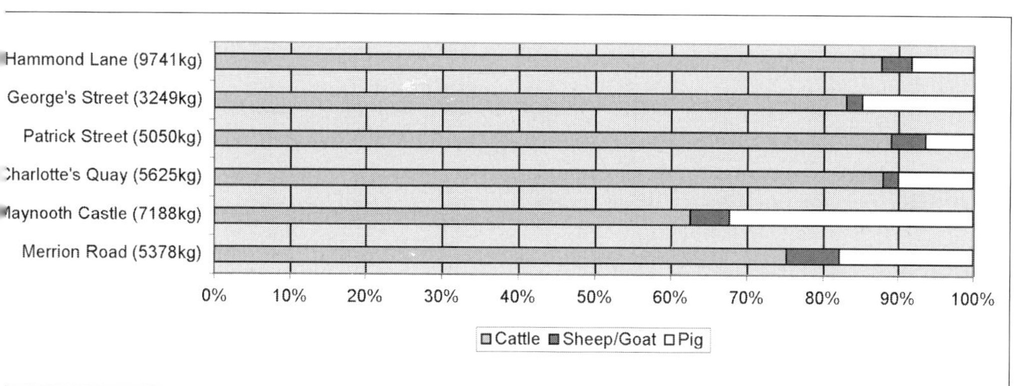

4 Total weight percentage of the meat providing mammals

Other species
It is difficult to interpret the significance the other species would have had at Merrion Road. There seems to be relatively more horse bone in the material. Whether this reflects tannery activity on the site or just remains of the household horses that were buried is impossible to say. It does not seem, however, that any of the horse bones were found in articulation *in situ*. From the very few fish bones that were identified, it is however clear that marine food and possibly hare was part of the diet. Most fish bones are very small in size, so in order to retrieve a good sample of bones; it is usually necessary to sieve considerable amounts of soil, which was not done in this case.

Conclusions
The osteological analysis of the animal-bone assemblage from Merrion Road identified bones from cattle, sheep, goat, pig, horse, dog, cat, bird and fish. They are in general mainly slaughter waste, which indicates that the animals were slaughtered on-site or nearby. There is also a possibility that there was some tannery activity, but probably of secondary importance to the slaughter. The Merrion Road animal-bone material had most in common with the data from Maynooth Castle, which is both contemporary and from the same type of site. But the analysis also gave similar result as the materials from Charlotte's Quay in Limerick and Patrick Street, George's Street and Hammond Lane in Dublin which all are urban sites. Since Merrion Road was a manorial/castle settlement located in a rural context, the osteological information probably reflects life habits that would have been similar to the urban population of Dublin.

APPENDIX V: ANALYSIS OF THE CHARCOAL

by *Lorna O'Donnell*

Introduction
This report discusses the results of charcoal analysis from the Merrion Road excavation. The main features excavated on-site were pits and depressions. Artefactual evidence dates the site to the thirteenth/fourteenth century. The report is broken into sections, which deal with the methods used, and present the results of analysis. An interpretative section then considers the type of landscape from which the charcoal was derived, and compares the assemblage to environmental work from other medieval Dublin sites. The conclusions and advice for radiocarbon dating are then discussed.

Sampling and processing The samples were taken on-site as bulk soil and processed by flotation, whereby each sample was soaked in water in order to suspend the carbonized material; this was then poured off and trapped in a sieve (mesh size 300μm). This 'flot' (i.e., the floated material) was dried and stored in sealed plastic bags. Thomas Cummins processed the samples.

Identification of the charcoal Each charcoal piece was identified by a first selection under a Nikon binocular microscope at a magnification of 10x–40x. The pieces were broken to reveal their transverse, tangential and longitudinal surfaces. A binocular microscope was used with dark ground light and magnifications generally of 200x and 400x to identify the charcoal. The charcoal was identified by comparison with known material and keys (Schweingruber 1978).

Results Two samples were analyzed from Merrion Road. These were from F6, C1 and F86, C2. Both of these features were pits, with no obvious evidence of *in-situ* burning. The charcoal level from the two pits was low. Alder (*Alnus glutinosa*), hazel (*Corylus avellana*), ash (*Fraxinus excelsior*), wild/bird cherry (*Prunus avium/padus*), blackthorn (*Prunus spinosa*) and oak (*Quercus* spp.) were identified from the site. These are all native Irish trees. More charcoal was identified from F6 than F86. Wild/bird cherry, blackthorn, oak, ash, hazel and alder were identified from F6, while wild/bird cherry, hazel and ash were found in F86. The most frequent trees present at Merrion Road, as regards weight, were alder followed by hazel, oak and ash. There were no insect holes present in the charcoal, indicating that the wood was not stored for long periods of time before use. Most of the charcoal pieces were of medium growth, yet there were some instances where it was quite mixed. In some cases the first 2–3 years of the hazel are fast, with a subsequent decline in growth. This suggests it was coppiced. However, this has to be interpreted cautiously, as wood will shrink and warp during carbonization. During coppicing, the stump sends up shoots, called spring, and becomes a stool from which an indefinite succession of crops of rods, poles or logs can be cut at intervals of years. It is a very efficient and reliable way of establishing a new crop (Rackham 2001). As hazel will self-coppice, the presence of coppiced wood on-site does not necessarily reflect woodland management.

Origin of the wood Alder carrs are often found on the banks of streams and rivers, and also in damp woodland. The tree prefers soil where there is movement or seepage of water (Orme and Coles 1985). Hazel frequently grows in a dry-land situation, as a shrub or as woodland under storey, often with oak. It can flourish in a cleared situation, as scrub. It will tolerate a wide range of conditions, from dry to wet (but not waterlogged). There are two types of native Irish oak, Sessile (*Quercus Petraea*) and Pedunculate (*Quercus robur*). Sessile oak prefers lighter, more porous soils than the Pedunculate oak (Orme and Coles 1985). Ash is a light-demanding species that will grow well on chalk or limestone soils. It will flourish on moist soils but not on those that are permanently waterlogged. It requires a nutrient-rich soil. Cherry and blackthorn require light and can be found on forest edges and in hedges.

Interpretation The environmental information gained from the charcoal analysis can be viewed in two ways. The wood may have been transported onto site from other areas, and therefore may give no environmental information about Merrion Road at all. O'Sullivan feels it is certain that the demand for supplies of timber and wood would quickly have led to the continuance or invention of some form of woodland management strategy, and that by the early fourteenth century formal systems of woodland management were in operation in the vicinity of Anglo-Norman Dublin (1998b). Alternatively it is entirely possible that any wood used on-site could have come from the surrounding hinterland, as the site is quite rural. The trees found infer the presence of nearby wetlands, in the form of rivers, lakes or marshes. Other woods identified, such as hazel, oak and ash prefer a dry-land environment, and the trees could have been found on the ridge of high ground associated with the site. The hedge that delineates the site could have been a source for small amounts of cherry and blackthorn, if it was present when the site was in use. As the tree cover corresponds well with the excavator's description of the site topography, it is more likely the wood was gathered locally than from forests surrounding Dublin.

Comparative sites In recent years environmental work on a variety of medieval Dublin sites has been completed. Although they are not archaeologically comparable to Merrion Road, their wood assemblages can be compared. At Back Lane, house walls, fences, pathways and roof supports were excavated (Walsh 1993). Post and wattle samples analyzed show that the most regularly used wood was hazel, while smaller amounts of ash, alder and willow were used. A complex extraction system of underwood was identified by O'Sullivan, mainly including coppice rotation-cycles of 5 and 8 years (1998a). At Winetavern Street, where thirteenth-century post-and-wattle and brushwood waterfront structures were excavated, the preferred wood used was ash and hazel. O'Sullivan (2000) noted evidence for the extraction of underwood at 4, 7–8 and 10–11 years. The source of timber for these sites would differ from that of Merrion Road, given their urban situation. Vast amounts of wood would have been required for the buildings' construction, and this would have need to have been sourced from outside their immediate area as there would not have been a large enough supply nearby. The most likely source for these forests would be from the north Wicklow woodlands, such as at Glencree and Newcastle McKynegan (O'Sullivan 1998b).

Environmental work by Ellen O'Carroll (pers. comm.) on samples from Hammond Lane has shown that the main wood used on-site was hazel, and that it was particularly selected for hurdles. The surrounding hinterland is more comparable to Merrion Road than the other sites mentioned, as wood used on-site could have been collected from the nearby Oxmanstown Green. Wood analyzed from the three sites mentioned here is comparable to the Merrion Road charcoal in their native species composition, and utilization of coppiced hazel, whether it was from woodland management or adventitious exploitation of hazel coppices. This reinforces the growing body of evidence that shows there was a discrete tradition of woodland management in medieval Dublin, both from wood transported to urban sites and from wood collected near rural sites.

Conclusion A variety of native Irish woods were identified from two pits excavated at Merrion Road. The function of the pits is unclear, and the presence of charcoal in them probably indicates some form of backfilling. The identified charcoal is not directly associated with any particular function. The woods found indicate a mixture of wetland, with access to rivers and marshy ground, with nearby drier, high ground that could support trees such as ash, oak and hazel. The wood was probably gathered near the site. Some of the hazel pieces displayed evidence for coppicing, and are very comparable to other medieval Dublin sites in this respect.

Table 1. Identified charcoal from Merrion Rd (weight)

Alder	37%
Hazel	21%
Ash	17%
Cherry	3%
Blackthorn	1%
Oak	21%

APPENDIX VI: ANALYSIS OF THE CARBONIZED PLANT-REMAINS

by *Penny Johnston*

Introduction

Eleven bulk soil samples were taken during archaeological excavation at Merrion Road in Dublin (04E0272). The examined samples were taken from pit-fills, spreads and gullies. These deposits were examined for the remains of carbonized seeds and other easily identifiable charred plant-remains. All of the samples contained charred seeds, although in four samples these were only present in very small amounts. The text in this report is broken into the following sections: a methodology section outlines the procedures used to process the samples; a results section outlines the findings on a sample by sample basis; a plant-remains section explains the significance of each plant type found; an interpretation section investigates the assemblage on a site-specific basis; a discussion section compares the results to assemblages examined from similar sites, and the report concludes with a non-technical summary that repeats the salient points of interest. The tables and figures are presented at the end of the report.

Methodology

The samples were processed using a simple flotation technique, whereby each sample was soaked in water in order to suspend the carbonized material; this was then poured off and trapped in a sieve (mesh size 300µm), a process that was repeated until no material separated from the sediment. Each 'flot' (i.e., the floated material) was dried and stored in a sealed plastic bag. Sorting and identification of the plant remains in each sample was carried out using a low-powered binocular microscope (magnification x4.8–x56). Each identifiable charred seed was extracted, identified and counted.

Results: the samples

F6/C1 (S1) The upper fill in the south-western quadrant of a large sub-rectangular pit, this deposit included many cereal grains, predominantly wheat. Most of these grains were probably free-threshing wheat, such as bread wheat, but the difficulties involved in identifying wheat grains on the basis of morphology alone are evident, as many of the grains from this sample could not be definitely classified beyond their genus (*Triticum* species). There were also several small grass, pulse and weed seeds. However, the sample was generally uniform and appeared to have been relatively well cleaned after harvest, with most common types of field weeds eliminated. The deposit also contained charcoal, medieval pottery, shell and bone. Large frequencies of charred plant-remains in a deposit such as this suggest one of the following scenarios: an *in-situ* burnt storage deposit, an *in-situ* cache of grain that has been burnt during processing (such as in a kiln), or a burnt crop that has been cleared out after burning and thrown away as waste. As the deposit contained bone and pottery waste, the latter situation is probably the most likely explanation for the presence of high quantities of charred seeds in this deposit.

F6/C3 (S2) A middle fill from the same pit as S1; the charred seed assemblage from this deposit was much poorer than that from the upper fill, with only five cereal grains and three weed seeds recovered. This suggests that it was occasional reworked waste, rather than a deliberate dump in the pit.

F11 (S3) A sample from an isolated spread (S3) yielded seeds from several cereals, most of which were badly damaged and were therefore not identifiable to type (they have been classified as 'indeterminate'). The cereal grains were not particularly abundant and weed seeds were as frequently retrieved as crop-remains. This deposit appears to have formed in a natural depression at the site, and the charred plant-remains may have accumulated gradually from scattered waste at the site.

F12 (S4) This sample from the fill of a circular cut contained only the charred remains of one grass seed, no doubt reworked from activity at the site.

F14 (S5) A sample from F14, a large, shallow, curvilinear feature, contained a small quantity of charred seeds, all cereal grains. The amounts are so small that they are probably merely waste from general activity at the site.

F47 (S6) A pit-fill, F47, produced a moderately rich charred-seed assemblage, predominantly of wheat grains, but also with one pea seed and one charred remnant of a flax seed capsule.

F52 (S7) The sample from this pit-fill contained only three charred cereal grains, all identified as wheat.

F75 (S8) The fill of this post-hole/small pit contained several cereal grains, mostly wheat, and many weed seeds which were predominantly weeds of cultivated ground and waste places. There were also several fragments from pulses, including two peas.

F65 (S9) This sample from a linear feature was rich in plant remains, particularly cereal grains. Many of the cereal grains were classified as indeterminate cereals as the surface preservation of the grains was not good and it was difficult to pick out their distinguishing morphological characteristics. However, the only identified types of cereal grains from the sample were from wheat, and it is most likely that these indeterminate grains were also wheat. This sample also contained a flax seed capsule.

F86/C2 (S10) This sample was taken from an oval pit and it contained cereal grains that were exclusively identified as wheat, apart from some grains that could not be identified to genus and were therefore labelled as indeterminate. This failure to identify the grains was primarily due to poor surface preservation of the seeds, probably partly brought on by charring conditions, which were probably very aerobic and hot. The preservation was subsequently worsened by reworking; possibly when the deposit was discarded as waste into a pit. The composition of this sample was so uniform that it is unlikely that the seeds were general waste that accumulated gradually, and it is more likely to represent one charred crop that was discarded after burning. However, the cobbling in this pit suggests that it was not merely a waste pit.

F86/C2 (S11) Like the other sample from this feature (S10), the cereal grains from this sample are predominantly wheat, although these are not as frequent in this sample as they were in S10. There is greater variety in seed type in S11, including many weed seeds of the dock family, and a surprisingly large number of sedge seeds. S10 also contained a small amount of sedge seeds and it is possible that the crops from these samples were taken from a relatively damp field and therefore these plants characteristic of damp places, the sedges, were included with the crops when they were brought onto site.

Summary

Large quantities of seeds retrieved from S1, S9 and S10 suggest deliberate deposition of burnt crops, perhaps as waste that was cleared out after a fire. Scatters of burnt seeds found in all the other sampled deposits at the site suggest a generally high level of charred seeds present and indicate that handling of cereal crops (processing or storage or both) was common at Merrion Road.

The plant remains

Cereals The most common crop type found was wheat. The wheat was probably predominantly free-threshing wheat, although identification was difficult as a result of some distortion to the grains due to their subjection to high charring temperature. There are also general difficulties that accompany the specific identification of wheat grains from archaeological sites, as there is a range of closely related species that have evolved over several millennia of human selection and hybridization and wheat grains can vary greatly between different sites and different periods (Hillman et al. 1995). Wheat has been a staple crop in much of Eurasia since the beginnings of cultivation and in early historic Ireland it had a high value; several early Irish texts attach a higher value to bread wheat than any other cereal (Kelly 1998). The arrival of the Anglo-Normans changed the emphasis of Irish agriculture to an intensive cereal-production regime, with wheat being the staple crop in most areas under Anglo-Norman control (Nicholls 2003).

Dock family seeds The plants from this family are ubiquitous, both in the countryside today and in archaeobotanical assemblages. They tend to be weeds of cultivated land and are aggressive and successful colonizers of open and waste ground; thus they are frequently associated with anthropogenic activity. The only identifiable seeds of this family found in the Merrion Road samples were probably from Sheep's sorrel (*Rumex* cf *acetosella*), which today is common in dry grassland, rocky outcrops, shingle beaches, and on lime-poor soils (Ackeroyd 1999). The seeds in these samples are generally found in samples with relatively high frequencies of cereal grains, suggesting that these weed seeds were brought onto site with the grain, as contaminants in the crops.

Goosefoot family seeds These seeds are frequently found in archaeobotanical deposits, although the numbers recovered from Merrion Road are small. They are plants of cultivated and open ground. The leaves are edible (like spinach) and the seeds were possibly cultivated in the past (Stokes and Rowley-Conwy 2002) to be used as a food in their own right, or to be added to grain in years when yield was not good; the seeds have been retrieved from prehistoric bog-body gut-contents (Holden 1995). However, the low rate of recovery from Merrion Road suggests that we are dealing here with weeds of cultivated crops, rather than actual crops or gathered wild foods.

Legume (pulse) family seeds Interesting inclusions in the samples were legumes, such as peas. These are nitrogen-fixing and therefore help to rejuvenate the soil. Crop rotation, using legumes as one of the rotations, appears to have been common practice in England by the fourteenth century (Campbell 1995), and the recovery of small amounts of legumes among cereal remains in some of the samples from Merrion Road may indicate that this was also carried on in Ireland at this period if these legume seeds were remnants of crops from previous harvests that were self-sown in the field while the cereal crop was grown. Legumes were probably an important supplement to the human diet. Spencer's survey of historical documents pertaining to food in the period between the twelfth and fourteenth centuries in England suggests dried peas and beans were commonly made into flour, or in some cases used as part of a pottage, while dried and ground peas were used in 'pease pudding' a favourite dish of both rich and poor tables (Spencer 2002, 57).

Flax Traditionally, flax has been grown for use of its fibre, to make linen. In these cases the stems are used as the main crops and the flax was probably cut when the seeds were immature. However, the seeds were also used as a crop in their own right; the entire seeds may have been used as an ingredient in bread, as the variety known as linseed is frequently used today. The crushed seeds are also a good source of oil. Two seed capsules were recovered from samples at Merrion Road; both were very small, perhaps indicating that they were immature and suggesting the possibility of flax-drying at the site. There are few stages in flax processing that make the plant remains liable to come into contact with fire, and thus they are relatively unusual in charred-seed assemblages, and they have so far only been recovered in very small quantities. Some charred flax seeds have been found at the following sites: Ballymount, Co. Dublin, Bremore, Co. Dublin and possible examples from Ballygrennan, Co. Limerick (all medieval sites, the latter two both containing evidence of plant processing). It appears that some kilns, in a much later period, were specifically constructed for the purpose of drying flax (Gailey 1970, 56), although an early historic Life of St Ciarán of Saigir refers to drying flax on the inside wall of a house (Kelly 1998, 270). It nonetheless appears that flax may have required the artificial application of heat in order to dry it properly before beating and this may be why the bolls were recovered here. However, some varieties of flax can grow wild or as a field-escape and it is perhaps best not to extrapolate too much from the recovery of such a limited quantity of remains.

Mallow family seeds Mallow plants were frequently grown in the past for medicines and food; their leaves were commonly used in cough medicine, and in some parts were an ingredient in winter soups. The common mallow is widespread in dry and disturbed grassland and hedges and waysides (Ackeroyd 1999); some may accidentally have been collected with the crops in these samples.

Cleavers Cleavers are also commonly called goosegrass; the plants and seeds are widespread in the countryside today and it was also widespread in the past, as it is found in many archaeobotanical samples and from a great range of sites. The plant is very variable, and appears to have smaller seeds when it grows as a weed of cultivation (Ackeroyd 1999); the examples from these samples were indeed rather small, suggesting that they were collected with the crops in these samples. Each sample that cleavers were found in also included reasonable frequencies of cereal grains.

Plantain seeds Plantains are the most common and successful grassland weeds that tend to colonize areas that have been occupied by humans (Pilcher and Hall 2001; Ackeroyd 1999). Some variants are common weeds of cultivated ground and the seeds from these samples were no doubt, once again, weeds of cultivation.

Cornsalad/valerian seeds This is another group of wild plants that can be eaten, in these cases as salad. Common valerian also has medicinal uses (Ackeroyd 1999). The presence of only one seed of this type, however, renders it insignificant in our discussions here.

Daisy-family seeds These seeds are often dispersed by wind, and therefore can be incorporated into many different types of archaeological deposits. The types recovered from the Merrion Road samples included possible corn marigold and knapweed/cornflowers, weeds of cultivation and meadows; they are associated with samples that contain many crop-remains and were most likely taken onto the site with a harvested crop.

Sedge-family seeds Cyperaceae are grass-like plants whose habitat tends to be damp ground; their presence in some of these samples may indicate that at least some of the crops were grown in slightly damp, rather than well-drained, fields. This is possibly because the site is close to the tidal mark and the crops found were probably grown in nearby fields, where the environment was quite marshy in the past.

Interpretation: the crop-remains assemblage from Merrion Road

There was evidence of disturbance and truncation of the archaeological features due to subsequent cultivation and drainage of the lands. The archaeological features were generally identified as pits/depressions, post-holes/stake-holes, surfaces, gullies/ditches/drains and deposits and layers (Baker 2004; see also above). The lands around Merrion were granted to Anglo-Norman settlers in the twelfth century and presumably became part of an intensive agricultural system upon which feudalized regimes depended for their wealth (Mitchell and Ryan 2001, 303). It is likely that the excavated features were associated with the products of the land. The purpose of this section is to examine in what way the archaeological deposits may have been associated with the production and processing of crops from the surrounding lands. Identification of the crop-remains indicates that the predominant crop was wheat, probably mostly bread wheat. Bread wheat was considered high-status in the early historic period and it was the staple cereal crop of areas of Ireland under Anglo-Norman control. As its name suggests, it was used to make bread, and in both Ireland and Scotland during this period bread was considered a luxury food eaten by the rich, although historical records indicate that wheat was the standard food crop in the area of the Pale in the late middle ages (Nicholls 2003, 133).

In order to assess the stages of processing that the crops had gone through prior to carbonization, the weed-seed content of samples was analyzed following ethnographic models formulated by Jones (1987). This identifies the distinction between crop-processing stages using classifications of weed seeds. The seeds are classified based on their size (Big or Small), their tendency to remain in heads, in particular when threshed (Free or Headed) and their aerodynamic characteristics, especially weight (Heavy or Light). Only samples with appropriate numbers of cereals can be tested, and here only three samples with over 50 cereal grains (S1, S9 and S10) were selected. This small number of samples militated against the use of statistics to categorize the samples, an integral part of Jones's approach; however, the exercise of classifying the weed seeds in the samples obtained some interesting results. The weeds from the Merrion Road samples were almost exclusively classified as SFH (Small, Free and Heavy), or BFH (Big, Free and Heavy). They do not appear to be size-specific, but they are predominantly free and heavy, which suggests that some winnowing had already been carried out by the time they were charred. These are among the first stages of wheat-processing. Much of the chaff would have been removed from the crops during these first stages of processing, and indeed there were very few chaff fragments found. These bits of the cereal plant may also have been destroyed during charring, as chaff is burned away to ash more quickly than denser plant material such as cereal grains and weed seeds (Boardman and Jones 1990).

What caused the carbonization of these grain crops? There are several possibilities: burning fields and stores during raids was one of the common tactics of warfare during the period; less dramatically, the crops may have been accidentally charred during processing; or perhaps stored products may have developed infestations that needed to be curbed, and in these cases large quantities of crops would need to be burnt in order to eliminate the pests. Each suggestion will be dealt with in turn in the following paragraphs. While raids may have occurred (the historical records for the sites indicate that destruction by dispossessed Irish families was known; Baker 2004), the crop assemblage retrieved as the result of burning in the field would have been much more mixed than the relatively uniform assemblages that were found in these samples. If, however, stores were burned down during a raid and later the burnt waste was discarded in this area, it is possible that the assemblages could have resembled the composition of these samples. However, this is probably the least likely explanation for the presence of carbonized grain at this site.

It is more likely that the charred crop-remains were the results of accidents that occurred during crop drying. Drying was frequently required after Irish harvests as the damp weather did not always allow for grains to ripen and to dry fully in the field. Thus it is quite likely that the carbonized crop-remains in these samples are the result of accidents that occurred during the drying stage of crop processing. The suggestion that infestation caused widespread crop burning is a strong possibility, as some of the grains showed possible signs of insect bore-holes. Possible bore-holes were noted in particular in S1. Stored products such as grain are liable to infestation by insects. One of the common grain pests was the grain weevil (*Sitophilus granarius*), well-established by the medieval period (the earliest finding so far being from late Viking/early Anglo-Norman contexts in Waterford; Reilly 2003). The female grain weevil hollows out a small cavity in the grains and deposits an egg therein, closing the hole with a plug of gelatinous material (Bala 1997, 241–2). When this occurs, the entire store will frequently be destroyed by fire in order to contain the infestation. Buckland suggests that total spoilage was probably relatively frequent; it may have resulted in many rich deposits of charred grain being left on archaeological sites (1978).

As many of the samples appear to be reworked deposits of burnt grain, rather than *in-situ* burnt-grain deposits, it is likely that they are the discarded remnants of either accidentally burnt crops that were spoilt during drying, or deliberately burnt storage deposits that were destroyed in order to get rid of an infestation of pests.

Discussion: comparisons with contemporary assemblages

Rural Dublin sites Several medieval sites in the vicinity of Dublin where carbonized plant-remains were examined by this author are used here as comparisons for the Merrion Road material. Firstly, carbonized plant-remains from Nangor, Clondalkin, Co. Dublin were found in deposits from a field system, and the proportions of wheat, barley and oat varied from sample to sample, although overall wheat was the most common cereal (Johnston 2001a). Recovery of large amounts of Leinster cooking ware from many of these deposits suggested a thirteenth-century date (McCutcheon 2001), although a radiocarbon date from seeds in one feature proved that activity at the site spanned a broad range (Ian Doyle, pers. comm.). Similarly, at another medieval/early modern field system in Bremore, Balbriggan, Co. Dublin high proportions of wheat grains were recovered (Johnston 2002a). These results suggest that the results from Merrion Road conform to the general picture of arable agriculture being predominantly wheat crops in the areas around Dublin during the medieval period. In addition, kiln deposits excavated at the Coombe (93E0066) and James's Hospital (no dates provided) also produced cereal assemblages that were predominantly wheat (Johnston 2002b and Johnston 2001b).

Rural and urban crop-remains A comparison of this assemblage with contemporary urban medieval sites is difficult: rural and urban plant-remains assemblages tend to be extracted from different stages of the food chain (production versus consumption). Urban medieval plant-remains assemblages tend to be preserved in anaerobic conditions and are often extracted from features such as cess pits. They therefore provide direct information concerning diet. Rural assemblages are often carbonized remains of burnt crops, which furnish direct evidence of the crop economy and must indirectly reflect diet. However, by the time crops are consumed and later purged into pit-deposits in urban settlements they are often no longer in the form of seeds; grains are ground into meal and flour, for example. Thus, although wheat-based products may have formed a significant part of the urban medieval diet, they are not often found in cess deposits. One means of overcoming this problem is to examine cereal bran fragments that are sometimes preserved in urban cess-deposits. This requires training in identification methods and higher levels of magnification than those traditionally used to examine seed assemblages and, to my knowledge, the technique has not yet been applied to medieval Dublin deposits.

Very few carbonized cereal grains have been recovered from medieval Dublin deposits. Settlement and pit-deposits that post-dated Viking activity at Temple Bar West included barley and oat in very small amounts (Johnston 2001c). Deposits from excavations at Patrick, Nicholas and Winetavern Streets in Dublin produced small carbonized grain assemblages; for example, late twelfth-century deposits contained an oat grain, a thirteenth-century sample contained carbonized grains of both wheat and oats, while fourteenth-century deposits produced one charred grain of oat (Collins 1997, 228–9). Similarly small mixed assemblages have been retrieved from other urban medieval deposits. In thirteenth- and fourteenth-century deposits from Cork, wheat, barley, oat and some possible rye was identified (McClatchie 2003, 395) and in Anglo-Norman Waterford, Tierney and Hannon (1997, 890) found that oats were the most common crop plant, but that cereals such as hulled barley, bread wheat and rye grains were also important. In general, the remains from urban Dublin are too sparse to justify the identification of the most important crop type found within the city. However, the remains from medieval rural deposits surrounding the city indicate that the crop economy was undoubtedly focused on the production of wheat and it is likely that the area immediately surrounding the city was one of the main sources of staple foods in the urban diet.

Summary

The plant remains from medieval deposits excavated at Merrion Road, Dublin were identified as being predominantly from wheat, probably the free-threshing variety called bread wheat. The results indicate that these crop-remains were burnt either as they were being prepared for storage, or in some cases the deposit may represent a stored crop that had to be burned in order to control an infestation of stored product pests such as the grain weevil. There are parallel medieval rural sites around Dublin where crop assemblages suggest a crop economy predominantly focussed on the production of wheat and the assemblage from Merrion Road conforms to this established picture. Unfortunately, the differences in evidence-type reduce the validity of comparisons between plant-remains assemblages from rural and urban sites and renders discussions of an urban/rural divide difficult. However, the reliance of the medieval town on nearby rural production-sites such as Merrion Road must be a strong likelihood.

ACKNOWLEDGMENTS

The Merrion Road excavation was carried out under the auspices of Margaret Gowen and Company Ltd., financed and facilitated by Michael McNamara Ltd. All due thanks to the on-site crew, post-excavation team and office personnel of MGL, especially to Linzi Simpson for her helpful comments on a draft this paper and Lindsay Delahunty for preparation of the illustrations. Special thanks to the specialists for their contributions: Clare McCutcheon (UCC), Conor Brady, Jonny Gerber (MGL), Lorna O'Donnell (MGL) and Penny Johnston (formerly of MGL). Note: abridgement of specialist reports was necessary for reasons of space—all errors are my own.

BIBLIOGRAPHY

Akeroyd, J. 1999 *The encyclopaedia of British flowers*. London.

Baker, C. 2000 Tullykane Co. Meath. Final Excavation report, forthcoming.

Baker, C. 2003 Archaeological assessment, Tara Hotel, Merrion Road (unpublished report); Archaeological assessment, Tara Hotel Carpark, Bellvue Avenue (unpublished report).

Baker, C. 2004 Merrion Road, Dublin (Licence no. 04E0272): stratigraphic report for Margaret Gowen and Co. Ltd.

Bala, B.K. 1997 *Drying and storage of cereal grains* Plymouth.

Ball, F.E. 1900 The antiquities from Blackrock to Dublin. *RSAI Jn.* 30.

Ball, F.E. 1903 *A history of the County Dublin*. Dublin.

Bessneck, J. 1969. Osteological differences between sheep (Ovis aries Linné) and goat (Capra hircus Linné). In D. Brothwell, E.S. Higgs (eds), *Science in Archaeology*. 2nd ed. London.

Blake, H. and Davey, P. (eds) 1983 *Guidelines for the processing and publication of medieval pottery from excavations*. London.

Boardman, S. and Jones, G. 1990 Experiments on the effects of charring on cereal plant components *Journal of Archaeological Science* 17, 1–11.

Buckland, P. C. 1978 Cereal production, storage, and population: a caveat. In S. Limbrey and J.G. Evans (eds) *The effect of man on the landscape: the Lowland Zone*. CBA Research Report 21, 43–5. London.

Butler, V. 2001 Report on the animal bones from Tullykane 00E0264. In C. Baker, *Final excavation report, Tullykane, Co. Meath. 00E0264*. Arch-Tech. Ltd.
Campbell, B.M.S. 1995 Ecology versus economics in late thirteenth- and early fourteenth-century English agriculture. In D. Sweeney (ed.), *Agriculture in the Middle Ages: technology, practice and representation*. Philadelphia.
Cohen, A. and Serjeantson, D. 1996 *A manual for the identification of bird bones from archaeological sites*. 2nd ed. London.
Collins, B. 1997 Plant remains. In C. Walsh, *Archaeological excavations at Patrick, Nicholas and Winetavern Streets, Dublin*. Dingle.
Connolly, P. and Martin, G.H. 1992 *The Dublin guild merchant roll, c.1190–1265*. Dublin.
Dillon, F. 1997 The lithic assemblages. In G. Eogan and H. Roche, *Excavations at Knowth* 2, Dublin: Royal Irish Academy.
Doyle, I. 2002 Final Report on archaeological excavations at Nangor townland, Clondalkin. Unpublished report.
von den Driesch, A. 1976 *A guide to the measurement of animal bones from archaeological sites*. Harvard, CT.
Edwards, N. 1990 *The archaeology of early medieval Ireland*. London.
Foley, C. 1989 Excavation at a medieval settlement site in Jerpoint church townland, County Kilkenny. *RIA Proc.* 89C, 71–126.
Gailey, A. 1970 Irish corn-drying kilns. *Ulster Folklife* 15/16, 52–71.
Gowen, M. 1988 *Three Irish Gas pipelines: new archaeological evidence in Munster*. Dublin.
Grant, A. 1982 The use of tooth wear as a guide to the age of domestic ungulates. In B. Wilson, C. Grigson, and S. Payne, *Ageing and sexing animal bones from archaeological sites*. BAR British Series 109. Oxford.
Green, H. Stephen 1980 *The flint arrowheads of the British Isles: a detailed study of material from England and Wales with comparanda from Scotland and Ireland*. 2 vols. BAR British Series 75(I). Oxford.
Habermehl, K-H. 1975 *Die Altersbestimmung bei Haus- und Labortieren*. 2nd ed. Hamburg.
Harcourt, R.A. 1974 The dog in prehistoric and early historic Britain. *Journal of Archaeological Science* 1, 151–75.
Hillman, G.C., Mason, S., de Moulins, D. and Nesbitt, M. 1995 Identification of archaeological remains of wheat: the 1992 London workshop *Circaea* 12 (2), 195–209.
Holden, T. 1995 The last meals of the Lindow Bog Men. In R.C. Turner and R.G. Scaife (eds), *Bog bodies new discoveries and new perspectives*. London.
Humphrey, R. 2002 Report on archaeological testing at former lands of the Sisters of Charity, Merrion Road, Dublin 4. Unpublished Report.
Hurley, M.F. 1987 Kilferagh, Co. Kilkenny. In R.M. Cleary, M.F. Hurley and E.A. Twohig (eds), *Archaeological excavations on the Cork-Dublin gas pipeline (1981–2)*, 88–100. Cork.
Ivens, R. 2001 Everted-rim and crannog ware. *Ulster Journal of Archaeology*.
Jackson, John 1991 The geology and raw materials of the Stone Age, in M. Ryan (ed.), *The illustrated archaeology of Ireland*, 33–5. Dublin.
Johnston, P. 2002a Analysis of the plant remains from Bremore, Balbriggan, Co. Dublin (Licence no. 01E0370). Technical report for Cultural Resource Development Services. Unpublished.
Johnston, P. 2002b Analysis of the plant remains from the Coombe, Dublin (Licence no. 93E0066). Technical report for Archaeological Projects Ltd. Unpublished.
Johnston, P. 2001a Charred plant remains from Nangor townland, Clondalkin, Dublin 22 (Licence no. 00E0754). Technical Report for Margaret Gowen and Co. Unpublished.
Johnston, P. 2001b Analysis of the plant remains from St James's Hospital, Dublin 8. Technical report for Margaret Gowen and Co. Unpublished.

Johnston, P. 2001c Macroscopic plant remains from excavations at Temple Bar West, Dublin. Technical report for Margaret Gowen and Co. Unpublished.

Jones, G. 1987 A statistical approach to the archaeological identification of crop processing. *Journal of Archaeological Science* 14, 311–23.

Kelly, F. 1998 *Early Irish farming*. Dublin.

Lehane, Daragh 1983 Part III: the flint work. In M.J. O'Kelly, R.M. Cleary and D. Lehane, *Newgrange, Co. Meath, Ireland: the late neolithic/beaker period settlement*, 118–67. Oxford: British Archaeological Reports, International Series 190.

Lydon, J.F. 1972 *The lordship of Ireland in the middle ages.* Dublin.

McClatchie, M. 2003 The plant remains. In R.M. Cleary and M.F. Hurley (eds), *Cork City Excavations 1984–2000* Cork.

McCormick, F. 1984 The animal bones. In A. Lynch, Excavation of the medieval town defences at Charlotte's Quay, Limerick. *RIA Proc.* 84C, 322–9.

McCormick, F. and Murphy, E. 1997 Mammal bones. In C. Walsh, *Archaeological excavations at Patrick, Nicholas and Winetavern Streets, Dublin*, 199–217. Dingle.

McCutcheon, C. 2000 Medieval pottery in Dublin: new names and some dates, in S. Duffy (ed.), *Medieval Dublin I*, 117–25. Dublin.

McCutcheon, C. 2001 The pottery from excavations at Nangor townland, Clondalkin, Dublin 22 (Licence no. 00E0754). Technical report. Unpublished.

McCutcheon, C. 2003 Pottery. In R.M. Cleary and M.F. Hurley (eds), *Excavations in Cork city 1984–2000*, 197–235. Cork.

McCutcheon, C. 2006 *Medieval pottery from Wood Quay, Dublin.* Dublin.

McCutcheon, C. in press The pottery. In E. O'Brien, *Excavations at Dundrum Castle, Co. Dublin.*

McCutcheon, C. in preparation (a) The medieval pottery. In M. Clinton, *Excavations at Carrickmines Castle, Co. Dublin.*

McCutcheon, C. in preparation (b) The pottery. In F. Myles, *Excavations at the Iveagh Markets, Dublin.*

McCutcheon, C. forthcoming (a) The pottery. In J. Carroll, *Excavations at 33 Patrick Street, Kilkenny.*

McCutcheon, C. forthcoming (b) The medieval pottery. In G. Egan, *Excavations at Coolamurry, Moneytucker to Jamestown Road, Co. Wexford.*

McEnery, J.F. and Refauusé, R. (eds) 2001 *Christchurch deeds.* Dublin.

McNeill, T. 1997 *Castles in Ireland.* London and New York.

MacShamhráin, A. 1994 The unity of Cóemgen and Ciarán: a covenant between Glendalough and Clonmacnoise in the tenth to eleventh centuries. In K. Hannigan and W. Nolan (eds), *Wicklow: history and society*, 139–50. Dublin.

Mitchell, F. and Ryan, M. 2001 *Reading the Irish landscape.* Dublin.

Moore, M.J. 1984 Irish cresset-stones. *RSAI Jn.* 114, 98–116.

Moore, M. 1997 The stone and pottery lamps. In M.F. Hurley and O.M.B. Scully, *Late Viking age and medieval Waterford: Excavations 1986–1992*, 432–6. Waterford.

MPRG 1998 *A Guide to the classification of Medieval Ceramic Forms.* Medieval Pottery Research Group Occasional Paper No. 1. Over Wallop.

Murray, E. 2000 The animal bones from Maynooth Castle, Co. Kildare. Technical report. Unpublished.

Nicholls, K. 2003 *Gaelic and Gaelicized Ireland in the middle ages*, 2nd ed, Dublin.

Ó Floinn, R. 1976 Medieval cooking pottery in Leinster thirteenth to fourteenth centuries. MA thesis. NUI, Dublin. Unpublished.

Ó Floinn R. 1988 Handmade medieval pottery in S.E. Ireland, 'Leinster cooking ware'. In G. Mac Niocaill and P.F. Wallace (eds), *Keimelia. Studies in medieval archaeology and history in memory of Tom Delaney*, 325–49. Galway.

Orme, B.J. and Coles, J.M. 1985 Prehistoric woodworking from the Somerset levels: 2: Species selection and prehistoric woodlands. In *Somerset Levels Papers*, 11, 7–24.

O'Sullivan, A. 1998a Woodland management and the supply of timber and underwood to Anglo-Norman Dublin. In G. de Boe and F. Verhaeghe (eds), *Environment and subsistence in medieval Europe*, 135–41. Scientific Institution of the Flemish Community. Doornveld.

O'Sullivan, A. 1998b Woodmanship and the supply of underwood and timber to Anglo-Norman Dublin. In C. Manning (ed.), *Dublin and beyond the Pale. Studies in honour of Patrick Healy*, 59–70. Bray.

O'Sullivan, A., 2000 The wooden waterfronts: a study of their construction, carpentry and use of trees and woodlands. In A. Halpin, *The port of medieval Dublin. Archaeological excavations at the Civic Offices, Winetavern Street, Dublin*, 62–92. Dublin.

Pearce, J.E., Vince, A.G. and Jenner, M.A. 1985 *A dated type series of London medieval pottery part 2: London-type ware*. London.

Pearson, P. 1998 *Between the mountains and the sea*. Dublin.

Peterson, J.D. 1991 From foraging to food production in southeast Ireland: some lithic evidence. *PPS* 56, 88–99.

Pilcher, J. and Hall, V. 2001 *Flora Hibernica* Cork.

Prummel, W. and Frisch, H-J. 1986 A guide for the distinction of species, sex and body side in bones of sheep and goat. *Journal of Archaeological Science* 13, 567–77.

Rackham, O. 2001 *Trees and woodland in the British landscape.* New York.

Reilly, E. 2003 The contribution of insect remains to an understanding of the environment of Viking-Age and medieval Dublin. In S. Duffy (ed.), *Medieval Dublin IV*, 40–62. Dublin.

Ryan, M.F. 1973 Native pottery in early historic Ireland. *RIA Proc.* 73C, 619–45.

Scannell, M.J.P. and Synnott, D.M. 1987 *Census catalogue of the flora of Ireland.* Dublin.

Schweingruber, F.H. 1978 *Microscopic wood anatomy*. Swiss Federal Institute for Forest, Snow and Landscape Research. Birmensdorf.

Serjeantson, D. 1996. The animal bones. In S. Needham and T. Spence, *Refuse and disposal at Area 16 east Runnymede. Runnymede Bridge research excavations Vol. 2*, 194–253. London.

Simington 1950 *The civil survey A.D. 1654–1656: County Dublin*. Dublin.

Simpson L. 2003 Dublin's southern frontier under siege: Kindlestown Castle, Delgany, County Wicklow. In Duffy (ed.), *Medieval Dublin* IV, 279–368. Dublin.

Spencer, C. 2002 *British food: an extraordinary thousand years of history*. London.

Stevens, C.J. 2003 An investigation of agricultural consumption and production models for prehistoric and Roman Britain. *Environmental Archaeology* 8(1), 61–76.

Stokes, P. and Rowley-Conwy, P. 2002 Iron-Age cultigen? Experimental return rates for fat hen (*Chenopodium album* L.). *Environmental Archaeology* 7, 95–9.

Strid, L. forthcoming (a) Report on the faunal remains from George's Street (99E0414). Technical Report. Unpublished.

Strid, L. forthcoming (b) Report on the animal and human remains from Hammond lane, Dublin (03E0721). Technical Report. Unpublished.

Sweetman, D. 1999 *The medieval castles of Ireland.* Cork.

Sweetman, H.S. (ed.) 1886 *Calendar of documents relating to Ireland, 1171–1307*, vol. V. London.

Teichert, M. 1975 Osteometrische Untersuchungen zur Bereuchnung der Widerristhöhe bei Schafen. In A.T. Clason, *Archaeozoological studies*, 51–69. Amsterdam.

Tierney, J. and Hannon, M. 1997 Plant remains. in M.F. Hurley, O.M.B. Scully, and S.W.J. McCutcheon (eds), *Late Viking Age and Medieval Waterford Excavations 1986–1992*, 854–93. Waterford.

Tobin R. 2000 Archaeological assessment, 185–203 Merrion Road. In I. Bennett (ed.), *Excavations.ie*.

Vretemark, M. 1997 *Från ben till boskap. Kosthåll och djurhållning med utgångspunkt I medeltida benmaterial från Skara. Del 1*. Skrifter från Länsmuseet Skara nr 25. Skara.

Walsh, C. 1993 Back Lane, Dublin. In I. Bennett (ed.), *Excavations 1992*, 16–17, Dublin.

Woodman, P.C. 1987 The impact of resource availability on Lithic industrial traditions in prehistoric Ireland. In P. Rowley-Conwy, M. Zvelebil, and H.P. Blankholm (eds), *Mesolithic northwest Europe: recent trends*, 138–46. Sheffield.

Wren, J. (forthcoming) Roof tiles. In A. Hayden, *Excavations at the Cornmarket, Dublin.*

An analysis of the environmental history of medieval County Dublin based on Archbishop Alen's Register *c.*1172–1534

TERESA BOLGER

> 'the natural environment cannot be fully understood in isolation from us and our interactions with it. But before our cultural relations with the natural environment can be considered in anything but a superficial way, we must understand that environment.' (Harrison et al. 1992, 6)

INTRODUCTION

In general, studies of the landscape of medieval Ireland have tended to concentrate on the 'cultural' landscape rather than on the environment per se (for example, Aalen 1978; Graham 1993; Lyttleton and O'Keeffe 2005); they focus on the physical remains of human activity in the landscape, and the interrelationship of those remains, more so than on the environment within and against which this activity was occurring and which was itself being modified by this activity. Discussions of the environment of medieval Ireland tend to be brief, general and to centre upon agriculture and agricultural practices, with little consideration of land that was not used directly for agriculture. Where any possible alterations in the environment are discussed, it is done from a national perspective, and only the most basic and general of conclusions about the state of the environment during the medieval period are put forward. Even agriculture is mainly discussed in terms of social organization, technological innovation and economic trends (for example, Buchanan 1973; Butlin 1978; Hall, Hennessey and O'Keeffe 1985; Glasscock 1997; Murphy and Potterton 2005), rather than in terms of the environmental systems which it creates or affects.

At present, the closest approximation of a study of the environment of Ireland, since prehistoric times, is the work of the late Frank Mitchell, in particular, his book *The Irish landscape* (1976). Even general discussions of the global environment fail to mention Ireland in any way, with regard to the medieval period, and give only a general outline of the situation on the neighbouring island of Britain (for example, Mannion 1991, 107–11). Admittedly, there has already been some work done specifically on the environmental history of Britain, unlike that of Ireland (for example, Astill and Grant 1988), with a definite focus on trying to reconstruct and interpret the evidence for the physical reality of the medieval countryside which survives in the documentary evidence. The basis of this study was very much an experiment in order to ascertain whether or not similar approaches to the analysis of medieval Irish historical material could be productive. It is an attempt to reconstruct a picture of an historic environment using documentary evidence and to consider how human activity shaped and influenced that environment.

SOURCES AND METHODOLOGY

The majority of the documentary sources for the history of Ireland in the medieval period stem from the colonial administration; certainly, all those relevant to the Dublin area at this time are of Anglo-Norman origin. There is a paucity of sources for this period in Ireland, when compared with the evidence stemming from England. This has been used in the past as a rationale for the lack of regionality in most studies of the period; however, latterly, region-specific studies have become more common (for example, Murphy and Potterton 2005; Lyttleton and O'Keeffe 2005).

No documentary source deals specifically with the environment, unlike areas such as land tenure or manorial organization; the relevant information occurs primarily as minutiae embedded in the incidental material in the sources. The only exception to this generalization is woodland, but it is a special case owing to its particular economic importance and also its legal position. Certain kinds of source material are obviously more fruitful in this regard than others. The forms of documentation most relevant to a study such as this are those concerned with land ownership and tenure, mainly manorial extents and surveys, but inquisitions *post mortem* can also prove very relevant. Other than the documentary sources, the main source of information on the nature of the environment in the medieval period comes via the discipline of archaeology, which has already incorporated the study of floral and faunal remains from excavations, as well as palynological studies of bog and lake sediments. Palynological studies offer a relatively broad perspective on the environment over time. However, when this is combined with studies of macroscopic remains on site, this more integrated approach has a greater potential for yielding interesting results.

As yet, the main body of information available in print in relation to the Dublin region is heavily biased towards the urban excavations (Mitchell 1987; Geraghty 1996). At present one of the main modules of the Medieval Rural Settlement research project within the Discovery Programme is focused on the analysis of the economy of the city of Dublin and its hinterland. This includes the assessment and integration of the results of the available environmental information from excavations in Dublin and its hinterland, although the initial analysis of the material is focused towards issues of economy and standards of living (Murphy and Potterton 2005).

This present study is confined to the examination of only one source of information, namely Archbishop Alen's Register (henceforth the Register). It is a parchment manuscript preserved in the Registry of the United Dioceses of Dublin and Glendalough and Kildare (Church of Ireland). An edited translation of the text has been published by Charles McNeill (1950). The Register was largely compiled in the first half of the sixteenth century and the records transcribed in it would appear to stem in the greater part from original documents, which were still in existence in the time of Archbishop John Alen (1528–34). Most of the entries are concerned with property and the temporal interests of the church, and the margins and blank spaces in the manuscript are filled with notes by Archbishop Alen. The entries with which this study is concerned are those which give details about the land to which they refer. Relevant references are scattered randomly through the Register; their only uniting factor is that they all occur in entries regarding land and land tenure. Specifically, the entries of interest are those where the type of land in question is indicated, whether arable, pasture, wood, moor, etc. Other significant entries detail the prohibitions relating to, for example, access to woodland. Also, references to changes in land use, land type and perceived changes in land quality are to be found.

The picture presented by the Register is not a complete one. When all the identified townlands relevant to the discussion are mapped (fig. 1), the sporadic nature of the source becomes quite clear. While several blocks of territory are apparent (corresponding with the main archiepiscopal manors), most of the townlands are quite scattered. Also, the entries included in the study in no way provide a compete picture of the environment of every townland; rather the map indicates those areas where at least a small amount of information on the environment can be reconstructed from the Register. Filling in these black holes would involve the investigation of further source material for County Dublin during this period. Also, while it was possible to identify the changes in certain areas over time, this was not possible on a county-wide basis or for all the aspects of the environment under discussion. As the source material is spread over several centuries it can be difficult to get an accurate picture of what is happening at any one time. For this reason, certain areas of the discussion have centred on particular entries or series of entries which give a good snapshot of what is happening in the county at a particular time with regard to the specified land type. While it is occasionally possible to trace the environmental progression of a particular area through the period covered by the source, such occurrences are rare in the Register

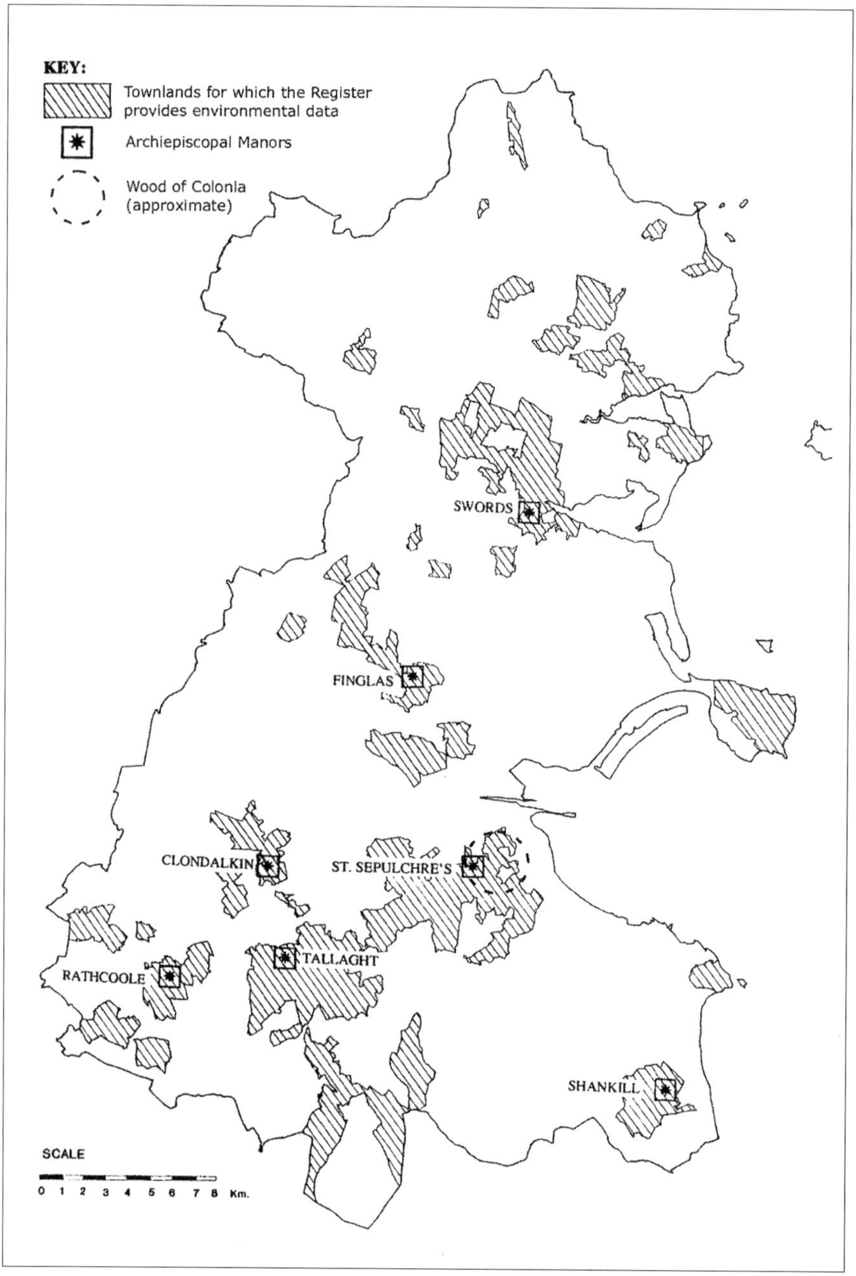

1 Map of Dublin indicating townlands for which the Register provides environmental data

and are the exception rather than the rule in this study. A study with a wider base of source material should, however, be well able to achieve this.

Bearing these limitations in mind, it was still possible to reconstruct many aspects of the environmental history of the county, and to identify factors which strongly influenced the nature of that environment during the later medieval period. One thing that becomes quite clear is that the environment of the county was far from uniform and one of the more notable aspects of this study is the identification of regionally-specific factors which were influencing the nature of the environment during this period. As well as reconstructing details of the environment it is also possible, to a limited degree, to identify contemporary attitudes to that environment. English studies of the environment of this period provided the main source for comparison and there are strong indications of the importation of English systems of natural-resource management into Ireland, as well as more widely recognized aspects of the manorial system.

AGRICULTURAL ORGANIZATION AND LAND USE

Human interaction with the environment creates environmental systems as well as destroying them. While the agricultural landscape is not a natural environment, nonetheless, it forms an environmental system of its own, albeit one closely controlled by humans.

The arrival of Anglo-Norman settlers in the Dublin area from 1170 onwards brought about a change both in the appearance and structure of the landscape, altering not only land tenure but also land use. An important point to remember when considering the impact of Anglo-Norman settlement on the Irish countryside, is that they were not arriving into virgin territory. Certainly in the case of what became County Dublin the land was already extensively settled and farmed by the Irish (Fagan and Simms 1992, 86).

There are some noticeable differences between the ways in which the land was exploited before and after the coming of the Anglo-Normans. The main sources for the study of the organization of Irish agriculture and farming in the pre-Norman period are the early medieval law tracts, which describe a very different system to that introduced by the Anglo-Normans, although involving the organization and control of the landscape on a similar scale (Kelly 1998). Arable cultivation, while an important part of the mixed farming economy in the pre-Norman period, appears to have had a lesser social significance than the raising of cattle. Another notable difference was that the Irish did not make hay, relying instead on winter grazing or foggage. Kinship appears to have been a very important factor in the organization of Irish agriculture. It is the key to the system of land tenure practised, and also to the concept of *comaithches* ('neighbourhood', 'relationship', etc.) upon which all social interaction regarding land and agriculture was based.

Feudal forms of land tenure and agricultural practice, in the shape of the manorial system, were introduced to County Dublin by the Anglo-Normans. The open field was the hallmark of this system of agriculture. Arable crops were cultivated in these, with dispersed unfenced strips of varying shapes representing the individual holdings. Crops were rotated on a two- or three-field system, and the latter appears to have been more popular in areas of rich soil. The word *sesona* is usually used to refer to these fields. While livestock was necessary to this system of agriculture, cattle, for example, did not retain the status they had under the Irish system, and the growing of arable crops had a higher priority. Pastureland was often held in common and strict controls were placed on the access to stubble-grazing. Under this system both pasture and meadow were at a premium in order to balance the requirements of the livestock necessary to manure fields, in order to retain their fertility, the goal being to maximize the potential of arable land.

In examining the agricultural land use of County Dublin, the most useful areas to compare in the discussion are the archiepiscopal manors—Swords, Finglas, St Sepulchre's, Tallaght, Clondalkin, Rathcoole and Shankill (fig. 1). The manorial extents of 1326 provide the best comparative information, to illustrate what is happening in different parts of County Dublin (see table 1). While the majority of information stemming from the Register does involve agricultural land, this series of entries provides the best snapshot of a large area of County Dublin at the same time. Though there are other entries in the

Table 1. Breakdown of land types/uses from manorial extents of 1326

Manors	**Arable**	**Pasture**	**Meadow**	**Wood**	**Imparked**	**Moor**	**Waste**	**Unspec.**
Swords	660a.	151.5a.	122a.	8a.	0a.	0a.	24a.	9522a.
Finglas	297a.	4a.	19a.	0a.	95a.	12a.	0a.	1326a.
St Sepulchre	203.5a.	48a.	13.5a.	66a.	0a.	0a.	242a.	390.5a.
Clondalkin	430.5a.	60a.	41.5a.	40a.	0a.	7a.	1356a.	939.5a.
Tallaght	132a.	14a.	19a.	60a.	0a.	0a.	399a.	687.5a.
Rathcoole	160a.	94.5a.	59.5a.	0a.	0a.	0a.	767.5a	218.5a.
Shankill	80a.	15a.	10.5a.	104a.	4a.	0a.	1483a.	189a.
Demesne Lands								
Swords	660a.	151.5a.	122a.	8a.	0a.	0a.	8a.	411a.
Finglas	297a.	4a.	19a.	0a.	95a.	0a.	0a.	8.5a.
Clondalkin	425.5a	60a.	31.5a.	40a.	0a.	0a.	4a.	4.5a.
Tallaght	111a.	19a.	14a.	0a.	0a.	0a.	49a.	5a.
Rathcoole	160a.	94.5a.	57a.	0a.	0a.	0a.	8.5a.	16a.

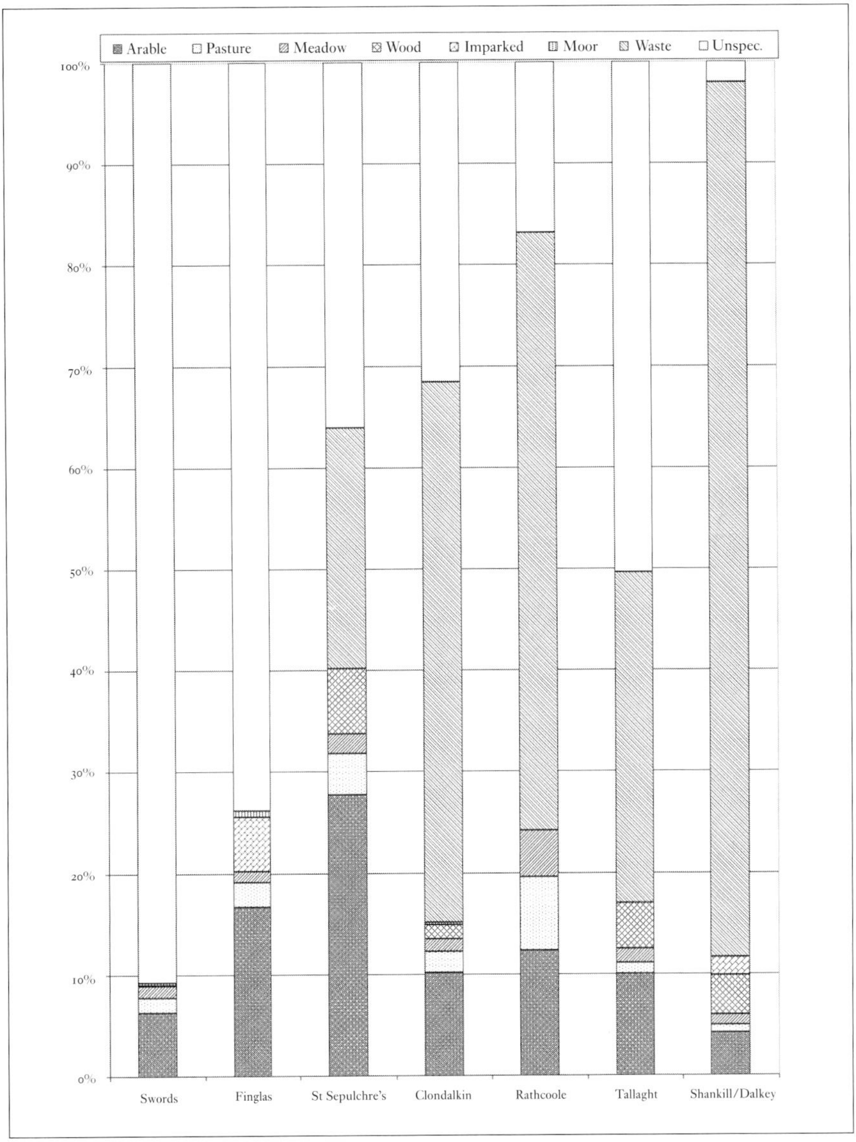

2 Comparison of the land uses recorded in the 1326 extents of the archiepiscopal manors

Register which give details about agricultural land use, these entries are scattered in time and location, and it would be difficult to integrate them into this picture. Only those lands for which a specific acreage is given in the extent were included, although there were occasions, most notably the pasture of the mountain of Slievethoul in Rathcoole, where references were omitted, as they could not be included in the analysis in any meaningful way.

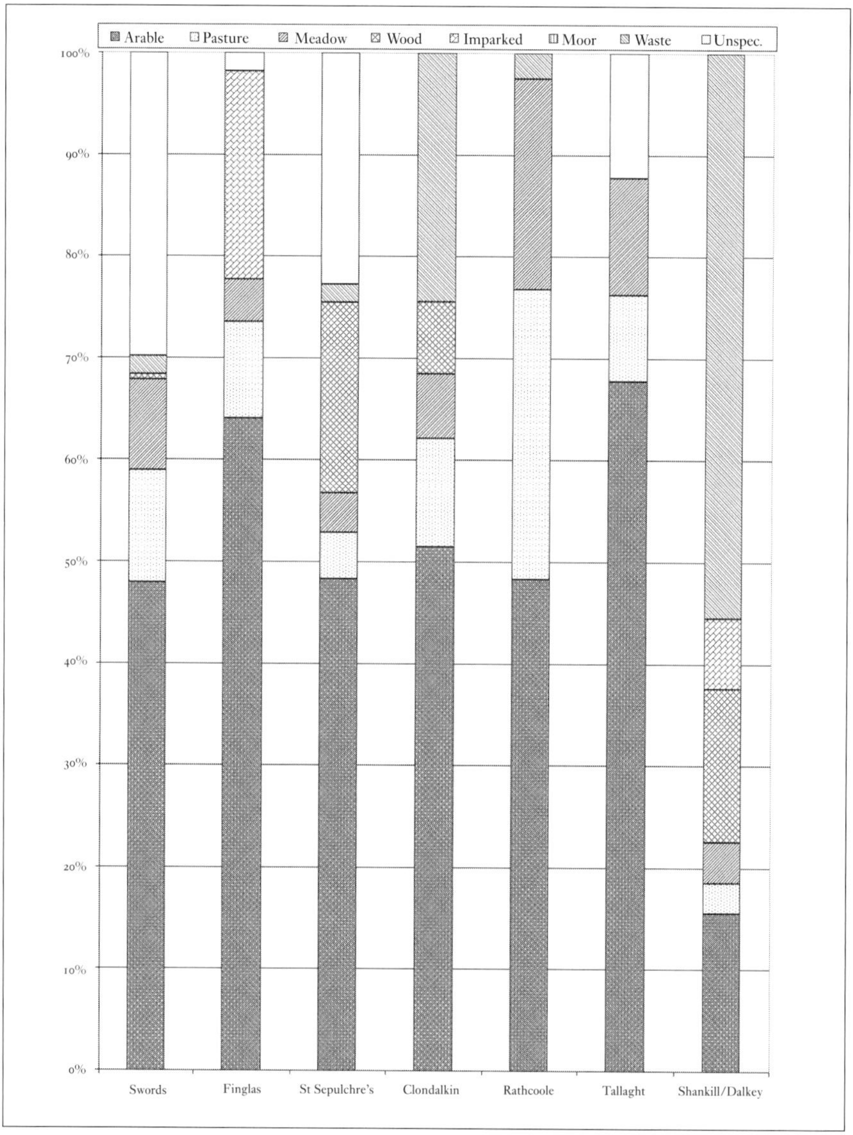

3 Comparison of the demesne lands of the archiepiscopal manors as recorded in the 1326 extents

The first major problem encountered when using the extents is that a high proportion of the land listed is unspecified, i.e. no details were given as to its condition or function. In the most extreme case, Swords, approximately 92 per cent of the acreage of the manor is unspecified (see fig. 2). This proved to be a problem in most manors where the percentage varies between 17 per cent (Rathcoole) and 76 per cent (Finglas). While it is most likely that the majority of this land is arable land, it does add an element of unbalance to any comparison. It is notable that the two manors north of the Liffey (Swords and Finglas) record the highest levels of unspecified lands. The reasons for this are probably two-fold – economic and political. Economically, it may be that the land north of the Liffey was generally of better quality, and was less prone to a loss in capability. Politically, the south of County Dublin was in an invidious situation, located close to if not in the March, and prone to the depredations of the Irish. Both these factors, ensured that the recording of the extents of the southern manors necessitated the provision of greater detail about the land to explain rent reductions and the abandonment of lands. However, the records of the demesne lands are much more complete and they provide a useful comparison both with each other and with the overall manor.

Arable land certainly seems to dominate the identified land types in all manors (although over three-quarters of the manor of Shankill is classed as 'waste', presumably this situation prevailed there also in more auspicious times). While pasture and meadow are recorded in all manors they comprise only a very small proportion of the agricultural land, usually less than 10 per cent in total. Woodland, although very important to the medieval economy, is recorded in the extents of only five of the manors, and only in the four southern manors (St Sepulchre's, Clondalkin, Tallaght and Shankill) is a substantial acreage recorded.

Material from archaeological excavations, particularly from the excavations in Dublin city (Mitchell 1987, Geraghty 1996), provides evidence for the kinds of plants grown – wheat (*tritium aestivum*), oats (*avena* sp.), barley (*hordeum* sp.), rye (*secale* sp.) and also peas (*pisum sativum*). However, this evidence says very little about the extent to which such crops were grown. When looking at the demesne lands, the dominance of arable land becomes quite clear (fig. 3). Up to three-quarters of the demesne lands of any of the manors were under the plough, and it is to be assumed that a similar situation prevailed in the manor as a whole, suggesting that the majority of unspecified land is arable land. The extents, in fact the Register in general, are not always very specific about what crop was grown in any given area. Details of crops grown tend to be sparse and incomplete, failing to account for all the acreage known to be under arable cultivation. For example at Swords

> There are in demesne in one *sesona*, 11 score acres, arable, in divers fields, 4*d*. an acre; 11 score acres in another *sesona*, 3*d*. an acre; 11 score acres in another *sesona*, fallow this year, for letting in pasture 1*d*. an acre and no more for want of beasts; … Of the arable demesne lands above, 10 score acres are this year sown with wheat and 5 acres with oats by the archbishop, and 10 score 1 acre with wheat and pease by him and the king. (McNeill 1950, 175–6)

Wheat is the most common crop referred to (at St Sepulchre's, Finglas, Swords, Tallaght and Clondalkin), and also appears to have been the most popular, based on those references where it is possible to compare it to the acreage given over to other crops. The sowing of oats is recorded at St Sepulchre's, Swords, Tallaght and Clondalkin. The sowing of barley is recorded solely at the manor of Tallaght, and peas solely at the manor of Swords.

While land is set aside in all manors specifically for pasturing animals, this was not the sole source of grazing land. Advantage was taken of moor, wood and upland pasture, as well as arable land which was being fallowed. There is no indication either in the extents or the Register as a whole of the size of animal herds on any of the manors, and indeed the only animals referred to specifically in the Register are rabbits (McNeill 1950, 44–5 and 178), which were first introduced into Ireland by the Anglo-Normans. Warrens were maintained on most of the manors and were considered a valuable asset. It is difficult to ascertain whether or not rabbits constituted livestock; certainly they would not in any modern context, but they may not have been held to be different from cattle, sheep or any other animal reared for its meat by medieval farmers. They are included by Stamper (1988) in the list of specialized livestock which were reared in parks. However, references to lands which were waste or of no value 'for want of beasts' in the manorial extents of 1326, indicates that, unlike in England (Dyer 1988), there may have been less difficulty in providing sufficient pastureland to support the livestock on the various manors.

Meadow was important to the economy of the medieval manor and was very valuable. Hay was the principal source of winter fodder for animals. However this did not protect meadows from damage and there are several instances where meadows were damaged by the digging of sods (for example McNeill 1950, 184). Though there were several alternatives to pastureland proper on which to graze animals, it is noteworthy that pasture outweighs meadow in almost all of the extents.

WOODS AND WOODLAND MANAGEMENT

Trees and their by-products were absolutely essential to the medieval economy, which meant that woodland was a closely controlled and greatly appreciated resource. Wood was necessary for construction, fuel, furniture and utensils, and woodland was a good source of animal fodder, particularly for pigs. Since such great demands were placed upon it, it is unsurprising to discover that careful regulations were applied to it during this period. Therefore, the limited amount which has been written on medieval Irish woodlands is surprising. The main general work on Irish woodlands by McCracken (1971) only examines the situation from the seventeenth century up until the present, and little is said about medieval woodland. While some specific work has been done based on pre-Norman sources, for example the early Irish tree-list (Kelly 1976; Kelly 1998), the only discussions of woods and woodland management during the Anglo-Norman period tend to be brief and to occur within the context of the broader debate on landscape and agriculture during this period (for example, Glasscock 1987). While recent articles (Rackham 1995; Hall 1995) have begun to redress this balance, these discourses remain broadly based and no detailed or comprehensive study of Irish woods and woodland management during the later medieval period exists, Kenneth Nicholls's relatively brief 2001 study being by far the most insightful contribution to the subject to date (Nicholls 2001). Therefore it is necessary to rely on studies of English woods and woodland management during this period to provide the relevant background information in order to explore this area.

There are two broad woodland systems which can be seen in operation in England during this period (Stamper 1988). First, managed woods, consisting of mature trees or 'standards' and coppiced wood, parts of which might be let for grazing, with animals being kept well away from the coppiced wood to prevent them damaging it. And second, wood pasture which consisted of rough grazing land interspersed with mature trees. Nuts from the trees were used to fatten pigs. Sometimes trees in the wood pasture were pollarded. Stands of thorns within the wood pasture were used to protect young trees from animals and wood thieves. This is a less intensive form of land use. The Register appears to provide evidence for the existence of the first woodland system in Ireland as well as for other features of English woods and woodland management not detailed above. The evidence for wood pasture in the Register is tenuous (although there are references to grazing in woods) appearing to bear out the argument (Rackham 1995) that the absence of oaks over 300 years old in Ireland is indicative of the absence of wood pasture.

There is not a great deal of information in the Register about tree species. However, several species are mentioned: oak (McNeill 1950, 175, 195, 265), ash (ibid., 265, 284), thorns (ibid., 175, 195) and apple-trees (ibid., 187). The composition of the tracts of woodland mentioned in the Register cannot be reconstructed from this source, and only individual cases can be commented upon. Three of the examples cited above refer to two species in association, oak and ash (ibid., 265) and more importantly oak and thorns (ibid., 175, 195). The association of oak and thorns in a grove in Swords (ibid., 175) and a park in Shankill (ibid., 195) is significant. According to Stamper (1988) clumps of thorns were an important feature of wood pasture, as they were used to protect young shoots from grazing animals and other predators, allowing timber trees to mature in safety. However, whether or not this is indicative of wood pasture in Ireland is more difficult to say. Both references specify the production of 'underwood'; certainly in English sources this is usually applied to coppiced wood. Its application to refer to pollarded wood is not common, though it does occur. The existence of coppiced wood in a wood pasture is highly unlikely as it would require constant protection from the grazing animals, which is why pollarding was generally associated with this form of land management in England.

There are references to underwood in many of the woodlands recorded in the Register, in Colonia, Swords, Clondalkin, Shankill, and Oldtown. Again it must be assumed that this is most likely to refer to coppiced wood – trees cut down to ground level so that they send up shoots, producing a wealth of straight poles suitable for wattling and fencing and also firewood. These poles were cropped on a 5- to 8-year cycle. The Register, unfortunately, gives no detail on the cycle employed in any wood recorded therein. Pollarding – where the tree is cut down to a point above the level of grazing animals, again to produce straight poles – would also have been practised. However, it is not distinguished in the Register, where underwood is the main term used. While some of the references could indicate pollarding, it is far more likely that they indicate coppicing; a broader analysis of the use of the term underwood in medieval Irish sources would serve to clarify this.

The English sources give evidence for certain well-defined rights of access to woodland (Stamper 1988), which are: agistment, pannage, herbage, firebote, housebote, fencebote, and ploughbote. However, the owners of grazing animals might have to pay a fee to ensure access to the wood and the rights to green wood were frequently much more limited than those pertaining to dead wood. These rights were applied both in woods and in forests and were closely controlled by the principal tenant; this practice was continued in Ireland (for example, McNeill 1950, 81–2). In the Register it is possible to identify some, though not all, of these rights. There are references to woods being grazed and let as pasture in Clondalkin, Colonia and Swords and in all cases a fee to the principal tenant was involved. Admittedly, at the time these entries were recorded (1326) the woodland in the first two was referred to as being 'waste'; however, they had presumably been grazed in the immediate past. Herbage (the right to ground-up vegetation, usually grass, collected by the individual and then removed from the wood for use as animal fodder) is referred to in several entries in the Register; however its practice does not appear to have been confined to woodland, as there is reference to the herbage of a garden in Clondalkin (McNeill 1950, 185–9). There is only one reference in the Register, dating 1228–44, which lists any of the 'bote' rights:

> He grants also the sites of mills to be erected on the lands named, and what applies to *housebote* and *heybote* and making a hearth from the wood next his great forest, by view of his foresters. (ibid., 70)

Heybote corresponds to hedgebote which is the term used in the English material consulted (Rackham 1990; James 1991), and means the right to use wood for enclosures, hedges and fences (Jäger 1983); housebote means the right to take timber or wood for construction.

In England, there were three categories of woodland ownership (Stamper 1988): woods owned by individuals, but within which others had common rights; woods which were entirely common; and woods which were entirely private. The Register only provides evidence for the first form of ownership – woods which were in the possession of an individual or the crown, but within which certain tenants had rights or within which areas were let for grazing or for underwood. The only evidence for private woodland is within parkland. There is no evidence for common woodland in the Register.

The practice of imposing conditions which limited how woods, or even specific trees, could be treated was common in England when lands were being leased (Stamper 1988), and this practice was continued in Ireland (for example, McNeill 1950, 265). The granting of specific rights to lessees, usually at least grazing and access to firewood, was normal practice with the standing timber being reserved for the lessor as well as access to the land and the trees for felling. Assarting (the creation of private farmland within woodland, commonage or forest) was penalized and discouraged; however, this did not prevent its occurrence.

THE WOOD OF COLONIA

It is possible to isolate specific areas of woodland within the manors of County Dublin. The precise location of these woods, however, proved problematic as references were at best precise only to the townland and there are instances (for example, at Shankill) of more than one area of woodland listed as being within a particular townland. Therefore, it was not possible to map the areas of woodland, solely on the basis of the evidence provided by the Register.

Only in the case of the wood of Colonia in St Sepulchre's (also known as the wood of St Thomas) are there entries referring to it consistently from the thirteenth century up until the sixteenth century when the Register ceases. Despite the wealth of entries the precise location of the wood remained elusive, though it was possible to identify the general area where it was located (fig. 1). The only other area of woodland which is referred to, in several entries, of varying date, is the archbishop's wood in Kilmasantan; however these entries are far fewer than those relating to the wood of Colonia and far less can be ascertained regarding the history of that wood.

The earliest mention of the wood at Colonia dates between 1228 and 1255 (McNeill 1950, 84–5). While it is referred to in a footnote to a grant from the 1180s, the wording of the footnote indicates that it is a later interpolation.

Most of the references to this wood are similar in nature; the wood is referred to as a fixed point in order to locate a particular landholding, as are most references to specific woods in the Register. However, there are some entries which provide a more detailed picture of the wood and its management.

The earliest of these is the undated inquisition which is given as an addendum to the 1326 extent of the manor (ibid., 172). The extent itself also provides much useful information regarding the wood of Colonia:

> At Colonia, … 66a. wood, no value either for letting in grazing or for selling in underwood, because wholely wasted … Hugh Brugge and Thomas de Hattyngleye hold 22 acres in the wood of Colonia at 14*s*. a year and suit of court from each. (ibid., 170–71)

From this it can be assumed that prior to 1326 the wood had been both grazed and coppiced. To successfully achieve this would involve the subdivision of the wood and the fencing off of areas to protect young shoots from grazing animals. It is possible, though unlikely, since underwood is specified, that the wood was pollarded rather than coppiced in order to protect the shoots from grazing animals. Certainly, the state of the wood in 1326 would suggest that the system of management used was insufficient to preserve the woodland resource, which was compromised by overuse. The second reference within the 1326 extent implies the existence of assarts within the wood. This must have taken place prior to the compilation of both the extent in 1326, and also the undated inquisition, as the area of the wood remains static in both. Another reference from 1330 also supports the existence of assarts within the wood:

> William Burg grants to Thomas de Hattnegley and Nicholas de Sueterby for ever 6 acres of arable land in the tenement of the archbishop of Dublin, lieing together in the wood of Colonia. (ibid., 201)

The latest reference to the wood occurs briefly in a list of remissions for the archbishop's holdings in Dublin and comes from the period 1529–34 (ibid., 296–7). It would appear that the damage to the wood in the early fourteenth century was temporary and that it had recovered from this setback and was being worked again by the date of this entry.

THE FOREST

It is necessary, at this point, to discuss the important distinction which exists during this period between 'wood' and 'forest'. As in the modern understanding of these terms, a wood may be a forest; however, in the medieval period, a forest was not necessarily a wood. Essentially, the term 'forest' is a legal one, referring to a tract of land where certain laws operated and within which there could be a range of land uses, and even, in certain English examples, a town (Rackham 1990, 166). In terms of land use and composition, forests were more closely related to wood-pasture than to woodland proper.

Primarily, forests were controlled by the king, but similar by-laws operated in favour of the magnates as well, although possession of forestal rights did not necessitate ownership of the land. Forest sizes varied considerably, and in certain English examples they encompassed a whole county, although they tended to be based upon large estates held by the crown and to include well-wooded and mountainous areas. Originally, these were more of a royal business than a hobby, as they produced the venison necessary to feed and support the king and his court, who toured the various royal forests, living off their produce. With the growth and development of royal bureaucracy, forests became encumbered with a great weight of officialdom in charge of the day to day running of the forest. One of their principal functions was the raising of revenue through the pursuance of forest fines, for breaches of forest law (for example, poaching or felling trees) and this revenue was principally expended in the support of the forest officers and bureaucratic structures. The increasing antagonism of the English populace towards forests and their attendant officialdom led to their decline from the early thirteenth century (Rackham 1990, 166), the abuses of forest rights being amongst those addressed by the Magna Carta of 1215. The economic benefits of using forests to feed the royal court became outweighed by public opposition to the legal constraints imposed on those who lived within the bounds of forests, and given the considerable size of many English forests this would certainly have comprised of a sizable proportion of the population. While the royal court remained the main consumers of venison, it ceased to tour the royal forests and found other ways to support itself.

There are three references to forests in the Register. The earliest grants the custody of the forest of Leinster to the archbishop of Dublin (McNeill 1950, 26); the precise bounds of this area are unclear, although presumably, given its nomenclature, it was of some considerable size. The most intriguing reference to a forest comes from the year 1229, and is particularly interesting given that the decline of the institution of the forest had already begun in England, by this time:

> King Henry [III] grants to Luke, archbishop of Dublin and his successors that all the underwritten lands shall be deafforested for ever both for venaison and all else pertaining to forest and foresters: the land called S. Keyuin's land, the land called Fertyr, the land called Coyllache, with appurtenances; these are all of the domain of the see of Dublin and formerly of that of Glyndelach and of Thomas sometime abbot of

> Glyndelach: on the east they extend to the King's lands of Obryn and Othethe, and thence on the south to Wykinnelou, the baron of Naas's land, and thence to Arclowe, Theobald Butler's land, and thence to Omaille, land of Philip son of Resius which is of the fee of Walter de Ryde[ls]forde, and thence on the west to the land of the Naas and thence to Radmore, Maurice fitzGerald's land, and thence on the north to the land of Tachsagare and thence to Balachclit, Walter de Rydelsforde's land, and thence to Creuache, Richard de Saint Michael's land and thence by brow of the hill to Senekyll, the archbishop of Dublin's land. Although all lands within these bounds were in forest in the King's ancestors' time and in his own, the archbishops may enclose their woods and make parks and take, give, sell and assart of their woods at will without view or opposition of foresters, vergers and other officers with liberty of chemin for ever, quit of waste reguard and view of foresters, vergers and reguarders: the residents are to be quit for ever of all suits of forest pleas and fines, of taking and expediment of dogs and all legal processes pertaining to the forest and foresters. (McNeill 1950, 62–3)

While this represents a significant change in the legal status and economic control of a substantial section of County Wicklow and south County Dublin, this is unlikely to have resulted in any immediate alteration to the environmental systems in place in this area.

Rather, what this grant represents is the handing over of absolute control of the resources of this area (both woodland and otherwise) to the archbishops of Dublin and the cutting off of any appeal to higher authority which the tenants and inhabitants of the area might make regarding any of the archbishop's actions and the removal of the land from the jurisdiction of the forest laws, as well as the removal of attendant forest rights. It is best viewed against the backdrop of the decline of the forest, already mentioned, with this grant being a direct result of that trend. Royal visits to Ireland were hardly so common as to ensure the preservation of royal forests for long after their decline in popularity commenced. Areas of woodland which are referred to at a later date in the Register, for example the archbishop's wood at Kilmasantan (McNeill 1950, 180–83) would appear to lie within the area outlined in the grant, and yet remained woodland, thus supporting this interpretation of the entry.

A later entry from 1290, however, indicates that the crown still held some land in forest in the south Dublin area (ibid., 152). No references to forests later than 1290 have been identified in the Register, which concords with the English evidence for the decline of the institution.

PARKS

The concept of imparking land developed from the deer-park, essentially an enclosed hunting ground. With the decline of the forest in the thirteenth century such enclosures became increasingly popular with the nobility. Deer-parks necessitated the construction of formidable enclosing features in order to prevent the deer from escaping. These enclosing features were expensive to maintain, so in practical terms, the larger the area imparked the more financially viable the park, owing to the greater ratio of enclosed acreage to enclosure circumference. Parks generally contained a combination of woodland and grassland and a typical park size would be around 60 acres. Though there are English examples of coppicing in parks, this was generally inconsistent with their original purpose, and this practice could only be maintained, in the long run, in parks large enough to be successfully compartmentalized (Rackham 1990). Mature timber trees were a particular feature of parks, in fact trees in parkland tended to be left standing for longer than in conventional woodland – great timbers for the construction of such buildings as King's College Chapel, Cambridge, tended to be sourced from parks (Rackham 1990, 158). Deer were not the only livestock maintained in parks, and other specialized features of English parks included rabbit warrens, stud farms and fish ponds. While those who imparked land did their best to eliminate all rights of access of tenants to that land, they were not always wholly successful, although in the main parkland was removed from the normal spectrum of agricultural land and woodland management.

In the Register there are references to parkland in the extent of the manor of Finglas and also the extent of the manor of Shankill, both taken in 1326. At Finglas there were two parks:

> and 24 acres of these demesnes which used to be *sub carucis* were imparked by the archbishop, no value, because nothing can be got from them; … a park there, 71 acres, the grazing extended at 2s. (McNeill 1950, 173)

While the conversion of arable land to park is not unprecedented, it was more usual to choose land already at least partially wooded. Archbishop Alen's footnote to this reference identifies this park with the 'lord's wood' then at Finglas. This reference would appear to be in keeping with the English material, as the park has been removed wholly from the spectrum of agricultural use.

The second park is more intriguing as it was still being let for grazing, so either it was not a deer-park – merely an enclosed wood pasture – or the archbishop was unable or unwilling to remove all rights of access to that land. There were also two parks recorded in the manor of Shankill (ibid., 195–6), neither of which parks would appear to fit the classic description of a deer-park: the second park (only 4a. in size) is clearly too small for such a purpose, and both were, to judge from this extent, intended for use as pasture. The larger (30a.) park was expected to produce underwood, and is too small to have been compartmentalized, although, as previously discussed the reference to oak and thorns could imply wood pasture. One of the parks had a rabbit warren, and this is the only feature referred to which is in any way concordant with the usual features of English parks.

Only in the case of the 24a. park at Finglas could one be comfortable in classifying it alongside the English examples, although the other three parks display features at least superficially from the English model. The nature and use of the word park in the Irish sources for this period is one which requires further study.

ORCHARDS AND GARDENS

Gardens were mainly used for the cultivation of vegetables and other plants such as herbs, and were as often kept by peasants as lords (Greig 1988). While fruit trees were grown in gardens, orchards were mainly used for their propagation and, in England, apples appear to have been among the most widely cultivated fruit (Greig 1988), although pears, nuts, damsons and cherries were among the other fruits grown.

In the Register there are many references to gardens, both suburban (e.g., McNeill 1950, 15), and also in many of the manors, such as Shankill, Swords, and St Sepulchre's. There is not much information given on what was grown in these gardens, but there are some hints. There are two references to gardens with 'fruit and grass' (ibid., 172, 178) and also to a garden with herbage (ibid., 187). Clearly, gardens were a source of animal fodder as well as vegetables.

There are only two references to orchards in the Register, one in Finglas and one in Clondalkin (ibid., 174, 187). The orchard at Finglas was let for herbage. However, the reference to the orchard in Clondalkin is a little more useful: 'a curtilage and old orchard, no value because unenclosed and without apple-trees' (ibid., 187). Obviously an orchard was expected to be enclosed, and, also, it could be assumed the apple-trees were a staple part of its composition.

MOOR AND MOUNTAIN

As in England, areas outside the structured agricultural landscape were utilized to provide pasture, fuel and other resources. In County Dublin this comprised primarily of areas described as 'moor' and also (in the south of the county) mountains. The Dublin mountains were an ideal area for upland pasturing of animals. Most upland pasturing was carried out in common, i.e., no one individual had any particular holding within the area of the pasture as in the case of Slievethoul (McNeill 1950, 184). However there are instances of individual holdings on mountains (ibid., 215) and woods could also be situated on mountains, as in the manor of Shankill (ibid., 195).

The term 'moor' is more difficult, and it may have encompassed a variety of land types from scrubland through to bog. Moor was most often used as pastureland, either in common or by individual tenants, for example, 'it used to render 33*s.* a year, no value now except 6*d.* for the grazing of a small moor within the said land' (ibid., 186). Moor was also a source of fuel, namely turf, and there is a reference to a 'moor of turbary' in Finglas (ibid., 174). Turf cutting was also practised on mountains (ibid., 84) and there is a reference to the granting of the right to cut turf to the tenants of the vicar of Howth (ibid., 75), although the source of this turf is not specified. The precise nature of moor is difficult to define based on the evidence contained in the Register; however, it probably implied some sort of non-agricultural, boggy, scrubland.

RIVERS AND WATERWAYS

Finally, it is worth considering the uses of and adaptations made to rivers and waterways by the Anglo-Normans. Watermills were known in Ireland from the early medieval period, and the Anglo-Normans as well as refurbishing and maintaining those mills already existing in County Dublin, also built many new mills. All the manors had at least one mill, usually a watermill, and it was a very valuable asset of the manor. There are references to the millpond at Swords (McNeill 1950, 177) and to millraces at Rathcoole and Taney. Not all rivers or parts of rivers would have provided suitable sites for watermills, so in many cases it must have been necessary to construct a millrace to power the mill, which may have brought about changes in the hydrology of an area.

Rivers and the sea provided fish. Fishing rights were carefully controlled and prized. There are many references to fishing rights in the River Liffey (ibid., 28–30, 145–6, 172). While those who lived directly on the coast might be able to fish more freely, they would still owe a duty to the local magnate as a reference from Howth makes clear:

> All fishermen of his land who go out to fish in that boat whether obliged to do so or not, while they are in its service shall be free from all exaction when they come to land; he will exact nothing unjustly from them, but if he wishes to buy from them, he will do it at their free will and for the same price as another. (ibid., 75)

WASTE AND DEGRADED LAND

The defining of land as degraded is subjective, usually closely linked to the perceived value of the land in question. The concept of the 'value' of land not only encompasses its inherent natural resources but also contemporary social and economic factors. This becomes quite clear in the Register, where the definition of land as waste or of no value, that is, degraded in some fashion, does not necessarily always indicate the loss of any intrinsic qualities in the land itself. Therefore it is difficult to judge changes in the quality of land based purely on its perceived value, and it is perhaps better to speak of the capability of land to sustain a particular environmental system rather than its value. According to Blaike and Brookfield, 'socially, degradation must relate to capability, and it is only if the degradation process under one system of production has reduced the initial capability of land in a successor system, actual or potential, that degradation is as it were, carried across the allocation change' (1987, 6–7). When land is transferred between systems, for example, from woodland to agricultural land, it may be more or less capable in its new context. When the system is changed the basis for judgement of capability changes, and it is necessary to think in terms of an area's ability to fulfil its new function rather than its old one.

Understanding the criteria used to determine whether land is degraded or wasted by any society can provide an insight into how that society perceives the environment. Again, the main sources for comparison here are the manorial extents taken in 1326, although these are not exclusively used. The reason why there may be discrepancies between the figures used to discuss wasteland and the more general discussion of land-use, is that while wood, for example, may be classified as waste in an extent, it may still, in actuality, be standing woodland. Therefore, when looking at the overall make-up of the landscape, it is self-defeating to regard such land as 'waste', and hence its classification as woodland for general discussion.

It is necessary to make a distinction between different rationales by which land is designated as waste since modern concepts of what constitutes degraded or waste land and medieval concepts are quite different. Also it may have significant implications for understanding and identifying the nature of the actual environmental system in operation. In fact there is a distinction between waste and degraded land which does not appear to be present in the medieval period. In modern terms, land described as waste is generally land which is not fulfilling any particular purpose, whether agricultural, industrial, recreational or functioning as an identified natural habitat. Land is recognized as being degraded when it has suffered a loss of capability, whether through human interference or natural processes, and any consequent loss in perceived value is coincidental rather than influential to this categorization. Modern

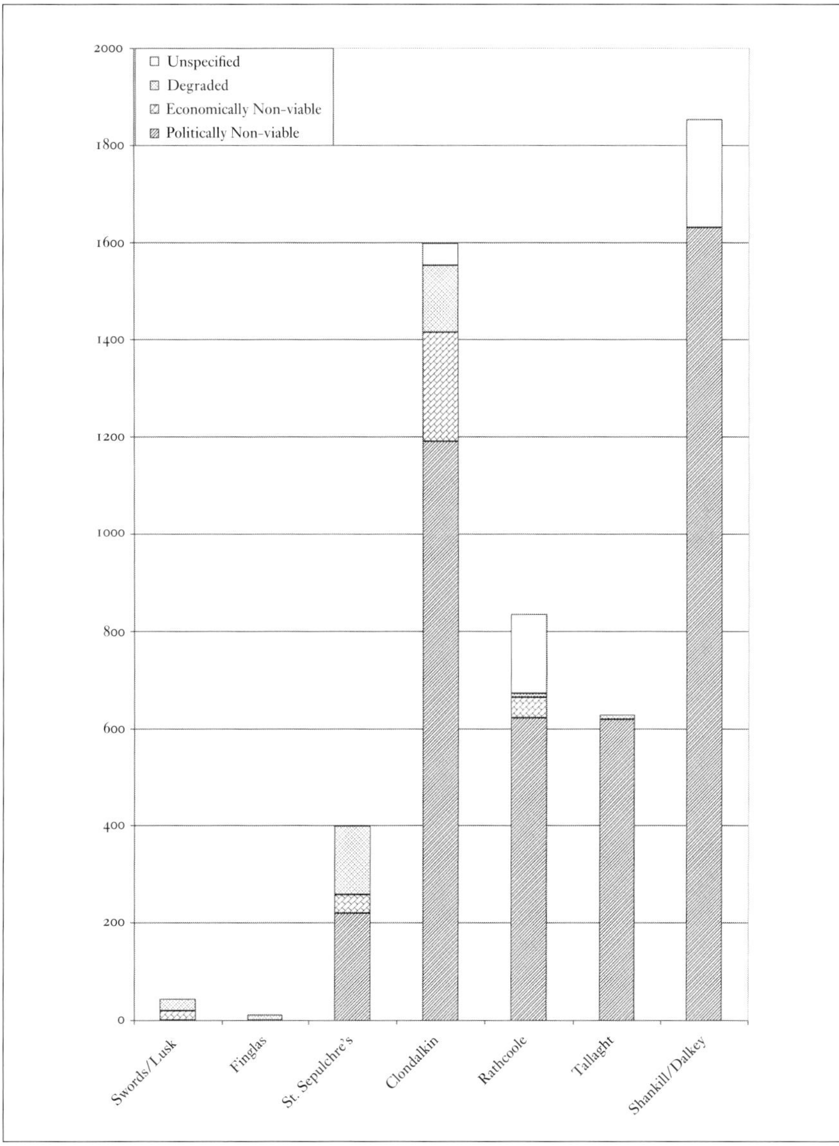

4 Comparison of the different categories of waste and degraded lands recorded in the 1326 extents of the archiepiscopal manors

perceptions of land degradation can be heavily influenced by the environmentalist movement; there is a perception that any environmental system which is converted from its 'natural' state to facilitate human activity is by definition degraded. While, more often than not, such an adaptation does incur a loss in capability, in practice, technically a change in function or system does not automatically imply degradation.

However, in the medieval period such adaptations in environmental systems were not recognized as having much bearing on land degradation. The guiding factor in their definition of what was degraded or waste is economic, based on the value of the land – the degree to which it was possible to exploit its natural resources to achieve an economic advantage. Put simply, land from which no income could be gained was classified as waste. As such a definition had relatively little to do with the capability of the land to fulfil its original designation, it is necessary to distinguish the reasons why a particular portion of land is designated waste. Land classified as 'waste' or of 'no value' in the Register falls broadly into three categories (fig. 4): politically nonviable, economically nonviable, and land which has suffered a loss in capability.

The first category is land which has been categorized as waste due to purely political considerations. As the boundary of Anglo-Norman control varied considerably from the twelfth to the fifteenth centuries, certain lands varied between being under English lordship and being under the control of the Irish. The early part of the fourteenth century was particularly unstable, significant areas of south Dublin passed back into Irish control, while, in others, continued Anglo-Norman settlement became untenable due to their proximity to the areas under Irish control. One of the most common phrases used to describe holdings in these areas is 'waste and among the Irish'. There is no evidence for loss of capability in most of this land and the only obvious reason for its designation as waste is that it is no longer within the political control of the Lordship or that its location in the border area makes it too dangerous to farm. This is seen at its greatest extreme in the case of the manor of Shankill, where almost all the land is described as being waste or of no value, as a direct result of its position in the March (McNeill 1950, 194–5). A later entry in the Register, dating from 1520, indicates that in the fourteenth and fifteenth centuries a good part of the holdings of the see of Dublin came to be regarded as waste or of no value. Some of these were subsequently alienated or let at less than their perceived value in the sixteenth century when, presumably, the political situation had stabilized somewhat:

> The possessions of the see of Dublin, once great, were wasted by rebellions and alienations under value by Richard Talbot and Michell Tregurry, late archbishops, and also a farm William Wise had of the same archbishops in Luske for nothing; which alienations and farm are annulled, saving the rights of the prior and the convent of the Cathedral Church of Holy Trinity of Dyveline, the college of St Patrick of Dyveline, Roger Finglas, Robert Sancte Larance, "seignioure de Howthe", Thomas Wendell, yeoman (now challenging the clause of distress contained in Archbishop Michel's grant to him, and that Thomas will do service while he can to archbishop John), Maistre John

> Bolande for his own person for life, and John Wycombe, provided he pay the ancient due as heretofore. (ibid., 265)

Politically nonviable land is only identifiable in the extents of those manors located south of the Liffey. Most of the manor of Shankill and large areas of the manors of Rathcoole, Clondalkin, Tallaght and St Sepulchre's are described as 'waste' or of no value, for purely political reasons (fig. 4). This is an important point to note as large tracts of south Dublin, previously under the plough or at least regularly grazed, may, in the early fourteenth century, have been reverting to scrub.

The second category of land is that which is economically nonviable, i.e., there were not the economic resources available in order to exploit it fully. Such land is usually described as being waste or of no value because 'there are not tenants to farm it or beasts to graze it'. One of the principal causes of this situation does relate to the resurgence of the Irish and the decline of the Lordship, which led to the abandonment of manors by English tenants. At the same time, it became increasingly difficult to persuade new immigrants to come from England. So, as the Lordship contracted geographically and politically it also contracted in population size. This land is distinguished from that which is politically nonviable because, while the root cause of its designation as waste or of no value is the same, this land appears still to be within the political control of the Lordship. While there are instances of such land being described as poor, particularly in the manor of Clondalkin, it is not clear that this indicates any loss in capability: 'At Corkagh four English tenants hold 7½ acres, formerly John de Castroknoc's, 7*s.* 6*d.*; 33a. of the same land are 'frisse' and untilled for want of tenants and the poverty of the land' (McNeill 1950, 186). It may be the case that in areas where the land as a whole was not of such good quality, it was more difficult to find tenants for it, with tenants gravitating towards the better-quality landholdings.

Again there is a strong southern bias in the distribution of such lands (fig. 4), which are recorded in the manors of Rathcoole, Clondalkin and St Sepulchre's. However there is no economically nonviable land recorded in either the manor of Tallaght or of Shankill which have, proportionally, the highest levels of politically nonviable land. While there is a southern bias, this category of land is not exclusively southern, as the following reference from Lusk indicates:

> Archbishop Richard with consent of both chapters reduces to 13*s.* 4*d.*, payable at the usual feasts, the rents of 13*d.* for a messuage in Luske and 12*d.* an acre for 26a. in the same vill, which Robert Bulloke and his ancestors held of him and his predecessors. The messuage and land lie waste and untilled, and the rent is so excessive that no one will take or till them for it; and so neither the archbishop nor his tenant have got anything for several years. (ibid., 240–41)

Clearly, what we have here is the medieval equivalent of a buyer's market. An important entry in this context is an undated extract from an inquisition of the manor of St Sepulchre's which is given as an addendum to the 1326 extent in McNeill's edition of the Register. Because the wood (at Colonia) appears to be in good condition in this extract, unlike in the 1326 extent of the manor, this suggests that it dates earlier than the extent. When it is compared with the equivalent passage in the extent they provide an interesting contrast (see table 2). The 1326 extent is clearly much more pessimistic in its estimation of the value of the land. Even those areas which have not been degraded, no longer carry the same rent, and the demesne lands are partially in the hands of tenants, unlike in the undated inquisition where it would appear they are still under the lord's plough.

Table 2. Comparison of the two extents for the manor of St Sepulchre's

1326, Extent of manor:	**Undated inquisition:**
At Colonia there are this year in one sowing (*sesona*) 50 acres arable, sown *sub carrucis* with wheat, extended at 3*d.* an acre, 12*s.* 6*d.* a year; there are in a sowing 48 acres sown with oats this year *sub carrucis*, at 3*d.* an acre, 12*s.*; in another sowing 68 acres, fallow, *sub carucis*, extended at 1*d.* an acre, 5*s.* 8*d.* and no more, as the land is exhausted and poor. There are of the same demesne lands in the hands of farmers four score acres, 40*s.* a year at 6*d.* an acre. At Brodemede, 10 acres meadow, at 4*d.* an acre, 3*s.* 4*d.*; in St Thomas's meadow 6 acres, meadow, 6*d.* a year, because near the king's way (wher Butler's acre lies, 8*d.*) and destroyed by carters; at Strifmede, 3½ acres, fallow, 7*d.* a year; at Crokemede, an acre and a half, meadow, 3*d.* a year: at Schenbalymore, 2 acres, meadow, 4*d.* a year. At Colonia, 16 acres, pasture, 16*d.* a year and no more for want of beasts, and most of the pasture is near evil-doers; 66 acres wood, no value either for letting in grazing or for selling underwood, because wholly wasted. (McNeill 1950, 170–71)	In the demesne of Colon[ia] are 12 score and six acres of arable land, by estimation; four score and twelve of these lie in the field called Shanbalymore, and 74a. in the field called Balymaregan and Barlycroft; there are 22a. of meadow, of which 5a. lie in St Thomas's field, worth 2*s.* an acre yearly, and 3½a. in Sigenesmede, worth 2*s.* an acre yearly; 1½a. in Crokedmede worth 3*s.* a year (the name of the 1½a. is le old hagard); and Brodemede, worth 2*s.* an acre yearly; 2½a. in divers parcels worth 5*s.* a year; 16a. of pasture worth 12*d.* a year; also Fosse and other appurtenances worth 4*s.* a year: the wood (Boscus), 66a., they extend at 20*s.* a year, with divers parks; likewise a garden by St Kevin's church worth ½ mark. (McNeill 1950, 172)

The third category, land which has suffered an actual loss in capability, is degraded both in medieval and modern terms. The principal cause for this loss in capability is human activity although there are also cases of land degraded through natural processes. For example, at Tallaght there were '20a.

in the archbishop's hand by escheat on the death of Adam de Stretton, formerly 13*s.* 4*d.*, now nothing, because the archbishop granted 12a. rent free to Ralph Aubine, and 5a. of the 20 are flooded by the Dodour' (McNeill 1950, 182); while at Lusk there were '24 acres pasture of little value, because the sea overflows them, 1*d.* an acre' (ibid., 176). Unlike in the other categories, not all land which has suffered a loss in capability is considered waste or of no value; in fact, in many instances, the land continues in agricultural use, though with lower yields. This can be seen in the case of a pasture in the manor of St Sepulchre's: 'in St Thomas's meadow, 6a. meadow, 6*d.* a year, because near the king's way (wher Butler's acre lies, 8*d.*) and destroyed by carters' (ibid., 170). Or a meadow in the manor of Rathcoole: 'Lesemourmede, 8½a., 1*d.* an acre, 8½*d.* and no more because wasted in time past by the digging of sods' (ibid., 184). Instances like these support the argument that there is nothing intrinsically wrong with land which is either politically or economically nonviable, other than the inability to exploit the land's resources for economic gain. Even though an area of land may have suffered an actual loss in capability, it continues in use within the agricultural system so long as it is possible to get a return on it.

Finally there are lands which are usually described as being 'waste' or 'all waste' with no qualification as to why this categorization has come about. While it has been itemized separately, in actuality it must clearly have fallen into one of the three main categories. The high proportion of politically nonviable land and the fact that most of these references are closely associated with references to such lands, leads to the conclusion that these lands mainly belong to that category also.

CONCLUSIONS

The picture of the environment of County Dublin which has emerged during the course of this study is complex. The most obvious point which has come across in the examination of most areas is of the existence of a general north-south divide. The two manors north of the Liffey – Swords and Finglas – provided the most stable and classical examples of manorial organization, with its attendant environmental systems. The primary land use of both manors was, by a considerable percentage, arable cultivation; pasture, meadow, and indeed wood would appear to have been at a premium. Very little wasteland is recorded north of the Liffey; even those areas which had suffered actual degradation (i.e., a loss in capability) were kept within the spectrum of agricultural usage as much as possible. Only in the case of the 24a. at Lusk which the sea overflowed (McNeill 1950, 176), is it possible that the land may have ceased to be used for agriculture; however, it is still accorded a value of 1*d.* an acre in 1326. By contrast, the demesne arable land of the manor of

Tallaght is only valued at 2*d.* an acre, despite the fact that it is recorded in the extent as being under wheat, oats and barley, at this time.

The picture which emerges of the manors located south of the Liffey – Clondalkin, Tallaght, Rathcoole, Shankill and St Sepulchre's – is much less stable. While superficially the proportion of arable land would appear to be only slightly less than in the north of the county, this is deceptive as the exploitation of much of that arable land was contingent on the political and economic stability of the Lordship. Large areas of the south of the county are described as waste in the manorial extents of 1326, in particular the manor of Shankill. While all the listed lands were undoubtedly being cultivated and exploited a century earlier, the information from the extents indicates that large portions of the south of County Dublin were reverting to scrub and wilderness. The long-term abandonment of this land would have brought about a considerable change in the ecology, with a greater variety of wild plants and weeds rather than the restricted range of plants associated with cultivated land. A detailed study of palynological evidence and macroscopic plant remains from the area may indicate such changes, if and when the opportunity for such a study arises.

The subject of woods and woodland management in medieval Ireland is one which is in need of detailed scholarship. The limited nature of the evidence from the Register provides only a partial picture of what is happening in this arena; however it is abundantly clear that even with so limited a source much can still be said. The evidence for the management and maintenance of woodlands tallies closely with that for medieval England, and while the Register does not provide evidence for the whole range of woodland practice which existed there, nonetheless it indicates that a very similar system was in operation in County Dublin, though perhaps with some divergences.

The north-south divide also crosses over into the area of woodland. By far the majority of woods and woodland in County Dublin, referred to in the Register, are situated in the south of the County, and appear to gravitate towards the upland areas at the Wicklow border. Also, there appears to have been a greater range of land quality in the south of the county: distinctions between different areas of pasture or arable land, for example, are more likely to have a basis in the capability of the given parcel of land. This is not necessarily indicative of degradation or loss in capability unless it can be established that the particular parcel of land had once been of better quality. In fact actual degradation of land is one of the few areas which does not illustrate this polarization. While both the manors of Clondalkin and St Sepulchre's show relatively high levels of land degradation, this trend is not continued in the other three manors located south of the Liffey where the levels of land degradation are similar to those in the manors north of the Liffey. One point which does not come across in the comparison of the manors is that areas of moor are slightly more common in the south of the county than the north. While the references to moors in the Register rarely indicate an acreage, locations south of the Liffey are more common.

Some of the differences between the north and south of the county clearly have an origin in the geography of the region – the upland areas in the south of the county would have been less amenable to arable cultivation, and would have had a more prevalent tree-cover – not all the differences can be so easily explained. The political and economic problems associated with the decline of the Lordship and the resurgence of the Irish had an important role to play. The population decline and loss of territory suffered by the Lordship as a result of these factors encouraged the abandonment of land and the greater prevalence of pastoral farming. Though there is an economic trend away from arable farming throughout Britain and Ireland generally from the early to the mid-fourteenth century, this does not appear to have been a prime motivating factor in the changes that take place in County Dublin. In the north of the county, which was not as strongly affected by the political upheavals, the manorial system continued little perturbed and there is no evidence to indicate any dramatic changes in the environment once the manorial system had been established.

One of the most important points to emerge, in terms of the overall environment, is that no area or aspect of the environment remained without interference; control was exercised over natural resources, not just agricultural land proper but also woods, moors, bogs, rivers, mountains and uplands. It was not possible to identify any area or land type within the county which was free from human interference during the medieval period.

To summarize, the north of County Dublin during the medieval period is characterized by a stable agricultural environment, composed of open arable fields interspersed with areas of pasture and meadow along with some areas of wood and moor. While the environment is in a constant state of flux there are no indications of dramatic changes in this area during the medieval period. In the south of the county however, the twelfth and thirteenth centuries saw the introduction of the manorial system, which would have produced an environmental system not dissimilar to that which existed north of the Liffey. By 1326, though, much of the south of County Dublin is recorded as having been abandoned by tenants and lords alike due to the increased levels of raiding by the Irish, and this territory would have reverted to scrub and wilderness. The manors of Clondalkin and St Sepulchre's display relatively high levels of land degradation at this time, and in particular the wood of Colonia had been severely compromised, presumably by overuse. Even in the more stable areas of the south, arable cultivation was not always as consistent as in the north. It is well into the fifteenth century before the reestablishment of intensive agriculture in those areas of the south which were abandoned can be definitely identified in the Register.

Finally, whether in areas of sustained agriculture or woodland or areas sporadically abandoned, it is human beings and their actions which are shaping and influencing the form and development of the environment of County Dublin throughout the medieval period. The motivations for this interaction are contained within the medieval perception of the environment: 'Humans' interactions with the natural environment can be understood only by considering their perception of it and their behavioural responses to it, both of which are conditioned by their cultural environment' (Harrison et al. 1992, 557). To put it more simply, how members of medieval society interacted with the environment and their perceptions of that environment are particular to them and are best understood within the context of that society and history. In the context of the environment of County Dublin this means that their interaction with and impact upon that environment can only be fully understood against the background of the Anglo-Norman presence and their activity within the county. Thus, the Register not only provides an account of the environment of County Dublin and of human interaction with that environment, but also goes some way towards elucidating medieval attitudes towards and perceptions of the environment generally.

Land value, in medieval society, is based wholly on that society's ability to exploit the natural resources of a given area to the maximum. If that ability is compromised in any way, whether by political, economic or environmental processes then that area of land is perceived as being lacking in value. Esoteric factors (beauty, convenience, rarity, etc.) have little relevance to this perception. This point is illustrated strongly in the Register, particularly in all the manorial extents of 1326, where land which has suffered a loss in capability continues in use within the agricultural spectrum (although it is valued at a lower rate), while in other areas perfectly viable agricultural land is described as waste and of no value due to political or economic obstacles preventing its exploitation.

There is a strong sense in which medieval legislation and control of the environment is concerned with the preservation of privilege and position rather than the preservation of environmental systems. Those to whom rights of access to resources are reserved are generally belonging to the upper echelons of society – the king, the nobility, and the church. While certain aspects of the regulation of the rights of access of individuals to certain resources within the environment, for example wood or fishing rights, might serve to preserve and conserve that environmental system, in the medieval period conservation of resources was in a sense self-interested: it was done purely with an eye to the long-term benefit of those in control of those resources, to ensure the constant supply of raw materials. A wood which continued to produce timber and underwood for several centuries was much more valuable and beneficial than a wood which was allowed to be grubbed out in the course of several decades. This point is further reinforced by the fact that, in England, common woods – woodland over which no one individual had authority – were most likely to suffer extreme damage through overuse, and least likely to survive for long into the later medieval period (Stamper 1988). This tendency is attributed to the fact that no individual had a financial interest in the survival of the wood, and that the close control of private and semi-private woodland reduced the peasantry to the over-exploitation of common woodland, where it existed. Opposition to the destruction or damaging of natural resources was based firmly in the sphere of economics, since such an area would produce less wealth, rather than that such destruction could destabilize or otherwise adversely affect the local environment.

This study indicates that the nature of Irish medieval documentation allows for a surprisingly detailed picture of the environment to emerge. While the guiding principles and methodology used in this study could be applied equally well to any area within the historic period, the main guiding factor as to the outcome of any study is based on the quality and range of the source material used. Despite the limitation involved in using only a single source, it has proved possible to achieve a fruitful picture of the environment of County Dublin during the medieval period. The actual depth and breadth of discussion made possible by the material in the Register was surprising in many areas. The quality and nature of the material dealing with agricultural land was to be anticipated; however, the evidence for topics such as land degradation or the social perceptions of the environment was an unexpected bonus. These issues are seminal to understanding the interaction of medieval Irish society with the natural world and, also, to understanding how and why they treated the environment in the way in which they did.

ACKNOWLEDGMENTS

This paper is based on a thesis submitted to the Department of Geography, UCD, as part of the requirements for the MPhil in Medieval Studies. I would like to thank my supervisor, Professor Anngret Simms, for her support and guidance throughout.

BIBLIOGRAPHY

Source

McNeill, C. (ed. and trans.), *Calendar of Archbishop Alen's register c.1172–1534*. Dublin, 1950.

References

Aalen, F.H.A., *Man and the landscape in Ireland*. London, 1978.

Aalen, F.H.A. and Whelan, K. (eds), *Dublin city and county: from prehistory to present.* Dublin, 1992.

Astill, G. and A. Grant (eds), *The countryside of medieval England.* Oxford, 1988.

Baker, A.R.H. and R.A. Butlin (eds), *Studies of field systems in the British Isles.* Cambridge, 1973.

Blaike, P. and H. Brookfield (eds), *Land degradation and society.* London, 1987.

Bolger, T., 'The environmental history of County Dublin in the medieval period (based on Archbishop Alen's Register *c.*1172–1534)'. Unpublished MPhil thesis, UCD, 1997.

Bradley, J. (ed.), *Settlement and society in medieval Ireland.* Kilkenny, 1988.

Buchanan, R.H, 'Field systems of Ireland', in Baker, A.R.H. and Butlin, R.A. (eds), Studies of field systems (1973) 580–618.

Butlin, R.A., 'Some observations on the field systems of medieval Ireland', *Geographia Polonia,* 38 (1978), 31–6.

Cosgrove, A. (ed.), *A new history of Ireland Vol. II.* Oxford, 1987.

Downes, K., 'Colonial society and economy', in Cosgrove, A. (ed.), *A new history of Ireland Vol. II* (1987), 439–91.

Dyer, C., 'Documentary evidence: problems and enquiries', in Astill, G. and A. Grant (eds), *The countryside* (1988), 12–35.

Fagan, P. and A. Simms, 1992, 'The villages of County Dublin: their origins and inheritance', in Aalen, F.H.A. and Whelan, K. (eds), *Dublin: city and county* (1992).

Geraghty, S., *Viking Dublin: botanical evidence from Fishamble Street.* Medieval Dublin Excavations 1962–81, Ser. C, vol. 2, Dublin, 1996.

Glasscock, R.E., 'Land and people', in Cosgrove, A. (ed.), *A new history of Ireland Vol. II* (1987).

Graham, B.J., 'The high middle ages', in Graham, B.J. and Proudfoot, L. (eds), *An Historical Geography of Ireland.* London, 1993.

Grieg, J., 'Plant resources', in Astill, G. and Grant, A. (eds), *The countryside* (1988), 108–27.

Hall, D.N., Hennessey, M. and O'Keeffe, T., 'Medieval agriculture and settlement in Oughterard and Castlewarden, Co. Kildare', *Irish Geography*, 18 (1985), 16–25.

Hall, V.A., 'Woodland depletion in Ireland over the last millenium', in Mac an tSaoir, S.S. and J.R. Pilcher, *Wood, trees and forests* (1995), 23–33.

Harrison, S.J., Motteshead, D.N. and White, I.D., *Environmental systems, an introductory text.* London, 1992.

Jäger, H., 'Land use in medieval Ireland: a review of the documentary evidence', *Irish Economic and Social History*, 10 (1983), 51–65.

James, N.D.G., *An historical dictionary of forestry and woodland terms.* Oxford, 1991.

Kelly, F., 'The old Irish tree-list', *Celtica*, 11 (1976), 107–24.

Kelly, F., *Early Irish Farming.* Dublin, 1998.

Lyttleton J. and O'Keeffe, T. (eds), *The manor in medieval and early modern Ireland.* Dublin, 2005.

Mac an tSaoir, S.S. and Pilcher, J.R. *Wood, trees and forests in Ireland.* Dublin, 1995.

McCracken, E., *The Irish woods since Tudor times.* Newton Abbot, 1971.

Mannion, A.M., *Global environmental change.* New York, 1991.

Mitchell, F., *The Irish landscape.* London, 1976.

Mitchell, G.F., *Archaeology and environment in early Dublin.* Medieval Dublin Excavations 1962–81, Ser. C vol. 1, Dublin, 1987.

Murphy, M. and Potterton, M. 'Investigating living standards in medieval Dublin and its region,' in Duffy, S. (ed.), *Medieval Dublin VI.* Dublin, 2005, 225–56.

Nicholls, Kenneth, 'Woodland cover in pre-modern Ireland', in Duffy, P.J., Edwards, D. and FitzPatrick, E., *Gaelic Ireland: land, lordship and settlement c.1250–c.1650* (Dublin, 2001), 181–206.

Rackham, O., *Trees and woodland in the British landscape*. London, 1990 (2nd edition).

Rackham, O., 'Looking for ancient woodland in Ireland', in Mac an tSaoir, S.S. and Pilcher, J.R. *Wood, trees and forests* (1995), 1–12.

Stamper, P., 'Woods and parks', in Astill, G. and Grant, A. (eds), *The countryside* (1988), 128–48.

Thirty years on: a personal memoir of the Friends of Medieval Dublin[1]

HOWARD B. CLARKE

In April 2006 the Friends of Medieval Dublin celebrated the thirtieth anniversary of their foundation. The first meeting took place in the Arts Club premises in Fitzwilliam Street, though for many years thereafter the Royal Society of Antiquaries of Ireland kindly offered the use of its library as a suitable venue for homeless people with little money and an academic bent, round the corner in Merrion Square. The founding members saw themselves essentially as a study group, focussed on a relatively neglected part of Dublin's long history. Back in the 1960s the Georgian city had come to public attention because of ruthless and widespread destruction of the surviving built environment.[2] The medieval past – far less visible in the streetscape than the Georgian one – was seen as having no defenders, at a time of unprecedented threat. This threat was directed towards underground rather than aboveground remains, towards an archaeological treasure-house of vast proportions and of both national and international significance. Excavation of part of the Wood Quay site (on the Winetavern Street side) had begun in 1969, but it was the much more extensive investigation under the directorship of Patrick Wallace from 1974 onwards that was yielding Anglo-Norman material that, qualitatively and quantitatively, far surpassed anything that had been discovered in Dublin before then. The story of the excavation programme down to the summer of 1976 is complicated and was characterized by a series of short (and ludicrously inadequate) time-extensions granted by Dublin Corporation and by totally irresponsible statements issued by the then director of the National Museum of Ireland to the effect that the work would soon be completed.[3] By early 1976 there was a perceived need to contextualize these discoveries, the better to understand their historical import.

My own contribution to the Arts Club meeting illustrates a well-worn principle – that to propose a 'good idea' is to be invited to carry it out. As an

1 In no sense is this memoir intended to serve as an evenly-balanced history of the group. Such an objective would best be undertaken by a well-informed external observer and should be based on extensive archival research. What follows is a mere fraction of what actually occurred, filtered through a single memory store. 2 Later catalogued to dramatic effect in Frank McDonald, *The destruction of Dublin* (Dublin, 1985). 3 All well described in Richard Haworth, 'The modern annals of Wood Quay', in John Bradley (ed.), *Viking Dublin exposed: the Wood Quay saga* (Dublin, 1984), pp 16–37, at pp 30–6.

1 Public poster advertising the march to save Wood Quay, 23 September 1978 (artist unknown). An estimated 20,000 people took part.

historian with a longstanding interest in maps, both as primary sources and as vital tools for historical inquiry, I suggested that the newly founded group should set as one of its immediate targets a large-scale map of the medieval city superimposed on a modern base. Thereby the archaeological discoveries at Wood Quay and elsewhere in the city centre would acquire an accurate historical context that was hitherto lacking.[4] The upshot in practice was two

4 Previous attempts to map medieval Dublin were deficient in various ways. On these, see H.B. Clarke, 'The mapping of medieval Dublin: a case-study in thematic cartography', in

versions, starting with an illustrated or pictorial one prepared by Peter Walsh, who was then curator of the Guinness Museum and Archive.[5] Peter was one of several people who assisted me in the process of compiling, from a position of egregious ignorance on my own part, a conventionally detailed or scientific map using a system of classification symbols.[6] The two maps were essentially complementary and were announced at an early stage by the Old Dublin Society.[7] Even before it had been published, the detailed map was to have a crucial walk-on part in the unfolding drama: in the trial of the action taken by F.X. Martin, in the high court in late June 1978, it was exhibited as evidence of the historicity of the Wood Quay site. Contextualization was vital to the argument that led to the declaration of the entire site as a national monument. As such it needed to be 'saved' from both developers and politicians (fig. 1), and people-power was mobilized.

As is well known, the supreme court's decision in the spring of the following year, 1979, enabled Dublin Corporation and its political masters in a government led by Charles Haughey to exploit a loophole in the National Monuments Act (1930) and to proceed with the building of the Civic Offices. In practice, yet more time was granted for further excavations that finally came to an end, still unfinished, in March 1981.[8] These last years of archaeological excavation by the National Museum were extraordinarily productive: in the words of the site director, Patrick Wallace, they 'were of such proportions that they altered previous impressions, gave rise to new ideas and generally made it necessary to rethink previous conclusions'.[9] A high percentage of all the Viking houses found in Dublin were excavated at that time, hence the dedication in the definitive work on these buildings to 'Fr F.X. Martin whose belief made everything possible'.[10] Accordingly the Wood Quay campaign conducted by the Friends and their Associates had a fundamental impact on the city's archaeological record and on the wider issue of urban conservation.[11] The state's own

H.B. Clarke and Anngret Simms (eds), *The comparative history of urban origins in non-Roman Europe: Ireland, Wales, Denmark, Germany, Poland and Russia from the ninth to the thirteenth century*, 2 pts (British Archaeological Reports, International Series, 255, Oxford, 1985), ii, pp 617–43. 5 P.J. Walsh, *Dublin c.840 to c.1540: the years of mediaeval growth* (Dublin, 1977). This was republished with a coloured overlay by the Irish Map and Poster Company in 1988. 6 H.B. Clarke, *Dublin c.840 to c.1540: the medieval town in the modern city* (Dublin, 1978). Both maps were published by the Ordnance Survey (now Ordnance Survey Ireland), by courtesy of the assistant director, Maurice Walsh. The detailed map was reissued, with additions and corrections, as an ancillary publication in the Royal Irish Academy's Irish Historic Towns Atlas series in 2002. 7 Anon., 'Mapping medieval Dublin', *Dublin Historical Record*, 30 (1977), 145–7. 8 A major doubt exists as to whether pre-tenth-century Viking-age levels at Fishamble Street were in effect never uncovered and therefore were subsequently destroyed. 9 P.F. Wallace, 'A reappraisal of the archaeological significance of Wood Quay', in Bradley (ed.), *Viking Dublin exposed*, pp 112–33, at p. 112. 10 P.F. Wallace, *The Viking Age buildings of Dublin*, 2 pts (National Museum of Ireland, Medieval Dublin Excavations, 1962–81, ser. A, 1, Dublin, 1992), i, p. iii. 11 For the long-

institutions were found to be sadly wanting in some (though not all) respects and the archaeological deficit was being made up from a combination of courageous freelance archaeologists and representatives of other academic disciplines.

By the same token, the campaign had a profound effect on the Friends themselves. First, the chairman emerged as a national figure – charismatic, heroic and resourceful. In those early critical months, F.X. Martin was ably assisted by the group's first secretary, Anngret Simms, who was then a geographer at University College Dublin blessed with drive, ingenuity and vision. Their tireless collaboration is symbolized by a somewhat grainy black-and-white photograph of the pair of them 'defending' with steely determination the medieval city wall.[12] Secondly, a number of founding members resigned, out of disapproval of the legal action initiated in November 1977. The least surprising of these resignations was that of none other than the late Sam Stephenson, the architect of the Civic Offices. As a result, the spectrum of membership was diminished and the battle formations became more clearly defined. There was, it is true, a dramatic though temporary broadening of that spectrum at the time of the occupation of the Wood Quay site for 'twenty glorious days' in June 1979.[13] The occupying group represented cultural, educational, political, religious and social aspects of Dublin life, including the local community in the Liberties. After those heady days, however, the group's membership tended to be more narrowly focussed.

Besides the archaeology of the ancient medieval core of the city, the Friends had another progenitor – the Dublin Arts Festival held each March in the 1970s. The decision to meet at the Arts Club was taken in the home of Ian Broad, one of the leading organizers, at a reception to mark the end of the 1976 festival. Two years later, half the programme of events was devoted to the medieval period, in association with the Friends, and I was invited to commission and to edit a small collection of scholarly essays entitled 'Focus on medieval Dublin'.[14] One of these, written by Anngret Simms, contained a map of the walled city subdivided into three zones representing twelfth- and

term context, see H.B. Clarke, 'The city of Dublin and its satellite townships', in E.P. Dennison (ed.), *Conservation and change in historic towns: research directions for the future* (Council for British Archaeology, Research Reports, 122, York, 1999), pp 145–57, at pp 149–52. 12 In the course of time both scholars, being held in high regard in many quarters, were presented with a volume of essays in their honour: John Bradley (ed.), *Settlement and society in medieval Ireland: studies presented to F.X. Martin, O.S.A.* (Kilkenny, 1988); H.B. Clarke, Jacinta Prunty and Mark Hennessy (eds), *Surveying Ireland's past: multidisciplinary essays in honour of Anngret Simms* (Dublin, 2004). More recently a posthumous volume of essays of a different character was also published: H.B. Clarke and J.R.S. Phillips (eds), *Ireland, England and the Continent in the middle ages and beyond: essays in memory of a turbulent friar, F.X. Martin, O.S.A.* (Dublin, 2006). 13 Vividly described in Bride Rosney, 'Occupation diary', in Bradley (ed.), *Viking Dublin exposed*, pp 68–92. 14 In Cobblestone Press, *Dublin Arts Festival, 21–30 April 1978* (Dublin, 1978), separately paginated.

thirteenth-century expansion from an original Viking core; this map has since influenced the way in which the topographical development of medieval Dublin is viewed.[15] Around the same time the Curriculum Development Unit at Trinity College produced a textbook that incorporated much of the new material and many of the new ideas that were beginning to circulate.[16] The fruits of archaeological discovery and the Wood Quay controversy were starting to be made available to a wider reading public, including a younger one, in conformity with the original intentions of the Friends of Medieval Dublin.

After the high drama of the Wood Quay campaign, the group's members continued to keep watch. Even in those pre-Celtic Tiger years, new developments in what was still an architectural wasteland occurred from time to time. To deal professionally with these issues on a regular basis, the Friends agitated for the appointment of a city archaeologist – a concession that was eventually made in 1991. Public lectures were delivered and seminars organized. In due course, the story of the Wood Quay campaign itself came to be told, initially in a volume of essays written by members and non-members of the group.[17] The book ended with a policy document based on recent experiences and a set of nine recommendations drafted by Richard Haworth and myself.[18] The other version of the story was told by a complete outsider from North America.[19] Based on a series of interviews and on extensive reading, this was a commendably forthright and objective assessment of 'one of the most intense battles ever waged by the public to save any archaeological site anywhere'.[20] It amounted to a powerful demonstration, if such were needed, that in the essential thrust of their campaign the Friends had been right. Meanwhile a spectacular set of reconstruction drawings focussed on Wood Quay from the same angle through the ages helped to keep the spirit of the campaign alive.[21]

The year 1988 was declared by Dublin's then city manager to be the 'millennium' of its birth. No amount of argument on my part could dissuade

15 Ibid., p. 13, fig. 7. It was reproduced as part of a more extended discussion in Anngret Simms, 'Medieval Dublin: a topographical analysis', *Irish Geography*, 12 (1979), 32, fig. 2. 16 Curriculum Development Unit, *Viking settlement to medieval Dublin* (Dublin, 1978). I was unsuccessful in dissuading the publisher from employing this tautological title, derived from customary archaeological periodization. 17 Bradley (ed.), *Viking Dublin exposed*. This was published by the O'Brien Press, Michael O'Brien having been himself one of the nine defendants against the temporary injunction granted to the building company on 13 June 1979: Rosney, 'Occupation diary', pp 83–5. 18 The Friends of Medieval Dublin 1984, 'A policy for medieval Dublin', in Bradley (ed.), *Viking Dublin exposed*, pp 168–77. 19 T.F. Heffernan, *Wood Quay: the clash over Dublin's Viking past* (Austin, TX, 1988). 20 Ibid., p. 1. 21 Jonathan Bardon and Stephen Conlin, *Dublin: one thousand years of Wood Quay* (Belfast, 1984). Three years later, quite independently of these developments, the Royal Irish Academy published the first volume in one of three coordinated series of specialized reports based on the excavations at the Wood Quay site in its larger sense: G.F. Mitchell, *Archaeology and environment in early Dublin* (National Museum of Ireland,

him from pursuing this notion, even though the event that gave rise to it did not fit the bill and, in any case, occurred a year later in AD 989.[22] Nevertheless a number of publications were launched in that year of celebration, three of them with contributions by members of the Friends of Medieval Dublin. The late John de Courcy, professor of engineering at University College Dublin, teamed up with artist Stephen Conlin to produce a sequential description of the River Liffey and its immediate environs, accompanied by an exhilarating panoramic view 169cm by 30cm in size.[23] We see graphically the twin towers at Wood Quay without the quayside extension built later. The excellent Historical Documents series issued by the National Library of Ireland under the editorship of Noel Kissane focussed this time on maps of Dublin.[24] Here the four medieval reconstruction maps were drafted by Anngret Simms and myself. Finally, the first two essays in a chronologically arranged one-volume collection were written by a member and a former member of the Friends.[25] The decade ended with the publication of two volumes of reprinted articles grouped into four thematic sections with elements of updating in the notes.[26] Given the lack of a large-scale history of the medieval city (which still obtains), this wide-ranging compendium was intended to advertise the scope of the subject, as well as to bring together some of the seminal contributions made by scholars past and present.[27]

The final recommendation of the policy document of 1984 was that a museum of Dublin should be established in which, among other things, the results of the archaeological excavations would be communicated to citizens and to visitors. As chairman of the Friends, I asked Anngret Simms to investigate any possibilities there might be. In due course she made contact with an independent group that in the 'millennium' year 1988 had begun the process of forming the Medieval Trust. This body, under the chairmanship of Craig McKinney of the Woodchester Bank, acquired a site in Golden Lane with the intention of building a theme complex designed to illustrate aspects of town

Medieval Dublin Excavations, 1962–81, ser. C, 1, Dublin, 1987). **22** That is, the second capture of the Viking settlement by Máel Sechnaill mac Domnaill, king of Mide and of Tara (high-king): *Chronicum Scotorum: a chronicle of Irish affairs … to AD 1135, with a supplement … to 1150*, ed. W.M. Hennessy (RS, London, 1866), pp 232–3. One of the murals in the ceiling of the rotunda of City Hall features the high-king receiving tribute from the townsmen and the explanatory panel (since removed) cited the given year (988) rather than the corrected one. **23** John de Courcy and Stephen Conlin, *Anna Liffey: the river of Dublin* (Dublin, 1988). **24** Noel Kissane, *Historic Dublin maps* (Dublin, 1988). **25** H.B. Clarke, 'Gaelic, Viking and Hiberno-Norse Dublin' and James Lydon, 'The medieval city', in Art Cosgrove (ed.), *Dublin through the ages* (Dublin, 1988), pp 4–24 and 25–45 respectively. **26** H.B. Clarke (ed.), *Medieval Dublin*, i: *The making of a metropolis*; ii: *The living city* (Dublin, 1990). I should like to take this opportunity to express my gratitude to Michael Adams for agreeing to come to the rescue and to have this landmark collection published by the Irish Academic Press. **27** The lengthy introduction printed in both volumes provided a referenced context for the entire contents and their authors.

life in the Middle Ages. In the event, the planning application was rejected (on reasonable grounds) and the outcome was that the Trust purchased instead the former Synod Hall on St Michael's Hill. Anngret Simms, Patrick Wallace and I became the first academic directors of the Trust and *Dublinia* was born as a subsidiary company, opening its doors in the spring of 1993. Accordingly there was an organic link between the Friends of Medieval Dublin and the Medieval Trust, and most of the academic content of the *Dublinia* exhibition was provided by members of the former body. *Dublinia* was, and remains, a major undertaking; it has become a highly visible cultural asset located at the principal road junction in the medieval city where the market-cross once stood.[28] By agreement with the National Museum of Ireland, a small museum component displaying a classified selection of artefacts from Wood Quay was included, complementing the much larger collection in the Kildare Street premises.[29]

From the mid-1990s onwards, a more substantial body of original publications by members of the Friends of Medieval Dublin began to emerge. One was a comprehensive dictionary of persons and places associated with the River Liffey, with a foreword by F.X. Martin.[30] This volume was the culmination of John de Courcy's lifelong interest in the river of Dublin. The same year witnessed the appearance of a history of the street bordering the Wood Quay site on the west.[31] This enterprise was sponsored by one of the main teaching unions, the Association of Secondary Teachers of Ireland, whose new headquarters occupy a post-modern edifice on the opposite side of the street. The book was launched by Ruairí Quinn TD, who had been one of the original backers of the Medieval Trust and who has a strong track-record of being supportive of cultural institutions in Dublin. Two years later a handsome and wide-ranging volume of essays in honour of one of the founding and most committed members of the Friends was published.[32] My own contribution featured a hitherto neglected aspect of the medieval city – the very extensive suburbs that lay outside the defensive walls in all directions.[33] Since 1998 archaeologists have been paying much more attention to the extramural city in the Middle Ages.

By the late 1990s the world of archaeology had been transformed by a proliferation of rescue excavations ahead of almost relentless, tax-driven pressure to redevelop land in the city centre and by a corresponding

28 A late eighteenth-century drawing of this monument is the subject of H.S. Crawford, 'The market cross of Dublin', in Clarke (ed.), *Medieval Dublin*, i: *The making of a metropolis*, pp 252–3. 29 Some years later, in 2000, Dublin Corporation (as it still was) installed its own visitor experience, The Story of the Capital, in the brick-vaulted basement of City Hall. 30 J.W. de Courcy, *The Liffey in Dublin* (Dublin, 1996). 31 Emer Purcell, *A short history of Winetavern Street and its environs* (Dublin, 1996). 32 Conleth Manning (ed.), *Dublin and beyond the Pale: studies in honour of Patrick Healy* (Bray, 1998). On Paddy Healy, see the beautifully-composed appreciation by Rob Goodbody: ibid., pp viii–ix.

proliferation of archaeological contract (or so-called 'private-sector') companies. In earlier days, prior to the appointment of the first city archaeologist, a vital role performed by members of the Friends and a regular item on their agendas was to monitor the proposed redevelopment of sites within the zone of archaeological potential.[34] The last old-style crisis arose in the early 1990s in relation to the construction of Jury's Inn and its associated car-park on the south side of Christchurch Place. Given its central location opposite the cathedral and especially in view of the spectacular quality of the archaeological strata uncovered by Breandán Ó Ríordáin years earlier,[35] it was reasonable to assume that similar material would have been preserved in that entire street block. Representatives of the Friends took part in a hearing by An Bord Pleanála, but they were unable to prevent this large and intrusive development from being allowed to proceed. Concessions of a kind were that the new buildings should rest on piles and that limited archaeological excavation around pile caps could be conducted, together with a watching-brief. These small-scale investigations duly confirmed what had been anticipated about the importance of this site,[36] and stimulated a debate about the long-term consequences of piling for surviving archaeological strata. These consequences remain largely a matter of speculation, partly because ground-conditions vary so much in practice.

The existence of a city archaeologist from 1991 onwards, the veritable explosion of archaeological activity, and the increasingly obvious deficit in the publication of the results all suggested a new role for the Friends of Medieval Dublin. This took the form of a series of annual symposia held in Trinity College in April or May, where many of the invited speakers were archaeologists of recent (and even not so recent) excavations whose findings were unpublished. It was a condition of speaking on such occasions that a text and (if appropriate) illustrations be provided for publication a year later. The outcome has been a continuous and continuing *Medieval Dublin* series, of which this is the eighth volume. The very first article was totally apposite – a substantial survey of forty years of archaeological excavations in the city.[37]

33 H.B. Clarke, '*Urbs et suburbium*: beyond the walls of medieval Dublin', ibid., pp 45–58. 34 This was based largely on documentary evidence combined with topographical considerations and was marked as a broken orange line on the 1978 Ordnance Survey map. 35 Still inexcusably and scandalously unpublished, having been excavated in 1972–6, apart from a more broadly-based treatment of the buildings in Hilary Murray, *Viking and early medieval buildings in Dublin* (British Archaeological Reports, British Series, 119, Oxford, 1983). 36 See the unpublished preliminary post-excavation report produced by Margaret Gowen in 1992. Two published reports are available for the southern part of this street block: Claire Walsh, 'Dublin's southern town defences, tenth to fourteenth centuries: the evidence from Ross Road', in Seán Duffy (ed.), *Medieval Dublin II* (Dublin, 2001), pp 88–127; Alan Hayden, 'The excavation of pre-Norman defences and houses at Werburgh Street, Dublin: a summary', in Seán Duffy (ed.), *Medieval Dublin III* (Dublin, 2002), pp 44–68. 37 Linzi Simpson, 'Forty years a-digging: a preliminary synthesis of archaeological

Equally apposite were the concluding words: 'the abiding goal must be publication'.[38] To this end, the Friends have made a vital contribution far exceeding their numbers or resources. Here I should like to give due recognition to three parties in particular: to John Fitzgerald, until recently Dublin's city manager, who established the precedent of funding the production-costs of the series; to Four Courts Press, which has produced all of the volumes to date; and to the current chairman, Seán Duffy, who has worked indefatigably both to make arrangements for the symposia and to edit the series. The 1990 volumes gave us reprints of older scholarship; the present series is providing a critical mass of new work, based both on archaeological investigation and on documentary analysis. Four volumes have been dedicated to deceased members of the Friends: no better memorial to their verve and vision could have been erected.[39]

The *Medieval Dublin* series has coincided with a number of other landmark publications. One of these arose from new excavations on part of the Civic Offices site conducted by the city archaeologist, Andrew Halpin, in 1993.[40] These excavations had the effect of compressing the previously established chronology of land-reclamation in the thirteenth century and of emphasizing Wood Quay as *the* port of Dublin at that time. Two years later, in 2002, the Royal Irish Academy published the first of a four-part atlas of the city of Dublin.[41] Here the interpretative essay, the fully referenced topographical information, and the historical reconstruction maps all take account of the work of the Friends and of others in recent times. That same year *Dublinia* produced a generously illustrated and attractively designed book of its existing exhibition, with financial assistance from Dublin City Council.[42] This won the Best Publication Award 2003 from the Heritage Council and the Northern Ireland Museums Council. One of the new generation of contract archaeologists prepared an invaluable guide commissioned by Dublin City Council in association with the Heritage Council.[43] This included an analytical digest of the primary historical records designed to cater for the specific needs of archaeologists.[44] In the following year the Friends

investigations in medieval Dublin', in Seán Duffy (ed.), *Medieval Dublin I* (Dublin, 2000), pp 11–68. **38** Ibid., p. 65. This remains the case, as was apparent at an archaeological forum held in the Royal Irish Academy on 14–15 September 2006. **39** F.X. Martin (vol. 1), Paddy Healy (vol. 2), Leo Swan (vol. 3) and J.W. de Courcy (vol. 6). The fourth volume was dedicated to that fine medieval scholar Philomena Connolly, while the seventh recognized the unfailing support of John Fitzgerald on the occasion of his retirement. **40** Andrew Halpin, *The port of medieval Dublin: archaeological excavations at the Civic Offices, Winetavern Street, Dublin, 1993* (Dublin, 2000). **41** H.B. Clarke, *Dublin, part I, to 1610* (Irish Historic Towns Atlas, 11, Dublin, 2002). **42** H.B. Clarke, Sarah Dent and Ruth Johnson, *Dublinia, the story of medieval Dublin* (Dublin, 2002). **43** Judith Carroll, *Dublin city: sources for archaeologists*, ed. Ruth Johnson and Donncha Ó Dúlaing (Dublin, 2003). The editors were (and still are) the city archaeologist and the city heritage officer respectively. **44** H.B. Clarke, 'Primary historical sources', ibid., pp 21–4.

themselves, in association with Dublin City Council, produced a single-sheet guide to three walks around the medieval city.[45] This features a reproduction of the dramatic scale-model of Dublin *c.*1500 that acts as the centrepiece in the *Dublinia* exhibition. Finally, 2006 saw the welcome publication of a major contribution to the National Museum of Ireland series, devoted to the ceramic discoveries at Wood Quay.[46]

What all of this amounts to is a transformation that is nothing short of astounding. The sheer quantity of published material relating to the medieval city – both archaeological and documentary – is now enormous and increasingly challenging to trace, let alone to master. One obvious requirement is a full bibliography, made available online and kept up to date. The story of medieval Dublin has been told in traditional book format, in the tangible shape of a scale model with a sound commentary in six languages, and most recently on DVD.[47] But another part of that story is actually 'modern', in the sense that the medieval past was rediscovered by the present generation in a dramatic combination of developmental initiatives, public debates and confrontations, and amicable resolutions. At the centre of so much of what has come to fruition were the Friends of Medieval Dublin, an eloquent testimony to what can be achieved by a small, under-resourced group of men and women equipped with little more than conviction, determination and professional integrity.

APPENDIX

Right from the foundation of the Friends of Medieval Dublin, the chief officers were the chairman and the secretary. Since no subscription system was ever implemented and since accommodation for regular meetings was provided free of charge by the Royal Society of Antiquaries of Ireland, by Christ Church cathedral and latterly by *Dublinia*, the role of honorary treasurer has usually been minimal and straightforward. At the time of the Wood Quay campaign, necessary fundraising was undertaken by the subsidiary group known as the Associates of the Friends of Medieval Dublin. On their disbandment, the remaining balance was kindly donated to the Friends and was transferred to a special savings account earmarked to

45 H.B. Clarke, Ruth Johnson and Linzi Simpson, *Walks around medieval Dublin* (Dublin, 2004). 46 Clare McCutcheon, *Medieval pottery from Wood Quay, Dublin* (National Museum of Ireland, Medieval Dublin Excavations, 1962–81, ser. B, 7, Dublin, 2006). A significant number of other important volumes in this three-part series are well advanced. 47 *Medieval Dublin from Vikings to Tudors: an interactive experience*, DVD produced by The Farm Media Group Ltd (Dublin, 2008), commissioned by Dublin City Council in partnership with OPW, *Dublinia*, Christ Church cathedral, and NMI.

subsidize future publications. Accordingly only the chairmen and secretaries are listed below.

Chairmen

F.X. Martin, O.S.A., 1976–84
Rhoda Kavanagh, 1984–6
Howard Clarke, 1986–98
Seán Duffy, 1998 to present

Secretaries

Anngret Simms, 1976–8
John Bradley, 1978–84
William Doran, 1984–7
Gearóid O'Keeffe, 1987–9
Mark Hennessy, 1989–90
Tadhg O'Keeffe, 1990–1
Gearóid O'Keeffe, 1991–5
Emer Purcell, 1995–9
Stuart Kinsella, 2000–5
Claudia Köhler, 2005 to present